Models of a Man

Models of a Man

Essays in Memory of Herbert A. Simon

edited by Mie Augier and James G. March

The MIT Press
Cambridge, Massachusetts
London, England

Set in Stone sans and Stone serif on 3B2 by Asco Typesetters, Hong Kong.

Library of Congress Cataloging-in-Publication Data

Models of a man : essays in memory of Herbert A. Simon / edited by Mie Augier and James G. March.
p.   cm.
Includes bibliographical references and index.
ISBN 978-0-262-01208-9 (hc. : alk. paper), 978-0-262-54649-2 (pb.)
1. Simon, Herbert Alexander, 1916–2001. Economists—United States—Biography.
3. Economics. I. Augier, Mie, 1972– . II. March, James G.
HB119.S47M63 2004
330′.092—dc21   2003052776

dedicated to Dorothea Pye Simon

Contents

Preface

Herbert A. Simon died on February 9, 2001. He was 84 years old and had devoted more than 60 years to a distinguished career as a social and behavioral scientist. The idea of this book arose in the warm sentiment of the Carnegie Mellon memorial service honoring Herb. It was obvious that a sense of loss and awe was shared among many people who knew him or knew of him.

One spontaneous indication of Herb Simon's position is found in the outpouring of short articles and tributes published to honor him. Another indication is this book. The idea was to gather a collection of short original essays by Herb's friends and colleagues. The book is a tribute to him by some of those whom he affected. It is eulogy, a remembrance, and a reminder of his special place in the history of twentieth-century science.

The book is not primarily a biography or an intellectual inventory. It is a collection of essays that combine personal feelings and stories with intellectual tributes. The precise mix between reminiscence and analysis varies from author to author, but they all communicate a measure of an extraordinary man.

In order to organize contributions of such diversity, we invoked two arbitrary rules. First, we asked each author to identify the one book or paper by Simon that had been most influential with him or her.

We have arranged the essays in four parts according to the authors' responses, resolving any ambiguity (a few authors didn't respond to the question; a few responded with more than one choice) with our own guesses. The essays in part I are by authors who cited *Models of Man*, the individual articles reprinted therein, and one article that might have been. Those in part II are by authors who cited *Administrative Behavior* and *Organizations*. Those in part III are by authors who cited articles and books dealing with relatively technical aspects of economics and operations research. Those in part IV are by authors who cited *The Sciences of the Artificial*, "The Architecture of Complexity," and articles on scientific discovery. Second, within the four parts we have ordered the contributors alphabetically by surname. The result has, we believe, a certain charm, a modicum of order, and perhaps a few surprises, but the contributions can be sampled profitably in any order. The prologues include an essay by Simon's eldest daughter, Katherine Simon Frank; the epilogue is a poem by James March.

When we proposed the book, we speculated that Herb Simon was probably the only person who could have read all of the contributions with comprehension. In retrospect, that is probably not true; but it is not true at least in part because he taught us to see the unity among disciplines rather than their separateness. As the collection of contributions attests, he had an impact that was extraordinary in breadth and depth. This book is a small acknowledgment of a large debt.

Acknowledgments

We are particularly grateful to the contributors, each of whom paused in a busy life to remember a friend. We are also very indebted to friends and colleagues who commented on the idea of this collection, influenced its direction, and supported its execution: Kenneth Arrow, William Cooper, Richard Day, Giovanni Dosi, Edward Feigenbaum, Yuji Ijiri, Kathie Simon Frank, Paul Samuelson, and Oliver Williamson. Robert Prior of The MIT Press was very encouraging from the beginning.

Several people have helped with finding pictures for this volume; and we are thankful to Katherine Simon Frank, Edward Feigenbaum, and David Klahr.

For helpful assistance with Simon's papers, private and archival, we would like to thank Janet New Hilf, Jennifer Benford, and Gabrielle Michelek, all of Carnegie Mellon University. The Simon letters quoted in this volume are quoted with permission from the CMU library archives.

Our work on the project has been supported by the Spencer Foundation and the Danish Social Science Research Council. All editors' and authors' royalties from sales of the book have been assigned to support the Herbert A. Simon Collection at the Carnegie Mellon University Library Archives.

Models of a Man

Prologues

Herbert A. Simon, Scientist

Mie Augier and James G. March

The death of Herbert A. Simon in 2001 marked the end of an era in the history of social science. His role in shaping twentieth-century social science was unparalleled. He exemplified the best that the era provided. He was totally committed to a demanding vision of social research that emphasized quality and embraced the fundamental tenets of scientific endeavor.

The Man

"In describing my life," Simon reflected in the final chapter of his autobiography (1991b, p. 367), "I have situated it in a labyrinth of paths that branch, in a castle of innumerable rooms. The life is in the moving through that garden or castle, experiencing surprises along the path you follow, wondering (but not too solemnly) where the other paths would have led; a heuristic search for the solution of an ill-structured problem. If there are goals, they do not so much guide the search as emerge from it. It needs no summing up before living it." Herb Simon left his own summation in the minds he graced by his role in shaping them.

Simon was a scientist's scientist and received major awards from many different science communities. These included the A. M. Turing

Award (in 1975), the National Medal of Science (in 1986), and the Nobel Prize in Economics (in 1978). He received the James Madison Award, the Dwight Waldo Award, and the John Gaus Lecture Award from the American Political Science Association, and he received the Gold Medal Award for Life Achievement in Psychological Science from the American Psychological Association. He was a Fellow of the Econometric Society and was elected to the American Philosophical Society, the National Academy of Sciences, and the American Academy of Arts and Sciences, as well as many foreign honorary societies. He was awarded honorary doctorates by many universities in the United States and abroad, including Harvard University, Columbia University, Yale University, and the University of Chicago.

Some of the respect that Simon earned from his colleagues is evidenced by this book. The list of contributors is an honor role of twentieth-century social and behavioral science. He made important contributions to economics, psychology, political science, sociology, administrative theory, public administration, organization theory, computer science, cognitive science, and philosophy. He received high honors from several different disciplines, and they all claimed him, but he was resistant to demands for disciplinary loyalty. "If you see any one of these disciplines dominating you," he said in conversation, "you join the opposition and you fight it for a while."

He was an indefatigable advocate for social science. He served on the Committee on Science and Public Policy (COSPUP) and as a member of the President's Science Advisory Committee. Simon's original appointment to the committee was not as a social scientist but as an expert in artificial intelligence, because it was then thought that the Soviets were making great strides in AI (Simon 1991b, p. 294). However, from his bases in COSPUP and PSAC he argued for the use of social science in matters of national policy (Simon 1989b).

Simon was an exemplar of a modern scientist. For him, science was all about "finding simple generalizations that describe data approximately under some set of limiting conditions" (1968, p. 443). Always searching for a pattern in what he saw, Simon created models of human decision making that were "beautifully simple" but at the same time "full of possibilities" (Feigenbaum, this volume). Simon believed that "to 'explain' an empirical regularity is to discover a set of simple mechanisms that would produce the former in any system governed by the latter" (1968, p. 445). In the Simon cosmology, such simple mechanisms are grounded in universally valid (though not necessarily universally relevant) laws of nature. Such laws exist and are discoverable by human reason. Indeed, even unique phenomena are subject to the sovereignty of such laws. He wrote: "When nature behaves in some unique fashion—deals a hand of thirteen spades, so to speak—this uniqueness, even if approximate, cannot be accidental, but must reveal underlying lawfulness." (ibid., p. 443). More specifically: "Human beings, viewed as behaving systems, are quite simple. The apparent complexity of our behavior over time is largely a reflection of the complexity of the environment in which we find ourselves." (1969, p. 110)

Simon's best-known books include *Administrative Behavior* (1947), *Organizations* (with James G. March, 1958), *The Sciences of the Artificial* (1969), *Human Problem Solving* (with Allen Newell, 1972), *Models of Bounded Rationality* (three volumes, 1982 and 1997a), and his autobiography, *Models of My Life* (1991b). Decision making was the core of the work. Simon was initially a student of public administration, and birth rights go properly to political science. For a relatively brief but enormously productive time as a young man he labored to bring behavioral realism to the theory of organizations and the firm, and that period can properly be claimed by economics. The last and longest part of his career was devoted to cognitive science, and his mature years belong properly to psychology. But for Simon these periods were all of one piece. He was a student of human decision making. "In the eighty-odd years I've known of Simon," he said in his last paper, published posthumously, "I've heard a great deal about him. I've read, I think, everything he has written. Collecting some of the things I had learned, I once even published a book about him [Simon 1991b]. Out of this

experience has come a picture of Simon as a complete monomaniac."
(Simon 2001)

Simon's doctoral thesis, later published as *Administrative Behavior*
(1947), became the basis of his other contributions to public administration (such as Simon, Smithburg, and Thompson 1950). That book's
focus on decision making was maintained in Simon's best-known
papers in economics, such as "A formal theory of the employment
relation" (1951) and "A behavioral model of rational choice" (1955),
which, together with "Rational choice and the structure of the environment" (1956), challenged major elements of the neoclassical view
of rationality. Similarly, decision making was the foundation of his
contribution to organization studies, in which, with James March, he
organized an inventory of organizations research around the idea of
decisions (March and Simon 1958), and of his work with Allen Newell
on individual problem solving (Simon 2001). The notion that humans
made decisions and might be imagined to make them better was the
basis of his interest in artificial intelligence and the hierarchical organization of knowledge.

Simon's quest to understand human decision making led him to
contribute to fields as disparate as political science, public administration, economics, management science, organization theory, psychology, and computer science. His work was multi-disciplinary in the
sense that it contributed to many different fields, but for Simon it was
very focused. Reflecting upon his career, he said: "A problem I found in
1935 has lasted [with] me. I have never had to find another." (Simon
1989a, p. 378). Or, as Allen Newell expressed it (1989b, p. 433):

Once upon a time when the world was young,
Oh, best beloved.
There came to the banks of the Monongogo river,
All muddy and brown,
Oh best beloved,
A Dijnn who was one thing on the inside
But many things on the outside.

The Work

Decision Making in Public Administration

Simon was born in Milwaukee and attended public schools there until he went to the University of Chicago. The university's intellectual character suited him, and he thrived. Several lifelong friendships were formed during Simon's years in Chicago. In particular, Bill Cooper and Harold Guetzkow, both of whom became colleagues with Simon later at the Carnegie Institute of Technology, first met him during the Chicago years. (See their chapters in this volume.)

During his undergraduate years, Simon took a graduate course on price theory taught by Henry Simons. This course, Simon said, "gave me a glimpse of the applications of rigor and mathematics to economics" (1991b, p. 39). Simon then "resolved to major in economics," but his resolution faltered in the face of a requirement that he take a course in accounting. He switched to political science (ibid.).

He described himself as having been inspired by Henry Schultz's book *The Theory and Measurement of Demand*, feeling that it provided an example of the possibilities for applying mathematics to the study of human behavior (1991b, p. 51). Simon also took courses in logic with Rudolph Carnap and with the mathematical biophysicist Nicolas Rashevsky—the latter, he noted (1988, p. 289), "to get my math up to speed." "My objective from the time I was in college," he said, "was to find ways of using mathematics to describe social phenomena," thinking that the fields needed "a little stiffening up."[1] His four preliminary examinations for his doctorate reflected very little of any of those interests, however. They were in public administration, statistics, constitutional law, and politics.

Many of the ideas that Simon elaborated during his career were first formulated within the context of political science and public administration (Augier and March 2001a; Bromiley, this volume; Egidi and Marengo, this volume). Simon was influenced by the attitudes of the political science department at the University of Chicago in the 1930s, in particular by the general conviction that deliberate coordination was necessary for effective collective action, and that it was possible to apply methods of rational planning to the allocation of public resources (Simon 1991b).

A series of papers written with Clarence Ridley were published in the journal *Public Management,* and the collaboration culminated in the book *Measuring Municipal Activities* (Ridley and Simon 1938). Simon's work on city management was linked to the municipal reform movement and to Ridley's conviction that professional management was an important instrument for improving the efficiency of local governments (Simon 1991b, p. 70). The research was dedicated to making municipal government more efficient in relatively standard economic terms, a perspective that anticipated the much later interjection of economics into the public sector under the label "The New Public Management." From Ridley, Simon learned that effective organizations can be powerful tools for human rationality in pursuit of collective goals (Simon 1947).

Simon never wavered from this goal of improving human rationality. When Simon received the Nobel Prize, James March (1978b, p. 858) described him as "an unrepentant knight of the enlightenment." However, the experience working on city management affected his view of economics considerably. He became a steady critic of pure rationality as a description of human behavior. Much later, he wrote: "The big problem for me, from the very beginning of my work with Clarence Ridley, was to reconcile the way that decisions were actually made in organizations with the way that the economists pretended that they were made." (Simon 1988, p. 286) He tried to use the perspective of utility maximization to understand budget decision problems in organizations, and he concluded that such a perspective was "hopeless" (ibid.). The disillusion established his research agenda. "Now," Simon recalled (1989a, p. 376), "I had a new research problem: How do human beings reason when the conditions for rationality postulated by the model of neoclassical economics are not met?"

In 1939 (at the age of 23), Simon moved to the University of California's Bureau of Public Administration in Berkeley to direct a study of the administration of state relief programs. In the course of this work, he studied the economics literature on taxation, eventually publishing his conclusions in a leading economics journal, the *Quarterly Journal of Economics* (1943). Much later, Simon suggested that his conclusions in this first publication in economics could be interpreted as questioning some aspects of the assumption of rationality found in conventional economic theory (1991b, p. 83). The article attracted little attention, however, and rationality was unscathed by it.

Simon's fame within political science and public administration depended neither on the Ridley and Simon report nor on his *Quarterly Journal of Economics* piece on taxation. Rather, it depended on his writings in the 1940s and the 1950s, particularly *Administrative Behavior* and *Public Administration* (the latter a collaboration with Donald Smithburg and Victor Thompson). He thought that the field lacked the powerful measurement techniques and concepts necessary to develop a useful theory. The idea that theories should be both empirically relevant and technically sophisticated became a consistent theme of his work (1991a, 1997b). In *Administrative Behavior*, Simon made a frontal assault on the received doctrine of public administration, criticizing existing theories and principles of administration as being worse than useless as guides to practical action because of vagueness and contradictions. He called them "proverbs" and consigned them to a Carnapian hell.

The attack on the principles of administration attracted considerable attention (Frederickson 2001), but the longer-lasting influence of *Administrative Behavior* stemmed more from its identification of decision making as a basis for the reconstruction of administrative theory. Decision making, as it is portrayed in *Administrative Behavior*, is purposeful, but not rational. In Simon's view, *Administrative Behavior* contained both the foundation and "much of the superstructure of the theory of bounded rationality that has been my lodestar for nearly fifty years" (1991b, p. 86). Simon argued that organizations make it possible to make decisions by constraining the set of alternatives to be considered and the considerations that are to be treated as relevant.

Other ideas important to Simon's later work can be found in *Administrative Behavior*. For example, he discussed organizational identification, a theme to which he returned much later in complaining about the emphasis on opportunism and conflict of interest in some analyses of organizations (1991a, 1997b). In the same book, he took the idea of inducements and contributions from Chester Barnard and developed it into the rudiments of a theory of hierarchical authority and the employment contract, a set of ideas he would later apply to the study of employment relations in a well-known article (1951).

Understanding these first experiences in public administration is important to interpreting Simon's later research and his general orientation to the study of decision making (Goodin, this volume). Ideas about the hierarchical organization of problem solving that became central to Simon's paper "The Architecture of Complexity" were first hinted at in *Administrative Behavior*. He recognized the prima facie efficiency of a hierarchy of decisions, where one stage in the hierarchy influences the next step, and so on, and purposeful action is achieved through a hierarchical chain of decisions guided by general goals and objectives (1947, pp. 4–5). The hierarchical ordering of decisions in administrative organizations led him to speculations about hierarchically organized decision processes more generally and a view of problem solving as constructed around hierarchies of ends and means. This theme also became very important to Simon's later work on near-decomposability, causality, and complex systems (1952, 1953, 1969). It influenced the work in computer science, where he saw the underlying structure of computational memory as hierarchical (1977), and in problem solving, where he saw problems as generally decomposable into hierarchical structures (1989a). In his research on artificial intelligence—for example, the General Problem Solver (Newell, Shaw, and Simon 1962)—Simon used an implementation of means-ends analysis as a computational tool for problem solving.

Administrative Behavior was first published in 1947. The thesis version was defended by Simon when he returned to Chicago in 1942 as a faculty member at the Illinois Institute of Technology. Simon taught topics in political science, such as American political institutions and ideas, constitutional law and administrative aspects of planning (1991b, p. 94). In 1946 he became chairman of the Department of Political and Social Sciences. The department was joined by Donald Smithburg and Victor Thompson, and the three of them extended the framework of *Administrative Behavior* into a textbook on public administration. Their book *Public Administration*, published in 1950, became a text used by the "young Turks" of public administration.

Cowles and Organizational Economics

Early in his career, Simon became a part of a community of distinguished social and behavioral scientists associated with the Cowles Commission and the RAND Corporation. The Cowles Commission assembled a group of exceptional mathematical economists doing pioneering research in econometrics, linear and dynamic programming, and decision theory (among other things) (Christ 1994). Seminars were held regularly to discuss current research on these issues. Participants included such subsequent luminaries as Kenneth Arrow, Roy Radner, Paul Samuelson, Franco Modigliani, Jacob Marshak, Tjalling Koopmans, and Gerard Debreu. As Simon noted in his autobiography, his interaction with Cowles made him into "almost a full time economist" (1991b, p. 140). Several members of the Cowles Commission group became his friends, and several have contributed chapters to this volume. Among the works discussed at the Cowles seminars were those of Paul Samuelson, Lawrence Klein, and John von Neumann.

One result of Simon's interaction with the Cowles Commission was his work on causality (1952, 1953). He was searching for an operational definition of political and organizational power. He argued that in order to understand (organizational) power it was necessary to understand causality, for power of one part of an organization can be defined operationally only if it is the cause of some effects in other parts of the organization. Also at Cowles, Simon became involved with a study on atomic energy that Jacob Marschak and Sam Schur were doing. They asked Simon to write the macroeconomics part of that project (Simon 1991b, p. 103). Simon had few illusions about the influence of this study: "If the atomic energy study ever had a large impact on the world," he said, "I have not detected it."[2]

The more significant effects of the Cowles experience on Simon were on his involvement in mathematical social science and his exposure to economics. With respect to the former, he wrote: "The greatest impact of the Cowles exposure on me was to encourage me to try to mathematize my previous research in organization theory and decision making—especially the theory developed in *Administrative Behavior*." (1947, p. 4) With respect to the latter, he observed that without the participation in the Cowles seminars, he "would surely not have had a full command of the tools of economic analysis" (ibid., p. 3). Simon believed that his association with the Cowles Commission brought him into the mainstream of economics and brought his papers to the attention of that mainstream.[3] In particular, Simon mentioned three papers that were significant with respect to his influence in economics and that grew out of his Cowles experience. Each of these papers used the tools of economics, yet communicated the idea that limits to rationality ought to be part of the analysis of decision making.

"A Behavioral Model of Rational Choice" (1955) was written in part at the RAND Corporation, where Simon (along with an impressive list of other major figures in modern economics and psychology) spent some summers in the early 1950s. Beginning with the assumption that decisions are reasoned and intendedly rational yet subject to cognitive constraints, Simon built on conventional decision theory ideas about alternatives, payoff functions, possible future states, and information about the probability distributions of outcomes conditional on a choice (ibid., p. 102). In models of rational choice, he observed, the organism must be able to "attach definite payoffs (or at least a definite range of payoffs) to each possible outcome" (ibid.). Simon described this as fanciful, arguing that "there is a complete lack of evidence that, in actual human choice situations of any complexity, these computations can be, or are in fact, performed" (ibid.). Because their computational power is inadequate for the complexity of the choice situation, decision makers have to simplify their decision procedures.

One of these simplifications is satisficing—the idea that decision makers interpret outcomes as either satisfactory or unsatisfactory, with an aspiration level constituting the boundary between the two. A decision maker, looking for a satisfactory solution, searches until a solution that is good enough is found. Simon summarized the argument this way: "The player, instead of seeking for a 'best' move, needs only to look for a 'good' move." (1955, pp. 107–108) This was Simon's first adoption of the idea of an "aspiration level," which had been introduced earlier into the psychological literature by Sidney Siegel and Kurt Lewin and which was important to Simon's later work (see, e.g., March and Simon 1958, pp. 47–52).[4] This early article influenced many social scientists, ranging from psychologists to economists working on theories of rational choice and games (see the chapters in this volume by Gigerenzer, Kahneman and Frederick, and Selten).

The second paper singled out by Simon as important from his years at Cowles was "A formal theory of the employment relation" (1951). This paper was influenced particularly by Jacob Marschak's views on the role of liquidity under uncertainty. It emphasizes authority, a concept that was central to *Administrative Behavior*. In an employment relation, Simon said, an employer expects to exercise a certain amount of authority over an employee, for which he pays a wage. The employee accepts this authority within certain "acceptance zones" (ibid., p. 295). This incomplete contract vision of employment ultimately became important, but Simon was not fully satisfied with it at the time. He noted that it was still ripe for extensions because it still was "highly abstract and oversimplified, and leaves out of account numerous important aspects of the real situation" (ibid., p. 302). He observed that, although the model appeared to be considerably more realistic than others in the way it conceptualized the nature of the employment relationship, it was still about "hypothetically rational behavior in an area where institutional history and other nonrational elements are notoriously important" (ibid.).

The third paper that Simon mentioned as growing out of his Cowles experience was "A comparison of organization theories" (1952–53), which compared the economic theory of the firm with organization theory, the latter emphasizing that organizations need only survive, not maximize profits, and participants receive inducements to make contributions (an echo of Barnard and *Administrative Behavior*). As Simon told the tale, traditional theories of the firm ("F-theory") were marked by an emphasis on production functions and the maximization of profits, whereas organization theory ("O-theory") was distinguished by its emphasis on conditions for organizational survival (ibid., p. 4). As in his work more generally, Simon paid homage to those students of institutions and organizations "who have perhaps been in closer contact than traditional economic theorists with the empirical phenomena" (ibid., p. 5).

Carnegie, Behavioral Economics, and Organizations

In 1949 Simon accepted a position at the Carnegie Institute of Technology. He stayed at Carnegie until his death 52 years later despite numerous offers from many other prestigious universities. He thrived at Carnegie and had little patience for those who were surprised at his resistance to moving. March (1978b, p. 861) put words into his mouth in describing his probable reaction to those who were surprised at his resistance to moving: "A discipline that finds ordinary behavior surprising probably ought to spend a bit more time looking at ordinary behavior, and a bit less time contemplating its theories." Simon himself rarely deigned to provide reasons for his constancy, preferring, in effect, to suggest that those who were captivated by reflected status should explain their behavior rather than ask him to explain his.

Carnegie both molded Simon and was molded by him. Under the leadership of G. Leland Bach and Richard M. Cyert, the Graduate School of Industrial Administration (GSIA) became the site of significant contributions to areas such as behavioral economics, operations research, experimental economics, and theories of the firm (Day and Sunder 1996). It also created a model that was widely adopted across the United States and (later) Europe, and that continues to stimulate interdisciplinary research in business schools (Kreps, this volume). GSIA found allies, particularly at the Ford Foundation, which championed the GSIA model in the United States and abroad and provided substantial financial incentives for its dissemination and adoption. In the 1950s the foundation set up a program area for the development of the behavioral sciences, supporting Carnegie projects that led to two major books: *Organizations* (March and Simon 1958) and *A Behavioral Theory of the Firm* (Cyert and March 1963).

When Simon first arrived at Carnegie Tech, he believed that research in the areas of organizational psychology and sociology was necessary to understand human decision making. He was also enthusiastic about mathematical approaches to the study of human thought and action, though more as a stimulant to imagination than as a demonstration of truth. "For me," he wrote in his autobiography (1991b, p. 43), "mathematics has always been language of thought.... When I am working on a problem, I am sure that I do not usually think in words, but in terms of a more abstract representation that is perhaps partially pictorial or diagrammic and partially symbolic. Mathematics—this sort of non-verbal thinking—is my language of discovery. It is the tool I use to arrive at new ideas. This kind of mathematics is relatively unrigorous, loose, heuristic."

Simon and his colleagues sought to build a group at Carnegie that would combine mathematics and quantitative techniques with economics, organizational sociology, and social psychology. The social and behavioral scientists who were attracted to GSIA in the 1950s and the 1960s, either as students or as faculty, included Albert Ando, Richard Cyert, Julian Feldman, Edward Feigenbaum, Harold Guetzkow, Charles Holt, Yuji Ijiri, Harold Leavitt, Michael Lovell, Robert Lucas, James March, Allen Meltzer, Merton Miller, Franco Modigliani, John Muth, Allen Newell, Richard Nelson, William Starbuck, Victor Vroom, Oliver Williamson, and Harrison White. During those years, Simon participated in many collaborations and projects, including work with Yuji Ijiri on skew distributions and the sizes of business firms (Ijiri and Simon 1977) and work with Albert Ando on near-decomposability (Simon and Ando 1961). In particular, the work with Ando applied Simon's ideas on causality and identification to the analysis of dynamic models and led to the important work on decomposable systems (Ando, this volume), and the work with Ijiri extended ideas that Simon had developed in a 1955 *Biometrika* paper on the Yule distribution (Ijiri, this volume).

Simon's contribution to decision making and behavioral economics in that period included three projects.

The first was a project led by George Kozmetzky and funded by the Controllership Foundation. In addition to Kozmetsky, the project involved Harold Guetzkow, Gordon Tyndall, and Simon. The study considered problems in the organization of the controller's function in large business organizations (Simon, Kozmetsky, Guetzkow, and Tyndall 1954). It examined issues such as organizational effectiveness; problems and advantages in centralization and decentralization, what kind of accounting system to use in organizations, and how to structure manufacturing reports. It also explored issues of organizational authority, which had been of interest to Simon since *Administrative Behavior.*

The second project was a study of decision making under uncertainty carried out by Simon along with Charles Holt, Franco Modigliani, and John Muth and sponsored by the Office of Naval Research. Led by Holt, this team examined the Springdale plant of the Pittsburgh Plate Glass Company. Several models for handling complex inventory and production decisions were developed and reported in the resulting book, *Planning Production, Inventories and Work Force* (Holt, Modigliani, Muth, and Simon 1960). As Muth, Holt, and Michael Lovell note in the present volume, Simon's participation in this project had a curious role in the early development of the idea of rational expectations. His work on certainty equivalence was important for Muth in developing his 1961 rational expectations paper. Although Simon diverged from rational expectations theory in many respects, he never questioned its importance to economics and never questioned that it deserved the Nobel Prize (although he thought that Muth deserved to share that honor with Robert Lucas).

The third GSIA initiative involving Simon was a response to a request from Bernard Berelson at the Ford Foundation for an inventory of propositions covering what was known about organizational behavior. The project involved Simon with James March and Harold Guetzkow and led to the book *Organizations*. The book expanded and elaborated Simon's earlier ideas on behavioral decision making, search, and aspiration levels. It also elaborated Simon's ideas on the significance of organizations as social institutions in society.

In general, Simon and the GSIA group tried to develop the rudiments of an understanding of how decision making took place. They focused on uncertainty, ambiguity, heuristics, norms, routines, learning, and satisficing. The ideas initiated at GSIA helped to establish a foundation for modern ideas in economics, such as bounded rationality, adaptive and evolutionary economics, transaction-cost theory, behavioral economics, and experimental economics (March 1978a; Simon 1991b; Conlisk 1996; Day and Sunder 1996; Williamson 1996, 2002; Day

2002; Earl and Potts, this volume; Leijonhufvud, this volume).[5] Simon did not do it all. Indeed, he did not always agree with everyone else. But he was a major presence who influenced everyone in the group. As Oliver Williamson recalls in this volume, "it was hard to be around Herb without becoming infected."

In subsequent years Simon published less in economics, but in occasional forays he continued his advocacy of his basic ideas and of an empirically relevant microeconomics (1997b). He continued to criticize assumptions of global rationality in economics (1976, 1978), and he argued that organizations should have a much more central place in economic theory. Contemporary economies, he asserted, are not market economies but rather economies of organizations and markets (1991a). His complaints about contemporary economics extended to those elements of organizational economics that seemed to him to exaggerate self-interested strategic actions, for example transaction-cost economics (see the chapters by Loasby and Dosi in this volume). He argued that altruism, converted into organizational loyalty, was an important source of effectiveness in organizations (1993). This interest in altruism and organizational identification—as both scientific and moral ideas—placed Simon at least partly in opposition to students of organizations who emphasized opportunism and conflict of interest (Williamson 2002; Augier and March 2001b).

Carnegie and the Psychology of Problem Solving

In the early 1950s, at RAND, Simon began his collaboration with Allen Newell, an association that would continue, though less intensively after 1972, at Carnegie Mellon (primarily in the Department of Psychology) until Newell's death in 1992. It was in the context of his collaboration with Newell that Simon began his long-time fascination with the computer as an instrument of behavioral science and intelligence. "Whatever the conceptual power of the mathematical models of operations research," said Simon (1960, p. 60), "their actual use in practical schemes for decision making hinged on the fortuitous arrival on the scene of the digital computer." At RAND, computers were used in solving problems of military strategy, and for pursuing the implications of new formalisms available in the social sciences, such as game theory, linear programming, and dynamic programming; and they were mostly used to work on constrained optimization problems. Simon saw them as a major new instrument for developing more realistic and powerful models of decision making.

Simon and Newell met at RAND, where both men had been invited to do studies related to the organization of early warning stations for air defense (Simon 1991b). Simon's work on organization theory was already well known, and Newell, before meeting Simon in person, had used Simon's theory in RAND working papers (Newell 1951; Newell and Kruskal 1951). In particular, he had commented on Simon's ideas relating to the employment relation. "The meat of the Simon theory," said Newell in Keen 1950, "is in the construction of the organization ... by means of the employers satisfaction function (getting different organizations depending on which type of 'rationality' the employer indulged in) and the psychology function by means of the worker's satisfaction function."

When Simon met Newell, he immediately saw a potential partner. As he recalled, "it became obvious within a few minutes that we had very similar views although we had very different ways of expressing them. And so, he was talking about information processing and I was talking about decision making and we decided that it was the same thing." By then, Simon had come to believe that detailed studies of the psychology of decision making could provide empirical evidence for his theories of decision making. He often used expressions such as "problem solving" and "information processing" to highlight the psychological side of decision making; however, decision making and problem solving were essentially the same for him (Newell 1989; Simon 1988, 1989a; Simon and Newell 1972; Augier 2001).[6]

In the summer of 1954, Simon learned to program the IBM 701, and he and Newell began trying to simulate human problem solving

(Simon 1991b, p. 201). In the beginning of 1956, they (along with J. Clifford Shaw) produced the Logic Theorist, the first Artificial Intelligence program (Newell and Simon 1956; McCorduck 1979; this volume). The Logic Theorist was an adaptive computer program designed to solve problems and prove theorems by selective search. The implementation of the program was done on the RAND Jonniac computer (named after John von Neumann, its creator). The first execution of the program occurred on December 15, 1955—the day on which Newell and Simon hit upon the conceptual scheme for the program, leaving only the implementation to be worked out. Simon persistently celebrated that day as the birth of the Logic Theorist. (See, for example, Simon 1991b.)

The next significant step was the first test run of the program. Simon involved his family as well as his colleagues and students to this important event:

While awaiting completion of the computer implementation of LT, Al and I wrote out the rules for the components of the program (subroutines) in English on index cards, and also made up cards for the contents of the memories (the axioms of logic). At the GSIA building on a dark winter evening in January 1956, we assembled my wife and three children together with some graduate students. To each member of the group, we gave one of the cards, so that each person became, in effect, a component of the LT computer program—a subroutine that performed some special function, or a component of its memory. It was the task of each participant to execute his or her subroutine, or to provide the contents of his or her memory, whenever called by the routine at the next level about that was then in control.... We were able to simulate the behavior of LT with a computer constructed of human components. Here was nature imitating art imitating nature.   (Simon 1991b, pp. 206–207)

The actual target program, written in the computer language IPL-II, ran for the first time on the Johnniac at RAND on August 9, 1956. Newell, Shaw, and Simon were eager to spread the word of the Logic Theorist to their colleagues. "Our light was hidden under no bushel," Simon recalled (1991b, p. 211). Their primary audience was people working on artificial intelligence problems (Marvin Minsky, John

McCarthy, Nathanial Rochester, Claude Shannon, Oliver Selfridge). However, they also wrote to Bertrand Russell to let him know that the Logic Theorist had (in the August 9 run) produced its first proof of a theorem in the *Principia*. Russell responded that he was pleased to know that the proofs could be accomplished by machine, and that he wished that he had known of the possibility "before [Whitehead and I] wasted ten years doing it by hand" (Simon 1991b, p. 208). After the discovery, as reported by Feigenbaum (1989 and this volume), Simon walked into his classroom declaring: "over the Christmas Holiday, Newell and I invented a thinking machine."

The Logic Theorist demonstrated the possibility of applying an information-processing model to problem-solving tasks. However, Newell, Shaw, and Simon were interested in more than just producing a machine capable of proving theorems. "The letters to Russell," Simon reflected in his autobiography (1991b, pp. 189–212), "show that from the beginning we were interested in simulating human problem solving, and not simply in demonstrating how computers could solve hard problems." A few years later, the General Problem Solver—a program measuring the difference between its current state and an aspiration level, and engaging in search to reduce this difference—was invented. In Simon's mind, the emphasis on trial-and-error processes of search guided by heuristics distinguished this work from more algorithmic efforts undertaken by others in the field (ibid., p. 202). Rather than dictating a unique outcome, Newell's and Simon's heuristics created a space in which search could take place. In that sense, they operated in much the same way that aspiration levels had operated to define a space of possibilities in organizations (March and Simon 1958).

In 1958 Simon wrote: "There are now in the world machines that think, that learn, and that create. Moreover, their ability to do these things is going to increase rapidly until—in a visible future—the range of problems they can handle will be coextensive with the range to which the human mind has been applied." (Simon and Newell 1958,

p. 387) He made a famous (and considerably optimistic) forecast of when the world chess championship would be held by a computer program, a forecast that he later described as basically correct but off slightly with respect to the timing. Simon had profound confidence that the research used to produce the Logic Theorist could be applied both to developing computer programs that solved difficult problems (artificial intelligence) and to advancing our understanding of human problem solving (often labeled cognitive science) (Simon 1991b, pp. 217–218).

Simon and Newell made efforts to communicate their results to a wider audience, in particular to psychologists.[7] For Simon, artificial intelligence and psychology were always connected, with human psychological phenomena acting as data against which theories, framed as AI programs, were to be tested. In a paper published (with Newell and J. Clifford Shaw) in *Psychological Review* in 1958, Simon attempted to translate the language of the Logic Theorist into psychology. This line of work ultimately resulted in the General Problem Solver (Newell, Shaw, and Simon 1962). Newell and Simon continued to work along the same lines in the 1950s and the 1960s. In 1972, hoping to present their integrated thoughts as a major treatise in the area (Simon 1991b, p. 225), Newell and Simon published *Human Problem Solving*. In that book they attempted to specify a general theory of human problem solving which conceptualizes both humans and computers as symbolic information processing systems and "views a human as a processor of information" (Newell and Simon 1972, p. 5). Their theory was built around the concept of an information processing system, defined by the existence of symbols, elements of which are connected by relations into structures of symbols. To understand the system (and make it work), it was necessary to understand the internal representation of information processing through the creation of symbols and through learning which works to transform external information into human memory (Simon 1991b, p. 229). The work underlying *Human Problem Solving* became as influential in cognitive science and artificial intelligence as Simon's earlier work had been in economics and organizations.

Carnegie and The Sciences of the Artificial

In 1968, four years before the publication of *Human Problem Solving*, Simon published *The Sciences of the Artificial*, a book based on his Karl Taylor Compton Lectures delivered at MIT. He viewed those lectures and that book as central to most of his other work—in organizations, economics, and psychology—but they became especially influential to thinking in artificial intelligence. *The Sciences of the Artificial*—which ultimately included (in its third edition) Simon's paper "The architecture of complexity"—made his most precise argument about the role of hierarchy in the organization of knowledge and the execution of problem solving.

Simon saw networks of human intelligence as organized hierarchically, both as a matter of fact and as a matter of efficiency (Sunder, this volume). The ideas were already in the Simon oeuvre, but "The architecture of complexity" and *The Sciences of the Artificial* gave them a precise and manifestly persuasive form. In keeping with the idea that heuristic search allowed problem solving and decision making in the face of constraints, Simon argued that complex behavior was not the result of complex plans or complex ideas, but rather the use of simple heuristics in a complex environment. It was a point that he had made earlier (March and Simon 1958, p. 178). Simon liked to use the example of an ant running: the path may twist and turn and switch, but this is done simply to avoid environmental constraints. This applies to human behavior too: intentional behavior, which appears to be complex, often is directed by a very simple goal and appears more complex than it is only because the environment prevents a straightforward path. Of course, behavior wasn't always governed by heuristics applicable to ants, and humans, as they became experts in certain types of problems, applied more complex strategies for making decisions—strategies they had collected through experience.

As an outgrowth of work on verbal learning that he had begun with Edward Feigenbaum, Simon was involved in precursors of expert systems (specialized computer programs that can make expert judgments in particular fields). For example, EPAM (designed by Feigenbaum) exhibited aspects of expert capabilities by recognizing and sorting stimuli and producing responses from its data memory (Feigenbaum and Simon 1963). This research influenced subsequent work on expert systems (see Feigenbaum, McCorduck, and Nii 1988; Feigenbaum 1989). Simon also worked on BACON and DALTON (Langley, Simon, Bradshaw, and Zytkow 1987), two AI programs that tried to extract laws from regularities in empirical data (Simon 1991b, pp. 371–372), and on KEKADA (Kulkarni and Simon 1988), a program that designed sequences of experiments and adapted each new experiment to the findings of the previous ones. In this work, Simon returned strongly to the spirit of his earliest efforts to reform practice, now focusing not on attacking inefficiency in city management but on attacking inefficiency in human problem solving, including the creative work of scientists.

Simon's earlier work in economics, political science, artificial intelligence, and the philosophy of science echoed in the work on scientific discovery. Although most of the papers were published in the 1980s and the 1990s, his first systematic exploration of issues of scientific discovery appeared in 1966. Working with several co-authors, Simon studied scientific discovery as a form of heuristic search through problem spaces. In keeping with the spirit of *The Sciences of the Artificial*, Simon argued that the apparent complexity of scientific behavior did not necessarily imply that the underlying processes were also complex. Nor did it imply uniqueness of scientific thinking. "The mechanisms of scientific discovery are not peculiar to that activity," Simon and co-authors wrote (Langley et al. 1987, p. 3); they are instead "special cases of the general mechanisms of problem solving." This work was often developed in the form of computational models (see the chapters by Langley and Valdez-Perez in this volume). The ability to define computational models that reproduced scientific outcomes (e.g., theorems and hypotheses) constituted for Simon a reasonable demonstration that the models represented the nature of scientific discovery. In this domain, he tended to adopt an "as if" demonstration strategy for theory validation that resembled the familiar strategy of classical economic theory that he sometimes criticized. The difference, he maintained, lay in the more solid empirical basis for the axioms of his work on scientific discovery.

The Legacy

Living in a scientific community involves exposure to many intelligent and creative minds. Nevertheless, knowing Simon was a unique experience. His standing was unsurpassed. During his career, he received every conceivable honor that his profession, his country, and his colleagues around the world could confer on him. It was not his honors that most distinguished him, however. It was his style. He was a classic twentieth-century scientist. He was dedicated to science with a brilliance, intensity, and single-mindedness that made him a paragon of uncompromising commitment to the life of the mind. He believed in a classical conception of the scientific endeavor. Although he did little empirical research, either on his own or in collaboration with others, he was an unremitting advocate of empirical studies. He believed that the pursuit of truth was a worthy pursuit, that it was possible and desirable to increase knowledge through the systematic confrontation of speculation with empirical observation and by means of a continual winnowing of ideas through scientific discourse.

He organized his life around his work, infecting his friends, his colleagues, and his family with his commitment to a scientific perspective that was unremitting. He was a proud and loving husband and father, a man who liked to walk (though he disliked most sports), and a skillful chess and piano player, among many other things. These were, however, not separate compartments of his life—each seemed to flow into the others and into his scholarship. Simon was always alert to the possible scientific significance of everything he saw or did, converting mundane events into intellectual experiences.

Intellectual curiosity was, for him, the essence of science. The dedication of his first single-authored monograph, "Fiscal aspects of metropolitan consolidation," read: "To my Mother and Father; Who taught me that curiosity is the beginning of all science." Aware of his own curiosity, he titled a 1992 talk given at Carnegie Mellon "The cat curiosity couldn't kill." In testimony before the House Committee on Science, Space and Technology, he called curiosity "[the] major driving force of science, and a noble goal" (1989b, p. 1). As a result of being curious, he had a strong desire to produce something genuinely novel and to be a revolutionary. He was not averse to claiming priority.

Curiosity was the womb of science for Simon, but argument was its lifeblood. He often engaged in spirited exchanges, both public and private, and he rarely let a critical comment on his work go unchallenged. Although he was conscious of the possibility that he might occasionally, though very rarely, be wrong, he believed that logic, evidence, and argument would naturally convert intelligent minds to the proper view (his) and that persistent opposition was the result of an unwillingness to think through a particular problem. After an exchange with Simon, Dwight Waldo wrote (1952, p. 501): "Professor Simon seems to me that rare individual in our secular age, a man of deep faith. His convictions are monolithic and massive. His toleration of heresy and sin is nil. The Road to Salvation is straight, narrow, one-way and privately owned." George Miller, in the present volume, recalls: "I never won an argument with [Simon], not even when I was right."

Simon combined ferociousness and effectiveness of argument with a genuinely gentle spirit. A heated argument would often begin with the words "Look, friend," as if he wanted to convey that what was to follow and the disagreement on a particular idea would not affect a relationship (Kotovsky, this volume). With his informal style, he treated everybody from every field, undergraduates and Nobel Prize winners, alike and with respect (Feldman, this volume). As John Conlisk writes in the present volume, he was a teacher and a scholarly friend to all. His students found his mind terrifying but his manner always polite and supportive. The pieces in this book give several examples of how Simon combined sympathy and rigor in his dealing with others. For example, he wrote the following to one friend (a former student): "Since I found so much to agree with in your book, I set to wondering why, whenever I mention your work in print I tend to carp about it and accuse you of pouring the old wine into new bottles.... Perhaps one criticizes one's friends because they are so near to the truth, and neglects the others because they are hopeless."[8]

When Herb Simon died, science lost one of its purest disciples and most elegant practitioners. He occupied a position in the social and behavioral sciences of the twentieth century that was without parallel. Herb Simon was our friend and colleague. And when we recall the twentieth century, we will recall him as a model scientist, one of the glories of the age, and one of the masters of his craft. His mark is on us all, and we are exalted by it.

Acknowledgments

This chapter borrows extensively (and with permission) from both the ideas and the texts of Augier and March 2001a and Augier and March 2002.

Notes

1. Pamela McCorduck, interview with Herbert A. Simon, October 28, 1974 (Herbert A. Simon archives, Carnegie Mellon University), p. 3.

2. Herbert A. Simon, note from Simon to Clifford Hildreth, "Inquiry on Cowles Commission," August 2, 1982. Herbert A. Simon papers, Carnegie Mellon University Library.

3. Herbert A. Simon, note from Simon to Clifford Hildreth, "Inquiry on Cowles Commission," August 2, 1982. Herbert A. Simon papers, Carnegie Mellon University Library.

4. Simon wrote a companion paper to his behavioral model of rational choice, titled "Rational choice and the structure of the environment" (1956), in which he introduced the ideas that the environment influenced decision making as much as information processing abilities do. Here he no longer uses maximizing assumptions; he wants to examine the influence of the structural environment on the problem of "behaving approximately rationally, or adaptively" in particular environments (p. 130). We mention this paper in a note because it wasn't intended for economists per se and it isn't mentioned in Simon's own recollections of his Cowles influences.

5. Day and Sunder (1996, p. 140) noted that Carnegie Mellon in the 1960s "was marked by an extraordinary congregation of men and ideas. In another place and time, these diverse ideas might have clashed and retreated to their own cubicles of academic disciplines. It was, perhaps, the fortuitous presence of unique personalities in this group of scholars that closed the exits for retreat and forced the ideas to clash—even spark—then fuse and generate new disciplines and lines of research." For similar enthusiasm about the early spirit at GSIA, see Williamson 1996 and Williamson, forthcoming.

6. The best history of Simon's involvement in AI and his work in this area is McCorduck 1979.

7. To Simon, this was a rather natural choice, because he felt the research on the Logic Theorist "had borrowed more from psychology to advance artificial intelligence than from artificial intelligence to advance psychology" (1991b, p. 219).

8. Simon, letter to Oliver Williamson, September 29, 1993.

References

Augier, M. 2001. Sublime Simon. *Journal of Economic Psychology* 22, no. 3: 307–334.

Augier, M., and J. G. March. 2001a. Remembering Herbert A. Simon (1916–2001). *Public Administration Review* 61, no. 4: 396–402.

Augier, M., and J. G. March. 2001b. Conflict of interest in theories of organization: Herbert A. Simon and Oliver Williamson. *Journal of Management and Governance* 3–4: 223–230.

Augier, M., and J. G. March. 2002. A model scholar. *Journal of Economic Behavior and Organization*.

Christ, C. 1994. The Cowles Commission's contributions to econometrics at Chicago, 1939–55. *Journal of Economic Literature* 32: 30–59.

Conlisk, J. 1996. Why bounded rationality? *Journal of Economic Literature* 34: 669–700.

Cyert, R. M., and J. G. March. 1963. *A Behavioral Theory of the Firm*. Prentice-Hall.

Day, R., and S. Sunder. 1996. Ideas and work of Richard M. Cyert. *Journal of Economic Behavior and Organization* 31: 139–148.

Day, R. 2002. Adapting, learning, economizing and economic evolution. In M. Augier and J. March, eds., *The Economics of Choice, Change and Organization*. Elgar.

Feigenbaum, E., and H. A. Simon. 1963. Brief notes on the EPAM theory of verbal learning. In C. Cofer and B. Musgrave, eds., *Verbal Behavior and Learning*. McGraw-Hill.

Feigenbaum, E. 1989. What hath Simon wrought? In D. Klahr and K. Kotovsky, eds., *Complex Information Processing*. Erlbaum.

Feigenbaum, E., P. McCorduck, and H. P. Nii. 1988. *The Rise of the Expert Company*. Times Books.

Frederickson, G. 2001. Herbert Simon and Dwight Waldo. *Public Administration Times*, March, p. 8.

Holt, C. C., F. Modigliani, J. F. Muth, and H. A. Simon. 1960. *Planning, Production, Inventories, and Work Force*. Prentice-Hall.

Ijiri, Y., and H. A. Simon. 1977. *Skew Distributions and the Sizes of Business Firms*. North-Holland.

Keen, C. 1950. A translation of the Simon Employment Relationship into the Kruskal-Newell language. RAND report RM-544.

Kulkarni, D., and H. A. Simon. 1988. The processes of scientific discovery: The strategy of experimentation. *Cognitive Science* 12: 139–175.

Langley, P., H. A. Simon, G. Bradshaw, and J. Zytkow. 1987. *Scientific Discovery: Computational Explorations of the Creative Processes*. MIT Press.

March, J. G., and H. A. Simon. 1958. *Organizations*. Wiley.

March, J. G. 1978a. Bounded rationality, ambiguity, and the engineering of choice. *Bell Journal of Economics* 9: 587–608.

March, J. G. 1978b. The 1978 Nobel Prize in economics. *Science*, November 24: 858–861.

McCorduck, P. 1979. *Machines Who Think*. Freeman.

Newell, A. 1951. Experimenting with organizations. RAND report D(L)-991.

Newell, A. 1989. Putting it all together. In D. Klahr and K. Kotovsky, eds., *Complex Information Processing*. Erlbaum.

Newell, A., and J. Kruskal. 1951. Formulating Precise Concepts in Organization Theory. RAND report RM-619.

Newell, A., C. Shaw, and H. A. Simon. 1962. The process of creative thinking. In H. Grubert and W. Wertheimer, eds., *Contemporary Approaches to Creative Thinking*. Atherton.

Newell, A., and H. A. Simon. 1956. The Logic Theory Machine. *IRE Transactions on Information Theory* 3: 61–79.

Newell, A., and H. A. Simon. 1972. *Human Problem Solving*. Prentice-Hall.

Radner, R. 2000. Costly and bounded rationality in individual and team decision-making. *Industrial and Corporate Change* 9, no. 4: 623–658.

Ridley, C. E., and H. A. Simon. 1938. *Measuring Municipal Activities*. International City Manager's Association.

Schultz, H. 1938. *The Theory of Measurement and Demand*. University of Chicago Press.

Schur, S., and J. Marschak, eds. 1950. *Economic Aspects of Atomic Power*. Princeton University Press.

Simon, H. A. 1943. The incidence of a tax on urban real property. *Quarterly Journal of Economics* 57: 398–420.

Simon, H. A. 1947. *Administrative Behavior*. Macmillan.

Simon, H. A. 1951. A formal theory of the employment relationship. *Econometrica* 19: 293–305.

Simon, H. A. 1952. On the definition of the causal relation. *Journal of Philosophy* 49: 517–528.

Simon, H. A. 1952–1953. A comparison of organization theories. *Review of Economic Studies* 20, no. 1: 40–48.

Simon, H. A. 1953. Causal ordering and identifiability. In W. Hood and T. Koopmans, eds., *Studies in Econometric Method*. Wiley.

Simon, H. A. 1955. A behavioral model of rational choice. *Quarterly Journal of Economics* 69: 99–118.

Simon, H. A. 1956. Rational choice and the structure of the environment. *Psychological Review* 63: 129–138.

Simon, H. A. 1957. *Models of Man*. Wiley.

Simon, H. A. 1968. On judging the plausibility of theories. In B. van Rootselaar and J. Staal, eds., *Logic, Methodology and Philosophy of Sciences III*. North-Holland.

Simon, H. A. 1969. *The Sciences of the Artificial*. MIT Press.

Simon, H. A. 1976. From substantive to procedural rationality. In S. Latsis, ed., *Method and Appraisal in Economics*. Cambridge University Press.

Simon, H. A. 1977. *Models of Discovery*. Reidel.

Simon, H. A. 1978. Rationality as process and product of thought. *American Economic Review* 68: 1–16.

Simon, H. A. 1979. *Models of Thought*, volume 1. Yale University Press.

Simon, H. A. 1982. *Models of Bounded Rationality*. MIT Press.

Simon, H. A. 1988. Nobel laureate Simon "looks back": A low-frequency mode. *Public Administration Quarterly* 12: 275–300.

Simon, H. A. 1989a. The scientist as problem solver. In D. Klahr and K. Kotovsky, eds., *Complex Information Processing*. Erlbaum.

Simon, H. A. 1989b. Social and Behavioral Science Programs in the National Science Foundation. Testimony of Herbert A. Simon, March 14, 1989, House Committee on Science, Space and Technology.

Simon, H. A. 1991a. Organizations and markets. *Journal of Economic Perspectives* 5: 25–44.

Simon, H. A. 1991b. *Models of My Life*. MIT Press.

Simon, H. A. 1993. Altruism and economics. *American Economic Review* 83, no. 2: 156–161.

Simon, H. A. 1997a. *Models of Bounded Rationality*, volume 3. MIT Press.

Simon, H. A. 1997b. *An Empirically Based Microeconomics*. Cambridge University Press.

Simon, H. A. 2001. On simulating Simon: His monomania, and its sources in bounded rationality. *Studies in the History and Philosophy of Science* 32, no. 3: 501–505.

Simon, H. A., and A. Ando. 1961. Aggregation of variables in dynamic systems. *Econometrica* 29: 111–138.

Simon, H. A., P. F. Drucker, and D. Waldo. 1952. Development of theory of democratic administration: Replies and comments. *American Political Science Review* 46, no. 2: 494–503.

Simon, H. A., G. Kozmetsky, H. Guetzkow, and G. Tidal. 1954. *Centralization and Decentralization in Organizing the Controller's Department.* Controllership Foundation.

Simon, H. A., D. W. Smithburg, and V. A. Thompson. 1950. *Public Administration.* Knopf.

Waldo, D. 1952. The development of theory of democratic administration. *American Political Science Review* 46, no. 1: 81–103.

Williamson, O. E. 1996. Transaction cost economics and the Carnegie connection. *Journal of Economic Behavior and Organization* 31: 149–155.

Williamson, O. E. 2002. Empirical microeconomics: Another perspective. In M. Augier and J. March, eds., *The Economics of Choice, Change and Organization.* Elgar.

He's Just My Dad!

Katherine Simon Frank

When Mie and Jim asked me to contribute a chapter to this memorial book, I began to sift through my memories of my father, my stories about him, and my experiences with him. It is so arbitrary, one's view of another. But one's father? If either of my siblings were to write this, each would tell different stories and give entirely different pictures of our father. Here's mine. I am solely responsible for my perception and portrayal of my father, Herbert A. Simon.

Just after my father won the Nobel Prize in Economics, he referred a reporter to me who wanted information about the family. "What was it like growing up with a famous father?" was his first question. I was silent for a long time, as I processed his question. Finally, I blurted: "I don't know what you mean. . . . He's just my dad!" I never experienced my father as famous—he wasn't famous to me. This was the first time that I was starkly aware that people thought my father was truly different, not just as a man, but also as a parent.

But how different? When we were small children, he crawled on the floor and growled when we played "Dinosaur." He lay on the floor, resting his chin on his hand, and played dominoes, checkers, Clue, marbles, chess. He read stories to me. He took me on walks as I walked my doll in her carriage. We built sand castles. We splashed in the ocean waves. We walked to the Bookmobile for library books. These were things that went on in all homes, weren't they? To me, he was just like other fathers. He was a man much like all others, yet distinctive in his own special ways.

My father was a very private person. His privacy about personal and family information never seemed false or unsuitably modest. His belief in keeping family matters in the family was expressive of his upbringing and his generation. We were taught that our parents' ages, family affairs, and family's finances were nobody else's business. We weren't told these were secrets, just that polite people didn't talk of such things. His privacy extended to his intellectual life, as well, though one often had the impression that intellectually he was completely open. He loved a good debate. He always had facts to back his arguments. But the debates were a game for him—the game of Devil's Advocate. He could so convincingly argue a case he didn't believe in at all that he appeared to promote just the opposite of what he actually believed. After satisfying himself that his opponent had sufficiently defended his or her side with relevant facts, he would reveal his personal opinion, and then engage in intense intellectual exchange of a personal nature. This practice was as true with his children—at least this child—as with his students, colleagues, and friends.

He loved his family and his friends—and he had many good close ones, ones he trusted and enjoyed and much spent time with. Still, he rued that sometimes people didn't get to know him at all. They were inhibited by The Famous Person Syndrome, he said. People who knew him only as A Famous Person worshipped the hero they made him out to be. They couldn't see past the facade that they created of him. This saddened my father, who was so authentic and who wanted nothing more than to be known as himself.

So after my father died, I was delighted when friend after friend expressed a consistent view of him: they knew his humorous side, his loyalty, his intensity, and his inquisitiveness. They said "Your father once said to me . . ." and they'd quote something they remembered my father telling them. Something different had struck each one. This, they told me, had influenced them in some significant way that they described. I was delighted, but also amazed. And then, one night shortly after his death, I found a document on his computer labeled "Adages" that indicated he had been working on it as recently as the day before he entered the hospital. I remembered a conversation my brother and I had with our father in the hospital less than a week before he died in which we talked about family sayings we had grown up with that inspired our personal perspectives.

I opened the six-page document. I recognized many of them as quotes his friends had shared with me. Some were part of the repertoire I inherited from my dad in conversations or in his letters to me. Some were those we had spoken of in the hospital the week before. As I read them, and now as I write about my father, I hear his voice in my mind's ear. Since the adages were so much a part of my father, you'll find a sprinkling of them in this chapter, and, no doubt as you read them you will hear Herbert's voice in your mind, as well.

I was lucky to know Herbert A. Simon for $58\frac{1}{2}$ years—my whole life. He inspired and motivated me from as far back as my conscious memory goes. It is from him that I developed my love of nature and the out-of-doors generally; the sun, moon, planets, and stars; music; reading; walking; intellectual inquiry; tennis; deep conversation; board games and crossword puzzles; bird watching; art; an understanding of right and wrong; the interconnectedness of everything in our lives; and oh, so many other bits that enhance life. True, sometimes I thought he was difficult, especially when he engaged me, an unwilling participant, in a debate while he took on his usual role as Devil's Advocate. Almost always when those debates ended he was glad to note that I had held my own and had been successful in defending my viewpoint. It was his way of teaching, and he loved nothing more.

Forty of my $58\frac{1}{2}$ years, I lived away from my father and mother. I left home at 18 to attend college, and never lived there again. In the intervening years, my mother provided me with weekly letters recording their social events and trips and life-as-usual. I also treasure my father's annual birthday letters to me, in which he mused about all manner of subjects, including his thoughts about family and friendship. I met many of my parents' friends when I was home for visits and I liked them. But, even so, when my father died I was unprepared for the outpouring of deep love and admiration his friends expressed. I had not expected the wealth of stories they shared. All different. All genuine. All deeply personal.

None of this, so far, seems so different from what I've observed other people experience with their fathers. But I remember even as a young child that I had the sense that other people thought there was something different about my father. That puzzled me very much. I understood one difference: he was a college teacher. Most of my friends' parents were business or trades people, so just what a professor did was a mystery to them. But, like all the fathers I knew, he went to the office every morning and came home just before dinner. So what was so different?

He talked more than many of my friends' fathers. And he listened well, always interested in what we children had to say. While my mother prepared dinner and I worked on my homework on the breakfast-nook table, he paced around the kitchen "talking shop," as he was fond of saying. I'm sure I heard about many controversies without knowing it. Only if he were furiously angry with someone would he say anything negative, and even then he was respectful of the person, while he disagreed with their behavior or ideas. I never heard him say anything negative or critical about friends. (Knowing how intensely my father felt about things, I can't believe there were never conflicts, so he must have moderated his shop talk, saving shocking news for private times with my mother when our little ears weren't tuned in.) Even when dinner was put on the table, he wasn't talked out. But when we were all together, he turned to other topics: he questioned how school was that day, who we had seen, what we had learned. Then he initiated discussions about current events or intellectual ideas. Not infrequently someone left the table momentarily to get the dictionary, the atlas, the almanac, or a volume of the *Encyclopaedia Britannica* so we could define a word, resolve a question, or locate a place. These were upbeat conversations, lively, intellectually challenging, and mostly impersonal. We children were included in the discussions and encouraged to contribute, but the conversation did not revolve around the children. Nor was it pitched at children's level.

My father's name and photograph also appeared in the newspaper from time to time. Why, I was never quite sure, but I gathered it was related to his job at Carnegie Tech: the development of a new program, receipt of an award, or announcement of a new book or discovery. One of my friends would inevitably ask why my father's name and picture were in the newspaper. I lamely replied that he taught at Carnegie Tech, thinking that would explain it. When I went home, I read the newspaper to find out why. My father and mother never made a big deal—or any deal, for that matter—about his appearances in the newspaper. I wouldn't have been aware of his public exposure if it hadn't been for other people's questions and attention. This continued throughout his life. Occasionally my mother sent me copies of articles that mentioned or featured my father and his work, but often she didn't. Instead, if I heard about his achievements, it was usually from my friends and colleagues. Did my parents want to shield their children from Father as a Famous Person, or were they truly casual about this public coverage of my father's professional life? I don't know. At any rate, I grew up with very little sense of the impact my father's work had on furthering the understanding of the world.

Before it was announced, I was totally unaware that my father had been nominated for the Nobel Prize. So imagine my confusion when the telephone rang before 5 A.M. central time on October 10, 1978. In a groggy half-sleep, I answered the phone, "Hello?"

I heard an excited voice: "Hello! Kathie! This is Dick. Congratulations. Imagine! Your father won the Nobel Prize!"

In my half-awake state, I could make absolutely no sense of this except that my friend must have lost his mind. All I could think of was that it was 5 A.M. and nobody calls anybody at 5 A.M.! "This is not a funny joke," I said. "Do you know what time it is?"

Dick was obviously very embarrassed as he uttered, "I'm sorry. Don't you know about this? Uh, perhaps I made a mistake.... I thought I heard it on the radio just now. First they said that Herbert Simon won the Nobel Prize, and then they announced that John Paul was appointed the new pope. Perhaps I heard it wrong. I'm really sorry to call you so early."

I struggled to sound gracious as I answered, "Oh, that's okay, I'll check it out and let you know."

I stumbled out of bed, found the phone number of one of our big news stations in the phone book and dialed it. "Do you have anything on your ticker tape about Herbert Simon winning the Nobel Prize?" I asked.

I waited while the man at the station looked at the incoming AP news releases. He returned to the phone and breathlessly said, "Yes, here it is. Herbert Simon was awarded the Nobel Prize in Economics...."

I thanked him; as I hung up I heard him shout, "Wait! Who is this? What's your connection?"

But I was off the phone. Without thinking, I picked up the phone again and dialed my parents. It wasn't uncommon for my father to be up and alert this early (it was now after 6 A.M. Eastern Time). When my father answered, I told him what I had heard. He affirmed that it was true, but, he admitted, he had not heard the news officially. The reporters in Pittsburgh were not on the job yet, it seemed. My dad said he learned unofficially late the night before from a friend in Europe that the official announcement of the economics prize would come from the Nobel Committee the next morning. True to form, my pattern of hearing first from friends about my father's achievements rather than from him continued.

Later in the day I phoned my friend back to thank him for alerting me to the news and to apologize for my early-morning crossness. He was relieved, as he teased me: "I'm glad to hear this. For awhile after I talked with you, I thought that maybe I had got it wrong—that maybe he had been appointed pope!"

How else was my father different? I became aware early on that our family was different because, in the early years, my parents did not own a car. Unlike all our neighbors, we did not vacation in Florida, but spent summers in California or shorter vacations in Maine, Georgia, North Carolina, Colorado, the Southwest, Wisconsin. My father did not attend team sporting events, nor did he listen to them on the radio or television. In fact, rarely did my father listen to the radio for any reason. My parents only bought a television in 1957 after peer pressure from my younger sister prevailed, but I was never aware of his watching it—ever.

However, he read avidly, almost anything he could find. This included the daily newspaper, which he read each day devotedly, grumbling all the way through about how you couldn't believe what you read. Since he had amassed years of experience in which newspaper reporters misquoted him in interviews about his achievements, he had reasonable doubts about the accuracy of what he read. He read, he said, to get the gist of what was going on in the world, but, he repeated every day, you can't believe everything you read. You have to collect data yourself to ascertain what is true. After his disturbing morning newspaper reading, he soothed himself by completing the daily crossword puzzle (in later years, two). Most Sunday afternoons he and my mother enjoyed the challenge of the *New York Times* puzzle, which often took hours to complete, including many trips to the bookshelf for peeks into his reference books.

My father was also different because of the ways he spent his spare time. Evenings he sat in a chair in a corner of the living room after putting a record on the phonograph, often something by Beethoven, Bartok, Mozart, sometimes Stravinsky or his college friend Ellis Kohs. Then he chose a book, now and then in one of the dozen or so languages he knew or a new one he was learning, and read for a couple of hours. About learning languages he said: "Anyone can learn quickly to speak a foreign language, badly but effectively, if she or he has no shame." He would stop reading periodically to help me with my homework, or to discuss an interesting aspect of the current chapter in history I was reading, or to answer a question about a physics or math problem I was struggling with. Mid-evening, he climbed upstairs to his study to write on his typewriter, later his computer. Sometimes he played the piano for an hour or so before we went to bed. Bach preludes and fugues, and Mozart and Beethoven sonatas were his favorites; he executed them all with great skill and feeling on the Steinway baby grand that he inherited from his pianist mother in the 1950s.

We had strange art on our walls: a large print of Van Gogh's wheat fields hung over the sofa; an elegant Egyptian bitch with large teats hung between the front windows (as a teen, I demanded that my parents remove this, because I was so embarrassed to have my friends see it); a giant red modern original oil by my parents' friend Sam Rosenberg. As the result of a bathroom leak that left a large irregular abstract stain on the living room ceiling, my father painted the large shape in shiny red enamel. Voila! ceiling art (quite a conversation piece) that stayed for several years until the ceiling was finally repaired. Gradually my parents began to collect other art, occasionally representational, but, more often, abstract or whimsical.

My father loved beetles. He knew their Latin names, and he knew facts about their habits and where they lived. Most of my friends, like many people, loathed beetles, so I realized this was something unusual about my father. I also learned to appreciate the beetles' beauty because of my father's deep fascination with them, as well as with the birds and tiny rodents that we saw when we hiked in various parts of the country. My father believed that we humans are not unique and set apart from nature; we are an integral part of nature. Our task, he believed, is not to use our intelligence to dominate nature, but to learn how to live in harmony with all of nature on this fragile planet that we share.

Growing up I sometimes thought that my father could have been more directive. I realize now that he was a superb (and subtle) guide. Rather than telling this child what to do, he asked questions, made proposals and suggestions (always many)—laid out the options, the possibilities. He sought to learn my opinions and encouraged me to express them. He taught me to think for myself, to have the confidence to make decisions and to live with the consequences, to know that I am responsible and that I can trust my basic inner essence. In not telling me what to do, I was not able to rebel against him. But in guiding me, by mentoring me, he gave me tools for the rest of my life. I phoned him from college in my freshman year when I was so miserable that I wanted to drop out or transfer. I asked him what I should do. Gently he answered: "I know you'll make the right decision." I was infuriated! I didn't want to make the right decision! I wanted him to tell me what to do! In time I realized he was right. His confidence in my ability to make a good decision for myself has stayed with me all my life. Over the years, when, in my mind's ear, his voice, returning again and again in vastly different situations, says: "I know you'll make the right decision," I am thankful for that voice. That is perhaps the greatest gift he could have given me.

He was also the strongest advocate of self-competition and cooperation I ever met. He taught me to focus on doing my very best regardless of what other people were doing. He taught me that working with others would accomplish more than working competitively alone. He said: "Avoid zero-sum games. Don't mire yourself in a game where you lose whatever others win and win only what others lose. Non-zero-sum games are not easy to design. They require that winning be measured only against your own performance, past, present, or future, and not by comparison with the performance of others. If humankind is to survive, we must invent a non-zero-sum game that we (including both human and non-human life) can all play together."

Many people said Herbert was the most rational person they knew. Yes! he lived what he believed: he was realistic about the demands of life and he knew how he liked to spend his time. He believed that "people satisfice because they do not have the wits to maximize" and "information is not the scarce resource; what is scarce is the time for us humans to attend to it." To maximize time for learning and teaching and talking with students, scholars, family, and friends, he needed to streamline less important activities. Once, early on, he made two decisions: what to eat for breakfast every day, and what to eat for lunch every day, thereby eliminating two daily decisions he would have had to make about something he considered trivial and uninteresting.

Another example of his reasoning occurred when we moved to Pittsburgh in 1949 when Herbert was hired at Carnegie Tech as Head of the Department of the Graduate School of Industrial Administration (GSIA). We moved into a wonderful house on Northumberland Street. It allowed a lovely walk, exactly one mile long, down many blocks on a tree-lined street with large brick houses spanning a half-century of architecture, across a golf course with a breathtaking view of the hills across the river to the south, and the steepest hill I have ever had to negotiate outside of San Francisco. My father walked the round trip every day, year round, in all weather, "down" to the office in the morning, home in late afternoon. Some neighbors along the route have been heard to say that they set their clocks when he passed by each day. This was his thinking time, so I felt especially honored on those occasions when he invited me to trot along and talk beside his measured stride the mile down to school. He was fond of telling people that the way he and my mother chose the location of our house was to draw a circle on the Pittsburgh map, the center on the corner where GSIA stood and a radius of a mile. They only considered houses for sale within that circle. I prefer to think that they only considered houses for sale *on* that circle (satisficing in the ultimate sense of the word). What did he figure out as a result of this decision? "I hold one world record. Nearly every day for 47 years I walked back and forth to the university, a total of about 25,000 miles, the distance around the world. Who else has walked 25,000 miles on Northumberland Street in Pittsburgh?"

So, you see, Herbert Simon was just my dad—no famous person, he. I know how widely he touched my life, though I admit that until recently I was rather oblivious to the extent of his influence on the wider community. From my vantage point, he played games with me, listened to me practice my piano and violin lessons, accompanied me on the piano when I played the recorder, reviewed my homework assignments and term papers and critiqued them only when asked, discussed my newly assigned history chapter, woke me at daybreak on cool summer mornings to play tennis, patiently instructed me how to drive, taught me to identify trees, beetles, birds, and stars on our family's hikes, initiated outings to art exhibits at the museum. He was steady and made sense. I viewed him as being just like everyone else. Maybe not. I guess that's how it is with people who are deeply in your life—you interact with them, you know them so well that you don't realize their uniqueness, and you don't think how the process of being together works.

Herbert enjoyed his life. He did what he thought was important in a manner he felt proud of with people who shared his vision and his desire to do good work. He died as he lived: rationally, intensely, thoughtfully, peacefully, and with dignity. All of us who knew him reaped the benefits of his gifts to us.

I   *Modeling Man*

Is Bounded Rationality Unboundedly Rational? Some Ruminations

Kenneth J. Arrow

Herbert Simon was extraordinarily fecund and had ideas and concepts in a large variety of directions. His variety of specific applications to many aspects of governmental and business administration would alone have earned him a major place in the fields of political science and administration. To the scholarly world, however, there is one concept that is most strongly associated with his name, the hypothesis that human reactions are "boundedly rational." Individuals, especially in social contexts such as the economic or the political, do indeed seek to do "better," whatever that means in a specific context, but they do not succeed in doing so.

The explication of bounded rationality occupied many of Simon's papers, and subsequent research, such as that of Amos Tversky and Daniel Kahneman (1974), and of the increasing group of behavioral economists who follow up specific hypotheses of incompletely rational behavior. The objection that mainstream economics imputed improbable computational capacity to humans was already raised by Thorstein Veblen (1908) in some of his choicest sarcastic language.

There are many questions that such a hypothesis raises, for example, the implications for economic behavior, the implementation in specific areas or the different ways in which full rationality fails. In this essay, I simply want to discuss the possibility of reinterpreting the proposition in terms of a more comprehensive definition of rationality. I do not come to a definite answer; rather, this is an essay in exploration.

If we ask why individuals do not engage in fully rational behavior, one and perhaps the most usual answer is that full rationality is simply too complicated. For example (Simon 1972, p. 164): "[R]ationality can be bounded by assuming complexity in the cost function or other environmental constraints so great as to prevent the actor from calculating the best course of action." (Simon does give other reasons for bounded rationality on pp. 163–164, though they do not seem as convincing.) He repeatedly uses the example of chess, in principle a perfectly solvable game, whose solution vastly exceeds any present or prospective computing power.

This answer suggests a general tendency, noted, for example, by the sociologist W. J. Goode (1997): when a departure from rationality is observed, humans seem to have an inherent tendency to seek an explanation which amounts to finding some consideration relevant to a full rationality which had not been taken into account before. (Goode's statement is especially interesting because he is basically an opponent of rational-choice models.) Simon (1978, p. 446) had much earlier made a similar point, that functional explanations for deviant and apparently dysfunctional behavior in anthropology, sociology, and, perhaps more strikingly, psychoanalysis were essentially appeals to rationality.

The hypothesis suggested, then, is that boundedly rational procedures are in fact fully optimal procedures when one takes account of the cost of computation in addition to the benefits and costs inherent in the problem as originally posed. I will bring together a number of remarks, none definitive; but in sum I am inclined to feel that one could not, even as a matter of principle, deduce actual problem-solving as the optimal response to computational costs.

Knowledge: Axiomatics and Costs

Rationality, whether substantive as in neoclassical economics or procedural along the lines stressed by Simon, is a process of logical inference (every computation is such a process). It proceeds from knowledge of a problem to knowledge of an answer to it (in the sense of a method of handling it). It raises questions such as what is meant by "knowing" something and in what sense can we infer or otherwise proceed from knowing some propositions to knowing others.

An approach which has found favor among game theorists interested in the epistemological foundations of their subject is the use of modal logic.[1] A set of axioms are stated for an operator K which is interpreted, "I know that." (The game theorists extend this formalism to having a number of knowers, but that extension is not necessary here. See Bacharach 1994 and Aumann 1999.) Among the assumptions is one usually referred to as, "logical omniscience": if Kp and K(p implies q), then Kq. In words, if a proposition p is known and if it is also known that p implies q, then q is known. It is easy to conclude from this that if one starts with a set of assumptions taken as known, then any proposition that can be inferred from these assumptions is known. In terms of computations, the statement means that given any problem for which there is a solution in a finite number of steps, then the solution is known.

Since mathematics consists of deduction from known axioms, it follows that all of mathematics must be known, at least in the usual meaning of the word 'deduction', which is taken to mean provable in a finite number of steps. In fact, of course, the mathematical consequences even of well-studied axiom systems are clearly not exhausted by current knowledge.

Obviously, the word 'known' has some ambiguity in it. There needs to be a time subscript on the knowledge operator. Propositions and computations which in some sense could be known are not however known at any given moment of time. The process of knowing is time-consuming. Therefore the process is resource-consuming, since time is a resource. In fact, time can be traded off against other resources by using more or faster and therefore more expensive computers or by investing in the development of new algorithms.

I cannot refrain from a trivial empirical example, i.e., a personal anecdote. Almost forty years, I was invited to give a lecture at a Belgian university well known in the United States for having been destroyed in two world wars; to Americans, it was the University of Louvain. I spent two days elsewhere in the country before going to the university and was brought to realize the intensity of the language question, with virtually every town being designated as Flemish or French but not both. I arrived by train to find that the sign at the station read Leuven. I immediately (and correctly) inferred that the town was Flemish-speaking. The university, it turned out, was a shell that contained two universities, one French-speaking and one Flemish-speaking. (The French-speaking component was subsequently moved to a linguistically more hospitable location.) I was greeted and told where my lecture was to take place the next day. I was shown a map and noted that the lecture was on rue des Doyens (a French name).

The next day I started out from the hotel and realized that I had forgotten to ask directions. I stopped a passerby. I had the view that speaking English in Europe displayed arrogance, so I asked directions in French. Thus, even though I knew that town was Flemish and that one never speaks French in a Flemish town, I was unable to draw the inference "Don't speak French." My interlocutor promptly replied (in English), with clear annoyance, that he preferred that I speak in English. I still had the problem that I only knew the French name of the street; but as I spoke, the word 'Dekanstraat' emerged from my mouth, thereby contradicting another usual axiom of knowledge theory: if Kp, then KKp, i.e., if you know a proposition, you know you know it. (I can only assume that the map I saw must have had the street names in both languages, but I certainly would have denied knowing the Flemish name if I had been asked been asked before the encounter.)

The processes of logical inference, computation, and problem-solving in general then certainly consume resources. Nevertheless, it is not easy to say what that cost is. For any particular problem, with specified values of the parameters, there is a shortest or cheapest solution; but to know which this is may well be a problem which is more difficult than some imperfect single solution. More basically, delay in solving a problem is itself a cost in terms of forgone possibilities of action. While the tradeoff between delay and resources can, in principle, be formulated explicitly, it must be recognized that sufficiently delayed information may be completely useless. Beyond a certain point, there is no tradeoff. Beautiful examples of this possibility have been given by Radner (1993). If bounded rationality means taking actions that have lower payoff than might be attained with infinite time for computation and analysis, then bounded rationality becomes a logical necessity.

The Possibility of Paradox

With this background, let us return to the question: can bounded rationality be modeled in some effective way as full rationality when one takes into account both that logical inference and computation take time and that the value of a decision also depends on the time it is taken? It has struck me that there is the possibility of a logical paradox in this approach. We start with a problem, say an optimization problem, which either cannot be solved within the appropriate time constraints or can be solved but at a considerable cost. Call this the first-order problem. We now want to reformulate the problem either as optimizing subject to a constraint on computation time or as optimizing a modified maximand in which costs of computation are subtracted. Call the reformulated problem the second-order problem. The second-order problem would appear to be more difficult in time or cost than the one we started with, the one we could not effectively solve. To solve this, then, we would again seek a boundedly rational solution and try to justify this solution as the optimal solution with time constraints and computation costs. This procedure obviously leads to an infinite regress.

We are led then to the hypothesis that a boundedly rational solution cannot be described as the optimal solution to an optimization problem in which computational delays or costs are included in the formulation of the problem.

It seems to me that there is the making of some logical paradox here, but on reflection it is not universally true. If I am using long division to determine a ratio and have only enough time to take one step, I can present the result (say, in decimals) by taking the outcome and then adding 5 in the next lower decimal place. Thus, if in the first step of a long division of a into b we get $c \times 10^r$, I can present the result as $c \times 10^r + 5 \times 10^{r-1}$. This can be derived by minimizing the maximum possible error. Thus, here the second-order problem (the solution rule) does not seem more difficult than the original one.

Nevertheless, one would suppose that the principle that bounded rationality is not sophisticated optimization must hold usually if not always.

Algorithm as Capital

I have one more variation on this theme. Consider again the second-order problem, that of optimization taking account of computational costs and delays. There are many circumstances in which solving the second-order problem actually provides a solution to many first-order problems. Surely the analysis which led George Dantzig (1963) to develop the simplex method for linear programming took a great deal of effort and time, not to mention computing costs. Yet the solution, once found, could be and was used for an enormous number of first-order problems. In that case, the "paradox" might have a different kind of resolution. The second-order problem, in this case that of finding an algorithm for optimizing solutions for linear programming problems, is indeed much more costly to solve than any given first-order problem. However, the solution of the second-order problem, like any knowledge, is a durable good. It can be used over and over again with no additional cost. The cost is thus distributed over an indefinitely large number of first-order problems and so becomes bearable.

In the case of linear programming, to be sure, we are achieving a first-best, an unboundedly rational solution. But the same kind of thinking can be applied to finding imperfect solutions whose choice reflects computational costs. In a way, any statistical sampling procedure is an optimally chosen balance between costs (say, of taking samples) and benefits in terms of improved statistical accuracy. This argument clearly cannot be universal. The second-order problem is really the simultaneous optimization of a large number of first-order problems which have such similar structure that the solution to one easily gives the solution to many others.

Are Problems Well Defined?

In a way, all the discussion to this point and many of Herbert Simon's discussions too start with a well-specified problem. The typical examples are combinatorial problems whose exact solution would be very lengthy. But much of bounded rationality in the real world is a reaction to problems which are not at all well specified. An explorer in an unfamiliar land has to find passes through mountain ranges which he or she has never seen before or embark on rivers whose course is unknown. Even a manufacturer processing raw materials that have unknown variations does not have a clearly defined problem. The actor or the analyst can impose some structure by assigning probabilities to the unknown alternatives, but in many cases even the set of alternatives is not known or cannot be well specified. No amount of past experience in the Alps will prepare one for the Rockies or the Himalayas.

With ill-specified problems, unbounded rationality has no meaning at all. The knowledge underlying any analysis is, at least in part, tacit, not consciously known but revealed in practice. Yet some limited kind of rationality is clearly evident in many of these examples.

Conclusion

The idea of optimization is very attractive if for no other reason than that it appears to be a definite theory. Of course, in practice, the implications of the optimality hypothesis depend on the model of the world we assume that the agent holds, so there is a lot of room to match reality. The rationality hypothesis of consumer demand is notoriously weak. Still, the hypothesis that individual agents optimize provides a uniform approach to descriptive modeling in specific areas and has certainly shown itself to be occasionally useful.

It is obvious to everyday observation and confirmed in experiments and to some extent in observations on the economy and the polity that rational-choice models have implications that are falsified. The problem with accepting the hypothesis of bounded rationality is not its reality but its adequacy as a theory. I am sufficiently an old-fashioned positivist (as was Herbert Simon) to hold that a theory that cannot be falsified is no theory. The gap is filled in practice by specific hypotheses about the particular form the bounds on rationality take in different contexts. But there is no general criterion for determining which limit on rationality holds in any given context and therefore the building of a complete theory of the economy on the basis of bounded rationality is a project for the future.

The idea of defining bounded rationality as rationality in a broader context of costs of inference would be one way of getting to a more useful theory. I conclude, though tentatively, that this project is not successful.

Note

1. I agree thoroughly with Simon's statements, in other but not unrelated contexts (1969, pp. 59, 67), that modal logics are unnecessary and that everything needed can be accomplished by ordinary declarative logic.

References

Aumann, R. J. 1999. Interactive epistemology 1: knowledge. *International Journal of Game Theory* 28: 263–300.

Bacharach, M. 1994. The epistemic structure of a theory of a game. *Theory and Decision* 37: 7–48.

Dantzig, G. B. 1963. *Linear Programming and Extensions*. Princeton University Press.

Goode, W. J. 1997. Rational choice theory. *American Sociologist* 28: 22–41.

Radner, R. 1993. The organization of decentralized information processing. *Econometrica* 61: 1109–1146

Simon, H. A. 1969. *The Sciences of the Artificial*. MIT Press.

Simon, H. A. 1972. Theories of bounded rationality. In C. B. McGuire and R. Radner, eds., *Decision and Organization*. North-Holland.

Simon, H. A. 1978. Rationality as process and as product of thought. *American Economic Review* 68, no. 2: 1–16.

Tversky, A., and D. Kahneman. 1974. Judgment under uncertainty: heuristics and biases. Science 185: 1124–1131.

Veblen, T. 1908. Professor Clark's economics. *Quarterly Journal of Economics* 22. Reprinted in T. Veblen, *The Place of Science in Modern Civilisation and Other Essays*. Routledge.

On Rational Satisficing

William J. Baumol

I must admit that I did not know Herb nearly as well as I would have liked, but our paths did cross, and we got on very well. There are two occasions I remember well, and two other associations that seem worth noting.

One association occurred in an emergency, when Congress threatened to cut the social sciences, including economics, completely out of the budget of the National Science Foundation. I was asked by the American Economic Association, and he by another group whose identity I do not recall, to go to Washington to do what we could, to save the situation. We first met and planned strategy, then visited some influential representatives and senators to explain to them that the social sciences were, in Benjamin Franklin's words, creating "useful knowledge," and that despite some much publicized examples of bizarre-sounding studies, the funding of research in the field did not constitute yet another "fleecing of America." Testimony before the immediately pertinent committee found them surprisingly receptive. But then the chairman of the committee complained: "... but no one has given us a number. How much should be provided in the next year's budget?" The staff members of the social science associations who were there, assigned to support us, seemed shocked, but we quickly responded, as though it was what had been intended all along,

that it should be at least the same as last year, with a suitable adjustment for inflation, and with a little help, were able quickly to come up
with a figure. We were amazed to find, as I recall, that this was the
amount that was actually provided. We felt afterwards that this time
our colleagues, so to speak, owed us one.

When Herb had been selected to receive the Nobel Prize, in accord
with standard practice, an essay on his achievements was commissioned, and I was very happy to be assigned the task. Rereading many
of his papers for the purpose turned out to be even more instructive,
stimulating and pleasant than I had expected.

But more directly pertinent to the brief essay that follows was a
debate I attended, between Herb and Milton Friedman. The subject was
the role of rational calculation in economic decisions, Milton arguing
the rationality of the optimization premise and Herb defending the
reality and reasonableness of satisficing. Milton suggested that satisficing was just a form of camouflaged rationality, entailing a careful
weighing of the costs of improved information and that of more
sophisticated calculation, while Herb responded that this view dodged
the substance of the issue, simply incorporating the one position into
the other by terminological sleight of hand.

It was this continuing line of argument, on that platform and elsewhere, that led Dick Quandt and me to prepare a paper on the rationality of following rules of thumb as one form of attempt at what we
called "optimally imperfect" decision making. This is the general subject on which I will offer some comments here.

Is There Really a Difference?

Frank Knight was fond of calling attention to "an irrational passion for
dispassionate rationality." And both Herb and Milton were in agreement that one cannot accept models in which behavior is assumed
consistent with this description. But this does not mean that they were
saying the same thing, and merely differed in the words they selected

to represent the situation. But what really is the difference? We all would agree that information is costly to acquire and that, even with computers and with the data available, optimality calculations can become complex, time consuming and perhaps even significant in cost. Clearly, there comes a point when further expenditure on either of these of time, effort and money will entail a cost greater than anything the calculator can hope to derive from increased accuracy. Indeed, we must reconcile ourselves to the fact that, whatever we do, our data and our calculations are condemned to be imperfect. The result is that it can never be optimal, and particularly in economic matters, to pursue determinedly a result that can pretend to be perfectly optimal. There must always be a rational compromise—at best, an optimally imperfect decision.

But this is something that is undoubtedly consistent with both the Simon and the Friedman position. If that were all there is to the matter, the two would have been in the position of doing the reverse of agreeing to disagree. Yet there is more to the matter, as Simon was at pains to emphasize. It is not in the recognition that results are condemned never to be perfectly optimal that the difference is to be sought. Rather, the distinction is to be found in the next step: what do decision makers do about it? And here it seems to me that there are indeed two different avenues that can be pursued.

The first is the Friedman avenue, approximative optimization. The price setter may be well aware that his cost and demand information is imperfect. He may nevertheless have his subordinates devote some effort to checking and refinement of the data, or including a longer time period in regressions, and then, judging that too much is, indeed, more than enough, bring the process to a halt. He may then have estimated admittedly approximative demand and cost functions, using methods that deliberately compromise between cost and sophistication, and come out with the price that, according to these data and calculations, with all their warts and blemishes, indicate the one that will maximize profits, if that is the objective. Generally, such a result will then be examined and modified on the basis of judgment and experience. Alternatively, he can employ an even more primitive approach, say, using a meeting of colleagues for what is (barbarically) labeled a "brainstorming" session. There, a series of alternative candidate prices are considered in turn, and opinions elicited on their plausible profitability, with each price possibly assigned a likely profit figure or perhaps with the prices only ranked in terms of profits. One can readily think of other such procedures, all somewhat crude, but all clearly qualifying as attempts at (rough) optimization, in which the costs and hurdles of more refined calculations are implicitly or explicitly taken into account. It seems clear that any and all of these qualify as optimization procedures.

What, then, is left for satisficing? Does anyone ever make decisions using procedures that do not resemble what has just been described? And, if so, must such decision makers be considered irrational? My answer, in terms of my own experience is that there are many decisions made in such other ways in reality, and that there is nothing inherently "irrational" about such a course of action. There is a general feature that distinguishes the two approaches. In an optimality calculation, explicitly or implicitly, the calculator must lay out a range of alternative possibilities, must then estimate the consequences of each and must then select the one that scores highest in terms of a preselected goal, or on some weighted average score for several such goals. The essence of optimization, then, is (possibly implicit) listing of the available alternatives, or at least some of them, and comparison of their expected performance.

Satisficing proceeds quite differently. The term is intended to convey the characterization not of the decision procedure itself, but of its termination rule. That rule involves two parts: first the selection of a state of affairs that is to be considered acceptable—with which the decision maker is just willing to live. Second, the search among alternative possibilities until she finds the first one that convincingly promises to meet that acceptability requirement. She may, for example, enter a stationers in which hundreds of fountain pens are on display. She has neither the time nor the inclination to try them all. So she tries out a half dozen, all of which prove to be unacceptably scratchy, but the seventh is not. End of search. She is well aware that there are surely pens on display that will suit her even better, but she makes no effort to find them. She is satisfied.

In practice even that may entail too complex a procedure. The firm's advertising agency for next year is chosen to be the same as this year's. Why? Because management likes the ads it has designed, likes where they have been placed and the expenditure that was entailed, and is pleased with the rate at which the firm's sales are increasing. No search and evaluation of other agencies is undertaken. The agency is, in fact, reassured that it can expect to be retained so long as its performance remains satisfactory.

But How Can Satisficing Be Rational?

Once it is granted that there is a real and substantial difference, a second question raises itself. How can satisficing possibly be rational? After all, optimization means achievement of the best, and the reasonable approach that has been suggested, one that gives appropriate weight to the added cost of search for further improvement of the optimization process, and stops before getting in too deeply, should presumably yield the best that can be expected in this world of costly and imperfect calculation. Is it not irrational to reject the best in favor of anything different?

But, once again, that is not how things generally work out in reality. I shall show now that there are circumstances, conditions that are fairly common, in which there are reasons to expect satisficing to constitute the more promising choice, and one that is surely not irrational. Paradoxically, then, optimization does not necessarily constitute the optimal approach to decision making. There are at least three reasons for this. First, the optimization calculation may trade the devil we do know for one that we don't. It may point the decision maker to options that, though promising on paper, are further from the range of his experience than those he would be led to by satisficing. Second, the very reliance on optimization of any variety may introduce transactions costs that are smaller or do not arise under a satisficing approach. Finally, the available information may be so imperfect that the comparison of options that underlies the very concept of optimization may have little point. Let me expand on each of these briefly.

Risks of Optimization as a Guide

The point that is pertinent here comes out most clearly in a situation in which satisficing calls for little or no change in the current structure of decisions. There the decision maker is not driven to conjecture about the unknown and previously untried. She will be opting to continue with the courses that she has already experienced and not found wanting. By definition, they will have lived up to her standards, and in the absence of any substantial and unexpected developments their results will continue to be satisfactory. That alone can be reason enough for preferring the satisficing approach, but where the decision maker is a delegated agent (for example, a company officer in a corporation) this approach has the added attraction of providing protection against stockholder dissatisfaction. If the optimizing solution is something of a gamble *ex ante* and proves disappointing *ex post*, she can be blamed for gambling with the company's future, whereas if she sticks to the tried and true, she is in a much better position to defend herself from stockholder attack.

This all holds to some degree even if the satisficing solution does call for a departure from current arrangements, for the standards of acceptability can include a reasonable degree of assurance that the selected course of action has some clear familiarity and a minimum of risk.

Transactions Costs of Change and of Planning for Change

The second advantage a satisficing procedure can offer is avoidance of costs that in some cases can be critical. The most obvious saving is the avoidance of the data gathering and analysis costs that optimization can require. But that is likely to be negligible. A much more significant cost difference is likely to stem from the distinct possibility that optimization can require more radical change than satisficing. For the latter entails an implicit promise to current employees and current subcontractors that so long as their performance and developments in general continue to go satisfactorily, no changes will be made. Neither employees nor subcontractors will be dismissed.

Not only can this contribute to morale and loyalty to the firm. It may also make it attractive to subcontractors and employees to undertake investments that improve the quality of their service and that will pay off eventually, but only if current relations with the firm continue. It is to be noted that this feature of satisficing is not only appreciated in a business environment. When a university admits a graduate student into its program and offers him financial support, it is often understood and sometimes stated explicitly that the support will be continued for the next several years, so long as the student's performance continues to meet standards of acceptability. We do not normally hold an annual contest among students in the current student body and outside it, re-allocating funds completely to the students who in that year are deemed most promising. The point is that there is value to commitment, and the university that can offer a conditional support commitment to students it is seeking to attract makes its money go further, but uses a satisficing approach to protect itself from the consequences of serious errors in the allocation of its student support funds.

More generally, what is implied here is that the very announcement that the decision maker proposes to act using an optimization procedure can exact some costs from which satisficing is immune.

Seriously Inadequate Information

For an economist who has not worked with business firms it may be difficult to imagine how incomplete is the information of business enterprises on matters that the silence of the textbooks can lead students to believe that the firms routinely possess. When a firm is faced with a lawsuit under the complaint that it has engaged in predatory pricing because its prices were allegedly lower than marginal costs, it is usually recognized both by managements and the courts that no one has any data on the magnitudes of those costs, let alone on their variations from product to product and from year to year. As a result, to arrive at a workable test of predatory pricing, the common procedure is to substitute data on average variable costs for the unknown marginal cost figures. But the data on average variable costs are also usually unavailable. So it is common for both defendants and plaintiffs to hire consulting firms, who undertake to estimate these figures at a cost often in the range of hundreds of thousands of dollars. Moreover, the estimates provided by the plaintiffs' consultants rarely are close to those of the defendants. Information on demand functions is in an even sorrier state, and the estimates of elasticities and cross elasticities required by Ramsey theory and other analyses remain a figment of academic imagination. More than once I have had chief financial officers of well-known firms make remarks such as "I assume you have never worked with a company whose data are as bad as ours!"

But these are just the data that, we are rightly told by economic theory, are needed for optimality calculations. When there is so little with which to calculate anything that can be claimed to approximate an optimum, is it irrational not even to try? Is it not more rational, then, to aim simply at viability—to engage in satisficing?

But, Then, Are They Not the Same, After All?

At this point it is tempting for advocates of the optimization premise to return to their original position, but reentering this time by the back door. One may well concede the validity of the description just offered of business calculations in reality. But then, one may add, all of them amount to recognition both of some true costs (like damage to work-force loyalty) that may be omitted in more naïve optimality calculations and to adaptation to the high cost of better information that in some cases may be virtually infinite. If so, is not the satisficer optimizing after all? Is not the satisficer then in the position of Moliere's protagonist who discovers that he has all along been speaking prose?

To concede this is to deprive the discussion of substance and to settle the issue via tautology. One can indeed define "optimization" to be just another term for "rational decision making" (though as behavioral economics has taught us, "rationality" itself is not so easily defined here, nor is it casually to be equated with actual behavior). But surely, whatever else one may choose to say about such wordplay, one must concede that it does remove any substantive issue from the discussion, and one may well add that it deprives "optimization" of operational meaning.

It is just for that reason that I began this discussion with an attempt to define both the concepts at issue operationally. In particular, I proposed to call a procedure to constitute even approximative optimization only if it entails explicit or implicit (as via the differential calculus) consideration of the members of a set of the relevant alternatives at issue and comparison and ranking of their estimated consequences. That is a concrete type of procedure, and it should be clear at once that in any particular circumstances it may or may not be the rational way to proceed. There may well be better criteria than I have proposed with which to frame the debate. But failure to adopt some such workable distinction surely qualifies as unwillingness to face up to the substantive issue.

In saying all this, I do not mean to imply that optimization is a useless hypothesis about behavior. Perhaps it can be shown to hold approximately in some discoverable and relatively broad varieties of cases. Perhaps in other cases it may prove to be the wrong description that dependably is approximately correct in its answers—in its description of the consequences of actual decision making procedures. At the very least, optimization can provide a standard of comparison— an indication of what is forgone in reality as a result of the uses of alternative decision procedures. Whatever the outcome of a discussion in such terms, however, it remains clear, first that theoretical analysis based on an optimization premise is not useless, second, that there is a real difference between optimization and satisficing and, third, that at least casual observation suggests that the latter is at least sometimes, and probably quite often, the more accurate description of the actual state of affairs. I suspect Herb Simon would have been willing to accept these conclusions, or at least to consider them seriously.

Memorial to Herbert A. Simon

William W. Cooper

This is a memorial to Herbert A. Simon, the Richard King Mellon University Professor of Computer Science and Psychology at Carnegie Mellon University, who died on February 9, 2001 at age 84 in Presbyterian University Hospital in Pittsburgh. This is a great—very great—loss to the world, especially the world of ideas. It is an even greater loss to friends who will miss his warmth, his wise counsel and his ever-present great good sense of humor. The greatest loss is, of course, to his wife, Dorothea, and their children Kathleen, Peter and Barbara—to whom our hearts go out in deepest sympathy.

I have known Herb Simon since 1935, when we both lived in the Burton Court dormitory at the University of Chicago. Our relations were social as well as intellectual even to the point of my arranging the date on which he first met Dorothea, his lovely wife of 63 years.

In this memorial I draw on my many memories of Herb's impact and influence on me and on others. Other friends of Herb's will bear witness to his qualities as an outstanding human being. I will focus on some of his many intellectual accomplishments and contributions since I think this is one way in which he would like to be remembered. I leave aside, however, his contributions to national science policy in his service on PSAC (the President's Science Advisory Committee under Presidents Johnson and Nixon) and as chairman of the Social Science

Research Council and Council Member of the National Academy of Sciences—as well as his many contributions to the professions and professional societies such as his services as a founding member and first vice-president of the Institute of Management Sciences (TIMS).

I also leave aside Herb's numerous contributions to higher education, not only as associate dean of the Graduate School of Industrial Administration at Carnegie Mellon University but also as an advisor to various foundations, such as the Ford Foundation, as well as government agencies such as is represented by his chairing the Committee on Pre-College Education for the National Science Foundation. My aim is directed mainly to Simon's research activities and accomplishments.

To start from the personal side, I should add that Herb and I shared the background provided by the survey courses which were required of all students during the intellectually exciting days when Robert Maynard Hutchins was president of the University of Chicago. These courses, which occupied the first two years of college, were designed to cover, broadly, the entire field of human knowledge in four separate packages consisting of the humanities, the social sciences, the physical sciences, and the biological sciences. Herb and I thereafter parted when we went into the upper divisions of the university. Herb went into political science and then into public administration. I went into chemistry and then into economics. Nevertheless, these survey courses made it possible to communicate easily with each other since they continued to provide a broad basis for understanding what we were each doing (and learning) both in the university and thereafter.

One way to view Herb's research is to refer to the fecundity (or intellectual productivity) that is exhibited by the nearly 1,000 publications listed on his home page. Another way is to note the breadth of these contributions, which range from psychology through economics and other social sciences and on into biology, the physical sciences, operations research, statistics, management, and the management sciences. However, this view does not do full justice to his amazing ability to quickly rise to the top of each of the fields in which he was working.

I illustrate by what happened when I returned from Washington toward the end of World War II to teach at the University of Chicago. Herb had also returned from his position as director of the Administrative Measurement Studies Division of the University of California's Bureau of Public Administration to teach at the Illinois Institute of Technology (previously the Armour Institute of Technology) in Chicago. Knowing that I had a lot of catching up to do, I suggested that we organize a once-a-week seminar on recent developments in economics. This took some persuasion, since Herb was occupied with two very imposing tasks. First, he was writing a textbook on public administration with Donald Smithburg and Victor Thompson—a text that took a new approach and subsequently became a classic in the field. The other task was to "axiomatize" classical physics. "The axioms of Newtonian mechanics," published in *Philosophical Magazine* in 1947, has led to exchanges with leading logicians and philosophers of science (available at Simon's web site).

I had majored in economics at both Chicago and Columbia, so I naturally took the lead in our once-a-week seminar which included Thompson as well as Herb and myself. However, this lead did not last very long. I was soon overtaken by Herb not only because of his critiques of the then-new mathematical material we were trying to master but also because this led him to better alternatives that he was able to synthesize. The latter soon led to publications, some of which produced what are now known as the "Simon-Hawkins theorems" on the conditions for macroeconomic stability. See, for example, D. Hawkins and H. A. Simon, "Note: Some conditions of macroeconomic stability," *Econometrica* 17 (1949): 245–248.

Through my acquaintance with Jacob Marschak, we next came in touch with some similarly oriented but broader-based seminars being conducted at the newly formed Cowles Commission for Economic Research, which was operating under Marschak's direction at the University of Chicago. The work of Paul Samuelson became one of the subjects of these seminars. Another was the work of Lawrence Klein, who was initiating research on large-scale econometric models. Outside visitors who presented work at this seminar included John von Neumann, who led a very lively discussion on his recently completed *Theory of Games and Economic Behavior*, published with O. Morgenstern —a book which Simon then perceptively analyzed from a social science perspective in a review which he published in the 1945 issue of the *American Journal of Sociology*.

At about this time, 1946, I left to accept an appointment at the Carnegie Institute of Technology (now Carnegie Mellon University) in Pittsburgh. Herb continued to attend these Cowles Commission seminars in Chicago, however, and this brought him into contact with the important work of Trygve Haavelmo, Tjalling Koopmans, and others in the new approaches to statistical estimation that were being developed at the Cowles Commission. Once again Simon rose to the top by reinterpreting this work in terms of a concept that he called "causal ordering." This work not only cast new light on these new statistical approaches but also related them to long-standing problems involved in interpreting causal relations in science and philosophy which Simon subsequently published in the 1952 issue of the *Journal of Philosophy* in an article titled "On the definition of the causal relation." An excellent summary of this work is provided in Simon's 1957 book *Models of Man*.

In his autobiography, *Models of My Life*, Simon notes that this (and subsequent) work with the Cowles Commission "almost made [him] into a full-time economist." Full-time or part-time, however, the importance of this work was later recognized by the Nobel Prize in Economics which was awarded to him in 1978.

Events again came to the fore. About this time, Carnegie Tech received a substantial grant from William Larimer Mellon of the Gulf Oil Company, headquartered in Pittsburgh. The objective was to provide an endowment for Carnegie Tech to found a new kind of school of business to be known as the Graduate School of Industrial Administration (GSIA). After much effort, Dean G. L. ("Lee") Bach and I were finally able to persuade Herb to join us in this endeavor as head of the

Department of Industrial Administration and as Associate Dean of the new school we were trying to form.

The contributions of this school to business education in the United States (and elsewhere) have been documented in great detail, in monographs and other studies commissioned by the Graduate Management Admissions Council. Hence I can comfortably continue to concentrate on Simon's research contributions.

At the time of his appearance in Pittsburgh, Herb was joining some of his earlier interests in biology in a new endeavor to study skew distributions in statistics (also known as Zipf distributions). The result was a series of articles in *Biometrika* arguing that these kinds of statistical distributions were more pertinent than the extensively used "normal distributions" introduced by R. A. Fisher (and others) for analyzing phenomena such as evolutionary behavior in biology.

Much was also happening in GSIA, which quickly became a research center for newly forming fields such as "operations research" and "management science." This was especially interesting and important for the school which had just received a large grant from the U.S. government for research directed to developing computer-oriented mathematical-modeling approaches to management. Herb soon turned his attention to these efforts. Arrangements were made to conduct his part of this research in the context of scheduling the production of paint at the Springdale plant of the Pittsburgh Plate Glass Company (now PPG industries). This was the "application oriented" context in which Simon, in cooperation with Charles Holt, Franco Modigliani, and Jack Muth (of GSIA) undertook research that led to their now-classic book *Planning Production, Inventories and Work Force*. Published by Prentice-Hall in 1960, this book contained a series of earlier publications and papers. Some idea of its impact can perhaps be seen from the fact that one of these original papers was rejected by the *Journal of the Operations Research Society of America* (now *Operations Research*) as being "not operations research"—possibly because the editors and the referees were steeped in the military operations research of World War

II where such topics had not been addressed. Now, however, the journal, Operations Research, has become a major outlet for such "scheduling" problems and, indeed, it is now experiencing competition from other journals devoted to what is now identified with Operations Management as a separate branch of knowledge. Finally, the importance of this (and other) work by Simon was given explicit recognition by the John von Neumann Theory prize jointly awarded to him by the Operations Research Society of America and the Institute of Management Sciences in 1988.

At about this time this school, GSIA, also received a grant from the Controllership Foundation to study the controllership function (and how it ought to be performed) in private business firms. This took the form of a large field study conducted by Simon with George Kozmetsky (recruited to GSIA from the Harvard Business School), Gordon Tyndall (a GSIA economist), and Harold Guetzkow (of GSIA), a psychologist experienced in large-scale field studies. The resulting report left the Foundation unhappy because of its science-based rather than practical orientation. Nevertheless it led to Centralization and Decentralization in Organizing the Controller's Department, a book published by the Controllership Foundation which has had considerable impact on the literatures of cost and managerial accounting.

Simon also received a grant from the Ford Foundation which enabled him to attract Jim March, a sociologist, to a joint effort that (with the aid of Harold Guetzkow) laid the foundations for a new (science-oriented) approach to the study of organizations. Based on extensive field research as well as an extensive knowledge of the pertinent literatures, this work led to their jointly authored book *Organizations*, which, on the one hand, attempted to "systematize" organization theory and, on the other hand, attempted to introduce new methods to test that theory. The latter included field research methods to further extend the boundaries of that knowledge in manners that were thereafter to effect the way research was done in the discipline that is now called "organization research." Finally, this book proved to be seminal not only in reorienting research in administration (private as well as public) but also in bringing the topic of organization research into prominence in the sociological literature as well.

Partly under the influence of Harold Guetzkow and partly as a result of his dissatisfaction with the literature on decision making (in organization contexts), Herb began to turn his interests in the directions of cognitive processes in human thought. As described in his autobiography, *Models of My Life*, Simon's contacts with the Cowles Commission in Chicago were augmented by contacts with the RAND Corporation in Santa Monica, another very active center of research involved in developing the new concepts and new methodologies coming into existence at that time. This led to Simon's fateful contact with Allen Newell and thus to the work that helped to bring the field of Artificial Intelligence into being and led to new (computer-oriented) approaches to the study of cognitive processes in psychology. This work, including its origins, is well developed in Simon's autobiography. Hence I need not describe it further in this memorial. I only need to note that whole new fields have emerged from Simon's research, as exemplified by the development of artificial intelligence (in computer science) and whole new approaches to existing fields have also emerged from the work of this remarkable man, as exemplified by his computerized approaches to the study of cognitive processes (in psychology). See also his book *The Sciences of the Artificial*, which extends the ideas of sciences of the natural world to sciences of the artificial such as the designs of physical, social, and psychological systems and processes.

The importance and the breadth of Simon's work can again be easily documented by noting that the American Psychological Association accorded him its Distinguished Scientific Contributions award in 1969 and that the Association for Computing Machinery gave him (and Allen Newell) its A. M. Turing Award in 1975. The Nobel Prize in economics (1978), the James Madison Award of the American Political

Science Association (1984), the Frederick Mosher Prize of the American Society for Public Administration (1974), the Contributions to Management Award of the American Academy of Management (1983), and the John von Neumann Theory Prize from ORSA and TIMS (1988) provide added testimonials, if they are needed, to the significance of Simon's contributions to each of these disciplines. In 1986, in recognition of the cross-disciplinary and policy implications of his work, President Reagan awarded Simon the National Medal of Science.

I might now best conclude this memorial by reporting that Herb Simon remained irrepressibly productive to the end. Working from his hospital bed, a day before his death, he supplied me with valuable comments and critiques on a paper I had been invited to write for the fiftieth-anniversary issue of *Operations Research*.

Now Herbert Simon is no longer with us. We are all poorer because of this loss, but we can be thankful that we had him as long as we did.

Consilience, Economic Theory, and the Legacy of Herbert A. Simon

Richard H. Day

Consilience is defined as "a jumping together of knowledge by linking facts and fact-based theory across disciplines to create a common groundwork of explanation." In a book devoted to this process, Edward O. Wilson (1998) describes how the physical and biological sciences have progressed in linking physical, chemical, and biological processes in a hierarchical ordering of knowledge and how together they form a coherent and consistent understanding of much of the natural world.[1] Wilson then contrasts this achievement with the situation in the social sciences, whose practitioners—to paraphrase him—by and large spurn the idea of a hierarchical ordering of knowledge, seldom examine their premises closely and never embed their narratives in the physical realities of human biology and psychology. Having thus accused the social sciences in general, Wilson turns to economics. Generously recognizing the difficulties that burdens our discipline, Wilson nonetheless charges that economics has not "even attempted serious consilience with the natural sciences."

Wilson then lists a number of biological elements that must be recognized in developing a consilient foundation for the theory of social and economic behavior, among them that "the brain is not a swift calculator." He then quotes or paraphrases the person whom we remember and honor here today: "Satisficing is one strategy for making up one's mind in complex settings with incomplete information." Without himself elaborating on it, Wilson brings us to Simon's effort to ground economics in psychological and sociological fact.

Herbert Simon began his academic career in political science, which led him to administrative, business, and general economics, to psychology, and to computer science. He was motivated by the view that empirical, systematic, and logically consistent theory could improve effective choice, action, and coordination in ongoing human organizations. From the beginning his intention was to separate scientific theory from the practical principles that dominated the literature on organization.

Simon's commitment to a scientific approach led him to consider the nature of scientific methodology, the logical content of causality, the possibility for identifying causal structure, and the foundations of human reason.[2] His examination of rational choice began in his thesis (the bulk of it written in 1942), which later became *Administrative Behavior* (1947). That project had grown out of his involvement in the administration of a New Deal program in San Francisco, an experience that had a profound impact on his desire to ground theory in reality. Later, in his 1955 *QJE* article "A behavioral model of rational choice," he focused his ideas precisely on economics and economic theory. I do not recall that he used the term "bounded rationality" in these seminal works, but he did use the term "intendedly rational" to distinguish what he had in mind from non-rational thinking. He recognized, of course, that non-rational thought and action play important roles in human life but felt that—given the heavy emphasis those aspects received by psychologists—it was a superior understanding of human rationality *in action* that was most needed.

Reason, Organization, and Evolution

Given the Nobel committee's installation of Herb Simon into the Valhalla of economists, there can be no doubt about the consilient embedding of economics into the realities of human biology and psychology. But for the benefit of our critics in the other sciences and for those within the discipline who have not yet gotten the message (if indeed there are any left), the following is a brief exegesis of Simon's central ideas and the implications he drew from them.[3]

Rationality

Rationality is limited for two fundamental reasons. First, it is instrumental: it operates on factual and value input (evoked alternatives and preferences). Any ambiguity or error in perception can lead to erroneous choice no matter how faultless the ratiocination. Any differences or changes in values lead to varied and conflicting choices. The resolution among them cannot be obtained by rational thought itself. To illustrate, Simon suggests that Hitler's arguments in *Mein Kampf* were quite up to the standards we expect in partisan political discourse. The principle defense against them could not have been reason itself but contrary factual beliefs and values. Second, reason is fallible and works more or less serially on one problem at a time. It can usually find only proximate solutions to mental problems or models that themselves only approximate the real-world problems at hand. Consequently, the goodness of rational decision depends more on the adequacy of the approximating assumptions and data supporting them than on the computation of maximizing values.

The Behavioral Model

The behavioral decision model emphasizes three points: (1) Decisions are made among partial, locally specific alternatives at anyone time. (2) Detailed scenarios about the future are not worked out. (3) Attention is focused sequentially on one decision problem after another. Given these characteristics it is unlikely that a single, comprehensive utility function is used as a criterion for all decisions. Rather different values are evoked in different choice contexts. The result is that "great inconsistencies can result from fluctuating attention" (p. 18). Therefore, attention must be "focused." Simon suggests that one mechanism for doing so is provided by the emotions which assure that "new problems of high urgency (obtain) a high priority on the agenda" (p. 21).

Intuitive Rationality and Pattern Recognition

Simon explains how "intuitive rationality" seems to be based on the brain's "elaborate discrimination net that permits recognition of any one of tens of thousands of different objects or situations" (p. 26). The ability to exploit this capability requires preparation, which in the case of "world class expertise" requires about ten years of intensive learning and practice. The intuitional mode of rational thought is quite compatible with the behavioral mode because "all serious thinking calls on both ... search-like processes and the sudden recognition of familiar patterns ... without (which) search through complex spaces would proceed in a snail-like fashion" (p. 28). This process provides an explanation for Friedman's widely cited "as if" hypothesis and Michael Polanyi's concept of "tacit knowledge" that was so effectively introduced into economics by Nelson and Winter (1982).

Emotion

Simon emphasizes the role that emotion plays in learning, expressing the view that "most human beings are able to attend to issues longer, to think harder about them, to receive deeper impressions that last longer, if information is presented in a context of emotion." (p. 32). To the example of Hitler's apparently mesmerizing diatribes, one might add Marx's genius at exploiting emotive words and phrases. Simon observes that though "works capable of evoking emotion have special value just by virtue of that capability, if we wish to use them to educate we must evaluate ... their scientific validity" (p. 33).

Organization

Simon's intendedly rational-choice forms the psychological foundation for a theory of the firm based on a sociological perspective: that is, the firm as a collection of interacting individuals with overlapping and sometimes conflicting interests. It explains the basic attributes of organization and administration: specialization of function, lines of authority and communication, incentives for cooperation, and mechanisms for the resolution of conflict. It is this organizational, informational, and procedural structure that permits a business organization made up of boundedly rational workers and managers to perpetuate their cooperative efforts. Simon emphatically rejected the use of game theoretic equilibrium concepts as a basis for his theory, not because he found them conceptually wrong, but because they do not describe the procedural aspects of behavior in a cooperative endeavor, or explain how people achieved viability when—from top to bottom—not one of them knows how the whole system works in all its complex detail.[4]

Selection and Evolution

Simon compares rational behavior and organizational process with biological evolution, juxtaposing Darwinian variation and selection and his own "alternative-generator-outcome-test" mechanism of rational choice. Without posing them directly, Simon raises in our minds three questions: (i) Can one draw inferences about the long-run character of social evolution by analogy with the long-run character of the biological process? (ii) In particular, if evolutionary variation and selection lead eventually to rational, equilibrium solutions is it not possible that boundedly rational satisficers might also do the same? (iii) Is a regime of "tooth and claw" competition most conducive to the (possible) long-run result or is there a role for altruism to augment the pursuit of private advantage? Not having put them this way, he does not answer them directly but their answers emerge from his concise summary and critical appraisal of evolutionary theory.

It is often held that evolution produces an optimal distribution of specialized species through the efficient filling of environmental niches. Simon argues that this idea is wrong. This is because evolving organisms create new niches. ("There could be no fleas until there were dogs.'') Moreover, the mechanisms of genetic restructuring are now known (through discoveries of quite recent vintage) to provide the Darwinian process with a virtually inexhaustible source of continued variation.

Selection forces are entirely local and foster fitness to local, current conditions. Instead of survival of the fittest, there is "[temporary] survival of the fitter!" As these local changes unfold new niches emerge that are hospitable to variations not yet generated, whose presence if and when their potential existence is realized will further modify the environmental terrain. Thus evolution does not produce a stationary, "rational" equilibrium even in the long run, but only "lots of local adaptations to the current environment, and at the same time constant movement toward a target that is itself continually moving" (p. 22).

Cultural evolution allows for ever more complicated patterns of adjustment including—indeed primarily involving—Lamarckian acquisitions of cultural traits among phenotypes. Thus, it is likely that boundedly rational satisficers driving and being driven by the forces of behavioral rationality will share the same long-run dynamics as the rest of nature; namely, endless search and unending change. In the process "pure altruism" cannot survive, but "weak altruism" or "enlightened self-interest" can give groups, with a sufficient number of individuals who are governed by it, a competitive edge.

Government and Collective Action

Government is a response to the existence of externalities that can only be dealt with by collective action. By means of appropriate institutions, it enhances the ability of people to form stable estimates of the consequence of individual behavior. Limitations of government are, however, to be emphasized. First, organizations, like individuals, can only give serial attention to big problems. While routine administration of simultaneous policies can be dealt with in parallel, crises require the focus of attention. This leads to faddish, single issue orientations, a tendency that is greatly exacerbated by the popular media. Second, multiple, sometimes conflicting values cannot be subsumed under a social welfare indicator. Third, the mechanisms of rationality and cooperation are "brittle in the face of uncertainty about the actions of another party when there is partial conflict of interest" (p. 86).

Institutions can be strengthened, however. The use of markets for routine exchange can be extended by appropriate mechanisms for "internalizing externalities" (as it has been put by others). Adversary proceedings within the judicial process can be extended to involve all who are significantly affected by the outcome. Management science and operations research techniques can be advanced. Their success will be based on the ability "to model the main interactions among the many facets of problems and hence, to think clearly about tradeoffs." Institutions can be made to work better if individuals have a better knowledge of their function. But because "it is probably reasonable to assume . . . that people will act from self-interest . . . a major task . . . is to create a social environment in which self-interest has reason to be enlightened" (p. 107).

In broad outline at least, such are the main ideas that formed Simon's theory of the socio-economic process. No doubt, much remains to be done. A very large segment of the profession, however, has taken up research aimed at the out-of-competitive-equilibrium, behavioral, evolutionary world of adaptive economizing. It now forms a second mainstream.

Adaptation and Adaptedness: The Dual Nature of Economic Theory

New or different perspectives require distinctive terminology. It is regrettable, however, that the terms "intended" or "bounded rational- ity" are necessary to remind us that, after all, there is only one kind of rationality that we humans know: our kind. It is based on filtered observation, limited memory, and fallible cognition. It is, nonetheless, one of our species' most distinctive means for adapting to the world around us and to each other.

Throughout Simon's development of the adaptive, behavioral point of view he expressed an intensifying belief in the irrelevance of general equilibrium and game theory, a growing resentment of its influence, and an increasing frustration at the lack of appreciation in so-called "mainstream economics" for the behavioral foundations that he explored. Those of us who have struggled to advance the development of the adaptive point of view must share some of these feelings. Yet, in my opinion, criticism of equilibrium theorizing should be tempered by the realization that the two approaches, when properly interpreted, are complementary, not contradictory.

General equilibrium is a rigorously consistent model of how an economy of decentralized households, whose preferences are fixed, and firms, who only know their own possibilities and limitations, can—on the basis of a special system of prices—independently choose the best feasible actions without considering any information but that about their own situation while simultaneously existing in a state of perfect coordination. For the economist it is a state in which all the niches are filled. It solves the classical conundrum about the sources of exchange value and simultaneously answers challenges by the proponents of authoritarian centralization because it is a theory of complexity based on individual discretion and voluntary exchange as opposed to centralized command and obedience to authority.

In contrast, adaptive economic theory has as its goal an explanation of how an economy of decentralized households and firms function simultaneously when they have something to learn about their preferences, possibilities and limitations, when at least some of them must figure out which prices are to be asked or offered, and what they should do when some of their plans are inconsistent.

To see why these theories are complements or duals of one another, recall the dual nature of mathematical reasoning in general: If answered in the affirmative, the question "Does a problem have a solution?" implies the question "Can a procedure for finding it be constructed?" Algorithms for constructing solutions of optimization problems may or may not succeed in finding an optimum just as the psychological process of arriving at a choice may or may not produce the best among those possible. Analogously, adaptive decision making and market mechanisms may or may not converge to a competitive equilibrium, but may instead wander around one, as Walras thought, or lurch from one to another, as Schumpeter thought, or eventually self-destruct, as Marx argued.

Some contemporary economists may not be aware that few, if any, important theorists of Simon's time—we think of Hicks, Samuelson, Koopmans, Arrow, Debreu, Morishima, and Nikaido, among others— claimed that the formal conditions of optimality and equilibrium characterized economic *behavior*. Indeed, it was generally understood that optimality described the conditions for an individual agent to be in a state in which further benefit could not be gained by *changing* behavior—at least not without making someone else worse off. It was *not* a theory of how an individual arrived at such a point. That would require a description of how stationary preferences emerge, how an individual came to know the complete product space and equilibrium prices, and how best choices are derived. Early theorists were quite explicit in recognizing this duality. Walras, for example, observed that "groping takes place naturally in the market under free competition because under such a system the price of services rises when demand exceeds offer and falls when offer exceeds demand." Here, by the founder of general equilibrium theory, is a precise expression of markets working out of equilibrium. Indeed, all of the great mathematical economists of Simon's era (including those mentioned above) implicitly recognized the behavioral aspect of the theory by investigating stability properties of Walras's tâtonnement process of adjustment out of equilibrium.

Thus, the existence of an equilibrium implies the problem of finding it; the process of adjustment outside equilibrium implies the question of the existence (and stability) of an equilibrium stationary state. For this reason, theoretical analysis of one of the dual theories will ultimately lead to questions about the other.

I think Herb agreed with this way of putting it but inveighed against the empirical relevance of the equilibrium concepts. It was the uncritical application of idealized concepts of unbounded rationality and of interpersonal equilibrium as theories of people, organizations, and economies in vivo that he found deficient.

Activity Analysis, Organizational Decision Making, Trigger Effects, and Adaptive Economizing

Activity Analysis

Simon's intellectual adventures brought him into contact with most of the great economic theorists of the mid twentieth century, of whom some, including Koopmans and Samuelson, reformulated economics in terms of activity analysis. It seems strange to me that Simon drew so little on these and on the related computational algorithms for constrained optimization models. Koopmans had founded the theory of production, not on the production function that relates inputs directly to outputs, but on the production *activity*, which he referred to as "the basic atom of technology," and which *generated* inputs *and* outputs. The economic production function then became an "efficient combination of activities." In this way, he implicitly established consilience with engineering and the agricultural sciences and hence, indirectly, with physics and biology. This consilience is explicit in the mountain of applied work produced in the two or three decades after World War II involving empirical studies of firms, industries, agricultural regions, and entire economies. Among the sins committed by contemporary economics is the virtual abandonment of this powerful modeling technique and the lapse into obscurity of Koopmans's great compendium *Activity Analysis of Production and Resource Allocation*, as well as Dorfman, Samuelson, and Solow's superb *Linear Programming and Economic Theory*.

Decentralization Algorithms

Not only was activity analysis used in widely varied industries; in a manner directly related to Herb's theory of organization, it was used to model the multi-level structure of decision and information flows, thus providing a way to formalize the *social* architecture of business firms and leading to the design of operational algorithms that decentralize overall decision problems into a sequence of recursively connected, iteratively solved, simpler optimization problems. In the hands of mathematicians and economists such as Danzig, Geoffrion, Kornai, and Hurwicz such algorithms mimic the flow of information and decision making within a complex organization. Some were (and are?) used in actual business firms.

We might have expected Herb to have drawn on those models and their corresponding algorithms in his own research, but apparently he did not. Obviously, even a man of such wide interests and varied talents could not follow up on all the related ideas being explored by others, let alone all of his own. Indeed, others can enjoy a sense of discovery by pushing further along one or another of the paths into which he ventured but from which he withdrew to explore other, to him, more intriguing territory.

Trigger Effects

However, Herb did in fact consider in some depth *one* aspect of activity analysis—a general property of inequality constrained optimization problems. It involves the discrete jumps in the activity levels that arise from continuous variation in objective functions or constraint coefficients. This phenomenon is particularly important in the linear programming case which yields step functions for the response of activity levels to changes in prices, and hence, to step functions of the supply of outputs and the demand for inputs. A similar discrete effect occurs if a new technology is introduced with modified coefficients that enter a constraint or objective function. Small coefficient changes simply modify activity levels without changing the activities involved. Large enough changes lead to the abandonment of some while activating one or more of the others. In his paper Koopmans 1951, Herb referred to these as "trigger effects." I had seen that paper in the Koopmans collection even before starting graduate school, but did not have the motivation or the background at the time to do anything with it. Later, after studying Goldman and Tucker's (1956) elegant, purely algebraic theory of linear programming, I saw how all the extreme solutions were represented by dual systems of equated constraints. I used this idea to characterize the multiple-phase, dynamic character of activity levels when the current limitations and/or objective function coefficients depend on past activity level solutions, as in the recursive programming models I developed to describe agricultural and industrial behavior when multiple technologies were available with different input-output characteristics. Herb's paper did not consider an explicitly dynamic model, but, using a comparative static analysis, he focused on the algebra of the switching mechanisms that produced the "trigger effects." He also illustrated such trigger effects using an agricultural example and showed how such effects could induce dramatic changes in resource utilization. It was that prominent example to which my initial application of recursive programming would later be addressed (Day 1967).

Adaptive Economizing

Recursive programming models are in effect formal representations of Herb's characterization of a "behavioral decision model" (summarized above). Based on activity analysis, they can use biological and engineering data directly and surveys of actual practice to characterize production activities. In addition to resource limitations, choices can be constrained by behavioral limits on the search for profit-maximizing solutions. These restraints form a neighborhood of current practice. As the activity levels chosen change from year to year in response to changes in prices and resources, this neighborhood or *zone of flexible response* changes around them. In this way, immediate adjustments are limited, but they can accumulate rapidly if developing conditions continue to favor them. A formal version of the approach was published in Day 1971. I believe the empirical studies summarized in Day and Cigno 1978, together with the examples described in Cyert and March 1992, remain the most extensive tests with real-world industrial and agricultural data of adaptive economizing theory.

Later (Day 1996), I developed a formal characterization of the adaptive economizing theory and in that context derived regularity conditions for the existence of a conventional competitive equilibrium, in this way exemplifying the dual aspects of economic theory outlined above.

On Science and Deconstruction

Herb's dedication to consilience and the scientific mission rested on a deep personal integrity and a fundamental belief in Truth. For the scientist Truth is obtained from facts. Facts are expressions of perception and experience that have been tested by rules and procedures for verification and that are provisionally accepted as such by reasonable people. They can always be challenged and modified on the basis of new perceptions and tests, but the scientists' faith rests on Truth's existence; his commitment is to the discovery and formulation of facts and to their use as the basis of theoretical understanding.[5]

Theories, like all ideas, are expressed in words and symbols whose usage and interpretation evolve. The scientist, however, does not accept the argument that scientific truths are solely subjective. But scientific knowledge transformed beyond its basis in fact escapes the domain of science and enters a different intellectual realm.

Religious scriptures abound in moral and spiritual precepts that arrive in some mysterious process of revelation, sometimes without warning, sometimes in a dream or vision, sometimes announced by a voice, sometimes pronounced by an apparent speaker. The mental processes underlying such experiences are possibly related to invention and discovery in music, art, poetry, and even to the formulation of mathematical theorems and scientific theory, just as Poincaré described in his celebrated essay on mathematical discovery. But for any idea to pass muster as scientific, it must run a gauntlet of empirical verification.

Certainly, it is a fact that people conceive and believe ideas that have no apparent basis in fact. And this is the paradox: *the fact that non-facts are believed; that they motivate behavior.* We may hypothesize that it is belief in the truth of one's ideas that motivates the attempt to express them as theory, to verify their basis in logic, to test their basis in fact, and to derive their logical implications. When myth and revelation motivate behavior that enhances the quality of our lives, we may rejoice in this paradox. So it is that the ability to believe ideas that do not as yet have a basis in fact plays a vital role both for the scientific enterprise and for the coherence of social living.

But there is a dark side to this human potential. It is the fact that people dissemble and deceive. The paradox we are talking about is illustrated in partisan rhetoric of political demagogues. Its greatest champion, Joseph Goebbels, elevated it to a principle: the bigger the lie, the greater the likelihood that people will believe it. A less diabolical adherent to that principle was P. T. Barnum, who estimated that a sucker was born every minute.

Herb developed a deep concern about the use of non-facts to represent truth and to influence people, a topic we discussed in correspondence in the weeks immediately before his passing. It is now common practice to re-interpret a work so as to modify its intended meaning while at the same time investing the new meaning with the authority of the original author. That practice was anathema to him. Such deconstructive activity runs rampant in the media, in legislative bodies, in our courts, in the halls of academia. Herb strongly objected to this practice. It was the articulation and understanding of fact and theory consistent with fact that he championed.

Conclusion

Scientific economics needs its champions. It has produced them in mathematical economists like Samuelson, Koopmans, Arrow, and Debreu who demanded precision in the formulation and derivation of theoretical concepts. It has produced them in empirically oriented theorists such as Commons, Schumpeter, Kaldor, Keynes, and Hayek,[6] who asked that the basic premises of economic theory be grounded in observation and fact. By bringing a new precision and logical clarity to the study of economizing behavior in organizations, Simon was in fact a champion of both camps. This kind of champion is invariably needed but always in short supply. When one is lost, we are all the less for it.

Had Edward Wilson read more of Simon, he would have recognized a kindred spirit in the ancient philosophers' consilient game of crossing disciplines to create unity of knowledge. Moreover, he would have seen that Simon, as much as any other theorist of his era, *built his work precisely on a close examination of the basic premises upon which economic theory is built*. He did this in terms of the psychology of individual choice and the social architecture of decision making in organizations. Mathematical economists such as Paul Samuelson, Gerard Debreu, and Kenneth Arrow were also examining the basic premises of economic theory, but they were concerned primarily with formal expression and logical implications of the neoclassical premises rather than behavioral characteristics.

By adding the observations about activity analysis, by taking account of the burgeoning literature on adaptive, evolutionary processes, and by recognizing the important insights of institutionalist research contributed by the empirically oriented theorists, economics has made and is making great strides in establishing consilient connections along the disciplinary boundaries of psychology, sociology, law, and many other scientific disciplines. The problem is our own bounded rationality. Each of us can only master a part—a relatively small part—of the work that has been done and the work now being done. It may only be in the mature reflection of especially gifted scholars that a real measure of consilience is actually achieved. That is why we admire Herb Simon and his gems of scientific and wise human understanding.

Simon's writings do not contain many references to the literature that touched on or developed similar ideas. He was an independent thinker, inspired by others certainly, but quite capable of developing ideas completely on his own that others may have thought of before or after. He was a keen observer of life around him. That was the real basis of his theoretical approach. It was that attribute that gives even his most mathematical work its unusual character and relevance.

Edward Wilson observed that "the world economy is a ship speeding through uncharted waters, strewn with dangerous shoals. There is no general agreement on how the economy works." If the shoals are to be avoided, a better understanding of how the economy works must be acquired. That understanding will be based on facts about how we think and how we act in private organizations, in markets, and in public institutions. It will be achieved when those facts can be orchestrated into rigorous theory that comprehends them. To achieve that understanding was Herb Simon's work. His spirit lives in those who pursue that arduous quest.

Notes

1. Wilson tells us that the quotation is from Whewell's 1840 treatise *The Philosophy of the Inductive Science.*

2. See Simon 1957.

3. This section draws in part on my review (Day 1985) of Simon's *Reason in Human Affairs.* The page references below are to that book.

4. We recognize in this theory a similarity to the work of John R. Commons, whose Legal Foundations of Capitalism and Institutional Economics were built on the same

behavioral foundation but who emphasized the legal and negotiational mechanisms of conflict resolution rather than the administrative architecture of cooperation that Simon emphasized. (Simon, somewhere acknowledges his debt to Commons.)

5. Simon (1992, pp. 35–36) argued that "we can observe with reasonable objectivity" and that "scientific knowledge can be public and objective." But he recognized that it could be so "only in a matter of degree" and that our observations "will always be subject to modification."

6. See especially Hayek 1952 for his unique attempt among economists to provide a theory of bounded rationality based explicitly on neurophysological grounds.

References

Cyert, Richard, and James March. 1963. *A Behavioral Theory of the Firm*. Prentice-Hall.

Day, Richard H. 1967. The economics of technological change and the demise of the sharecropper. *American Economic Review* 57: 427–449.

Day, Richard H. 1978. Modelling economic change: The recursive programming approach. In R. Day and A. Cigno, eds., *Modelling Economic Change*. North-Holland.

Day, Richard H. 1996. Satisficing multiple preferences in and out of equilibrium. In R. Fabella and E. de Dios, eds., *Choice, Growth and Development*. University of the Philippines Press.

Dorfman, Robert, Paul Samuelson, and Robert Solow. 1958. *Linear Programming and Economic Theory*. McGraw-Hill.

Georgescu-Roegen, Nicholas. 1951. Multiple phases in a dynamic input-output model. In T. Koopmans, ed., *Activity Analysis of Production and Resource Allocation*. Wiley.

Goldman, A. J., and A. W. Tucker. 1956. "Theory of Linear Programming." In H. Kuhn and A. Tucker, eds., *Linear Inequalities and Related System*. Princeton University Press.

Hayek, Friedrich von. 1952. *The Sensory Order*. University of Chicago Press.

Koopmans, Tjalling, ed. 1951. *Activity Analysis of Production and Resource Allocation*. Wiley.

Simon, Herbert A. 1951. The effects of technological change in a linear model. In T. Koopmans, ed., *Activity Analysis of Production and Resource Allocation*. Wiley.

Simon, Herbert A. 1955. A behavioral model of rational choice. *Quarterly Journal of Economics* 69. Republished in Simon 1957b.

Simon, Herbert A. 1956. Rational choice and the structure of the environment. *Psychological Review* 63. Republished in Simon 1957b.

Simon, Herbert A. 1957a. *Administrative Behavior: A Study of Decision Making Processes in Administrative Organization*. Free Press.

Simon, Herbert A. 1957b. *Models of Man, Social and Rational*. Wiley.

Simon, Herbert A. 1992. Colloquium with H. A. Simon. In H. A. Simon et al., *Economics, Bounded Rationality and the Cognitive Revolution*. Elgar.

Wilson, Edward O. 1998. *Consilience: The Unity of Knowledge*. Knopf.

Interdisciplinary Reasoning and Herbert Simon's Influence

Yuji Ijiri

I came to Carnegie Mellon University in January 1961 as a Ph.D. student, having earned a masters' degree at the University of Minnesota a few weeks earlier. I have been with CMU since then, with the exception of four years on the faculty of the Stanford Business School in the mid 1960s.

I knew nothing about CMU while at Minnesota. I owe my start at CMU to Martin Bronfenbrenner of the Minnesota economics department, who strongly suggested that I go to Carnegie Mellon ("Carnegie Tech" at that time) and wrote a letter of recommendation to Bill Cooper, a founding faculty member of CMU's Graduate School of Industrial Administration. Later, I learned that Martin, Bill, and Herb Simon were all together at the University of Chicago's Economics Department in the 1930s.

I had Bill Cooper as the supervisor of my dissertation, which was finished in 1963 and published in 1965 (Ijiri 1965). My dissertation work benefited tremendously from Bill's expertise as one of the leading pioneers of Operations Research as well as his strong background in accounting, having been influenced by his mentor, Eric Kohler, a two-time president of the American Accounting Association.

I was able to get Herb Simon on my dissertation committee by special permission from Jim March, the director of Ph.D. program at that time.

When I consulted with Jim about the composition of my committee, he said "Normally, you cannot have both Bill and Herb on the same committee as they are sought after by many doctoral students, but I will see what can be done." He later approved the committee consisting of Bill, Herb, Kal Cohen, and Neil Churchill.

Herb's interdisciplinary scholarship and pathbreaking contributions in so many fields are indeed awesome. I have been greatly influenced by him.

Skew Distributions

Among many valuable courses I took at CMU, the most influential one for me was Herb's Mathematical Social Science course. The course had about a dozen doctoral and masters' students as well as a couple of faculty members. Some of the chapters in *Models of Man* (Simon 1957) were used in class along with other materials he brought in.

What made this course so influential for me was the unusual breadth of materials covered, as a glance at *Models of Man* can indicate. In addition to social sciences and mathematics, the class included natural science fields such as physics and biology. It took me several years to realize just how much this course and, more generally, Herb's interdisciplinary scholarship, affected my thinking and my work. After returning from Stanford to CMU in 1967, I got the privilege of teaching this course jointly with Herb.

When I took his class in 1962, I was particularly interested in an article in *Models of Man* called "On a class of skew distribution functions," which was originally published in *Biometrika* in 1955. I decided to use this article as a basis for the term paper for the course. This article starts as follows:

It is the purpose of this paper to analyse a class of distribution functions that appears in a wide range of empirical phenomena—particularly data describing sociological, biological, and economic phenomena. Its appearance is so frequent, and the phenomena in which it appears so diverse, that one is led to the conjecture that if these phenomena have any property in common it can only be a similarity in the structure of the underlying probability mechanisms. The empirical distributions to which we shall refer specifically are: (A) distributions of words in prose samples by their frequency of occurrence, (B) distributions of scientists by number of papers published, (C) distributions of cities by population, (D) distributions of incomes by size, and (E) distributions of biological genera by number of species.

Herb credits G. Udny Yule (1924) as the first to develop a particular form of skew distribution functions based on the Beta function. Yule used this mechanism to explain the distribution of biological genera by numbers of species.

Herb's contributions in this *Biometrika* paper lie in his developing, based on two simple assumptions, an elegant and plausible stochastic model whose steady state distribution is the Yule distribution. He is also credited for linking the results in biology with those in numerous other fields, as the above five examples indicate.

He sets up the following two assumptions using terms in word frequency distributions. The first assumption is "Gibrat's Law of Proportionality," which postulates that the expected percentage rate of growth in size is independent of the size already attained (Gibrat 1931). Here, 'size' means the number of times a given word appeared in a given text.

Assume that in a given text containing, say, 10,000 words, the word 'that' appeared 100 times and the word 'what' appeared 10 times. During the next series of adding more words to the text, both words have the same expected percentage rate of growth, say a 10% growth to 110 times for the former and to 11 times for the latter.

The second assumption is that there is a constant probability, α, that the next word added to the text is a new word, a word that has not occurred up to that point in the text. Herb derived the Yule distribution based on these two assumptions.

When the words in a text are ranked from the largest (rank 1) to the smallest (size 1, appearing only once in the text) and are plotted on the log-log scale with log of rank on the *x* axis and log of size on the *y* axis, the plot tends to conform to the Yule distribution. They show nearly a straight line sloping downward to the right, with the slope at the intercept with the *x* axis frequently very close to 45°.

Herb suggested that I might explore the impact of altering the first assumption by introducing a discount factor γ ($0 < \gamma < 1$). Without discounting, two words with the same size have an equal chance of increasing its size by one at the next round. With discounting, a word that appeared in the recent part of the text has a better chance of increasing its size than a word with the same size that appeared in the older part of the text. This is intuitively appealing because of our tendency to prefer coherence in writing, instead of randomly shifting among a large number of topics.

I ran computer simulations under a variety of combinations of parameters γ and α. While the slope of the curve at the intercept with the *x* axis varied, they all showed the characteristics of the Yule distribution. We were pleased to find the robust nature of the Yule distribution. The efforts resulted in my first joint paper with Herb (Ijiri and Simon 1964).

This started a collaboration with Herb on the subject of skew distributions. We produced four more papers (Ijiri and Simon 1967, 1971, 1974, 1975), the last of which dealt with an extension of the applicability of the Yule distribution from contagious phenomena in living systems to those in particles. We thought, as long as matters are attracted to each other, it really should not matter whether it is by affection, by gravity, or by any other forces. This extension was done by linking the theory behind the Yule distribution with the "Bose-Einstein statistics" used in describing the statistical behavior of a collection of certain kinds of particles.

The Bose-Einstein statistics deals with seemingly odd phenomena. Stated in marketing terms, suppose that two customers are attracted equally to two identical, adjacent stores, selling the same goods at the same price. Normally, we expect that each store will have a $\frac{1}{4}$ chance of getting both customers, a $\frac{1}{2}$ chance of getting only one, and a $\frac{1}{4}$ chance of getting none. Under the Bose-Einstein statistics, these three possibilities are equally likely, a $\frac{1}{3}$ chance each!

To understand the phenomena, we used the following metaphor of a storefront expanding linearly as the store gets more customers. Originally, both stores have the same unit-size storefront with no customers. When one of the two stores gets the first customer (probability $\frac{1}{2}$), the size of the storefront increases by one unit. This makes the store twice as attractive as the other store, increasing the probability to $\frac{2}{3}$ of getting the second customer. Hence, this store has a $\frac{1}{2} * \frac{2}{3} = \frac{1}{3}$ chance of getting both customers. The same $\frac{1}{3}$ chance is available for the other store to get both customers; and thus the chance of each store getting one customer is also $\frac{1}{3}$. This leads to the "contagious" phenomenon: a customer attracting more customers.

Incorporating the constant probability α of a new store with a unit-size storefront being introduced at each round, we showed that the Bose-Einstein statistics leads to the Yule distribution. Later, we published a book (Ijiri and Simon 1977) that put together these and other papers on skew distributions.

The research on skew distributions that Herb started in 1955 began receiving more attention in the late 1980s and the 1990s. Among authors in this line of research, Paul Krugman of MIT's economics department gave Herb the most deserving credit: "In fact, Herbert Simon proposed such a story more than 40 years ago, in one of those papers that should have been extremely influential but that somehow, whether because they did not fit the zeitgeist or because they were written in the wrong style, were largely ignored. . . . And Simon's model is so wonderfully elegant an approach that I continue to regard it as the best game in town." (Krugman 1996, pp. 44, 97). After Herb passed away, I received a couple of articles that he would certainly have enjoyed reading (Axtell 2001; Kou and Kou 2001).

Double-Entry Logic

I now would like to turn to my own research in accounting that has been greatly benefited from Herb. While this makes it necessary to give some details of my research in "double-entry bookkeeping," I shall try to condense them as much as possible.

I was 15 years old when I first learned about double-entry bookkeeping in order to keep my father's books for a small bakery store in a little town not far from Kyoto. I was immediately fascinated by its logic. As I learned more about its structure, I began to wonder why it would not be possible to logically extend it to "triple-entry bookkeeping." This became a mystery in accounting that has challenged me for the next four decades.

Initially, I was not very serious, just a curiosity. But soon I became obsessed with the mystery. When I was a junior in college, I visited a pottery shop near the Kiyomizu Temple in Kyoto with a monk, whom I had known for ten years, and his artist friend. We all wrote our wish on teacups and had them processed in the kiln while we were waiting at the store. I wrote my wish: "From Two to Three!" A half century later, I still have this teacup.

After coming to the United States in 1959 and finishing my masters at Minnesota, I got my curiosity about the mystery rekindled. During my dissertation work at CMU, Bill Cooper introduced me to the writings of the nineteenth-century British mathematician, Arthur Cayley, in particular to his booklet on double-entry bookkeeping (Cayley 1894). In the preface of the book (p. v), Cayley stated: "The Principles of Book-keeping by Double Entry constitute a theory which is mathematically by no means uninteresting: it is in fact like Euclid's theory of ratios an absolutely perfect one, and it is only its extreme simplicity which prevents it from being as interesting as it would otherwise be."

I was very pleased to see such a nice praise given to double-entry bookkeeping, but at the same time I was somewhat disappointed since if it would indeed be "absolutely perfect," it would not likely be extensible to triple-entry bookkeeping. But still I could not give it up.

After finishing my doctorate, I joined the Stanford Business School faculty. Soon thereafter, I made it a rule to audit a course in different fields in each quarter to expand my interdisciplinary perspectives, undoubtedly stimulated by Herb. I started auditing courses in physics and mathematics. A course on "Metamathematics" taught by a Polish logician, Andrzej Ehrenfeucht, was most interesting and helpful, although it was very difficult to understand initially and I had to retake it. It started with axiomatic set theory, which turned out to be very useful for thinking about accounting transactions at the most abstract level. This led to an axiomatic formalization of accounting processes which was later included in my book (Ijiri 1967).

My fascination with the number 3 also led me to study many-valued logic, hoping that it might possibly help solve the triple-entry problem by extending the customary two-valued logic into three-valued logic. (On many-valued logic, see Rosser and Turquette 1958.) While this pursuit turned out to be not directly applicable, my studies in logic somehow resulted in an invitation to be an abstract writer for the mathematical logic section of *Zentralblatt für Mathematik*, for which I served for about ten years.

Going back to Cayley's statement mentioned earlier, Euclid's theory of ratios that Cayley mentioned seems to refer to the fact that ratios as a mathematical entity always have two sides, the numerator and the denominator. Both must coexist to be a ratio, and collectively they cover all rational numbers. Then by "an absolutely perfect one," Cayley must be referring to the fact that under double-entry book-keeping, each and every transaction must have one debit account and one credit account. (Composite transactions can all be decomposed into a set of simple transactions, each of which requires only one debit account and one credit account.)

I then ran into Peano's axiomatic system for natural numbers. Peano (1889) first defines the concepts of the "1" and the "successor," from which all natural numbers are derived, setting the basis for mathematical induction. I thought: Can't I define the 1 and the successor in double-entry bookkeeping? This was the first turning point in my endeavor.

Cayley's comment made me consider "dichotomy" as something that was untouchable or "divine." Therefore, "trichotomy" sounded like something even more divine as in "Trinity." What Peano's system did to me was to demystify the matter. The "3" is just a number that follows the "2"; nothing sacred about it!

I learned that the balance sheet existed during the single-entry period and what was newly added by the emergence of double-entry bookkeeping was a set of income accounts, along with an income statement that summarized them. Before learning about Peano's system, I was exploring the trichotomy of the past, the present, and the future that may be captured in three statements, the income statement for the past, the balance sheet for the present, and the budget statement for the future. While this line of relating and integrating the three statements can offer a highly useful form of financial reporting, it just did not generate any new concepts.

Using Peano's system, I refocused on the income accounts. They made it possible to require every transaction to have a debit account and a credit account by letting an income account "explain" why net wealth (assets less liabilities) changed.

This recording of "what happened" and "why it happened" in tandem is, I realized, what is at the core of double-entry bookkeeping. It forces accountants to think in tradeoffs and causal linkages among seemingly independent events. This reasoning is required, not just when accountants wanted to explain, but on each and every transaction; otherwise debit and credit do not balance. Imagine a mundane event like a room temperature going up by 3°. It would be a recordable event for any scientists, engineers, or economists, but not for account-ants who must first find out a reason for this event before it can be recorded in double-entry.

This reminded me of the Japanese and other Asian languages in which there is one word for "elder brother" and a totally different word for "younger brother," with no word to express just "brother." (The same goes for most other family relationships.) Thus the language forces people to respect seniority since otherwise they have to expose their ignorance in public. The double-entry system does exactly the same for causal reasoning.

The first publication on double-entry bookkeeping is due to Luca Pacioli, an Italian monk and mathematician (Pacioli 1494). This book was published more than a century before the shift in emphasis occurred in science from reasoning to prediction. This shift is said to have been triggered by Kepler's laws that predicted planetary motions extremely well but no one could explain why. Yet, ignoring such a shift in science, double-entry bookkeeping has continued its hammering of reasoning in accountants' minds, just like Asian languages remained unchanged even after respect for seniorities started waning.

If income explains the reason for a change in net wealth, the next higher level of explanation must mean something that explains why the income has changed! I then realize what I had to do next.

A balance sheet is a stock statement, stating the financial position of the firm at a single point in time, while an income statement is a flow statement, stating the total amounts of flows between two points in time. Can we develop a new "stock" statement that is linked to the income statement and another "flow" statement that explains changes in this "stock" statement? If so, like a sliding ladder, I can reach the third floor, so to speak.

This is where I am most thankful to Herb and his 1962 course that got my interest in physics started. I considered whether the principle of impulse and momentum might be a useful framework upon which to develop this necessary "ladder." It did have the "right smell," the phrase Herb pointed out to me when he was describing Feigenbaum's constant in chaos theory (Heppenheimer 1986).

A new accounting framework was developed starting with a "momentum statement" which is the time-derivative of the income statement at a single point in time. Then an "impulse statement" was introduced to explain changes in net momenta. Under the principle of impulse and momentum, both measurements are in the same unit and impulse does explain the reason for a change in momentum. This was the second turning point in my endeavor.

When momentum accounts are integrated over time, they produce income; when impulse accounts are integrated over time, they produce what may be called "action" (though its usage is not completely the same as the one in mechanics) which state the reasons for changes in income accounts. Thus, the logical extension to triple-entry book-keeping was made possible—Action, such as an introduction of a new product or opening of a new market, is the reason for a change in income and, in turn, income is the reason for a change in wealth. Here, "reasoning" serves as the "successor" in Peano's system.

The last hurdle was the measurement unit. Journal entries under momentum accounting must all be carried out, not in a monetary unit, but in a monetary unit per unit of time, such as "dollars per month." I never thought such accounting would be meaningful, but the fact that momentum as well as impulse can be meaningfully added in physics, encouraged me that they must also be meaningfully added in account-ing, which turned out to be true. This was the third turning point.

A host of new ideas started flowing from such a new system of accounting that preserved the essence of double-entry bookkeeping but applied it at a higher level. A new notion of "status quo" that emerged from this new system, in a manner analogous to the Newton's first law of motion, turned out to be very useful in accounting and business.

Under the conventional system, management performance is mea-sured by income. Every dollar increase in income is viewed as management's contributions, in a manner analogous to pre-Newtonian mechanics which viewed that a force must be applied continuously for motion to continue. Under the new system, impulse is the performance measure. If the impulse is zero, that means there was no change in net momenta during the year, hence zero performance, even if income is earned steadily by the passage of time. The management just rode on the momentum created earlier.

I put all these ideas together in a book (Ijiri 1989), which I dedicated to Bill Cooper on the occasion of his 75th birthday as a small token of my deep appreciation for his continual encouragement and support during and decades after my dissertation work.

I am also greatly indebted to Herb for giving me the "courage" to search even in physics to solve accounting problems. Interdisciplinary research has its inherent "risk" as one must get into a new field without full knowledge commonly shared by the specialists in the discipline. Yet, the payoff potential is great because it allows one to view the problem from a broader perspective. Herb encouraged me to be a risk-taker in this regard, for which I am most grateful. I now believe that it is this inherent risk, over and above the risk common to any research, that makes interdisciplinary research so challenging and exciting.

Molecular Biology

In the fall 2001, Jonathan Minden of CMU Biological Sciences Department offered what he called "Faculty-to-Faculty (F2F) Seminar on Foundations and Frontiers of Biology" in 12 weekly sessions in the evening during the semester. I signed up for it and was accepted—luckily, since there were twice as many applicants as Jon had expected.

Jon stated three reasons why he was offering this course. One is, for more complete understanding of biology, he felt it necessary to look at biology from many different standpoints and this called for inter-disciplinary participation. The second reason is he loves to talk about molecular biology because of its complexity. The third reason is Herb Simon; Jon came to CMU because of its interdisciplinary orientation, and Herb was at its center, he said.

The seminar was indeed most fascinating. Using as a reference a textbook in molecular cell biology (Lodish 2000), Jon went over foundational as well as cutting-edge matters in molecular biology.

There were many concepts and processes in biology that can be related with those of accounting and auditing. At the moment, they are relatively shallow, point-to-point analogies. But I hope I can gain more knowledge and insight in the future to extend them to structure-to-structure analogies, like the one I found in mechanics and accounting. At least, however, I can state a few observations.

A cell is an organism and, as such, it seems to share the same key elements such as micro-intelligence, preference for safety-in-numbers, and mutation capabilities. These elements are also shared by humans and, incidentally, by double-entry bookkeeping, too.

The term 'micro-intelligence' is used here to mean intelligence good enough to manage the system internally but is not enough to comprehend and adapt fully to the changing macro-environment of the system. Organisms seem to supplement their deficiency in intelligence by cooperating with each other, preferring, as it seems, to decide under the rule of safety in numbers. Finally, they seem to have mutation capabilities to guard against a sudden change in the environment, trading off returns in favor of reduced risks.

The double-entry system has all these ingredients. It organizes information about the firm using prices generated internally through transactions. It allows thousands of accountants working in a firm to be myopic in recording the transaction. Applying prices in the macro-environment of the firm may be easier but risky because they lie outside the firm.

Hence, it seems to make sense for the organism called a firm, limited by its micro-intelligence, to use only costs, that is prices at which goods are actually bought or sold by this firm.

Finally, the double-entry system is now undergoing a mutation as the use of cost is being replaced, step by step, by market prices outside the firm. This is because investors are more and more interested in predictions and anxious to get data that reflect the future, not the past, and the market price is closer to the future price than the cost.

Unfortunately, this particular mutation is a risky one. Not only market price is often subjective for non-standard assets, market price accounting amplifies boom and bust in the economy enormously by a chain reaction: a stock price increase in firm A is reflected in a profit increase in firm B which holds firm A's shares. This in turn is reflected in a stock price increase in firm B stock, with chain reactions continuing many rounds.

Nevertheless, mutation capabilities are important in accounting, too, and I am hoping that a new hybrid system of accounting might emerge as a result of our experience in both systems of cost-based and price-based accounting, complementing each other by means of a dual presentation in financial statements.

One unexpected benefit of the seminar is that I now seem to have regained child's eyes in looking at human systems including double-entry bookkeeping. I have been so used to these human systems that I had lost curiosity about them.

If Martians were to exist and capable of observing humans on earth with a large telescope, they may be seeing humans just like cells in a microscope. Undoubtedly, they would be greatly amazed by the systems that humans, in spite of individually limited intelligence, were able to collectively create in the science, in the arts, and in numerous other fields. Our fascination with molecular biology can indeed be transferred to human systems, giving us fresh, new insight into the living system as a whole.

When Herb received his Nobel Prize for Economics in 1978, he was cited by the Swedish Academy of Sciences for "his pioneering research into the decision-making process within economic organizations" (Swedish Academy of Sciences 1978).

"What is new in Simon's idea," the Academy stated in the citation, "is, most of all, that he rejects the assumption made in the classic theory of the firm as an omniscient, rational, profit-maximizing entrepreneur.... In his epoch-making book *Administrative Behavior* and in a number of subsequent books, he described the company as an adaptive system of physical, personal and social components that are held together by a network of intercommunications and by the willingness of its members to cooperate and strive towards a common goal." (See Simon 1947.)

I learned Herb's Principle of Bounded Rationality in his 1962 class and from *Models of Man*, where he stated: "The capacity of the human mind for formulating and solving complex problems is very small compared with the size of the problems whose solution is required for objectively rational behavior in the real world—or even for a reasonable approximation to such objective rationality." (p. 198) This is very much in line with the lessons I learned from Jon's seminar.

After his seminar was over, Jon told me about Herb's insight into cell biology and the way he viewed living systems in a hierarchical way. Herb's Principle of Bounded Rationality seems to have had roots not only in human organizations but also in a host of living systems. I must say that Jon's seminar opened my eyes to molecular biology as well as to the depth of Herb's intellectual wealth from which he generated his numerous path-breaking theories.

Interdisciplinary Reasoning

These three examples of interdisciplinary studies and research highlight the power of "interdisciplinary reasoning."

Being interdisciplinary does not mean just a larger collection of diverse knowledge in different disciplines; otherwise all "universities" will be interdisciplinary by definition. Such knowledge must be related and integrated by "reasoning," which is the essence of scholarship.

Interdisciplinary reasoning forces people to focus on bigger pictures across disciplines and create a new understanding of the phenomena at a higher level. Herb Simon was a master of this interdisciplinary reasoning.

Undoubtedly, however, this is a "reductionistic" way of looking at science. We must also consider a newer scientific approach such as the one proposed in a book by Jack Cohen and Ian Stewart, British biologist and mathematician, respectively.

This book discusses a newer approach, called "contextualism," that focuses on understanding and predicting emergence of "features," "patterns," and other qualitative characteristics of the phenomena. They serve as complements to traditional quantitative predictions, especially where they are difficult to make as in chaotic phenomena.

Cohen and Stewart (1994) explain the phenomena in which simplicity emerges out of internal complexity. Skew distributions are good examples of this. They caution us, however, that it is still internal: "... the real cause of large-scale simplicities is not internal complexity at all, but external constraints, which collapse chaos and render systems independent of much of their own internal complexity" (p. 399). They propose to use the newly coined term 'complicity' to describe such phenomena, in contrast to "simplexity," which is the emergence of large-scale simplicities as direct consequences of internal rules. Their emphasis is on complicity and outside contexts, not simplexity and internal contents or essence. They state that "the prime example of complicity is evolution" (p. 418).

Cohen and Stewart (p. 442) say that reductionism and contextualism must be combined and that "Richard Feynman speculated on the possibilities of devising such a theory." They quoted Feynman in the front matter of the book: "The next great awakening of human intellect may well produce a method of understanding the qualitative content of equations. Today we cannot. Today we cannot see that the water-flow equations contain such things as the barber pole structure of turbulence that one sees between rotating cylinders. Today we cannot see whether Schrödinger's equation contains frogs, musical composers, or morality—or whether it does not." (Feynman et al. 1963) This emphasis on understanding the predictive power behind equations seems to support the continued importance of "reasoning" in the future.

Viewed from the contextualism, interdisciplinary reasoning goes, not toward the intersection of the sets of knowledge in multiple disciplines, but toward their outer products and the emergence of new phenomena that occur as a consequence. Whether reductionistic or contextualistic, interdisciplinary reasoning will play an indispensable role in the future scientific endeavor.

The reason for mentioning the newer approach is that I have a strong hunch that Herb understood the need for the new approach even in 1960s, long before such an approach emerged. Herb emphasized external constraints in *Models of Man* (p. 197), the same emphasis placed in Cohen and Stewart. He mentioned many times in class and in private conversations the importance of context and emergence of patterns. In fact, I wondered, reflecting the reductionistic bias I had, why he was so rigorous everywhere else but still kept bringing up patterns and shapes which seemed so soft and ambiguous.

The Gardens

I now would like to mention Herb's serious interest in Japanese language and Japanese culture which put us together frequently. He showed me a series of ten small books on Japanese fairy tales, written in English and printed on well-preserved rice paper. They were passed on to Herb from his father, who received them as a gift from a friend. I recall Herb citing fondly from these fairy tales.

In a summer in the early 1970s, Herb and Dorothea went to Japan and traveled to Sendai, which is about 200 miles north of Tokyo. There, they ran into the "Tanabata Star Festival," the city's big celebration, following the beautiful Chinese legend of the two stars, Altaire and Vega, coming closest to each other, once a year at that time. Children are said to become good calligraphers if they write on "Tanzaku," which is oblong, multi-color cardboard and decorate bamboo trees with them during the festival.

Here, Herb learned the song of the festival, "Tanabata-sama," a very popular song among children. He liked it so much that he sang it at a gathering at a university in Japan. We also sang this song and other Japanese songs together on a number of occasions.

A few years ago, he saw a Japanese modern animation video called "Totoro," a story of a friendly monster by that name which can be seen only by children. As they get older, they lose the ability to see "Totoro." Herb liked the video very much and asked me about the origin and meaning of "Totoro." Luckily, my wife, Tomo, found a Japanese book by the author of the story, Susumu Miyazaki, who said "Totoro" was a symbol of dreams and creativity. We gladly presented this book to Herb and Dorothea.

Indeed, Herb was a person able to see "Totoro" at any age. He was a person who cherished single-minded, earnest efforts whether they are by children, by students or by faculty members. I treasure these memories of Herb so much.

A couple of months ago, I had an occasion to translate a Japanese song into English at the request from our alumnus. She and her husband saw a Japanese movie called *Madadayo* by Akira Kurosawa, which is about a Japanese college professor and his former students getting together once a year, decades after graduation. They were both impressed by the song in the movie, called "Aogeba Toutoshi" ("Looking Up To My Teachers)," a very popular Japanese song written in 1884. For many decades since then, it has been sung at graduation ceremonies of grade and high schools. (A Scottish song, "Auld Lang Syne," translated into Japanese, is also popular at these ceremonies.) Her husband wanted to get the translation of the song and send it to his teacher in England.

This is one of a few songs that still give me an emotional chill —nearly a half century after my graduations from grade and high schools. I wish to present it here in closing with the hope that the spirit of the song may nevertheless be conveyed in spite of my crude translation.

Aogeba Toutoshi (Looking Up To My Teachers)

Looking up to my teachers,
　To whom I owe so much.
Many years of studies,
　In the gardens of learning.
Time has passed so fast,
　These years and months.
Now, it's time to move on,
　So long, farewell.

Our friendship and affection,
　Our gratitude to all.
Let us never forget,
　Even long after we depart.
Toast to our success, to our fame,
　To our unceasing endeavor.
Now, it's time to move on,
　So long, farewell.

Day and night, our familiar place,
　At the windows of learning.
Using fireflies or deep white snow,
　As our precious reading light.
There is no way to forget,
　These passing years.
Now, it's time to move on,
　So long, farewell.

(source: *Grade School Song Book (Third Grade)*. Tokyo: Japan Ministry of Education, March 1884)

Carnegie Mellon University and its Graduate School of Industrial Administration, in particular, have indeed been small "gardens" of learning blessed with exceptional teachers and students. Yet there seem to be something more. The gardens seem to have a special way of letting people grow.

The key ingredient for this magic is, I am convinced, interdisciplinary scholarship. It is the belief that by means of reasoning, knowledge can be effectively condensed or cross-fertilized beyond disciplines, no matter how different they may look on the surface. This is what seems to have permeated the gardens over the past half century, helping people explore phenomena from deeper and broader perspectives, and thus reducing the inherent risk of interdisciplinary research mentioned earlier.

Herb Simon was indeed at the core of this interdisciplinary scholarship that benefited so many people around him. This essay is intended to offer one small testimony to his profound influence.

References

Axtell, Robert L. 2001. Zipf distribution of U.S. firm sizes. *Science* 293, September 7: 1818–1820.

Cayley, Arthur. 1894. *The Principles of Book-keeping by Double Entry*. Cambridge University Press.

Cohen, Jack, and Ian Stewart. 1994. *The Collapse of Chaos: Discovering Simplicity in a Complex World*. Penguin.

Feynman, Richard, Robert B. Leighton, and Matthew Sands. 1963. *The Feynman Lectures on Physics II-41–12*. Addison-Wesley.

Gibrat, R. 1931. *Les Inégalités Économiques*. Librarie du Recueil Sirey.

Heppenheimer, T. A. 1986. Routes to chaos. *Mosaic* 17, no. 2: 2–13.

Ijiri, Yuji. 1965. *Management Goals and Accounting for Control*. North-Holland.

Ijiri, Yuji. 1967. *The Foundations of Accounting Measurement: A Mathematical, Economic, and Behavioral Inquiry*. Prentice-Hall.

Ijiri, Yuji. 1989. *Momentum Accounting and Triple-Entry Bookkeeping: Exploring the Dynamic Structure of Accounting Measurements*. American Accounting Association.

Ijiri, Yuji, and Herbert A. Simon. 1964. Business firm growth and size. *American Economic Review* 54, March: 77–89.

Ijiri, Yuji, and Herbert A. Simon. 1967. A model of business firm growth. *Econometrica* 35, April: 348–355.

Ijiri, Yuji, and Herbert A. Simon. 1971. Effects of mergers and acquisitions on business firm concentration. *Journal of Political Economy* 79, March–April: 314–322.

Ijiri, Yuji, and Herbert A. Simon. 1974. Interpretations of departures from the Pareto Curve firm-size distributions. *Journal of Political Economy* 82, March–April: 315–331.

Ijiri, Yuji, and Herbert A. Simon. 1975. Some distributions associated with Bose-Einstein statistics. *Proceedings of National Academy of Sciences* 72, May: 1654–1657.

Ijiri, Yuji, and Herbert A. Simon. 1977. *Skew Distributions and the Sizes of Business Firms*. North-Holland.

Kou, S. C., and S. G. Kou. 2001. Modeling Growth Stocks via Size Distribution. Working paper, Department of Statistics, Harvard University.

Krugman, Paul R. 1996. *The Self-Organizing Economy*. Blackwell.

Lodish, Harvey, et al. 2000. *Molecular Cell Biology*, fourth edition. Freeman.

Pacioli, Luca. 1963. *Summa de Arithmetica, Geometria, Proportioni et Proportionalita: Distintio Nona-Tractatus XI, Particularis de Computis et Scripturis*. In R. Brown and K. Johnston, *Paciolo on Accounting*. (McGraw-Hill). Original published in Venice in 1494.

Peano, Giuseppe. 1889. *Arithmetices principia, nova methodo exposita*. Turin: Bocca, 1889. Cited in S. C. Kleene, *Introduction to Metamathematics* (North-Holland, 1952).

Rosser, J. B., and A. R. Turquette. 1958. *Many-Valued Logics*. North-Holland.

Simon, Herbert A. 1947. *Administrative Behavior*. Macmillan.

Simon, Herbert A. 1955. On a class of skew distribution functions. *Biometrika* 52, December: 425–440.

Simon, Herbert A. 1957. *Models of Man: Social and Rational*. Wiley.

Swedish Academy of Sciences. 1978. Citation for the 1978 Winner of the Nobel Prize for Economics.

Yule, G. Udny. 1924. A mathematical theory of evolution, based on the conclusions of Dr. J. C. Willis, F.R.S. *Philosophical Transactions* B 213: 21–87.

Beliefs and Tastes: Confessions of an Economist

David M. Kreps

I regret to say that I never met Herbert Simon. His influence on my intellectual development—especially through his classic 1951 paper on the employment relationship, "A formal theory of the employment relationship" (*Econometrica* 19: 293–305)—was certainly enormous. And his influence on my career in another way, which I will leave mysterious until the end of this essay, was even more profound.

I relearned both these lessons quite recently, when another of my intellectual heroes, Hugo Sonnenschein—who is also a friend—gave me an assignment. Sonnenschein, as president of the University of Chicago, was to play host in October 2000 to a meeting of the American Association of Universities, which, as he explained to me, is the "club" of presidents of major American research universities. The various presidents assemble twice a year to discuss common concerns, such as how to get along with head coaches, and Sonnenschein conceived that for one day, he would present them with a somewhat more intellectual program: He would ask one scholar from the physical sciences, one from the biological sciences, one from the social sciences, and one from the humanities, to take a guess at what the future held for their respective divisions, using their own careers as a focus. Sonnenschein asked if I would represent social science. The task was daunting, but since Sonnenschein is my hero, he knew I would try. So I set out to first write down and then present something appropriate.

What follows is an adaptation of what I wrote. I've edited it to fit the current occasion, although except for a brief autobiography, which I've remodeled, and the end, which I've redone to pay a final tribute to Simon, it isn't changed much at all. Thus as you'll learn, one thing is clear: If my speculations are correct, the future of the Division of Social Sciences is to realize just how prescient was Herbert Simon.

Economists and Other Social Scientists

About five years ago, I had the pleasure of participating in a conference put on by the American Academy of Arts and Sciences, which attempted to trace developments in Academe in the period since the Second World War. Four fields were represented: Comparative Literature, Philosophy, Political Science, and Economics. For each field, three "representatives" reported on the field from her point of view. One representative was of the generation that came to intellectual maturity in the 1950s, one from the 1960s, and one from the 1970s.

It turned out that the "middle-aged" economist sent in regrets the morning of the conference, so economics was represented only by the "old" (by Robert Solow) and the "young" (which was my job). But among the organizers and commentators at the conference was a third economist, Michael Woodford, so we economists had reasonably diverse representation.

I should also note that while primary presentations came from members of the four disciplines above, at the conference were a number of worthies from other fields in the humanities and social sciences, to comment and critique the primary presentations.[1]

A number of interesting observations emerged at the conference. But for current purposes, one observation in particular was telling: Economists seemed to be a distinctly different species of academic from everyone else at the conference. The other fields reported as common the phenomenon of generational conflict; each generation had spend a lot of time and energy in overthrowing the settled wisdom of their academic parents. Economics, on the other hand, had a well-developed orthodoxy, and while it was clear that things had changed intellectually over the fifty or so years, it was equally clear that "today's" economists respected and played by the basic rules set forth by earlier generations. And the other fields reported a great deal of uncertainty about where they were headed. We economists, on the other hand, were smugly self-satisfied that we had a clear conception of what we knew and what we didn't know, and how to work at the things unknown.

I suspect—but I certainly don't know for sure—that had there been natural scientists at the conference, the economists would have resembled them. (Being an economist, to whom money is meant to be the measure of all things, I can't help but note that when Stanford University publishes salary ranges by Divisions and Schools, the economists are lumped in with the natural scientists. I assume this is so that our colleagues in other social sciences won't be depressed by how much economists are paid. Perhaps this is a coincidence. But, as I'll argue, perhaps it is not.) I don't mean to suggest that economics is more "scientific" than is sociology or political science or anthropology. (For the record, I don't believe that it is.) Indeed, being in a business school, I have many colleagues who are sociologists or social psychologists by training, and I'm well aware that these colleagues view economics as being scientifically equivalent to alchemy; to these colleagues, at least, economics is based on basic assumptions and principles that have no connection to reality.

But while I don't think economics is more scientific than the other social sciences, I think economists resemble natural scientists because we have a strong, well-developed, and well-honed "paradigm"; a way of approaching questions in the economic and social realm, which we apply the way religious missionaries apply the catechisms of their faiths, namely without doubt or question. In my limited experience, physicists are unsurpassed for a smug assurance that they are smarter than everyone else (except perhaps mathematicians) and better able to solve all the problems of all other fields by a modest exercise of their way of thinking. But within the limited domain of the social sciences, in this competition economists surely take the gold medal, and the silver and bronze.

Robert Solow has summarized the economics paradigm as Greed, Rationality, and Equilibrium:

- Individuals are selfishly self-interested.

- They are also fairly far-sighted and devilishly clever in pursuing their self-interest.

- Where conflicts arise, institutions bring diverse and conflicting desires into equilibrium.

Certainly, the way we apply this paradigm has changed over the years.[2] But at least in microeconomics, I'd be fairly happy teaching first-year graduate students for at least the first semester out of books thirty years old. And books that are getting on for a half century in age—such as Arrow's *Social Choice and Individual Values* and Debreu's *Theory of Value*—remain almost vital primary reading for today's graduate students.

Why tell you all this? Because I am increasingly convinced that economists should—and will—have to change large pieces of the paradigm that has kept us relatively monolithic for the past fifty years. We'll increasingly look like and work with our colleagues in the other, "lesser" social sciences. (Presumably, this means that we'll soon be paid like our kin in the other social sciences, which is probably a welcome speculation to make in front of an assembly of university presidents.) To make these points, I'll begin with an extended example that illustrates the "errors" that I think the economic paradigm propagates. Then I'll give a bit of a history of developments in economics, tying this to my own research program. This leads to where I think ('hope' is the more accurate verb) that program is headed. And then I'll abuse the soapbox you've so kindly given me, to put in a brief plug for the role that well-managed professional schools might play in these developments.

Gary Becker on Prenuptial Agreements

One of the great economists of the past fifty years, Gary Becker, writes a column periodically for *Business Week*. Several years ago, he wrote on the topic "why every marriage should have a contract," where he gave economic arguments for why (serious) prenuptial agreements should be made mandatory.

Gary Becker is one of the luminaries of the so-called Chicago School, perhaps best known for his work on labor markets and employment. But he is also well known—and among sociologists at least, somewhat notorious—for applying economic logic to topics—for instance, marriage, the family, and crime—that are normally left to other disciplines. He isn't notorious for simply traipsing on the territories of other disciplines, but for doing so in the sure and certain knowledge that if we think of (say) marriage as an economic exchange and apply the economic paradigm, everything will become clear. (When Becker received the Nobel Prize, *The Economist* did a story on him in which they as much as said "Here, finally, is someone who is making sense out of topics that sociologists make into a hash." This did not endear him or *The Economist* to my friends from outside economics.)

Becker's argument for why every marriage should have a contract is best taken in two steps. First, marriage contracts are good, everything else held equal, because they allow individuals to fine-tune their specific relationship to their specific tastes, preferences, and circumstances. We don't expect one-size-fits-all when it comes to, say, contracts for the construction of buildings. So why expect that one size—the standard laws of divorce in a particular jurisdiction—will fit all marriages? Let markets operate—let couples fit their contracts to themselves and their circumstances—and efficiency will rise. Indeed, Becker goes so far as to say that the divorce courts and divorce lawyers will wither away, as couples become better at writing well-tailored contracts.

As a member of the Chicago School, Becker is supposed to believe that government interference in private relationships is an evil to be avoided. If he is right that detailed marriage contracts will enhance efficiency, then he ought to expect that clever individuals will recognize this and voluntarily enter into these sorts of arrangements. But with rare exceptions, we don't see these things. So Becker insists that we should *compel* parties to draft these contracts. Why?

This is the second step in his argument. He recognizes that markets can sometimes break down when parties have access to private information. When I know the quality of used car I'm selling, but prospective buyers are in the dark, it may be difficult for me to get full price for my excellent car, if my car is indeed excellent. In the case of marriage, a certain stigma attaches to one fiancé saying to the other "Let's go draft a prenuptial agreement." The second party may draw adverse inferences from this declaration, about the first party's degree of commitment to the relationship, for instance. So, Becker argues, despite their basic value in enhancing efficient marriage-transactions, we don't see prenuptial agreements widely used. Where such adverse inferences are not drawn—within (say) upper-class British society in the nineteenth century or today in Hollywood—we see these contracts in full flower. But right now, in American society at least, we are trapped by adverse expectations when one fiancé suggests that a contract be drawn up.

So, argues Becker, the state should take the minimal step of requiring specific contracts. No adverse conclusions can be drawn if the drafting of a contract is compelled by the state. And then all the efficiency-enhancing benefits of such contracts will be realized.

It may be correct that, by making such contracts mandatory, the "adverse expectations trap" will be defeated. But this is not guaranteed, at least in (economic) theory. An important area of research in economics over the past two decades has concerned the inferences drawn by uninformed parties in situations where the other party has private information. Since I've been one of the more active members of the group that conducted this research, I can be trusted when I assert that this research has been less than a raging success: Very little can be precluded in terms of such inferences, on the basis of purely economic arguments. If Becker is convinced that making these contracts mandatory will solve the adverse expectations problem, he must be convinced for reasons other than economics.[3]

But suppose that, empirically, making such contracts mandatory defeated the adverse expectations trap. Still, I have a second problem with Becker's argument that, I believe, is much more damaging to the standard economic approach to this question.

I've outlined Becker's general argument to colleagues who are social psychologists and sociologists, and they are generally aghast. Speaking somewhat in code, they respond that a detailed marriage contract would objectify the relationship between husband and wife. In closer-to-lay terms, generous behavior rooted in affection between the partners would be would be crowded out by calculative satisfaction of the contract. Of course, there is no guarantee that this would happen. But the possibility is there and it is real, and because of this possibility, requiring marriage contracts would cause more difficulties than these contracts might solve.

If there is one thing that economists have been good at for the past half-century, at least, it is developing logically coherent models of behavior and then pursuing the logical consequences of those models. For a column in *Business Week*, Becker is not going to write out the formal model that underlies his assertions. (I suspect that this is what led him to be a bit too optimistic about how making contracts mandatory would evade the adverse-expectations problem.) But his assertions are very well rooted in formal theoretical developments in economics over the past twenty-five years. So if my aghast colleagues are correct, Becker's "error," if I may call it that, must be rooted in incorrect underlying assumptions that he and economists more generally make about behavior. To understand where the economic paradigm has gone wrong—at least according to those who are aghast—requires some background.

Economists almost always assume that individual behavior is purposeful; driven by well-behaved preferences of the individual that are revealed by the individual's choices. As a matter of mathematical logic, if those preferences are sufficiently well behaved—as a binary relation among the objects of choice, complete and transitive, plus a technical condition such as continuity—the individual's behavior is observationally equivalent to maximizing some numerical index of well-off-ed-ness, the so-called utility function.

An immediate question is "What does the individual value?" Put formally, "What will lead to an increase in his or her utility?" Economists typically assume that individuals are narrowly selfish. In a marriage, the husband and the wife are each concerned with their own personal well-being and, except insofar as it enhances their personal well-being, they have no concern for the well-being of their partner.

Put it this way: Imagine that a husband was offered the opportunity to perform some task that requires effort and perhaps a modicum of discomfort, but that, if done, would greatly enhance the well-being of his wife. But—and this is crucial to the thought experiment—if he performs this task, she will never know that he did so. And if he doesn't, she will never know that he had the opportunity to do so and decided against. In other words, performance of this task is purely altruistic; the only benefit he might receive—in compensation for the effort and discomfort directly encountered—is in his personal knowledge that he has made her better off. He gets no "points" or "credit" for doing this, nor does he lose points or credit for failing to do this. The typical assumption on behavior made by economists in their models is that, in these circumstances, the task will not be done.

I need a term for behavior that would lead to the task being done. Genuine altruism is one possibility, generosity is another. Social scientists generally say that when one party takes actions that are personally costly but that benefit another, without any prospect of reciprocation (or penalty if the task is not done), the first party has internalized the welfare of the second. I'll use generosity and internalized welfare in what follows. Let me make two important but somewhat technical points about this sort of behavior:

- Because economists regard what a person does as that individual's revealed preference—that is, an individual's welfare is enhanced by the actions she takes, more or less as a tautology—the notion that an individual takes an action that runs against his or her own self-interest can be formally elusive. But with care, this idea is not impossible to pin down in the style of axiomatic choice theory; there are ways to differentiate between an individual's overall utility or welfare or well-off-ed-ness and his or her narrow self-interest. (Set the choice space as a full product space, where one component is the state of affairs for one person and the second is the state of affairs for the other. Assume weak separability of preferences, and fixing the state of affairs for the "other," you have the individual's self-interested preferences. And the tradeoffs between the two record the level of internalization. Indeed, it is easy with this setup to formalize purely benevolent altruism—the first person's overall welfare, holding her own state of affairs fixed, is increasing in the second person's self-interest preferences—from preferences that are more paternalistic.)

- The assumption in the thought experiment that the party taking the action (or not) does so with no prospect of reciprocation is vital. I may appear to be generous to a fault to someone else based solely on pure self-interest, expecting that if I am, she will reciprocate (perhaps in the belief that I will then reciprocate that—see the discussion following on the folk theorem—and perhaps out of a sense of gratitude) or, more negatively, that she will harm me if I am not generous. Genuine generosity or internalization of another's welfare isn't calculative in this fashion; the generous party sacrifices herself simply to improve the welfare of the other.

To reiterate, economists have tended, with a few exceptions, to assume that people are not generous in this sense. Any generous behavior we observe must be the result of calculative self-interest. And, to begin to identify Becker's "error," my aghast colleagues would observe that partners in a marriage are often genuinely generous towards each other, which can lead to efficient behavior—behavior that maximizes the parties' joint welfare—making an explicit contract unnecessary.

Given a right of reply, I believe that Becker would argue that this does not in the least affect his basic thesis. If a particular husband—wife pair have preferences/utility that are generous in this sense, the optimal marriage contract between them will be designed to reflect that. The contract between, say, two economists, who are professionally committed to self-interest, will be filled with specific-performance clauses; the contract between two social psychologists would be much vaguer and reliant on good will and generosity. Indeed, Becker could argue that this *strengthens* his basic point: To the extent that there is variation in the population along this dimension—some partners are more generous in this sense, but others less—having a single one-size-fits-all divorce law breeds inefficiency: Obviously, we should have different and tailored marriage contracts depending on the degree to which the partners are more or less generous in this sense. (I leave to your imagination the method by which we would elicit from young couples the information that, on balance, they are less generous towards each other in this respect.)

So if Becker has indeed erred, it isn't here, at least not directly. Instead, I think the "errant" assumption on behavior that Becker implicitly makes, and that has been implicit in almost all of economics, is that individual preferences are an immutable primitive for each individual; one can take these preferences as given and design a contract to fit.

My aghast colleagues disagree with this assumption. They believe that the existence or absence of a detailed contract will fundamentally change the preferences of the individuals involved. Preferences are determined to some extent by the social environment and to some extent by the specific experiences of the individuals involved.

Very specifically, they believe that a detailed and carefully calculated contract will reduce the extent to which husband and wife internalize each other's welfare. I won't take you through the social psychological constructions and terminology that underlie this assertion. But, roughly, the notion is that individuals look for ways to justify their own previous actions. When you take actions that fulfill a legal contract, you justify your actions as contract fulfillment, as in "I did X or Y to avoid breach, because of the unpleasant consequences for me of breaching the contract." But absent a formal contract, if you do a favor for someone, to justify your own actions, you decide that you did it because you value the welfare of the other party. In a virtuous cycle, your rationalization leads you to more good deeds, which when rationalized increase the degree to which you believe you internalize the other party's welfare (and thus do so, at least in the revealed preference sense), and so forth. In comparison, laying a formal contract on a marriage evokes a vicious cycle. Perhaps you begin by internalizing the welfare of your spouse. We can hope so, in any case. But when you take some action that benefits your spouse, rather than rationalizing this on your concern for his or her welfare, you rationalize it as "The contract forced my hand." Your level of internalization falls, making you more reliant, next time, on this rationalization. In the end, you follow the dictates of the contract, only.

And this, if it really happens, leads to inefficient marriages. Economists have studied agency and the topic of incentives extensively, we know that the combination of private information and hidden or unenforceable actions can lead to substantial inefficiency, even under the best extrinsic incentive scheme. Moreover, although economists haven't got the formal tools to back up this assertion, there is a general sense that in long-term relationships in which contingencies arise that are initially unforeseen and probably unforeseeable, the best extrinsic incentive schemes will be sorely lacking. In such circumstances, and a marriage is clearly an extreme case of such circumstances, perhaps it is better to rely on the good will and generosity of the individuals involved and, indeed, to do whatever is needed to enhance that good will and generosity, *avoiding* actions—such as drafting formal and detailed contracts—that lead to a loss of good will and generosity.

At this point, I want to tie all this to the development of economics, past and future. But before leaving Becker's analysis, I should say that he hasn't necessarily erred, at least insofar as he is making the tautological assertion that tailoring contracts to the individuals involved can be no worse than one-size-fits-all, since the optimal tailoring could always be the one size that otherwise fits all. If a formal and detailed contract would lead to a loss of good will and generosity, then the optimal contract will not be formal and detailed. But when it comes to implementing Becker's recommendation, if we put economists in charge of drafting these contracts, their mindset, bred out of the way that economists have done business for the past half century, would probably lead them to underestimate—or completely miss—the feedback from the contract to underlying preferences. And that, I think, would justify the attitude of my aghast colleagues.

Why Is This Important? Developments in Economics

Economists, by and large, are not concerned with perfecting the institution of marriage. Notwithstanding the high regard in which Gary Becker is held, I think most economists would be willing to leave marriage to other disciplines. But what I hope is fairly obvious in the case of marriage contracts is actually quite important, if a bit less obvious, in a lot of topics that have become mainstream economics and that, indeed, increasingly dominate economics.

To explain, I need to go back about fifty years, to the immediate post-World War II period. Economics as a monolithic and smugly self-satisfied scientific discipline traces, I believe, from that time, when the basic paradigms we continue to use today were laid down. In this period—in the 1950s and the 1960s—you find an enormous rise of mathematically based modeling in economic discourse. Gerard Debreu, in his presidential address[4] to the American Economic Association documents this. Economists use mathematics somewhat haphazardly and opportunistically—Robert Solow has termed the style as loose-fitting positivism[5]—but this use of mathematics has meant that the basic "rules" of economic discourse became fairly uniform. Before World War II, relations between the different branches of economics— labor economics, money and banking, industrial organization, etc.— resembled the relationships among the romance languages: there were certainly connections, but each tongue needed to be studied separately. But as mathematical modeling first rose and then pretty conclusively wiped out all other forms of discourse, the field became much more one of a single language, applied to different contexts. Ideas that appear in one field are now quickly imported into others; individuals move much more freely from one field to another. For instance, Jean Tirole, one of the leading theorists of the past twenty years, has made important contributions to methodology (game theory), industrial organization, public finance, the regulation of financial institutions, and organization theory, spilling over into labor economics and law and economics. Of course, Tirole is exceptional—no one matches his breadth or his productivity, except perhaps my former colleague Joe Stiglitz—but having one person write so broadly across so many fields is a tribute to how unified the overall subject has become. Macroeconomics used to be somewhat freestanding, but not anymore. Economic development and political economy are largely incorporated in the mainstream way of thinking. And even economic history is now a part of the greater whole.

And, perhaps needless to say, when a discipline achieves such remarkable unity and consensus, it gains both self-confidence and the ability, through unity, to defend itself and arrogate to itself particular perks and benefits.

The mainstream consensus is rooted in Solow's troika of greed, rationality, and equilibrium. Nearly everyone in economics does business according to these three principles. The models of individual behavior are common, both in terms of what people desire and how we think about the expectations they hold. And the notion of "the answer"—an equilibrium—is common. (The technical definition of an equilibrium varies depending on the type of model being used, but the general idea is as follows: Within the model, we imagine individual actors who choose actions or, in more complex settings, strategies. Depending perhaps on institutional arrangements, each array of actions/strategies—called an action or strategy profile—maps into an overall outcome. Individual actors evaluate the outcomes; they have well-behaved preferences among outcomes, usually modeled by a utility function. And an equilibrium—called in particular a Nash equilibrium when the model is of the variety of noncooperative game theory—is an action/strategy array where each actor *individually* is doing as well as he or she can, in terms of his or her utility, fixing the actions or strategies of the other actors.)

This is not to say that economics today looks like the economics of the 1950s and the 1960s. When the consensus first took hold, it was centered around price theory, the economics of large and impersonal markets. This sort of economics is powerful, but limited. There are many important contexts that are hard to think about, if your models are mostly about markets that are large and impersonal. But beginning in the 1970s, the consensus methodology expanded to look increasingly at contexts in which time, uncertainty, information, and small numbers all play a role. The methods of noncooperative game theory—formulating situations as games, and looking for Nash equilibria of those games—became an important part of the consensus way of doing business.

The methodological developments of the 1970s were crucial to allowing economists to maintain the consensus. For a while, there was plenty to do in working through the economics of large, impersonal markets. Work in these areas, especially concerning financial markets, continues. But a large share of interesting economics involves markets or other institutional settings where the number of "actors" or participants is small, uncertainty is rife, parties have access to private information, and one-time transactions are replaced by long-term exchange relationships. For instance, my particular interest over the past decade or so has been applied labor economics or, as it is known in business and in business schools, the subject of Human Resource Management. When talking about the employment relationship between, say, your professoriate and your institution, or the key professional employees of IBM or, even more, Apple Computer or a biotech startup, thinking in terms of large impersonal markets (hiring halls, and the like) just doesn't work. We think instead in terms of long-term employment relationships where employer and employee invest substantially in the relationship, investments that, because they are sunk, dilute the power of the market to determine terms of trade. (It is something of an article of faith in the popular press that employment relationships, especially in the New Economy, are increasingly short term. The data to support this article of faith are spotty, at best. And even if the assertion is true, employment is still long-term and complex enough so that thinking of it in terms of an impersonal large market can be very misleading or, at least, incomplete.) Terms like reputation and reciprocity become important. This is true not only in the context of employment relationships, but it applies to the contexts of competition between and strategic alliances among firms, trade relations among countries, microcredit organizations in developing economies, and so forth.

But this is where the problem arises. Solow's troika, as implemented throughout economics, makes considerable demands upon economic actors. In short, they have to know a lot about what they can and cannot get as they vary their actions. In the context of large and impersonal markets—especially markets for goods to be consumed immediately—these demands are considerable but not overwhelming. More complex large and impersonal markets—such as for financial securities and durable goods—introduce substantial uncertainty and begin to tax the forecasting powers of the actors. And when you move to the arenas in which one finds the most action today—where numbers are small, private information abounds, and economic relationships are enduring—the powers of reasoning we demand of economic actors, and the levels of rationality and stability of preferences that we suppose are simply incredible. It isn't hard to imagine that models of behavior originally deemed adequate for large and impersonal markets in consumables would begin to look somewhat inadequate for the much more complex settings of long-term employment or joint ventures between firms. The question is, what do we do about it?

The Folk Theorem and Its Uses

To explain more fully where the problem is, it will be helpful to describe one of the central technical results in game theoretic economics—the so-called folk theorem—so-called because the idea is so obvious that it seems always to have been known in principle, if not in detail—and how it is used.

Formally, the folk theorem is a mathematical result about repeated games. Rather than state the formal theorem, I'll give a caricature that illustrates what it says. Imagine a situation in which Sam must decide whether to trust Jan. If Sam decides not to trust Jan, both are given $0. If Sam trusts Jan, then Jan must decide whether to respond honorably or abusively. If Jan responds honorably, they both get $1. If Jan responds abusively, Jan gets $2 and Sam loses $5.

Played once and once only, with no subsequent interaction between Sam and Jan and under the assumption that both are selfishly self-interested, Sam cannot trust Jan. If Sam does trust Jan, then Jan can have $2 from abusive behavior or $1 from honorable behavior. Under the assumption that each is selfishly self-interested, Jan will choose abuse. Sam, anticipating this, understands that if she trusts Jan then Jan will act abusively and she will be out $5. Better to refrain from trust and get $0. This outcome is inefficient, because if somehow Jan could guarantee that he will act honorably, Sam can trust Jan, and both get $1, better for both than the $0 outcome.

To avoid the inefficient outcome, we might try to have the two form a binding contract in which, say, Jan suffers via court action by more than he gains directly from abusive conduct. But the folk theorem takes us in the direction of another solution to the problem. Imagine that Sam and Jan are engaged in this interaction repeatedly. To be precise, imagine that they play the game once, and then a random event is conducted so that, with probability 0.1, the full encounter is over, but with probability 0.9, they play again. After each round of play, the random event is conducted independently; each time there is a 0.1 chance that the round just played was the final round, and a 0.9 chance that the encounter continues. (Or, you can imagine they play infinitely often, and they discount their payoffs by 0.9 each round.) The basic idea is that there is always substantial probability that there will be future encounters, and each side places substantial weight on the possible results of future encounters, relative to today's winnings or losses.

Then there are many possible self-interested equilibria. For instance, imagine that Jan somehow gets the notion that Sam will behave as follows. If Jan is trusted and responds with abuse in a given round, Sam will not trust him for the following three rounds, if there are three more. But if Jan is trusted and responds honorably, Sam will continue to trust him. In essence, Jan believes that Sam, having been abused, withdraws from the interaction for a period of time.

If you do the math, you will find that Jan's best dynamic response to this strategy by Sam is to act honorably. And if Jan acts honorably in each round, the strategy we've suggested for Sam is among her many best responses.

That, essentially, is the folk theorem. Of course, it is a theorem, so it is much more general than this. But its message is that when encounters are repeated and when the individuals involved in the encounters think and act strategically, the power of reciprocity—I'll be good to you in the future if you are good to me today; I'll punish you in the future if you take advantage of me today—can expand considerably the range of possible selfish self-interest equilibrium outcomes.

The folk theorem generalizes this simple idea from the example to more general encounters involving more player/participants. And variations and emendations consider further complications. For instance, we might wonder how this idea would work if Jan did not encounter Sam repeatedly, but instead he interacted with a series of different trading partners. What happens if Jan interacts repeatedly with Sam, but Jan interacts simultaneously with a number of others, who differ in their characteristics? A very important variation concerns the impact of so-called noisy observables: Imagine that Jan has not a dichotomous response—honor or abuse—but instead a continuum of possible responses, of varying value to himself and to Sam, and Sam may not perceive his response to be what Jan intends it to be. That is, Jan takes an action, Sam sees a result, but there is noise interposed between Jan's choice and Sam's observation, so that Jan may have chosen a response that is basically honorable, and Sam perceives this as somewhat abusive. The inability to monitor exactly what the other party intends can make for a lot of trouble in trying to sustain trusting/efficient outcomes. If Sam perceives abuse, is this just noise? Or is Jan pushing the envelope to take advantage? Should Sam respond by punishing Jan— if he didn't intend abuse, mightn't that sour the relationship or, more formally, lead to a loss in value to each—or should she assume he intends honorable behavior and forgive him, which invites him to push the envelope?

While I don't want to take you into the technicalities of this result —I bring the folk theorem up to make quite a different point—it is probably useful to say what my brand of economist does with this formal result about repeated games. Having understood this result and its elaborations and emendations, we use it as a parable for repeated interactions in the real world. It is quite a stretch from this simple model to, say, the interactions between General Electric and Westinghouse in the Large Electric Turbine Generator market in the 1960s and the 1970s, but the leap is made. In trying to fathom the strategic actions taken by GE in 1964 (one of the most brilliant strategic moves in the history of industrial competition), the model of the folk theorem with noise orients one's thinking magnificently.

Or this parable can be used to understand employment practices in high-tech startups in Silicon Valley. In a very large empirical study, the Stanford Project on Emerging Companies, or SPEC, investigators found striking patterns of practices in the data. There does not seem to be one set of best practices in the Valley. Instead, there seem to be clusters of practices that complement one another and that complement the business strategy of the firm. The parable, very liberally read, rationalizes what we see in terms of communicating to employees both old and new what is expected of them—what behavior is "honorable" and what is not—both in general and specifically.

Dynamic Choice in Economics, or My Research Career

The folk theorem is about dynamic economic interactions, and so it is first of all about dynamic choices made by single economic actors. As I've already observed, economists nearly invariably assume that actors in their models act purposefully. Within the constraints imposed upon them by their resources and other conditions of their environment, they are assumed to work towards fulfilling specific and definite goals. Some very neat pieces of mathematical analysis show that as long as they act somewhat rationally, they act as if they were maximizing some numerical measure of how well off they are, called their utility. So in economic models, economists write down the utility functions of the actors and assume that their actions maximize those functions, subject to the constraints imposed by their environment. When economists define an equilibrium, the notion is that each individual, separately, maximizes his or her own utility, given the simultaneously optimizing choices of others.

Putting this in a dynamic context adds two crucial complications. First, in taking an action at a given date, the individual must forecast the future consequences of today's possible actions. At its simplest, this involves forecasting "objective" future events, such as the returns from some physical investment. An example the size of a crop that comes out of the ground, depending on how much seed the farmer plants, how much fertilizer he spreads and—outside of the control of the farmer—the weather. A degree more complex is forecasting future equilibrium values, where the equilibrium values depend on large masses of individuals. The farmer may need to forecast future (equilibrium) prices of corn, conditional on the size of his own crop. As we move towards situations with small numbers of parties, it increasingly becomes important to forecast the future actions and reactions of other specific individuals. (Think of the farmer trying to forecast how the local banker will react in terms of rescheduling the farmer's debt, in case the harvest is bad or corn prices are low.) When those others have access to information the first party lacks, the first party's forecast has to take into account the impact that information will have on the other's actions. Thus there is a problem—of increasing complexity the more small numbers, uncertainty, and private information are involved—of expectations.

These expectations can matter enormously. In my caricature of the folk theorem, I described an equilibrium in which Jan, somehow, concludes that Sam will respond to abusive behavior with three rounds of refraining from trust. How does Jan come to this remarkable conclusion? Indeed, in the equilibrium I described, Jan—suitably chastened by the thought—will never act abusively. So Jan never has any data about Sam's behavior after abuse. Yet his expectations in this regard are crucial to the equilibrium; he must believe that Sam will respond to abuse with sufficient severity, so that abuse is no longer a rational option for Jan. Or put it this way: I can adjust Jan's (and Sam's) expectations and come up with an equilibrium that is just as good an equilibrium on formal grounds, in which Sam never trusts Jan. And all this is in the ultra-simple world of my parable, with dichotomous choices and precisely repeated play. How does a large industrial company such as Westinghouse decipher the actions of a rival such as GE, especially when any explicit communication on the matter is illegal?[6]

The second complication is even more fundamental. How do we think about the sequence of choices that the individual makes? Do we model and conceptualize them as a sequence of choices "rational" according to economic precepts as a snapshot, but not connected together at all? Do we model them as a sequence of snapshot-rational choices that are loosely connected? Or do we think of them as pieces from a grand optimal strategy.

In the caricature of the folk theorem, Jan was going to the second stage, at least. Although abuse beats honor in the short run, Jan forecast that this would have adverse effects in the future, and so honor was better from the perspective of Jan's overall expected payoff from playing the game.

Economists invariably go with the third route. Dynamic choice is always (well, nearly always) a matter of finding the best dynamic strategy for behavior throughout the span of the situation being modeled. The chief mathematical tool for finding optimal strategies is dynamic programming, which is an important technical stop on the education of first-year graduate students in economics.

Even given a set of expectations about how others will act, solving these dynamic choice problems can be quite difficult. Teaching dynamic programming to first-year graduate students takes a couple of weeks, in most cases, and still the number of problems we can solve is extraordinarily limited. To give you a sense of this, imagine you are vacationing in a country house adjacent to a forest. Each day, you pack up a rucksack and take a walk in the forest. You've never been to this forest, and you aren't sure what should be carried. What might you encounter along the way, and how useful will be the various implements and goods you might carry? If I assume that you learn by experience, and I assume that you can only learn, or that you best learn, what items are good for if you carry them with you, I have described a dynamic decision problem that is in general completely beyond the abilities of anyone to solve. (For readers who know a bit of the lingo, this is a multi-armed bandit problem with non-independent arms, but with arms that have a very particular structure.) In fact, to the best of my knowledge, there are no known "useful heuristics" for solving this problem, unless you are going to be vacationing at this spot for a very long time, so learning what is useful swamps any short-run concerns about the weight of what you have on your back, or unless I make the very strong assumption that on each day on your walk, you can remove from your rucksack at most one item to use.

And if this problem sounds fanciful, it is formally equivalent to the problem of a university president maintaining a staff of, say, lawyers who have different but unknown skills, facing an uncertain but litigious world.

Now if you go on vacation, or if you have to maintain a staff of inside legal counsel, your inability to solve this problem precisely won't stop you from doing reasonably sensible things. But, my point in this, your decision process is, as far as anyone knows, very far from the way in which economists would model your behavior.

Let me emphasize: In mainstream economics, there are almost no alternatives to the standard assumption that parties are fully strategically rational. If you went to almost any practicing economist, pointed out the absurdity of the assumption that dynamic choice is nothing more than optimal choice of a full strategy for lifetime play, and then asked for alternative modeling strategies for dynamic choice, you'd be met with a blank stare. With very few exceptions, the issue isn't discussed. Graduate students, somewhere in the first year, move from models of large, impersonal markets in which choices are taken all at once (so the question doesn't arise) to models where actors are involved in dynamic decision problems. At that point, they are given the formal mathematical tools needed for finding optimal strategies in the few simple situations where optimal strategies can be found, and they are shown a few very simple examples that follow this modeling rule. And that's it. No questions, no doubts, no alternatives.

At this stage in my harangue, most of my colleagues in economics will mutter "Does it matter?" Economists are well known for at rationalizing patently ridiculous assumptions about behavior by observing that economists are positivists: It doesn't matter whether real-life economic actors consciously solve complex dynamic optimization problems. What matters is whether their actions are, to a first approximation, as if they did so. I suppose we can have an open mind to the possibility that this rationalization will hold up, although surely the onus is on the economist to give some reason to believe that this is so. And if social psychologists are right about endogenously changing preferences, I think the open mind should be fairly skeptical.

But let me suggest a different and more constructive approach to the question of dynamic choice. Think of the second route towards modeling dynamic choice: Choice at each date is reasonably rational in the usual terms of economics, coherent enough to be formally equivalent to maximization of some utility function, but the choices at different dates are only loosely coupled to one another.

This may still be asking for too much rationality and coherence. For instance, as I understand satisficing behavior, it involves the twin ideas that the individual carries around a sense of aspiration level—that's the coupling that connects past experiences and future choices—and the static rule that the individual chooses a convenient alternative that is "good enough." The second part of this—the implicit model of static choice in a dynamic setting—will pose problems for models that involve utility maximization, even at a single point in time.

But humor me for a moment about this, and think about models following the second route. The question becomes, How do the past experiences of the individual affect his current (and thus future) choices? What knits choice at different points of time, and the results of those choices, together?

This is where a bit of autobiography comes in handy. Most of my scholarly life, I've been involved in various aspects of economic models of dynamic choice. I've strayed a bit from the standard "route three" approach to the basic model, trying for instance to model choice by individuals who know there are contingencies they can't foresee and who, in consequence, value leaving themselves with the ability to respond flexibly to circumstances. And I've looked a bit at whether standard equilibrium concepts arise naturally as the end-product of adaptive learning processes. But if I have strayed, it hasn't been far.

About a decade ago, though, I embarked on a different intellectual venture. It began as a teaching assignment: Together with a sociologist colleague, James N. Baron, I was told to pull together a course for MBA students on Human Resource Management. The thesis for this assignment was that economists and organizational behavior types, mostly organizational sociologists and social psychologists, have utterly different conceptions of what is important to understand in the management of human resources, and it would be interesting to present to students a he-said—she-said sort of course. You might wonder whether the dean in question entertained sadistic thoughts about our students. But, in fact, Jim and I are friends, and we thought the exercise might be interesting for us and not too confusing for the students, once we sorted out the presumably different domains addressed by our respective disciplines.

In the event, things worked out quite differently. The economic framework we use is essentially the variation on the folk theorem, involving reputation, that Simon pioneered (decades before the folk theorem was formalized) in his 1951 *Econometrica* classic. The language is brought up to date, and the structure of the employment relationship is made more complex and adapted, as best we can, to the possibility of unforeseen contingencies. But the basic ideas come rather directly from Simon's formal model.

As with any folk theorem construction, there is the problem of too-many equilibria, depending on individual's *beliefs* about how others will act and react. And as with any economic model at all, there is the question of what *tastes* the various actors have; in essence, what at any given point in time constitutes the individual actor's utility function? How stable are these tastes? How are they affected by experience and by the institutional and social setting? The folk theorem—broadly speaking, the economic fulcrum for this, for Simon's conceptualization of the nature of the employment relationship—teaches us how important to final outcomes are tastes and beliefs. And it, and all of economics, is then silent on specifying these crucial ingredients.

This is precisely where Organizational Behavior as a discipline comes in. What is missing from the economics—the ways in which parties form and build their expectations, and the impact of outcomes and institutions on their preferences—is supplied in large measure by a host of ideas from social psychology and sociology. To take two examples, attribution theory and processes of escalating commitment from social psychology are hugely informative about how individual preferences adapt through time. Social comparison theory is very helpful in understanding the sorts of data workers will be drawn to, and how those data will be used, as workers how well they are being treated and whether the employer is keeping to "the deal." Jim and I wound up not with "he said—she said" or with "economics-says-this, but-O.B.-says-that," but instead with a fairly strong sense that organizational sociology and social psychology are strongly complementary to the economic approaches to these questions—at least if you take a somewhat nonstandard-to-economics view of dynamic choice—with each side filling in gaps in the other side's story.[7]

The Future

So where does this leave economics and other social sciences in the future? Economists are going to keep on working on dynamic interactions and situations involving small numbers, uncertainty, and private information. This is too big a piece of the economic universe to ignore; indeed, while I'm quite prejudiced, I think that labor exchange is the single most important economic transaction there is, and labor exchange is preeminently a subject in which these factors enter. Even more, labor exchange has another important characteristic; it is an exchange that has enormous social and emotional content. Those social and emotional factors must be attended to, if a particular labor transaction is going to be efficient.

To come to grips successfully with this sort of economic exchange, economists must do better in modeling the behavior of the actors involved, which means we must do better—get closer to reality, justify our models with something more than religious faith—modeling basic dynamic choice. We have to be more accepting of models in which, using the basic doctrine of revealed preference, preferences apparently shift endogenously. For transactions with emotional and social content, we have to be more open to how emotions and social forces color preferences and behavior. We clearly need to do better in modeling systematically how expectations are formed, and how individuals perceive and judge their own situations.

I'm certainly not alone in thinking of this as a future frontier in economics. Indeed, there is interesting work being done by more-or-less mainstream economists on models of dynamic choice that move from Route 3 to Route 2 style models. To mention a few favorites, there is the axiomatic work being done by Gilboa and Schmeidler on case-based reasoning, the work of Roth and Erev on simple reinforcement learning, Rabin's work on psychology and games, the superb experimental work of Selten and his associates on learning and communicating aspirations while playing games, and Fehr's work on the sorts of "social effects" I mentioned above.

At the same time, my experiences with Baron convince me that economists should become much better informed about how our colleagues in the other social scientists think about how expectations and preferences are formed and revised. Economists have tended to be somewhat disdainful of the efforts of our colleagues from the other social sciences, asserting that they are "low paradigm" thinkers. I've never completely understood what this means, but I think the notion is that sociologists and social psychologists are much more willing to formulate and test specific hypotheses that aren't linked together in some grand theory of how everything works everywhere. If that's what low paradigm means, I suspect economists interested in understanding how individuals act dynamically could use more of it.

This will require that economists get somewhat closer to their data. Happily, data both from the field and the laboratory is increasingly available to economists. It is perhaps worth saying here that experimental economics has become firmly established in the profession.

Let me be clear that I'm not advocating that economists become sociologists or social psychologists. In working with my colleague Baron, I learned a lot from him and his subject. But I think he learned a lot from mine. I think a good place to hang one's hat is on Herbert Simon's famous definition of bounded rationality: behavior that is intendedly rational, but limitedly so. The first part of this—*behavior that is intendedly rational*—is what makes this economics: people are by and large purposeful in their actions, and they can also be remarkably clever—more so than most observers might credit—in trying to achieve those purposes. But colleagues in the other social sciences have perhaps a better sense of where and how the limits come in, and how those limits play out operationally.

A Final Tribute

I will close with my other debt to Herbert Simon. In my mind, and I suspect in the minds of others, Simon is associated both with the scientific work he did and the magnificent institution, Carnegie Tech and later, Carnegie-Mellon Graduate School of Industrial Administration, at which he did it. I don't believe I demean the contributions of others, such as Lee Bach or Jim March or Richart Cyert, to say that Simon was a pillar of that institution.

My intellectual autobiography—and in particular my "career move" into the territory that lies between economics and sociology and social psychology—is very much the result of my having been at another great school of management, the Stanford Graduate School of Business. The nature of the institution—relatively intimate, with few departmental barriers separating people from different disciplines, and with a "bottom line"—the professional degree program—that draws people from different disciplines together, makes an ideal setting for inter- and cross-disciplinary work. I'm a huge fan of this sort of institution. I think it is a place whose architecture in the broad sense can make it an ideal setting for important and innovative work in the social sciences. But this only will happen if institutions of this sort, and their masters in university central administrations, take seriously the ideas that these institutions can be both professional schools *and* first-rank research institutions; that, in fact, the two roles are synergistic. When I made these remarks to the university presidents at the AAU, I said all this and asked them to treat their professional schools as more than cash cows; to abuse and switch the metaphor, the eggs these institutions can lay can be of much finer stuff than money; they can be of intellectual advance.

And in the current setting, when pointing out the advantages of this sort of institution as a laboratory for ideas, it is natural for me to observe: Herbert Simon's intellectual legacy in terms of his own ideas is great. But it is not impossible that the larger part of his legacy for the social sciences will be the role he played in shaping and leading a great research-oriented professional school of management.

Notes

1. The proceedings of this conference, first published in *Daedalus* (126, winter 1997), were republished as *American Academic Culture in Transformation*, ed. T. Bender and C. Schorske (Princeton University Press, 1998).

2. For one description of the changes, see my essay for the AAAS, referenced earlier.

3. The details of why Becker's assertion won't work are not important, but they are easy enough to illustrate, so I'll do so in this parenthetical remark. If you get married in Israel (or anywhere as an orthodox Jew), a marriage contract is required. At least in Israel, these are binding legal arrangements, recognized by the courts. And the default has been a very standard form Ketubah (contract) where the only option is an optional amount pledged by the groom for the wife's "security." Nearly everyone— at least among my acquaintances—executes this default contract, and to propose something that is serious tailored to the specific circumstances of the couple would have precisely the same chilling effect that Becker asserts would be lost by making contracts mandatory (which, in this case, they are). Thus, even if contracts were made mandatory in the United States, we would continue to have as a possible equilibrium one in which a very standard default contract is chosen by nearly everyone, because to ask one's spouse for anything else gives rise to adverse expectations.

4. Reprinted as "The mathematization of economic theory," *American Economic Review* 81 (1991): 1–7.

5. In "How did economics get that way? And what way did it get?" *Daedalus* 126 (1997): 39–58.

6. The strategic beauty of GE's actions stemmed, in part, from the way in which GE left for itself a means of communicating to Westinghouse it's displeasure with Westinghouse's responses. And the strategic beauty stemmed, in part, from the way in which GE left Westinghouse a pretty clear map of what it wanted from Westinghouse in response.

7. We turned this into the book *Strategic Human Resources: Frameworks for General Managers*, published by Wiley in 1999, which certainly doesn't pull these ideas together in a manner that one could publish in scholarly journals, but that, I think, shows pretty clearly how the two sets of ideas complement one another.

The Best Is the Enemy of the Good

Roy Radner

On December 29, 1979, at the annual meeting of the American Economic Association, there was a lunch in honor of Herbert Simon. At that lunch Richard Cyert and I gave short, informal talks about Simon's work. I do not have the text of Cyert's talk, and mine was never published. The publication of the present volume seems to me to provide an appropriate occasion to make my talk available to students of Simon's work and its influence on economic thought. The personal and informal style of the paper is also, I believe, consistent with the spirit of the volume. The second section of this chapter reproduces a very slightly edited version of the original talk. (Additions are bracketed.) In it, I summarize the main ideas of a paper that Simon published in 1951, "A Formal Theory of the Employment Relation," and then trace some of the subsequent related developments in economic theory, up to 1979. In the third section, I provide some additional references to related books and articles that have appeared since then.

The Best Is the Enemy of the Good

A quarter of an hour is clearly not enough time for a serious and comprehensive survey of the impact of Herbert Simon's work on economics. I have chosen, instead, to illustrate this impact with an example, in which two different threads of Simon's work eventually combined in a surprising, and I think fruitful, way. The choice of this example is perhaps idiosyncratic, but it has a significant personal basis for me, and I hope it is therefore appropriate to this occasion.

My first contact with Herbert Simon's work occurred when I was a graduate student (in statistics) at the University of Chicago. Simon had written a paper for the Cowles Commission, "A formal theory of the employment relation," and it was the Cowles Commission's practice to have its papers refereed before they were circulated externally. For this ostensible purpose, I was asked to read Simon's paper. As I remember it, I was being considered for a research assistantship at the commission, and I suspect that the paper was given to me more as a test of my own abilities than anything else. This paper was eventually published in *Econometrica* (1951), then reprinted in his 1957 book *Models of Man*. What I intend to do here is trace the subsequent history of the ideas in that paper.

First, I shall give a brief account of the substance of the paper. In his characteristic way, he set out to explain an empirical observation, in this case the institutional fact that "services are obtained by buyers in our society, sometimes by a sales contract, (and) sometimes by an employment contract. For example, if I want a new concrete sidewalk, I may contract for the sidewalk or I may employ a worker to construct it for me." Simon elaborated a model of employment contracts in which there was an agreement on a wage and on a set of alternative acceptable behavior patterns of the worker; the employer then observed some aspects of his environment (modeled as exogenous random variables), and on the basis of the observation decided which of the acceptable behaviors the worker should adopt. The set of acceptable behaviors constituted the *authority* that the worker relinquished to the employer, in exchange for the agreed-upon wage. The consequent utility to each of the parties to the contract depended upon the chosen behavior, the environment, and the wage (differently for the two parties, of course). A *sales contract* was modeled as a special case of an employment contract, in which the set of acceptable behaviors is narrowed down to a single behavior, specified in advance of the employer's knowledge of the environment.

In the framework of this model, Simon examined the following two conjectures:

1. The worker "will be willing to enter an employment contract only if it does not matter to him 'very much' which behavior (within the agreed upon area of acceptance) the employer will choose, or if the worker is compensated in some way for the possibility that the employer will choose a behavior that is not desired by the worker (i.e., that the employer will ask the worker to perform some unpleasant task)."

2. The employer will be willing to pay for the privilege of postponing the selection of the worker's behavior until he has observed the relevant aspects of the environment, and will be willing to pay more, the greater the (prior) uncertainty about the environment.

With the aid of some more precise assumptions about his formal model, Simon was able to confirm the correctness of his conjectures, and to characterize more precisely the conditions under which some (nondegenerate) employment contract would be preferred to a sales contract. He concluded his paper with a discussion of possible extensions of the model to explain the allocation of "authority" and decision making among the members of an organization, and of the application of these ideas to the theory of planning under uncertainty.

It is important for my subsequent remarks to mention another point. Simon noted that, in general, an employment contract would *not* result in a Pareto-optimal arrangement for the employer and worker jointly (and in particular, not in the presence of risk aversion). As Simon said, "the difficulty lies in the fact that, once agreement has been reached about (the wage and the acceptable set of behaviors), there is no way for the worker to enforce any (informal) understanding that the employer will ... subsequently choose a behavior that optimizes some joint utility rather than the employer's own utility (within the acceptable set, of course)." In other words, "the worker has no assurance that the employer will consider anything but his own profit in deciding what he will ask the worker to do."

Simon went on to note that "we might expect the employer to maximize (their joint utility) only if he thought that by doing so, he could persuade the worker, in subsequent renewals of the employment contract, to accept a wage sufficiently smaller to compensate him for this. Otherwise, the employer would rationally maximize (his own short-run profit). We might say that the latter behavior represents 'short-run' rationality, whereas the former represents 'long-run' rationality when a relationship of confidence between employer and worker can be attained. The fact that the former rule leads to solutions that are preferable to those of the latter shows that it 'pays the employer to establish this relationship."

Finally, in this paper, Simon did not use any explicit principles or mechanisms of "bounded rationality." Nevertheless, I might point out that the paper does not consider the problem of optimizing among the set of *all* possible contracts, but restricts its attention to a limited set of contracts, which are intended to model an important aspect of the institution of "authority."

Some of the ideas in this paper reappeared, in different forms or in different contexts, approximately twenty years later, in papers by Theodore Groves and by Stephen Ross. In his Ph.D. dissertation (1970) and his paper, "Incentives in Teams" (1973), Theodore Groves considered the problem of devising incentives (reward functions) that would induce the members of a team to use decision and communication rules that would be optimal from the point of view of the organizer (e.g., society, or an employer). The solutions and techniques he developed there led to, among other things, the well-known Groves-Ledyard mechanism for solving the "free-rider" problem in the allocation of public goods.

Ross (1973) formulated the "principal-agent problem," closely related to the problem studied by Groves. In a situation with moral hazard, a principal and his agent play a game in which the principal offers the agent a contract that is intended to induce the agent to act on the principal's behalf. Ross showed that, if the agent were more risk-averse than the principal, then the resulting "equilibrium" would not, in general, be fully Pareto optimal for the two parties jointly, although he was able to characterize (within his own particular model) those special conditions that would lead to full Pareto optimality. [Note that, reversing the usual interpretation of the principal-agent model, the worker is the *principal* and the employer is the *agent*.]

About the same time (or earlier), Leonid Hurwicz was developing his theory of decentralization and incentive compatible mechanisms, which explored, among other things, the nature of the potential conflict between decentralization and Pareto optimality. (Time does not permit me to trace all of the antecedents of these ideas, but, at the usual risk of offending the many left off the list, I should at least mention J. Marschak, K. J. Arrow, K. Borch, M. Spence, and R. Zeckhauser.)

The substantial development of these ideas that occurred during the period 1970–1979 essentially used the formulation of the theory of games, and in particular, the theory of "Cournot-Nash," or noncooperative, equilibrium. In this context, the conflict between equilibrium and Pareto optimality was not new, of course; just recall the "Prisoners' Dilemma Game," the simplest and most dramatic formal example of this conflict.

How are we to reconcile this considerable body of theory with the observation that cooperative arrangements pervade much of economic life, indeed, *cooperative arrangements that are not enforced by any formal contracts*? (The area of labor relations alone provides numerous illustrations.) A clue to one explanation can be found in the passage from Simon's paper that I quoted above, namely the establishment of *long-term relationships*.

Long-term relationships permit the use of self-enforcing combinations of strategies that sustain cooperative behavior. For example, in the Prisoners' Dilemma there is a unique noncooperative equilibrium pair of actions (in fact, a dominant-strategy equilibrium). There is also a Pareto-optimal pair that yields an outcome that is better for *both* players; no other action pair gives one player a better outcome without giving the other a worse outcome. Call this the *cooperative* action pair. Suppose that the Prisoners' Dilemma is repeated many times, and that each player uses the criterion of average payoff per period. A promising candidate for a pair of strategies would be the following: each player uses his cooperative action until the first time that the other player does not; thereafter he uses his noncooperative (equilibrium) action. Call this the *trigger-strategy pair*.

Unfortunately, if the number of repetitions of the Prisoners' Dilemma is finite, no matter how large, the trigger-strategy pair cannot sustain cooperation! This is easily seen by working backward from the end, since one player can obtain a benefit from breaking the cooperative agreement before the other does so. In fact, if one defines equilibrium strategy pairs for the long-run relationship suitably, then all equilibria result in noncooperative actions throughout the relationship. Thus, even equilibrium in a (finite) long-term relationship cannot explain sustained cooperative behavior in a Prisoners' Dilemma-like situation. This includes the employee relationship with which we started. [The equilibrium concept used here is that of a *subgame-perfect equilibrium* of a repeated game. However, if the repeated game is infinitely long, and the players use the criterion of long-run average payoff per period, then the trigger-strategy pair is a subgame-perfect equilibrium. See references herein.]

Here is where Bounded Rationality comes to the rescue. Notice that, in a long-term relationship, the trigger-strategy pair is almost an equilibrium, because the benefit from breaking the cooperative relationship is short-lived, and therefore can be advantageous only at or near the end. Furthermore, any benefit from breaking the cooperative agreement before the other player does will have a small effect on the average of the remaining payoffs if the end of the relationship is sufficiently distant. Hence, if each player is satisfied with a strategy that is *almost*, but not quite, an optimal response to the other player's strategy (technically, called an *epsilon equilibrium*), then a pair of behaviors in which each player uses a trigger-strategy until a certain distance from the end will be an epsilon equilibrium for the long-term relationship. This kind of reasoning can be extended to principal-agent situations in which the principal cannot perfectly monitor the agent's actions (moral hazard). Modesty would not prevent me from giving a reference for these results, but I have not yet published them. [However, see references to subsequent publications herein.]

So, we have joined two threads from Simon's earlier work, in an application that he may not have anticipated. Bounded rationality may be a glue that holds together cooperation in the face of threats of strict optimization. "The best is the enemy of the good."

I would like to conclude with a prediction. I did not go into sufficient technical detail here to make the point, but I am convinced that there are many more analytical tools (particularly from probability theory) suitable for exploring Herbert Simon's ideas that are more readily available to today's economist than was the case thirty years ago [now more than fifty years ago]. For this reason (and others), I am convinced that we shall soon see—or are already seeing—a new wave of applications and extensions in economic theory of his stimulating insights.

Epilogue

The prediction in the last paragraph of my 1979 talk has been amply confirmed in the succeeding twenty-three years. A full account of the relevant developments is beyond the scope of this chapter. The literature on the principal-agent model with moral hazard is reviewed in Dutta and Radner 1995. Material on this topic, on the Prisoners' Dilemma Game, and on more general formulations of repeated and dynamic games can be found in most recent game-theory textbooks. For an excellent introduction, see Dutta 1999. For more advanced treatments, see Fudenberg and Tirole 1991 and Osborne and Rubinstein 1994.

Applications of the epsilon-equilibrium concept to the repeated principal-agent model and the repeated Prisoners' Dilemma Game alluded to herein were published in Radner 1980 and in Radner 1986, respectively. Another application, to the theory of oligopoly, is in Radner 1980.

Simon's concept of bounded rationality goes far beyond, of course, epsilon equilibrium. (In fact, I am not aware that he ever proposed the latter concept.) This is not the place for an account of his contributions to the study of bounded rationality. For a brief historical review of the development of the concept in the context of individual and team decision making, with an extensive bibliography, see (Radner 2000, 2001); game-theoretic models of bounded rationality are discussed in (Rubinstein 1998). However, the field is hardly mature, and I am confident that the prediction in the last paragraph of my 1979 talk is still valid for the foreseeable future.

References

Dutta, P. K. 1999. *Strategies and Games*. MIT Press.

Dutta, P. K., and R. Radner. 1995. Moral hazard. In R. Aumann and S. Hart, eds., *Handbook of Game Theory*, volume 2. North-Holland.

Fudenberg, D., and J. Tirole. 1991. *Game Theory*. MIT Press.

Groves, T. 1970. The Allocation of Resources under Uncertainty. Ph.D. dissertation, University of California, Berkeley.

Groves, T. 1973. Incentives in teams. *Econometrica* 41: 617–663.

Osborne, M. J., and A. Rubinstein. 1994. *A Course in Game Theory*. MIT Press.

Radner, R. 1980. Collusive behavior in noncooperative epsilon-equilibria of oligopolies with long but finite lives. *Journal of Economic Theory* 22: 136–154.

Radner, R. 1981. Monitoring cooperative agreements in a repeated principal-agent relationship. *Econometrica* 49: 1127–1148.

Radner, R. 1986. Can bounded rationality resolve the prisoners' dilemma? In A. Mas-Colell and W. Hildenbrand, eds., *Contributions to Mathematical Economics*. North-Holland.

Radner, R. 2000. Costly and bounded rationality in individual and team decision-making. *Industrial and Corporate Change* 9, no. 4: 623–658.

Radner, R. 2001. Decision and choice: Costly and bounded rationality. *International Encyclopedia of the Social and Behavioral Sciences*. Elsevier/Pergamon 2001.

Ross, S. 1973. The economic theory of agency. *American Economic Review* 63: 134–139.

Rubinstein, A. 1998. *Modeling Bounded Rationality*. MIT Press.

Simon, H. A. 1951. A formal theory of the employment relationship. *Econometrica* 19: 293–305.

Simon, H. A. 1957. *Models of Man*. Wiley.

•

The Hawkins and Simon Story Revisited

Paul A. Samuelson

Before dealing with the important 1949 Hawkins-Simon conditions that are necessary and sufficient for an input-output system to be net permanently viable, I want to write briefly about Herbert Simon as a creative scholar and a person. I was born a year before him, about a hundred miles from his Milwaukee birthplace, and I overlapped with him at the University of Chicago; our careers were intertwined for more than six decades. Simon's many published works were part of my inventory of knowledge, as they were for any avant-garde theoretical economist of the post-1933 years.

While reading his 1991 autobiography *Models of My Life*, I was struck by some similarities in our personalities and careers. (The previous sentence represents considerable boasting and some wishful thinking on my part.) But there were certain differences also. Thus Herb, like E. O. Wilson, the eminent biologist, was an Eagle Scout, something that tells much about his energy and perseverance and contrasts with my lifelong habit of working hard only on the things that capture my central interest. But both of us were quick-off-the-mark bright boys with supportive families and roving intellectual interests. Thus, in the Simon bibliography it comes as no surprise to encounter the item on axiomatics of Newtonian rational mechanics; many of my own happiest hours have been spent on something seemingly light years away from economics, namely alternative deductive approaches to classical phenomenological thermodynamics.

I was a Chicago undergraduate from January 1932 to June 1935. Herb's years were from September 1933 until June 1936. Strangely our paths seem never to have crossed. Simon lived in the college dorms; I was a commuter. We were both in the social sciences and surfaced young as promising scholars with a bent toward mathematics. I knew well as undergraduates Jacob Mosak and Gregg Lewis, and as graduate students George Stigler, Allen Wallis, Albert Gaylord Hart, Milton Friedman, and Martin Bronfenbrenner. Perhaps our disconnect was because economics was then, and later, only one string in Herb's bow: his major was Political Science Administration, a field that at first blush might seem less amenable to an ordinary person's flair for deductive elegance. But of course Herbert Simon was not an ordinary person.

It was after my Chicago period that Herb fell in with the Cowles crowd at Chicago: Jacob Marschak, Tjalling Koopmans, Herman Rubin, Kenneth Arrow, and numerous European visitors. As he has said, this explains how—as something of an outsider to economics—he received an early unshared Nobel Prize in that subject.

Herb Simon was not only *not* solely *inside* economics; he regarded himself in a certain sense as against important new trends in mathematical economics. In contrast to maximization, he promoted "bounded rationality" and "satisficing." Leaning away from elegant and esoteric advanced Bourbaki mathematics, he preferred to look for simple Baconian regularities. When he reported that *Econometrica* averaged out to a higher degree of more intricate mathematics than *Physical Review*, Simon regarded this not as praise but as evidence of probable sterility. While building a distinguished department at Carnegie-Mellon in Management and Psychology, he was not at all tempted to imitate MIT's powerhouse in mainstream economics. Perhaps that helps explain why such stars as Franco Modigliani, Merton Miller, and Robert Lucas strayed away from the exciting Carnegie-Mellon environment.

A separate essay might be written about Simon's lovers' quarrel with economics. Cyclically, within this subject, tensions oscillate between proponents and opponents of doctrines and dogmas about rationality and irrationality.

The Hawkins-Simon Narrative

In 1948, David Hawkins, a philosopher who had returned from the Los Alamos bomb project to the University of Colorado, published in *Econometrica* a system of capitalist dynamics. This article seems to have had some roots in the Quesnay-like Tableaux of Reproduction and of Balanced Growth that were contained in the posthumous volumes II and III of Marx's *Das Kapital*. (See Samuelson 1974, where I describe this effort as the most novel of the many attempted contributions by Marx to fruitful economic theory.)

My Harvard mentor, Wassily Leontief, devoted his major lifetime energies to empirical and theoretical analyses of input-output systems. This was an outgrowth of his primitive studies in Russia of Marx, and of his advanced study in Berlin under the prolific Ladislaus von Bortkiewicz. Readers of Hawkins 1948 cannot tell whether he had then known of a similar 1941 statical version of Leontief's input-output system. However, the Leontief connection is explicitly referenced in Hawkins and Simon 1949. Neither Hawkins, Simon, nor Leontief had reason to know that the secretive Piero Sraffa had already in the period 1927–1960 been working sporadically in Cambridge on a similar input-output model. (See Sraffa 1960.) Indeed, during their long lifetimes Leontief and Sraffa, as far as I can learn, never once referred to each other—even though in the period 1960–1983 well-informed readers were aware of the major overlaps between their systems. This is hardly to the credit of these two justly admired scholars.

Hawkins's thirteen-page 1948 article devotes its last nine pages to a dynamic version of the input-output system. Strictly speaking, all of Simon's dialogue with him, and all of their corrected version of

Hawkins-Simon conditions, deal exclusively with the first four 1948 pages devoted to stationary-state matters. Therefore, I can explicate their basic joint contribution of the Hawkins-Simon conditions without having to delve deeply into the difficulties and ambiguities involved in trying to reduce macroeconomic multi-sector dynamics to a set of strictly linear differential equations.

Statically, when can a positive constant total of labor, $L = L_1 + L_2 + \cdots + L_m$, produce constant levels of gross products, $(Q_1 Q_2 \ldots Q_m)$, and produce at the same time one or more positive constant amounts of consumptions, $(C_1 C_2 \ldots C_m)$, when each Q_j needs for its production

$$L_j \geq \alpha_{0j} Q_j, \quad Q_{1j} \geq \alpha_{1j} Q_j, \ldots, Q_{mj} \geq \alpha_{mj} Q_j, \quad j = 1, \ldots, m, \quad \alpha_{ij} \geq 0 \quad (1a)$$

and obeys

$$C_j \leq Q_j - \sum_{i=1}^{m} Q_{ij} = Q_j - \sum_{i=1}^{n} \alpha_{ij} Q_j, \quad j = 1, 2, \ldots, m, \quad (1b)$$

$$0 < L \leq \alpha_{01} Q_1 + \cdots + \alpha_{0m} Q_m, \quad \alpha_{0j} \geq 0, \quad \Sigma_1^m \alpha_{0j} > 0. \quad (1c)$$

In equation 1 I have scrupulously introduced inequalities even where Hawkins and Hawkins-Simon would have used equality signs and would have written

$$L = \alpha_{01} Q_1 + \cdots + L_{0m} Q_m, \quad (2a)$$

$$C_1 = Q_1 - \alpha_{11} Q_1 - \alpha_{12} Q_2 - \cdots - \alpha_{1m} Q_m,$$

$$C_m = Q_m - \alpha_{m1} Q_1 - \alpha_{12} Q_2 - \cdots - \alpha_{1m} Q_m. \quad (2b)$$

For the "*open* version" of the Leontief and Sraffa systems, if Hawkins and Simon were writing today, they could have dealt exclusively with equation 2's $m \times m$ linear equations and $m \times m$ matrix

$$\alpha = [\alpha_{ij}] 10 = [Q_{ij}/Q_j] \geq 0, \quad (3a)$$

$$I - \alpha = [\delta_{ij} - \alpha_{ij}] = \begin{bmatrix} 1 - \alpha_{11} & \cdots & -\alpha_{1m} \\ \vdots & & \\ -\alpha_{m1} & \cdots & 1 - \alpha_{mm} \end{bmatrix}. \quad (3b)$$

The economic problem to be solved by Hawkins and Simon can be described by asking what are the necessary and sufficient conditions on the $I - \alpha$ matrix (with no α_{ij}s negative) so that all the elements of its existent inverse matrix, $[I - \alpha]^{-1}$, will be non-negative. (Some or all αs are allowed to be zero rather than positive: as Hawkins and Simon remark, it is harmless for their theorem if they choose to replace all zero α_{ij}s by arbitrarily small positive ε_{ij}s.)

Their beautiful 1949 theorem states:

If, and only if, all the *principal* minors of $I - \alpha$ are strictly positive will the input-output economy with constant level of positive labor be capable of sustaining positive stationary levels of *some* or *all* net consumption levels, $(C_1 C_2 \ldots C_m) \geq 0$, $(C_1/L) + (C_2/L) + \cdots + (C_m/L) > 0$.

For the one-sector case, $m = 1$, Hawkins and Simon require only

$$\Delta_1 = \det[I - \alpha] = 1 - \alpha_{11} > 0. \tag{4a}$$

For the two-sector case, $m = 2$, Hawkins and Simon require three inequalities

$$1 - \alpha_{11} > 0, \quad 1 - \alpha_{22} > 0,$$

$$\Delta_2 = \begin{vmatrix} 1 - \alpha_{11} & -\alpha_{12} \\ -\alpha_{21} & 1 - \alpha_{22} \end{vmatrix} = (1 - \alpha_{11})(1 - \alpha_{22}) - \alpha_{12}\alpha_2 > 0. \tag{4b}$$

For $m = 3$, we have, in all $2^3 - 1$ or seven principal minors—counting always $\det[I - \alpha]$ as itself a principal minor: then

$$1 - \alpha_{11} > 0, \quad 1 - a_{22} > 0; \quad 1 - a_{33} > 0, \quad (1 - \alpha_{11})(1 - \alpha_{22}) - \alpha_{12}\alpha_{21} > 0$$

$$(1 - \alpha_{11})(1 - \alpha_{22}) - \alpha_{12}\alpha_{21} > 0, \quad (1 - \alpha_{11})(1 - \alpha_{33}) - \alpha_{13}\alpha_{31} > 0$$

$$(1 - \alpha_{22})(1 - \alpha_{33}) - \alpha_{23}\alpha_{32} > 0$$

$$\Delta_3 = \begin{vmatrix} 1 - \alpha_{11} & -\alpha_{12} & -\alpha_{13} \\ -\alpha_{21} & 1 - \alpha_{22} & -\alpha_{23} \\ -\alpha_{31} & -\alpha_{32} & 1 - \alpha_{33} \end{vmatrix}$$

$$= (1 - \alpha_{11})(1 - \alpha_{22})(1 - \alpha_{33}) + \alpha_{12}\alpha_{23}\alpha_{31} + \alpha_{13}\alpha_{32}\alpha_{21}$$

$$-\alpha_{13}\alpha_{31}(1 - \alpha_{22}) - \alpha_{12}\alpha_{21}(1 - \alpha_{33}) - \alpha_{13}\alpha_{31}(1 - \alpha_{11}) > 0. \tag{4c}$$

Early on Leontief managed to handle statistically $m = 10$ economic sectors. That would imply in all $2^{10} - 1 = 1,024 - 1 = 1,023$ Hawkins-Simon conditions. Fortunately, it is not hard to prove that it is both necessary and sufficient to have only $m = 10$ positive equalities—since selected properly, those can already ensure that all the *other* $1,023 - 10 = 1,013$ conditions also get satisfied. The choosable m such conditions are

$$\Delta_1 > 0, \quad \Delta_2 > 0, \ldots, \Delta_m > 0, \tag{5a}$$

where the Δs are *naturally ordered* principal minors

$$\Delta_1 = |1 - \alpha_{11}| > 0, \quad \Delta_2 = \begin{vmatrix} 1 - \alpha_{11} & -\alpha_{12} \\ -\alpha_{21} & 1 - \alpha_{22} \end{vmatrix} > 0, \tag{5b}$$

$$\Delta_3 = \begin{vmatrix} 1 - \alpha_{11} & -\alpha_{12} & -\alpha_{13} \\ -\alpha_{21} & 1 - \alpha_{22} & -\alpha_{23} \\ -\alpha_{31} & -\alpha_{32} & 1 - \alpha_{33} \end{vmatrix} > 0$$

$$\ldots, \Delta_m = \begin{vmatrix} 1 - \alpha_{11} & -\alpha_{12} & \cdots & \alpha_{1m} \\ -\alpha_{21} & 1 - \alpha_{22} & \cdots & \alpha_{2m} \\ \vdots & \vdots & \vdots & \vdots \\ -\alpha_{m1} & -\alpha_{m2} & \cdots & 1 - \alpha_{mm} \end{vmatrix} > 0. \tag{5c}$$

Equations 5 state that it is necessary and sufficient that all the principal determinants be positive when one removes successively the last row and columns of $I - \alpha$ until none are left.

My use of αs as modern notations for Q_{ij}/Q_j avoids the authors' use of a_{ij} and b_{ij}, which might be confused with various other common present-day notational conventions.

Herbert Simon never met David Hawkins. When he read the 1948 exposition, Simon perceived that its derived major theorem was not quite correct for systems involving $m > 2$. He wrote to Hawkins, giving a counter-example (see Hawkins and Simon 1949, p. 246). Apparently Hawkins may already have sensed some doubt about his result, and both scholars were pleased to join together for a definitive correct statement.

The story of events told here, which I have gleaned from Simon's writing, is one that sheds credit on two noble characters. In present-day publish-or-perish academic times, customarily when A spots an error in B's publication, A rushes into print with a rebuttal and a correction. There have been exceptions in history, but not too many. Thus, the great mathematician Euler held up publishing some of his calculus-of-variations novelties until the young and brilliant Lagrange could publish his original version. Once the MIT physicist Victor Weiskopf published an important paper on the vexing normalization problem in quantum dynamics. Wendell Furry of Harvard wrote to inform that there was an error in it, traceable to one mistake in algebraic sign, which Weiskopf could correct in a simple erratum. Again, in early quantum physics, there is a Koopmans approximation that apparently still had some usage in 1975 when Tjalling Koopmans received a Nobel Prize in economics. When I asked him about it, he reported: "My Dutch mentor, Hendrik Kramers, was the midwife who helped pull it out of me. But being the character he was, he refused to put his name on the article as a joint author." In contrast, it has been gossiped that the great John Bernoulli once predated a document so that he could share in some glory with his son Daniel. It takes all types to people the Senior Common Room.

Clearly neither Simon nor Hawkins was familiar with the vast literature on Frobenium-Perron non-negative matrices, so often used in Markov-Frêchet probability theory and elsewhere. (Equation systems like those of Leontief and Sraffa appeared in Cournot 1838.) Also, the Keynes-Kahn-Chipman-Goodwin-Metzler dynamic multiplier expenditure models utilize those same matrices; and Hicks-Mosak-Mundell gross-substitute matrixes likewise are of a similar structure.

That is how science evolves: as the product of many independent and cooperating hands. Only a Carlylean believer in the single-great-man drama of history could believe that the achievement of Hawkins and Simon is at all diminished by the existence of this earlier related literature. The Hawkins-Simon theorem came just when it came to be needed. See the chapters on related equivalences in Dorfman, Samuelson, and Solow 1958.

Thus, a corollary to Hawkins-Simon is the matrix generalization of Malthus's geometric series: namely, for a Hawkins-Simon productive system,

$$[I - \alpha]^{-1} = I + \alpha + \alpha^2 + \cdots \alpha^{m-1} + \cdots \to [A_{ij}] \geq 0. \tag{6}$$

This generalizes the convergent scalar infinite expansions

$$\left(1 - \tfrac{1}{2}\right)^{-1} = 1 + \tfrac{1}{2} + \left(\tfrac{1}{2}\right)^2 + \cdots = 2 < \infty$$

or

$$[1 - x]^{-1} = 1 + x + x^2 + \cdots < \infty \quad \text{for } |x| < 1. \tag{7}$$

Why did not Leontief and/or Sraffa discover the Hawkins-Simon conditions long before 1948? Sraffa was no mathematician, and he never fully revealed to Ramsey, Besicovitch, and other star Cambridge mathematicians what economic models he explored. Leontief did understand why net production would be impossible if 1 of coal required more than 1 of coal input, and would also fail if 1 of coal required 1 of iron while 1 of iron required more than 1 of coal. Essentially, he understood that directly or indirectly no viable system could tolerate a good that directly, or indirectly through however many indirect paths, required more than 1 of itself as input. This satisfied Leontief, particularly since all his tableaux or non-negative cash interflows showed by their very existence that a viable circular flow did certainly obtain. (When trying to predict how an OPEC oil shortage might induce inventions of new technical α_{ij} coefficients, Leontief and his engineering co-workers would want to utilize something like the Hawkins-Simon computable conditions.)

Concluding Remarks

On the present occasion space precludes my more than sketching what David Hawkins did have in mind when exploring his linear dynamics. It was his suspicion that a multi-sector market system, even in the absence of exogenous shocks from technology or bubbles or bumbling governmental policies, might be capable from its very nature of self-generating endogenous instabilities. Karl Marx would have liked such a notion.

However, paradoxically Marx's own Tableaux of Steady or Expanded Reproduction could serve to prove the existence of, and the permanent persistence of, a steady-state equilibrium. The early-twentieth-century under-consumption dilemmas of the radical Rosa Luxemburg could, under favorable conditions, be shown to be escapable in *Das Kapital*'s Multi-Sector Tableaux dated in the 1860s and the 1880s. Those same Marxian constructions, if Marx had understood them, defended Adam Smith from Marx's tens of thousands of critical words arguing that Smith wrongly defined Income as the tripart sum of Wages + Interest or Profits + Land rents, which thereby allegedly erred by leaving out a fourth component of Depreciation of used capital items. Properly understood, Smith's value-added accounting was already correctly taking account of Depreciation when reckoning in the wage-interest-rent costs of replacing machines so that their stocks remain exactly at the stationary-state levels.

Hawkins, Leontief, and Sraffa insisted on a single set of α_{ij} production techniques for each and every good, which can sometimes remove essential ambiguity and achieve a set of *linear* differential equations with constant coefficients.

Even at this date it would be worthwhile to prepare a full and critical discussion of David Hawkins's purported dynamical analysis. However, since that is a complex and intricate task, and since Simon's role in Hawkins-Simon conditions seems to have no intrinsic connection with this dynamics, I desist from any further comment on it and refer only to Dorfman, Samuelson, and Solow 1958 and Solow 1959.

The pearl of Hawkins and Simon can shine autonomously alone.

References

Cournot, A. A. 1838. Recherches sur les principes mathématiques de la théorie des richesses. Translation: *Researches into the Mathematical Principles of the Theory of Wealth* (Macmillan, 1929).

Dorfman, R., P. A. Samuelson, and R. Solow. 1958. *Linear Programming and Economic Analysis*. Dover.

Hawkins, D. 1948. Some conditions of macroeconomic stability. *Econometrica* 16: 309–333.

Hawkins, D., and H. A. Simon. 1949. Note: Some conditions of macroeconomic stability. *Econometrica* 17: 245–248.

Marx, K. 1867, 1885, 1894. *Das Kapital*, volumes I, II and III (Penguin, 1976, 1978, 1981).

Samuelson, P. A. 1974. Marx as Mathematics Economist: Steady-State and Exponential Growth Equilibrium. In Horwich, G., and P. Samuelson, eds., *Trade, Stability, and Macroeconomics*. Academic Press. Reproduced as chapter 225 in *The Collected Scientific Papers of Paul A. Samuelson*, volume 4 (MIT Press, 1977).

Simon, H. A. 1991. *Models of My Life*. Basic Books.

Solow, R. M. 1959. Competitive valuation in a dynamic input-output system. *Econometrica* 27: 30–53.

Herbert A. Simon Opened My Eyes

Reinhard Selten

In 1958 I first read Herbert A. Simon's seminal papers on bounded rationality (1955, 1956) in his 1957 book *Models of Man*. I was immediately convinced by his arguments. I have remained his follower ever since. Simon opened my eyes to the realities of human economic decision making.

This happened very early in my academic career. After receiving my master's degree in mathematics in 1957, I became a research assistant of Professor Heinz Sauermann in the economics department of the University of Frankfurt am Main. It was my task to work on a project involving the application of decision theory to the theory of the firm. I began to investigate a model of a firm maximizing its long-run growth rate in a stationary stochastic environment. This research was progressing well, but in the light of my new-found enthusiasm for Simon's ideas about bounded rationality it seemed to be meaningless and I did not pursue it further.

Before I was exposed to Simon's writings, I accepted the usual assumption of economic theory that full rationality is a good approximation, even if it is not a correct description of actually observed behavior. Today I apply the label "naive rationalism" to this methodological position. Simon's work made me aware of the need for a different approach. It was necessary to develop a theory of bounded rationality.

When I studied mathematics I also pursued some extracurricular activities like taking psychology courses. My exposure to experimental psychology prepared me for a critical attitude toward naive rationalism. When I read Simon's papers, I had already begun to do oligopoly experiments motivated by the confusing multitude of supposedly rational solutions of the oligopoly problem. The results were reported in the paper titled "Ein Oligopolexperiment" (Sauermann and Selten 1959). From then on, experimental economics was one of my major research activities.

In another paper (1962), Heinz Sauermann and I developed an aspiration adaptation theory of the firm. This work was explicitly based on the ideas of Simon. The paper describes a firm pursuing multiple goals in a dynamic environment. The goals are not aggregated into a utility function. The search for alternatives is guided by an "aspiration adaptation scheme," a grid of possible multi-dimensional aspiration levels with adjustment priorities attached to them, and an "influence scheme" summarizing qualitative effects of possible action changes. Many years later, this theory became available in English (Selten 1998, 2001).

Aspiration adaptation theory was an attempt to elaborate the ideas of Simon. It has the virtue of presenting a plausible and coherent procedure for adaptive decision making without probabilities and utilities. However, I do not want to put too much emphasis on modeling details, since there is insufficient empirical support. Real progress in descriptive decision theory needs painstaking experimental work. I share the opinion of Simon that bounded rationality is an empirical problem.

In the year of 1961 I participated in a game theory conference at Princeton. After the conference I stayed in the United States for several weeks, and during this time I visited Pittsburgh for a few days. There I had the opportunity to talk to Simon for half an hour in his office. I explained to him the basic ideas of aspiration adaptation theory, and he reacted positively.

Many years later I met Simon at the house of John C. Harsanyi in Berkeley. We had an interesting conversation, but Simon probably did not remember me and my affinity for his views. We never participated in the same conference. Our main lines of research were different. Even if I contributed to descriptive decision theory, mainly by my experimental research, it is understandable that he was not aware of this, since I was much more known for my work on rational game theory.

Herbert A. Simon was a great man. He was the initiator of the theory of bounded rationality and a founder of two scientific disciplines: cognitive psychology and artificial intelligence. For me he was a famous figure to be admired from a distance. I did not expect to come into closer contact with him. Therefore, I was very surprised by a long letter he wrote to me on December 26, 1996. In the following I shall present some excerpts from this letter.

Dear Professor Selten:

I begin by apologizing for an overly long letter. In sending it, I presume upon our common friendship with John C. Harsanyi and our common interest in bounded rationality. With regard to bounded rationality three surprising things happened in 1996. First, I learnt about Tom Sargent's book bearing that title, published about two years ago. Then I received a copy of Professor Aumann's Nancy Schwartz Lecture. I wrote to both authors in a rather combative tone, indicating that what they were discussing did not much resemble what I thought of as bounded rationality, a major difference being their continuing tendency to introduce capricious limitations upon rationality on a priori grounds with little or no empirical motivation (I must confess also to feeling a bit of pique that they regarded my contribution as no more than pointing to the faults of neoclassical theory without suggesting any positive alternative— but more on this latter theme below).

Finally last week, I received from the publisher a copy of the Festschrift published in honor of your 65th birthday, and was further, but in this case very pleasurably, surprised by your comments on bounded rationality in the interview that opens the volume.

The letter continues with some remarks on game theory and then explains why Simon abolished his initial interest in it in favor of the "study of rationality by computer simulation of human thinking and problem solving in conjunction with psychological experiments." I will skip this part and return to the text of the letter at a later point:

What excited and pleased me most about your interview is that we seemed to have arrived independently at somewhat the same views about a priorism in economics and the need for more empirical emphasis especially at the micro level. When one occupies a minority position over a long period of years, self-doubts arise. Can the whole world of economists be wrong? Support coming from someone of your demonstrated abilities reassures me that, indeed, they can be wrong, and almost surely are. Of course we should not exaggerate our minority status: I regularly encounter wide-spread cynicism and doubts about neoclassicalism throughout the profession especially among the young. The chief factor which seems to delay open revolt is uncertainty as to whether there is anything that can replace the mythical structure of global expected utility maximization, rational expectations and all that.

In the remainder of the letter it is explained that "the raw materials for replacement are already at hand" but that "the economics profession is still largely unaware of the large body of evidence about actual human problem solving and decision processes that has been accumulated." Simon mentions some particular empirically based economic simulation studies and comes to the following conclusion:

So there is today a substantial body of common and consistent theory on these matters and the theory has been formalized in list-processing languages in a manner quite analogous to the formalizations of economics and physics in system of differential equations. (Alas, the discrete-time equations of cognitive theory cannot be solved in closed form, but must be studied by simulation, but that is a condition not unknown to physics once we go beyond the simplest functions and boundary conditions).

The letter closes with a statement of the need to expose graduate students to the new evidence about human decision making and to train them in the formalism of list processing and production systems in order to enable them to carry out their own empirical studies.

I did not reply to this letter in writing; instead I called Simon on the telephone. We had several very interesting long phone conversations in which we exchanged our views. He sent me some of his papers and I sent him some of mine.

Maybe I should add something to what I have said about Simon's influence on my own thinking. I was tremendously impressed by

Newell and Simon's 1972 book *Human Problem Solving*. In my course on bounded rationality, which I begun to teach in 1992, I also covered this theory. I think that it is of great importance, even if finding good economic applications for it is difficult. Economic problems are often less clear-cut. There is no definite solution. The theory needs to be complemented by aspiration levels which may be adjusted during the decision process. This is an example for the rich possibilities of further developments in the research program initiated by Herbert Simon.

In 1997 I tried to invite Simon to the workshop on the theory of bounded rationality (THEBORA) at Bonn. He told me by telephone that he had seen enough airports in his life and that he no longer traveled. I was sorry about this, but I think in spite of his not being present at this conference his spirit was very present there. I am convinced that the importance of his path-breaking work will continue to increase.

References

Newell, A., and H. A. Simon. 1972. *Human Problem Solving.* Prentice-Hall.

Sauermann, H., and R. Selten. 1959. Ein Oligopolexperiment. *Zeitschrift für die gesamte Staatswissenschaft* 115: 427–471.

Sauermann, H., and R. Selten. 1962. Anspruchsanpassungstheorie der Unternehmung. *Zeitschrift für die gesamte Staatswissenschaft* 118: 577–597.

Selten, R. Aspiration adaptation theory. 1998. *Journal of Mathematical Psychology* 42: 191–214.

Selten, R. 2001. What is bounded rationality? In G. Gigerenzer and R. Selten, eds., *Bounded Rationality: The Adaptive Toolbox.* MIT Press.

Simon, H. A. 1955. A behavioral model of rational choice. *Quarterly Journal of Economics* 69: 99–118.

Simon, H. A. 1956. Rational choice and the structure of the environment. *Psychological Review* 63: 129–138.

Simon, H. A. 1957. *Models of Man.* Wiley.

Monetary Rewards and Decision Cost in Strategic Interactions

Vernon L. Smith and Ferenc Szidarovszky

Traditional economic models of decision making in experiments have tended to assume that only the monetary rewards associated with the experimental decision task matter, while psychologists (Tversky and Kahneman 1978; Dawes 1988) have tended to assume that such rewards do not matter or matter little. Important exceptions to this characterization of psychologists include Siegel (1959), von Winterfeldt and Edwards (1986), and Knoll, Levy, and Rappoport (1988). In fact Siegel seems to provide the earliest of many experimental studies surveyed in Smith and Walker 1993a, in which payoffs were systematically varied as an experimental design treatment. A common reaction of economists, when the predictions of theory are not supported by experiment, is to hypothesize that the payoffs were not large enough for the predicted outcomes to matter. Specifically, this may be a consequence of the problem of flat maxima, or low opportunity cost of deviating from the optimum, an issue revisited more recently by von Winterfeldt and Edwards and by Harrison (1989). To our knowledge these problems were first proposed and explored by Siegel in the context of a game against nature, by Siegel and Fouraker (1960) in the context of bilateral monopoly bargaining, and by Fouraker and Siegel (1963) in bargaining and in duopoly and triopoly markets.

Standard theory, however, predicts that decision makers will provide optimal decisions regardless of how gently rounded is the payoff function, provided only that there is a unique optimum. This means that the theory is misspecified, and needs modification to take account of the common intuition that the size of payoffs, and payoff opportunity cost, should affect decisions. This intuition implies that there must be something else in agent utility functions besides monetary payoffs (Smith 1976, 1982). Smith and Walker (1993a) take a decision-cost approach in formulating the problem; i.e., a problem of balancing the benefit against the effort (mental labor) of reducing "error," the latter defined, not as a mistake, but as the deviation between the agent's actual decision and the optimal decision in the absence of decision cost. Thus, "when the theory is properly specified there should be nothing left to say about opportunity cost or flat maxima; i.e. when the benefit margin is weighed against decision cost, then there should be nothing left to forgo" (Smith and Walker 1993a, p. 245). Of course "proper specification" may involve much more than decision cost but this seems like a reasonable hypothesis with which to start the modeling effort. Their proposed model is consistent with the experimental data they surveyed: in several studies, the predicted optimum is at the boundary of a constraint set, and increasing rewards shift the central tendency of the data toward the optimum; in many studies, an increase in rewards reduces the variance of the data relative to the predictions of the theory; and increases in subject experience often improve performance at rates that are equivalent to large increases in monetary rewards. Camerer and Hogarth (1999) have extended the survey of Smith and Walker and also report results consistent with an effort (or "capital-labor") theory of cognition.

There is an important gap, however, in the Smith-Walker model: it is formulated in terms of a game against nature. Although many of the studies they survey fall into this category, others are market, bargaining, or oligopoly experiments largely conducted under private information on payoffs; i.e., each agent knows only his or her own payoff and nothing about the payoffs of others. It is well known that private (as opposed to complete) payoff information yields the condition most favorable to realizing a noncooperative equilibrium (Smith 1982; McCabe, Rassenti, and Smith 1997).[1] Here we modify the Smith-Walker model to allow for interactive decision in the n-person case and state conditions that permit one of the main theoretical results to be extended to the interactive case as follows: where standard theory predicts an interior optimum, increased payoff reduces the variance of decision error.

Historical Origins

The challenge of modeling the response to monetary reward in experimental tasks that are realistically expected to exhibit subjective costs of executing the task was first examined formally in the context of predicting Bernoulli trials by Sidney Siegel (1959). Siegel's motivation was attributed to an idea developed by Herb Simon:

... the necessity for careful distinctions between subjective rationality (i.e., behavior that is rational, given the perceptual and evaluation premises of the subject), and objective rationality (behavior that is rational as viewed by the experimenter) ... in the explanation of observed behavior.... If we accept the proposition that organismic behavior may be subjectively rational but is unlikely to be objectively rational in a complex world then the postulate of rationality loses much of its power for predicting behavior. To predict how economic man will behave we need to know not only that he is rational, but also how he perceives the world—what alternatives he sees, and what consequences he attaches to them ... We should not jump to the conclusion, however, that we can therefore get along without the concept of rationality. (Simon 1956, pp. 271–272)

Earlier, Simon had noted that "there is a complete lack of evidence that, in actual human choice situations of any complexity, these (rational) computations can be, or are in fact, performed ... but we cannot, of course, rule out the possibility that the unconscious is a better decision maker than the conscious" (1955, p. 104). The model we develop is very much in the spirit of Siegel's original work, inspired by the first Simon quotation. But the second quotation is entirely relevant as there should be no presumption that the subjects are aware of any implicit weighing of cost vs. benefit as their brain's expend increased effort when the reward centers signal greater value in doing so. If subjects implicitly take account of the effort cost of decision, then of course the subject's unconscious decisions are indeed better—superrational—than the conscious rational decision analysis predictions of the theorist/experimentalist.

Modeling Net Subjective Value

Consider a two-person experimental game with outcome π^i ($i = 1, 2$), which is converted into a monetary reward using the conversion constant λ ($\lambda > 0$). Let $C_i(z_i)$ be the subjective or mental cost of cognitive effort z_i. The subjectively experienced utility of player i can therefore be written as[2]

$$U_i = (1 + \lambda)\pi^i(y_1, y_2) - C_i(z_i), \tag{1}$$

where y_1 and y_2 are the decision variables of an interactive Nash game. When no cash reward is offered, then $\lambda = 0$, and the formulation (1) allows that there is some self satisfaction in maximizing the paper profit $\pi^i - C_i$. This is indicated by the common observation that subjects make reasonably good decisions—they do not choose arbitrarily or randomly—when there is no monetary reward.

Let (x_1^*, x_2^*) denote the Nash equilibrium computed by the theorist when net payoffs are π_i, and the cost term in equation 1 is ignored.

Now write each subject's decision in the error deviation form

$$y_i = x_1^* - s_i \xi_i(z_i), \tag{2}$$

where s_i is a random variable and ξ_i is some function of i's effort, z_i. Thus, $\xi_i(z_i)$ is i's production function for reducing error by application of cognitive or physiological resource effort.[3]

Neither z_i nor $\xi_i(z_i)$ is observable, but we do observe their effect on y_i and the deviation error, $x_i^* - y_i$. Under this assumption the utility of player i can be rewritten as

$$U_i = (1 + \lambda)\pi_i(x_1^* - s_1\xi_1(z_1), x_2^* - s_2\xi_2(z_2)) - C_i(z_i). \tag{3}$$

Let a pair (z_1, z_2) be an interior equilibrium of the two-person game with payoff functions (3). Then the first order conditions imply that

$$(1 + \lambda)\frac{\partial \pi^i}{\partial y_i}(x_1^* - s_1\xi_1(z_i), x_2^* - s_2x_2(z_2))(-s_ix_i'(z_i)) - C_i'(z_i) = 0 \tag{4}$$

for $i = 1, 2$. Assuming that the operations of expectation and differentiation are interchangeable (which is the case for sufficiently smooth π^i, we have

$$\frac{\partial E(\pi^i)}{\partial z_i} - \frac{C_i'(z_i)}{1 + \lambda} = 0 \tag{5}$$

for $i = 1, 2$. In addition, assume that equation 5 has a unique solution (z_1, z_2) with arbitrary $\lambda = 0$. Then z_1 and z_2 are functions of λ. Differentiate both sides of equation 5 with respect to λ to see that

$$\begin{pmatrix} \dfrac{\partial^2 E(\pi^1)}{\partial z_1^2} - \dfrac{C_1''(z_1)}{1 + \lambda} & \dfrac{\partial^2 E(\pi^1)}{\partial z_1 \partial z_2} \\[3mm] \dfrac{\partial^2 E(\pi^2)}{\partial z_1 \partial z_2} & \dfrac{\partial^2 E(\pi^2)}{\partial z_2^2} - \dfrac{C_2''(z_2)}{1 + \lambda} \end{pmatrix} \begin{pmatrix} \dfrac{dz_1}{d\lambda} \\[3mm] \dfrac{dz_2}{d\lambda} \end{pmatrix} = -\frac{1}{(1 + \lambda)^2}\begin{pmatrix} C_1'(z_1) \\ C_2'(z_2) \end{pmatrix}. \tag{6}$$

Using Cramer's rule, the solution of this equation is the following:

$$\frac{\partial z_1}{\partial \lambda} = \frac{D_1}{D} \quad \text{and} \quad \frac{\partial z_2}{\partial \lambda} = \frac{D_2}{D},$$

where

$$D = \left(\frac{\partial^2 E(\pi^1)}{\partial z_1^2} - \frac{C_1''(z_1)}{1 + \lambda}\right)\left(\frac{\partial^2 E(\pi^2)}{\partial z_2^2} - \frac{C_2''(z_2)}{1 + \lambda}\right) - \frac{\partial^2 E(\pi^1)}{\partial z_1 \partial z_2} \cdot \frac{\partial^2 E(\pi^2)}{\partial z_1 \partial z_2},$$

$$D_1 = -\frac{1}{(1+\lambda)^2}\left[\left(\frac{\partial^2 E(\pi^2)}{\partial z_2^2} - \frac{C_2''(z_2)}{1+\lambda}\right)C_1'(z_1) - \frac{\partial^2 E(\pi^1)}{\partial z_1 \partial z_2}\cdot C_2'(z_2)\right],$$

and

$$D_2 = -\frac{1}{(1+\lambda)^2}\left[\left(\frac{\partial^2 E(\pi^1)}{\partial z_1^2} - \frac{C_1''(z_1)}{1+\lambda}\right)C_2'(z_2) - \frac{\partial^2 E(\pi^2)}{\partial z_1 \partial z_2}\cdot C_1'(z_1)\right].$$

It is usually assumed that

$$\frac{\partial^2 E(\pi^i)}{\partial z_i^2} < 0 \quad (i = 1, 2),\tag{i}$$

which means that there are diminishing returns to effort, and

$$C_i'(z_i) > 0 \quad (i = 1, 2),\tag{ii}$$

which requires that the cost functions are strictly increasing in the neighborhood of the equilibrium.

In order to examine the signs of the solutions of equation 6, assume first that

$$D, D_1, D_2 \text{ are all positive.}\tag{iii}$$

Notice that $D > 0$ if the mixed partial derivatives $\partial^2 E(\pi^i)/\partial z_1 \partial z_2$ are small relative to the values of the differences

$$\frac{\partial^2 E(\pi^i)}{\partial z_i^2} - C_i''(z_i)$$

regardless of the signs of the mixed partial derivatives. This is the case if $\partial^2 E(\pi^i)/\partial z_i^2$ is sufficiently large with convex cost functions, or in the case of concave cost functions at least one of the quantities $\partial^2 E(\pi^i)/\partial z_i^2$ and $C_i''(z_i)$ have to be sufficiently large. The value of D_1 is positive if

$$\frac{\partial^2 E(\pi^2)}{\partial z_2^2} - \frac{C_2''(z_2)}{1+\lambda}$$

is negative and the mixed partial derivative is positive or a relatively small negative number. In the case when the difference

$$\frac{\partial^2 E(\pi^2)}{\partial z_2^2} - \frac{C_2''(z_2)}{1+\lambda}$$

is positive (that is, C_2 is very strongly concave) the mixed partial derivative $\partial^2 E(\pi^1)/\partial z_1 \partial z_2$ has to be positive and sufficiently large. Similar conditions can be given for D_2.

Alternatively we may assume that

D, D_1, D_2 are all negative. (iii')

The value of D is negative if the mixed partial derivatives have the same signs and are sufficiently large compared to the differences

$$\frac{\partial^2 E(\pi^i)}{\partial z_1 \partial z_2} - \frac{C_i''(z_i)}{1+\lambda}.$$

The value of D_1 becomes negative if either C_2 is concave with large second derivative or the mixed partial derivative $\partial^2 E(\pi^1)/\partial z_1 \partial z_2$ is a sufficiently large negative number. Similar conditions can be drawn for D_2.

Finally, assume that

$$\xi_i(z_i) > 0, \quad \xi_i'(z_i) < 0. \tag{iv}$$

Under conditions iii or iii' and iv, both derivatives $\partial z_i/\partial\lambda$ are positive.[4]

The discrepancy between the actual equilibrium (y_1, y_2) of the subject's experience, and the equilibrium (x_1^*, x_2^*) of the theorist is characterized by the component-wise discrepancies

$$\varepsilon_i = x_i^* - y_i = s_i \xi_i(z_i). \tag{7}$$

Simple calculation shows that

$$E(\varepsilon_i) = E(s_i)\xi_i(z_i) \quad \text{and} \quad Var(\varepsilon_i) = Var(s_i)\xi_i^2(z_i); \tag{8}$$

therefore

$$\frac{dE(\varepsilon_i)}{d\lambda} = E(s_i)\xi_i'(z_i) \cdot \frac{dz_i}{d\lambda}, \tag{9}$$

which is positive if $E(s_i) < 0$, negative if $E(s_i) > 0$, and vanishes if $E(s_i) = 0$. In the latter case the subject's error in cognition is unbiased. Notice that $E(s_i) < 0$ indicates that y_i is above x_i^* in the average and since $dE(\varepsilon_i)/d\lambda$ becomes positive, in the expectation, the discrepancy ε_i becomes smaller as λ increases. Similarly, if $E(s_i) > 0$, then y_i is below x_1^* in the average, and since $dE(\varepsilon_i)/d\lambda$ becomes negative, the discrepancy decreases again, in the average, if λ increases. These conditions open a rich theory of biased cognition error, its effect on expected observational error, and its interaction with payoff levels, issues that will not be explored here. Similarly,

$$\frac{dVar(\varepsilon_i)}{d\lambda} = Var(s_i)2\xi_i(z_i)\xi_i'(z_i) \cdot \frac{dz_i}{d\lambda} < 0, \tag{10}$$

showing that the variance of the discrepancy in the average must decrease if λ increases. This result corresponds to a principal characteristic of the data reported by Smith and Walker (1993a,b). Note that to get this empirical prediction, the multiplicative form of the error equation 2 was used.

We will next show that the conditions which guarantee that the solutions $\partial z_i/\partial\lambda$ of equation 6 are positive are closely related to the theory of M-matrices (Szidarovszky and Bahill 1988, pp. 467–468). Notice that the coefficient matrix of equation 6 can be written as $-\underline{H} - \underline{D}$ with

$$\underline{H} = \begin{pmatrix} -\dfrac{\partial^2 E(\pi^1)}{\partial z_1^2} & -\dfrac{\partial^2 E(\pi^1)}{\partial z_1 \partial z_2} \\[3mm] -\dfrac{\partial^2 E(\pi^2)}{\partial z_1 \partial z_2} & -\dfrac{\partial^2 E(\pi^2)}{\partial z_2} \end{pmatrix}$$

and

$$\underline{D} = \begin{pmatrix} \dfrac{C_1''(z_1)}{1+\lambda} & 0 \\[3mm] 0 & \dfrac{C_2''(z_2)}{1+\lambda} \end{pmatrix}.$$

If the diagonal elements of $\underline{H}$ are positive, the off-diagonal elements are non-positive, and the determinant of $\underline{H}$ is positive, then $\underline{H}$ is an M-matrix with positive inverse. If C_1 and C_2 are convex in the neighborhood of the equilibrium, then $\underline{H} + \underline{D}$ is also an M-matrix, so $(-\underline{H} - \underline{D}) - 1$ is negative. Since both right-hand sides of equation 6 are negative, the solution is necessarily positive.

Consider next the n-person extension of the same model. The utility of player i has now the form

$$U^i = (1 + \lambda)\pi^i(y_1, \ldots, y_n) - C_i(z_i), \tag{11}$$

and it is assumed that y_i is the same as given by equation 2 for all $i = 1, 2, \ldots, n$. Notice that equation 5 remains valid in the n-person case, and equation 6 can now be written in the more general form

$$(-\underline{H} - \underline{D})\frac{d\underline{z}}{d\lambda} = -\frac{1}{(1 + \lambda)^2}\underline{C}', \tag{12}$$

where

$$\underline{H} = \begin{pmatrix} -\dfrac{\partial^2 E(\pi^1)}{\partial z_1^2} & -\dfrac{\partial^2 E(\pi^1)}{\partial z_1 \partial z_2} & \cdots & -\dfrac{\partial^2 E(\pi^1)}{\partial z_1 \partial z_n} \\[2ex] -\dfrac{\partial^2 E(\pi^2)}{\partial z_2 \partial z_1} & -\dfrac{\partial^2 E(\pi^2)}{\partial z_2^2} & \cdots & -\dfrac{\partial^2 E(\pi^2)}{\partial z_2 \partial z_n} \\[2ex] \cdots\cdots\cdots\cdots\cdots\cdots\cdots\cdots\cdots\cdots\cdots\cdots \\[1ex] -\dfrac{\partial^2 E(\pi^n)}{\partial z_n \partial z_1} & -\dfrac{\partial^2 E(\pi^n)}{\partial z_n \partial z_2} & \cdots & -\dfrac{\partial^2 E(\pi^n)}{\partial z_n^2} \end{pmatrix},$$

$$\frac{d\underline{z}}{\partial \lambda} = \begin{pmatrix} \dfrac{dz_1}{\partial \lambda} \\[2ex] \dfrac{dz_2}{\partial \lambda} \\[2ex] \cdots\cdots \\[1ex] \dfrac{dz_n}{\partial \lambda} \end{pmatrix}, \quad \underline{C}' = \begin{pmatrix} C_1'(z_1) \\[1ex] C_2'(z_2) \\[1ex] \cdots\cdots \\[1ex] C_n'(z_n) \end{pmatrix},$$

and

$$\underline{D} = diag\left(\frac{C_1''(z_1)}{1+\lambda}, \frac{C_2''(z_2)}{1+\lambda}, \ldots, \frac{C_n''(z_n)}{1+\lambda}\right).$$

It is difficult and complicated to obtain simple general conditions that guarantee the positivity of the solution. Specific conditions can, however, be derived in the following way.

Assume that matrix $\underline{H}$ is an M-matrix, and all cost functions are strictly increasing and convex in the neighborhood of the equilibrium. Under these conditions $\underline{H} + \underline{D}$ is also an M-matrix, $(-\underline{H} - \underline{D}) - 1 < \underline{0}$, and since the right-hand-side vector is negative, all solutions are positive, implying that for all i

$$\frac{dz_i}{d\lambda} > 0.$$

Since $E(\varepsilon_i)$ and $Var(\varepsilon_i)$ remain the same, our previous conditions on the derivatives $dE(\varepsilon_i)/d\lambda$ and $dVar(\varepsilon_i)/d\lambda$ remain valid in the n-person case.

In Cournot duopoly, y_i is output by firm i. With linear demand and zero costs, profit is

$$\pi^i = [a - b(y_1 + y_2)]y_i, \quad i = 1, 2$$

where $a > 0$ and $b > 0$ are the linear demand parameters. Using data from Fouraker and Siegel (1963) for linear Cournot duopoly experiments, Smith and Walker (1993a) report mean square deviations from the optimum of 7.2 under low payoffs, and 5.5 under high payoffs. Using data from various versions of bilateral bargaining (simultaneous move versus sequential move and private versus complete information on cash payoffs), the mean square deviations vary from 2 to 27 times greater under low compared with high payoffs (Smith and Walker 1993a, p. 257). Double auction supply and demand experiments with perfectly elastic supply, and perfectly inelastic demand (yielding a competitive equilibrium at the supply price boundary) exhibit large differences, period by period in both the mean deviation, and the mean square deviation from equilibrium, when comparing weak with strong payoff motivation (ibid., p. 259). Finally, Smith and Walker (1993b) published new first price auction experiments that varied rewards, by letting $\lambda = 0, 1, 5, 10$, and 20 times the normal amounts paid to individual subjects, and reported a significant reduction in the mean square error for linear bid function regressions as λ was increased. They also report a large reduction in the mean square error linear bid function when subject experience is increased while controlling for payoff level. Experience is interpreted in the above model as lowering decision cost. As familiarity with a task increases, decisions become routine requiring reduced attention from higher cognitive resources. This is the brain's way of conserving scarce attentional resources.

Notes

1. Motivated by the general experimental findings, Kalai and Leher (1993) model private information as a Bayesian game in which players have a diffuse prior on each other's payoffs, showing convergence to Nash. This is an important development, but is much beyond the scope of what is attempted here.

2. Compare the following development with equations 1–9 in Smith and Walker 1993a.

3. The functions $\xi_i(z_i)$ and $C_i(z_i)$ have been assumed here to represent cognitive processes, but they can just as well be used to model the explicit cost and productivity of the time of paid consultants or others assigned a strategic decision task. In this way the stakes in a field application of game theory can be weighed against the cost and productivity of observable effort.

4. Given equation 2 and condition iv, the sign of $\partial^2 E(\pi^i)/\partial z_1 \partial z_2$ is determined by the sign of $\partial^2 E(\pi^i)/\partial y_1 \partial y_2$. The latter is controlled by the choice of $\pi^i(y_1, y_2)$ in an experiment. Consequently, we can choose the cross-partials of π^i so that they are complements or strong substitutes, and compare the predictions 9 and 10 for each of the two payoff environments by varying λ from low to high.

References

Camerer, C. F., and Hogarth, R. M. 1999. The effects of financial incentives in economic experiments. *Journal of Risk and Uncertainty* 17: 7–42.

Dawes, R. M., ed. 1988. *Rational Choice in an Uncertain World*. Harcourt Brace Jovanovich.

Fouraker, L., and Siegel, S., eds. 1963. *Bargaining Behavior*. McGraw-Hill.

Harrison, G. 1989. Theory and misbehavior of first-price auctions. *American Economic Review* 79: 749–762.

Kalai, E., and Leher, E. 1993. Rational learning leads to Nash equilibria. *Econometrica* 61: 1019–1045.

Knoll, Y., Levy, H., and Rapoport, A. 1988. Experimental tests of the separation theorem and the capital asset pricing model. *American Economic Review* 61: 500–519.

McCabe, K. A., Rassenti, S. J., and Smith, V. L. 1997. Behavioral foundations of reciprocity. *Games and Economic Behavior* 24, no. 1/2: 10–24.

Siegel, S. 1959. *Psychometrika* 24: 303–316.

Siegel, S., and Fouraker, L., eds. 1960. *Bargaining and Group Decision Making: Experiments in Bilateral Bargaining*. McGraw-Hill.

Simon, Herbert. 1955. A behavioral model of rational choice. *Quarterly Journal of Economics* 69: 99–118.

Simon, Herbert. 1956. Rational choice and the structure of the environment. *Psychometrika* 63: 267–272.

Smith, V. L. 1976. Experimental economics: Induced value theory. *American Economic Review* 66: 274–279.

Smith, V. L. 1982. Microeconomic systems as an experimental science. *American Economic Review* 72: 923–955.

Smith, V. L., and Walker, J. M. 1993a. Monetary rewards and decision cost in experimental economics. *Economic Inquiry* 31: 245–261.

Smith, V. L., and Walker, J. M. 1993b. Rewards, experience and decision costs in first price auctions. *Economic Inquiry* 31: 237–245.

Szidarovszky, F., and Bahill, A. T., eds. 1998. *Linear Systems Theory*, second edition. CRC Press.

Tversky, A., and Kahneman, D. 1987. Rational choice and the framing of prices. In R. Hogarth and M. Reder, eds., *Rational Choice*. University of Chicago Press.

von Winterfeldt, D., and Edwards, W., eds. 1986. *Decision Analysis and Behavioral Research*. Cambridge University Press.

II   *Organizations and Administration*

A Focus on Processes: Part of Herbert Simon's Legacy

Philip Bromiley

I did my thesis with Herbert Simon. While he had largely quit doing organizations and behavioral economics by the time I arrived at Carnegie-Mellon, I happened to be in his cognitive psychology class at the same time he was awarded the Nobel Prize. In addition, I planned to do the kind of work he recommended in economics. Consequently, he agreed to join Toby Davis in supervising my thesis. I studied the process by which large corporations determined the amount they would spend on capital investments (Bromiley 1986).

Simon fundamentally believed in explaining phenomena by understanding the processes that generate the observed phenomena. This emphasis goes all the way back to an article he wrote called "Proverbs of Administration" (Simon 1946). At that time, scholars sought general rules such as "a manager should supervise X employees" or "specialization increases efficiency." In this article, he argued that scholars shouldn't search for such general rules of administration. The search for general rules leads to vacuous or contradictory principles. Instead, Simon argued scholars needed to understand the processes by which organizations operate. Such understanding would require understanding what decisions individuals make and what influences they face in making such decisions. This leads directly into needing to understand what we later termed information processing in organizations. From a prescriptive stance, he argued that tying such understanding to decision criteria and performance outcomes might lead to meaningful understandings of appropriate ways to organize. In short, we need to understand organizational information processing in order to generate meaningful prescriptions.

This search for process continued throughout his career. *Organizations* (March and Simon 1958) offers a process understanding of how organizations function. It introduced the field to flow diagrams, a natural representation of processes. It emphasizes the interactions among individuals and the coordination of organizational behavior, as foundations for understanding organizations. And above all, it presents process representations of relationships.

Figure 1 (from *Organizations*) clearly demonstrates this process representation. The *level of aspiration* and *expected rewards* influence the level of satisfaction. Dissatisfaction results in search, which results in improved rewards. Expected rewards positively influence the level of aspiration.

This representation offers us several important methodological insights.

First, we can see it is most natural to think of this representation as a dynamic model. Many of these things take time so this calls for a

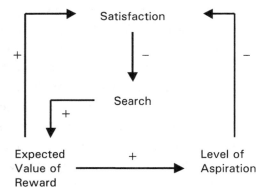

Figure 1
General model of adaptive motivated behavior (figure 3.5 in *Organizations*).

time series representation. Indeed, the text associated with this figure presents a time-based differential equation model for this system. Many areas of organizations scholarship are just learning the importance of time and dynamic understandings (see Zaheer, Albert, and Zaheer 2000; Goodman, Anacona, Lawrence, and Tushman 2001).

Second, this system can be examined as a cross-sectional equilibrium. With "a few additional assumptions" (March and Simon 1958) this model can be solved for an equilibrium. Thus, if in a particular empirical exercise we know we are observing a cross-sectional process that has reached equilibrium, a cross-sectional analysis could be productive.

Third, this process does not have to stabilize to an equilibrium. In his autobiography, Simon (1991) offers a story based on aspirations. In this story, the subject cycles between the lowering his aspiration levels because he cannot find appropriate rewards, and searching. When the aspiration level is low, the subject quickly finds satisfactory rewards, but this causes increases in future aspirations. At some point, the aspiration level becomes high enough that the individual cannot satisfy it within a reasonable amount of search and so lowers the aspiration level.

As most readers know, Simon spent his primary efforts over a large portion of his life working in the area of cognitive psychology. Here too we can contrast a process view with a cross-sectional view. Simon wanted to understand the detailed process by which people solved problems. He attacked this by exceedingly painstaking work using verbal protocols from people who were solving problems. From these verbal protocols, he and his colleagues generated computer programs that simulate the process by which individuals solved problems.

Compare the kind of work and knowledge that the cognitive processing people generate to the equally fascinating work in behavioral decision theory (see, for instance, Yates 1992). For the most part, behavioral decision theory ignores process and looks for patterns where individuals differ from rational decision processes as defined by economists. Thus behavioral decision theory consists largely of an inventory of heuristics or biases individuals display. These heuristics are exceedingly attractive because they lend themselves to relatively straightforward experimentation and to generalization to other areas. For example, a large literature in corporate risk taking and much of behavioral finance rely on the individual results on decision making under uncertainty (see examples in Bromiley, Miller, and Rau 2001 and Shefrin 2000).

In contrast, cognitive processing work seems to provide a deeper level of explanation, but less clear superficial predictions. We do not get a set of simple hypotheses that apply to any decision-making-under-risk task. However, this does not mean the process does not lead us to some fundamental understandings, for example the bounds on information processing tell us a lot about how display will influence decisions, the limits on how people can integrate information to make decisions, etc.

Perhaps most important, a process study of actual decisions helps us understand how individuals frame and solve such actual decisions. Often, individuals are actually trying to solve a problem that is not the problem scholars assume they are trying to solve. For example, Patrick Crecine's government budgeting work found that government budgeters were often concerned with shoehorning desired expenditures into an allowable totals that come from fiscal policy or revenue forecasts (Crecine 1967, 1969). This contrasts with an academic literature that largely explains government expenditures as responding to public demands for government services where such demand is represented by average income levels, demographics, etc.

One nice feature of process models is that they make a large number of predictions rather than simply predicting some final stage. For example, Gregg and Simon (1967) and Simon (1968) compare a process model of concept attainment learning to a stochastic theory. As Simon (1968) points out, not only can the stochastic model be derived deductively from the process model, the process model makes additional, testable predictions the stochastic model does not. These additional predictions, and the fact that the process model has no free parameters while the stochastic model has two free parameters, make the process model more easily falsifiable than the stochastic model. Simon argues that, if we take Popper's criteria of simplicity, the simpler theory is the one that is more easily falsifiable, then the process model is simpler than the stochastic model even though it appears superficially more complex.

In many cases, we may only be able to differentiate among theories based on their process implications. That is, we often have multiple theories that predict very similar behaviors at the aggregate or final level. For instance, Becker (1971) shows that the major implications of economic consumer behavior analysis come not from assumptions about information processing but rather lead directly from the assumption that households face a budget constraint. No finding about these implications can readily differentiate among models of consumer decision making—almost any model with a budget constraint will make similar predictions, and the budget constraint is simply an ancillary assumption rather than a core theoretical construct.

Thus, aggregate behavior often cannot differentiate among differing decision procedures. After all, most of our tests take the form "*X* positively influences *Y*." For most practical *X*s and *Y*s, a variety of reasonable models can lead to such an influence and finding such an influence cannot tell us which model is correct. While the association might let us choose among theories that predict specific magnitudes of influence, few of our theories make such predictions.

Coming back my study corporate capital budgeting, Simon clearly supported an understanding based on careful examination of the budgeting process. However, in parallel to most of the previous work in the field, he thought I should represent the process with a simulation model. With the advantage of coming after numerous fine process researchers, I suggested a research process that used qualitative data to generate explicit hypotheses about the quantitative relationships in the system. Then, these quantitative hypotheses could be tested using data from the system using conventional econometric techniques. After some debate, Simon agreed to this and later recommended the process (Simon 1997).

This need to follow process and to explain things with process constitutes a core of Herb's approach to scholarship. After I had been collecting data on processes within the Copperweld Corporation for several months, I was struggling to define the critical questions I would attempt to answer. I believed that at the end I needed to say something about a specific economic variable and how it should behave that would be directly comparable to the way other scholars had discussed this variable. I explained to Simon two different routes I could take with the thesis and he listened carefully. Then he asked "Will this decision change what you do this week?" I responded that it really wouldn't. He told me then that I didn't need to make the decision now, but at some point, taking a quarter out of his pocket and holding it as if to flip it, he said I probably have to make a decision.

All of this comes around to fundamental belief that if you use a good process to try to understand a process, good scholarship can result.

References

Becker, G. S. 1971. *Economic Theory*. Knopf.

Bromiley, P. 1986. *Corporate Capital Investment: A Behavioral Approach*. Cambridge University Press.

Bromiley, P., K. D. Miller, and D. Rau. 2001. Risk in strategic management research. In M. Hitt, R. Freeman, and J. Harrison, eds., *Handbook of Strategic Management*. Blackwell.

Crecine, J. P. 1967. A computer simulation model of municipal budgeting. *Management Science* 13: 786–815.

Crecine, J. P. 1969. *Governmental Problem Solving: A Computer Simulation of Municipal Budgeting*. Rand McNally.

Goodman, P. S., Anacona, D. G., Lawrence, B. S., and Tushman, M. L. 2001. Special topic forum on time and organizational research, introduction. *Academy of Management Review* 26, no. 4: 507–512.

Gregg, L. W., and Simon, H. A. 1967. Process models and stochastic theories of simple concept formation. *Journal of Mathematical Psychology* 4: 246–276.

March, J. G., and Simon, H. A. 1958. *Organizations*. Wiley.

Shefrin, H. 2000. *Beyond Greed and Fear: Understanding Behavioral Finance and the Psychology of Investing*. Harvard Business School Press.

Simon, H. A. 1946. The proverbs of administration. *Public Administration Review* 6: 53–67. Reprinted in J. M. Shafritz and A. C. Hyde, eds., *Classics of Public Administration* (Moore, 1978).

Simon, H. A. 1968. On Judging the Plausibility of Theories. In Van Roostelaar and Stall, eds., *Logic, Methodology and Philosophy of Science III*. North-Holland, 1968. Reprinted in H. A. Simon, *Models of Discovery* (Reidel, 1977).

Simon, H. A. 1991. *Models of My Life*. Basic Books.

Simon, H. A. 1997. *An Empirically Based Microeconomics*. Cambridge University Press.

Yates, F., ed. 1992. *Risk-Taking Behavior*. Wiley.

Zaheer, S., Albert, S., and Zaheer, A. 1999. Time scales and organizational theory. *Academy of Management Review* 24, no. 4: 725–741.

Herbert Simon as Friend to Economists Out of Fashion

John Conlisk

In my graduate courses in the early 1960s, I liked macro better than micro. The reason had nothing to do with level of aggregation, but rather with a difference in approach. In macro at the time, we would write down plausible behavioral relations, phrased as a difference equation system, and let the adaptive dynamics play out. What would happen? What would we learn? In micro at the time, we would write down a utility or profit function, maximize it subject to usual constraints, and interpret the first order conditions as describing behavior. We usually knew what would happen from the outset; different micro optimizations were much alike. The macro approach seemed closer to behavior and more open to novelty and imagination. I thought at the time that it would be the wave of the future.

A terrible prediction. In the years to follow, macro was taken apart; many parts were scrapped; and the rest was rebuilt to look like micro. Macro was to have a "sound grounding in micro optimization." As the optimizations progressed from (i) static to (ii) intertemporal to (iii) intertemporal with rational expectations, agents in the models were required to understand more and more. To handle rational expectations, an agent had to understand the entire economy, not just his or her own piece of it. Given the complicated optimizations, analytical tractability required that other model ingredients be simplified away.

Multiple agents, multiple sectors, and multiple markets were among the discards. The outcome was a bold and remarkable idea—the "representative agent" model of a macroeconomy.

In this model, there was but a single agent—call him Robinson Crusoe—living in isolation and producing a single good. Since Robinson's output was all there was, the model was proclaimed to be macroeconomic. Mathematical shadow prices at Robinson's optimum were proclaimed to be market prices, although there were in fact no markets; hence the model was proclaimed to be a general equilibrium theory. Through random shocks, Robinson was made to experience economic fluctuations; they were proclaimed business cycles, although there were no businesses. Since Robinson would work less in some periods than others, the model was proclaimed a model of unemployment. Real data were fit. For example, it could be shown that, for the right parameter values, Robinson's output would have roughly the same autocorrelations as United States output. In this way, a one-person model of a national economy could be judged a scientific success. I was continually amazed by all this. I became the slow boy in the seminar room, repeatedly asking, "Can a one-person model really describe a national economy?" The answer would be "yes," and by and by I stopped teaching macro.

Similar developments were unfolding in other parts of economics. In contrast to my prediction as a graduate student, universal optimization was routing behavioral hypotheses in the competition for journal space. Leading economists, editors, referees, and most of my own colleagues seemed content with the outcome. It was common to hear that economists should now convert other social sciences to such methods.

Although the tide has turned in recent years, universal optimization had a remarkably long run, about three decades, as the fashionable economic dogma. During this time, most of my career, I felt short of scholarly exchange, pressured to squeeze gratuitous optimizations into papers, and, worse, pressured to doubt that common sense about behavior even mattered.

Herbert Simon provided a rescue. Soon after my graduate school days, I began reading his work. In contrast to the dogma, he was an anchor of good sense. Although I never met him and doubt that he knew of my existence until quite recently, I viewed him as a teacher and steadfast scholarly friend. He was such a clear writer that I could have pleasant, imaginary conversations with him as I read his papers. I imagine there are many like me, people who never met Simon, but who felt close to him through his work. This is a mark of a great scholar.

Here are some of the lessons that Simon taught me: Cognition is a scarce economic resource, not an infinitely plentiful one. Cognitive power and problem difficulty can be roughly measured and compared. The context of a problem matters as well as its abstract character. Optimization is part of the tool kit for decision modeling, but only part; its use depends on context. In the strict optimization models of economics, predictions typically come from auxiliary assumptions on the objective function and constraints, not from the optimization hypothesis itself. The ratio of evidence to theory is far too low in economics. Economists have much to learn from psychologists. Decision making is typically a question of searching and stopping—how a person searches for an answer and how the person decides when to stop searching and take action. Search models can handle both imperfect reasoning and imperfect information.

Simon was not the only one making these points over the years (witness other contributors to this volume), but I think he was the earliest, clearest, and most consistent. It is striking that economists, after neglecting Simon's ideas for decades, are now close to accepting them, but still cite Simon only rarely. For example, Stigler is widely cited as the economist who brought optimal search theory into economics in the early 1960s, whereas Simon had already brought both optimal and satisficing search into economics in the mid 1950s.

In 1996, just after I had published a survey on bounded rationality, Simon wrote me about it. This was a signal event to me. Nobel laureates don't usually write (the rate thus far is once per century). The letter was generous, long, beautifully written, and deeply thoughtful. Simon was encouraged by the slow movement in economics away from optimization dogma, but worried that graduate students are still afflicted by "deep cynicism about their own research and about what they are being taught and asked to believe." "The cynicism," he wrote, "is not healthy (nor the behavior associated with it), and we must find ways to divert it to more constructive activity." The letter went on to discuss where economics could go from here. I will quote most of five paragraphs from Simon's letter:

> If there is any one thing that emerges with utmost clarity from the psychological research it is that you cannot predict decisional processes in any domain without discovering how people in that domain form their problem representations (alias problem spaces or problem contexts). No one before Newton used the calculus; no one after Newton could do serious physics without the calculus. If we study the history of chess from the time of Morphy (about 1860) down to the present—a little more than a century—we discover three or four major shifts in the way in which grandmasters conceptualize the game, and with each shift a change in style of analysis with consequent changes in how one has to think in order to win. There is no reason to suppose that the problem spaces in which people make their economic decisions are any less subject to temporal change. . . .

> So just as the behavior of an electron will be different, depending on the electrical and magnetic fields in which it finds itself, so the behavior of economic actors will be different depending on the social and historical context in which they find themselves. That is why the shift toward evolutionary theories (call them historical theories, in the sense of historical geology) is so important. If there are invariants, they will be found at the level of process, especially learning processes, not at the level of world representations.

> Economists are far from ready to accept this demotion of their science from true laws of motion (the physics envy that is so prevalent and that Paul Samuelson is so engagingly open about) to laws that are highly contingent on history, institutional structures and public opinion. Of course, as my electron example shows, the same kind of relativity is present in all the sciences: they simply talk of initial and boundary conditions (but insist on empirical procedures and not arm-chairing to fix them).

> But scientists generally do the kinds of research they have learned to do in graduate school, using the instruments and methods they have acquired there. Insofar as economists learn empirical methods at all (except for the current

activity in experimental economics), they learn to use statistics in order to look at the world through the wrong end of a telescope, using horribly inaccurate and aggregated data. They are ignorant of, or if not ignorant, opposed to, the methods (primarily field studies of a variety of kinds) that would bring them sufficiently close to the real world to observe how decisions are actually made, and what influences act upon them.

Therefore, the revolution is not going to gain full momentum until there is a revolution in the graduate curriculum to include in it training in methods of observing decision processes at close range and in detail....

By comparing Simon's paragraphs to mine above, we see that he thinks much more deeply than I do, which is the trouble with writing about a great man. That he would put such effort into a letter to help someone he never met displays a good man as well. Through his writings, he was, and is, teacher and scholarly friend to all, especially to economists out of fashion.

Herbert A. Simon and the Education of Managers

William R. Dill

In a book whose authors are almost all faculty and research colleagues or doctoral students of Herbert Simon, there should be room for a chapter that describes his role in educating master's students for practical careers. After all, Lee Bach and Bill Cooper lured him to Carnegie Tech in 1949 to launch a new Graduate School of Industrial Administration. William Larimer Mellon had made his endowment gift specifically to prepare engineers to become general managers and creative leaders in business.

Bach believed that education to lead in a world of rapid change should integrate across traditional disciplinary boundaries. It should draw from theory, empirical research, and analytic tools to stimulate new approaches to practice and problem solving. The goal was not to equip graduates with specifics for their first jobs, but to prepare them to learn and grow over their lifetimes. The Graduate School of Industrial Administration's planned approach contrasted sharply with typical M.B.A. programs of the day, which lectured students or used case discussions to convey current managerial wisdom and technique.

Simon did come to Carnegie with promises that he could draw on the Mellon grant to do empirical research about organizational behavior and that the new school's portfolio would eventually include doctoral programs. However, for the first five years (1949–1954) almost all

GSIA students were M.S. candidates who had their sights on managerial opportunities in companies like U.S. Steel, American Brake Shoe, Gulf Oil, Ford Motor, Kodak, and Westinghouse. Even when GSIA began to recruit a separate cadre of Ph.D. students in 1954–1956, at least half of them had originally come to the School with the master's and with business careers in mind.

GSIA's early reputation hung almost entirely on implementing its practice-oriented program well. Simon played a significant role in its success with applicants and employers and, after only a decade of existence, its recognition by the Carnegie Corporation and the Ford Foundation as an outstanding national model for the reform of master's programs in business.

Simon's role was not clear to me in 1951 when, as a master's applicant, I visited Carnegie for interviews with Bach and others on the initial faculty. I was arguing selfishly that GSIA's mission to educate engineers ought to be flexible enough to accept an English major who had taken calculus, statistics, and some extra science courses. Simon was friendly but tough. He and Bach pointed out that if accepted, I would need to overload in the first year with four semesters of engineering courses. He recommended I start over the summer with texts on design and on statics and dynamics. I bought and struggled with both, learning quickly that "introductory" to Simon meant "advanced placement" for anyone else.

Most of us in GSIA's first ten years had Simon as a teacher in only one course, a required second-year introduction to the workings of organizations, with his *Public Administration* and *Administrative Behavior* as texts. He had not yet published *Organizations*, *Models of Man*, or *The New Science of Management Decision*. A few master's students worked with him as graduate assistants. Herb was a regular at the afternoon student-faculty coffee hours. We appreciated his willingness to engage in things we wanted to talk about and the ease with which he lured us in other directions, even as far afield as his encyclopedic knowledge of beetles. He liked to spar over ideas and opinions. He joked that one of his books had first come out with a misprinted title page *(Pubic Administration)*. By the mid 1950s, he began to promise development of thinking machines and make what seemed at the time outrageous predictions about the impact of computers on business and society.

Faculty Leadership behind the Scenes

Only later as a GSIA faculty member did I appreciate that the most important things Simon did to insure a superior education for master's students were done behind the scenes. He once wrote that operating a professional school is "like mixing oil and water," and "left to themselves, the oil and the water will separate again" (Simon 1967).[1] He worked on the mix, intensively through the 1950s and intermittently into the 1990s, long after he had switched his interests to doctoral students and away from business to psychology and computer science. Herb used his stature as a researcher's researcher to seduce, jawbone, and shame discipline-focused faculty colleagues into stretching to achieve difficult aspects of the master's program design—particularly to back cross-field efforts to help students address applied managerial problems. His was a steady voice for an holistic view of what students should learn, a focus on problems rather than disciplines. Within disciplines he was an advocate that the best theories come from painstaking observation of how people and organizations actually behave.

Simon could be tough judging junior faculty hires who failed to finish their doctorates or who, whatever their rank and degrees, were not energetic and imaginative in their scholarship. But he demonstrated a wonderful indifference to academically correct credentials in helping Lee Bach to build a faculty. This shows in his autobiography, *Models of My life*, where he celebrated the maverick qualities of the other three people on the initial design team (Simon 1991, pp. 135–160):

▪ Lee Bach, whose most important trait may have been his tenacious ability to learn and help others learn by asking questions rather than by his ranking as an economist

- Bill Cooper, steered away from a boxing career to the University of Chicago by an accountant he had caddied for and still feisty enough later to walk away from a nearly completed doctorate because of disagreements with his committee over the appropriateness of his thesis

- Elliott Dunlap Smith, Carnegie's provost, a lawyer and self-educated industrial psychologist who had spent much of his career in management for a New England paper company.

Herb's tolerance for mavericks continued. GSIA's early senior appointments included George Kozmetsky and Melvin Anshen, products of the Harvard case teaching system that GSIA seemed determined to overturn; the established social scientists Harold Guetzkow, Alexander Henderson, and Franco Modigliani, for whom teaching prospective managers was an entirely new venture; and Leland Hazard, a retired corporate anti-trust lawyer and civic leader who had a vision for giving life to a stillborn segment of the master's curriculum, a broad-sweep course on the History of Ideas and Social Change. Two master's graduates who returned from many years in senior positions in industry to teach, Gerald Meyers and Jack Thorne, found in Simon an interested and supportive colleague.[2]

One reason for Simon's success in keeping oil and water mixed was that he did what he asked others to do. Many professors did not want advice about teaching responsibilities, just the freedom instead to run their courses as they pleased. They did not appreciate running appraisals of their classes or extras that truly involved working together.

Initially, there were regular meetings of professors teaching master's students to compare impressions of progress and to balance work loads among courses. For six complex "cross-course" business cases in the first year, students turned in written analyses and recommendations, which then most faculty members were asked to help grade. During the first several years the faculty administered a comprehensive examination at the end of the program to help determine which students would graduate. Many professors would have liked to escape these duties. Lee

Bach's insistence and Herb's willingness to put in his share of time and effort brought others around.

Bach and Cooper may have been the prime movers in getting a computer very early at Carnegie and having it installed in the basement of GSIA, with relatively open access for students. But Simon is remembered as the apostle promoting its use. Ann Preston, the School's first woman graduate, writes that learning to program with SOAP on the IBM 650 won her an opportunity to work with IBM's Service Bureau Corporation and soon to build her own company where she has not had to "worry about glass ceilings and power suits." She was only one of many master's students in the mid 1950s who heeded early predictions from Simon that information processing was the place for them to try to build their careers.

In the 1960s, GSIA introduced a required semester of involvement with the Carnegie Management Game—then and still, one of the most ambitious business simulation exercises. It was rich enough in the environment described and the problems posed to challenge teams of 8–10 players to differentiate roles, ponder questions of hierarchy, and attend to long as well as short-range decisions. It challenged students to apply analytic tools in making production, marketing, and financial decisions. It was realistic enough draw interest among "real-world" managers and professionals to engage with the student teams—e.g., entrepreneurs and executives to supervise as boards of directors, bankers to evaluate and act on live presentations of financing proposals, and union officials to negotiate labor contracts. Eventually Carnegie established a live market for students and faculty to trade in stocks of the firms.[3] New York University, a second major user, added more depth, particularly to the live role playing, and adapted the game to introduce American concepts of management to experienced managers in Hungary and Poland.

Developing the game was a large, messy project that over 3–4 years consumed the energies of a team of younger, untenured faculty (Cohen et al. 1964). Simon did not play a direct role. Behind the scenes, though, in senior faculty meetings Simon helped Dick Cyert, then dean and prime mover on the project, in three key measures of support. He accepted the game as a potentially important addition to the curriculum. He was on the side of giving members of the development team scholarship credit for their work on building and implementing the game, in lieu of some traditional expectations for publication. He supported expansion of the computer resources necessary to test and run the simulations.

As the game got going with live boards of directors, Simon again led by example. Even though he no longer taught classes to master's students, he did early turns as a board chair to help draw other faculty into various game roles and helped anchor the game within the master's curriculum.

The introduction of entrepreneurial emphasis to GSIA in the 1980s and the 1990s was an even later case of Simon's willingness to support changes that helped the master's program. By then he had little association with the School. He had turned his personal energies to cognitive studies and artificial intelligence and had moved his office to another part of the Carnegie-Mellon campus.

As a field, entrepreneurship was defiantly holistic and practical, and most academics scorned its potential as a field for serious research. At Carnegie and other major schools, the push from students was for teachers like Jack Thorne who brought success as entrepreneurs rather credentials as scholars. Most discipline and research-focused faculty thought that corporations were more interesting than new and small businesses to work with. GSIA's faculty tolerated Jack Thorne's initiative, but most did not see entrepreneurship as a mainstream investment.

Saras Sarasvathy, now a faculty member at the University of Washington, had come from India to earn a doctorate to do research in entrepreneurship. Failing to find a Ph.D. program that would welcome her interests, she enrolled for a master's at GSIA. With the hope of finding a way to launch her dream project of comparing the thought processes of entrepreneurs and bankers, she enrolled for an elective in cognitive psychology with Simon.

Herb stretched the specifications for his term paper assignment to let Saras try the comparative analysis. He acknowledged the quality of her work by encouraging her and guiding her to write it up for publication, and he offered to help her get into the doctoral program. He intervened with the dean, agreeing that since this was his request, he would chair her dissertation committee. Simon saw the mark of quality in Saras's work and had no problem acknowledging potential for research in entrepreneurship and a place for it within GSIA.

Simon helped even more when Jack Thorne proposed a research conference on entrepreneurship. He agreed to chair the conference and helped Jack and Saras build a lineup of speakers and panelists, including other Nobel Prize winners, whose accomplishments and reputations would draw doubters within the GSIA faculty to attend.

Simon would have had a significant indirect effect on the quality of teaching in the master's program simply by his leadership in research and in helping to hire and winnow faculty. He never ceased guiding other professors and sparring with recalcitrants about his major concerns: his disdain for narrow discipline-bound studies and his insistence that the best theory comes from careful empirical observation of how the world works. The latter comes out most clearly in his attempts to redefine economic man as "satisficer" rather than maximizer.

What master's graduates should appreciate is how much over the years, by support and participation, he intervened directly in the ways they were taught. Herb's support for the original program design and for faculty appointments and curricular changes that reinforced and refreshed it have been of great benefit over the years to all of GSIA's practice-oriented students.

Lessons from the Classroom

As a classroom teacher of organizational behavior to master's students, Simon did not leave memories as vivid as Lee Bach did with his intensive questioning drills; Bill Cooper, with his zealous embrace of new tools for making decisions; or Elliott Smith, with his "gotcha" role playing challenges in human relations. In a quiet and usually good-humored fashion Herb showed students ways of assessing organizations and managerial duties in behavioral terms. But he described a world and levels of involvement in it that most of us had not yet experienced. He did not engage us as much as many professors in discussion of specific case situations.

Although Simon had the right to sound very authoritative, he is remembered for downplaying the attention students should pay to his words. Blase Reardon recounts an experience that many students had on the first or second day of a Simon course:

HAS: Young man, what are you doing?

BR: Taking notes.

HAS: You did not pay good money to come here to take notes. You came here to listen to me. This is a 60-minute class. Keep your eyes on me and listen, writing only a cryptic note or two if necessary. At 53 minutes after the hour, signal and I will stop talking. At that point you can write down all the reflective notes or questions that come to you.

The job was not to absorb, but to develop the gumption to think for yourself. Simon's pets among master's and doctoral students were not passive disciples, but potential intellectual sparring partners.

Master's students from different classes experienced Simon's current enthusiasms in research. During GSIA's first decade, Herb was trying to expand what we could say with confidence about how organizations function. The work led in two directions. First were studies to document how business decisions were made. He began with an evaluative analysis of the controllership function in corporations: how it was and how it should be organized. Then came field studies involving three young faculty members that gathered interviews, observations, documents, and taped records of meetings over many months to map the making of complex decisions in different corporate settings.

These field studies did not provide neat additions to theory or crisp advice for practice.[4] But they demonstrated Simon's belief in empirical observation. Like Elliot Smith in his Management of Men course, Herb emphasized that if you want to solve problems of surviving in organizations, you had better look behind labels and models and try to understand how people interact and how systems really work.

The parallel research effort, which took more of Simon's personal time, was the collaboration with Jim March and Harold Guetzkow to assemble from psychology, sociology, political science, and other sources an inventory of tested and testable propositions about behavior in organizations. Ideas and examples from that effort showed up in his classes, and eventually in the book *Organizational Behavior* (March and Simon 1958).

Master's students took different lessons from the exposure. Some absorbed his priority for asking "What is?" before designing what ought to be. Some were struck in ways that continue to spur them to be inquisitive by the range and depth of Herb's curiosity and his abiding interest in how people learn.

Some alumni wish Simon had prepared them better to deal with politics in the workplace. But others found his way of viewing organizations just the ticket for addressing such questions. The Barnard-Simon model, a precursor to today's "stakeholder" formulations, saw organizations as systems of individuals and groups bound together by mutual efforts to offer inducements that would elicit contributions of work, resources, or other kinds of support from one another. Formal descriptions of hierarchies and division of authority and responsibility meant little. The job was to understand and learn to shape and manage networks of informal relationships.

Other concepts also stuck: the distinction that he and Barnard made between effectiveness and efficiency in organizational accomplishment; his interest in aspirations and expectations as the drivers of human behavior; his examples of similarities among management tasks in different institutional settings, such as business vs. government.

As computers came along, Simon became a guide to what they could mean to future managers. Ideas from his 1960 paper for GSIA's tenth anniversary symposium (Simon 1960a) and from his early simulations of human problem solving behavior found their way into class and coffee hour discussions.[5] Could a computer become the chess champion of the world? Would the job of managing shift from motivation and supervision of people to regulating computers that in turn would operate machines and robots? Might jobs in middle management disappear? As Bill Staley watched Disney replace his lifelong employer, U.S. Steel, in the Dow Jones industrial index, he recalled Herb's predicting that with more leisure, mass entertainment would grow into one of the country's largest industries.

But more than specific ideas about organizations, graduates recall more subtle lessons they learned about how to learn and live. Simon's comfort with messy complexity and his emphasis on the human side of organizations and markets shook up engineers like Bill Pounds, later Dean of MIT's Sloan School, who enrolled at GSIA "to learn about mathematics and economics and *only* those two subjects." Simon's bold speculations about computers helped open minds to the idea of startling changes as a natural way of the world and of the need to explore imaginatively and respond creatively.

Some of his strategies for problem solving took root. More master's students were intrigued than turned off by Herb's efforts to state propositions about human behavior as equations. If they doubted the practicality, they admired his preference for simplicity in his formulations. They appreciated that even when he spun out formal models, he emphasized the importance of building them from careful observation of how people really behave. From a graduate school which had perhaps too many salesmen for maximizing, many alumni like Lee O'Nan of Alcoa and John Dimling, CEO of Nielsen Media Research, carried away an appreciation of Simon's arguments in favor of satisficing as a framework for making and reviewing managerial decisions.

Cyrus Friedheim, Vice Chairman of Booz Allen and Hamilton, writes that Herb's value was the example of "a perfectly rational mind with an uncommon ability to listen and respond with hard common sense. It wasn't his business experience ... but his ability to understand so quickly what was important, where we missing the point, how our logic or facts or conclusions fell short. I also valued his ability to communicate so ... that we felt we were his colleagues, not his students. Herb was the ideal consultant, and a model which I have striven to emulate."

He especially drove home a key lesson that successful managers have to master: the need for focus and self-discipline in use of time to get essential work done. The Simon-March "Gresham's law of organization" warned that without great care, attention to the trivial will use up time that should be spent on the truly important. He reinforced the point in quirky ways:

- the suggestion that it is generally a waste of time to read newspapers

- the conviction that traveling teaches less about the world than a few hours in the local public library

- his boasts that he saved time every day, wherever he was, by ordering an almost universally available American cheese sandwich on white bread for lunch.

Humanity and Genius

Even within GSIA's stellar early faculty, even to students who came with superb academic records and egos to match, even before Simon acquired the aura of a Nobel Prize winner, Herb stood out for the quality and range of his intellect. It was intimidating to talk with someone who seemed to know more than you did about most of the things you tried to talk about and who viewed learning zoology, chess, Japanese, ALGOL, or the latest theories of econometrics as easy recreational pursuits. It was awesome to watch him up close, and it could be intimidating if you saw him engaged with other senior faculty in no-holds-barred intellectual debates.

Yet in many settings as students and later as graduates, master's alumni remember most fondly Simon's very human, almost "aw shucks" demeanor. Joe Redding, who met Herb on an airplane soon after he had won the Nobel Prize, commented on how modest and casual he seemed about the award. Tom Bromeley, a successful entrepreneur, remembered Herb as "a light-hearted and merry person who took neither himself nor the world at large overly seriously." As board chair for management game teams, Simon was appreciated for the way he questioned and critiqued. Cy Friedheim again:

He did it in a constructive, supportive way, so we never felt criticized or, worse, humiliated. He was part of the team—a member who said little but communicated tons, a member we could count on to backstop our enthusiasm and inexperience with wisdom and judgment.

His example, a couple of graduates said, made them more human. If Simon could be deal with them without being arrogant, their own tendencies toward arrogance deserved to be repressed.

The Difference Simon Made

I feel a kinship with views of GSIA's master's graduates even though I continued at Carnegie to work toward a doctorate and then become part of the GSIA faculty. I taught behavioral and policy courses, did studies of decision making and of managerial careers, and helped develop the management game. My career has been mostly based in universities—but for the past thirty years as an academic manager and leader: dean, president, trustee. Simon's observational wisdom about life in organizations has helped me diagnose problem situations and work out reasonable answers. His eclectic curiosity and enthusiasm for learning has rubbed off, not in comparable accomplishments, but in a willingness to keep zigging and zagging in new directions.

Three special things stand out to me as legacies that I hope I have lived by and can help pass on.

One was to develop a nose for talent and a passion for nurturing it. Herb had very high standards for how good he wanted students and colleagues to be, but a wonderful tolerance for diversity in what they undertook. Too many "great" professors and executives like to sur-round themselves with acolytes. Simon had an eye for raw talent. When he spotted it, as in students as diverse as Jack Muth and Saras Sarasvathy, he encouraged their curiosity, persistence, and independence. His goal was to help students and colleagues find their own ways.

Second was a missionary zeal to keep people from sealing themselves into comfortable compartments, whether functions, markets, or product lines in a business or the discipline-walled silos of academe. Jack Welch (2001) talks exuberantly about "boundaryless thinking," but Herb Simon exemplified it. Over his fifty years at Carnegie, Simon ragged everyone around him to look beyond the narrow and often fad-dish dimensions of fields like economics or operations research that were comfortable home bases for colleagues. His example kept giving me hope at New York University as I tried to goad a first-rate, but dys-functionally fragmented faculty into meeting the holistic needs of M.B.A. students and at Babson College to achieve mutual respect and real collaboration among humanities, science, and business professors.

Third was Herb's willingness until the end to keep emphasizing that the world is changing. Few people who have speculated recently about the future of business education have done as well as Simon. At GSIA's fiftieth-anniversary symposium he called for a completely fresh start—an exercise to design a new school from scratch, to address a freshly defined menu of future needs. He named three, but left the way for others to be added. His three were preservation and management of the natural environment, coping with the continued and ever expanding electronic revolution, and learning to manage organizations that can deal with frictions around human loyalties that are showing up all over the globe. Who else has been so succinctly prescient?

Notes

1. Many of Simon's experiences at GSIA are summarized from his memories and comments of others by Andrea Gabor in *The Capitalist Philosophers* (Times Business, 2000).

2. Meyers came back to GSIA after serving as chief executive of American Motors, and Thorne after being involved with the establishment of Litton Industries and later Scionics Corporation, a company of his own.

3. At least once, this resulted in accusations of insider trading and the very emotional situation of a student team deciding they needed to hire outside counsel to defend themselves before a hastily convened faculty court.

4. A wonderful case of information overload! Man-years and mountains of data produced the molehill—just one article: Cyert and March 1958.

5. See also Simon 1960b.

References

Cohen, Kalman J., et al. 1964. *The Carnegie Tech Management Game: An Experiment in Business Education*. Irwin.

Cyert, R. M., W. R. Dill, and J. G. March. 1958. The role of expectations in business decision making. *Administrative Science Quarterly*, December: 307–340.

March, James G., and Herbert A. Simon. 1958. *Organizations*. Wiley.

Simon, Herbert A. 1960a. The corporation: Will it be managed by machines? In Melvin Anshen and G. L. Bach, eds., *Management and Corporations 1985*. McGraw-Hill.

Simon, Herbert A. 1960b. *The New Science of Management Decisions*. Harper and Row.

Simon, Herbert A. 1967. The business school: A problem in organizational design. *Journal of Business Studies*, February: 1–16.

Simon, Herbert A. 1991. *Models of My Life*. Basic Book.

Welch, Jack, with John A. Byrne. 2001. *Jack: Straight from the Gut*. Warner Books.

A Very Reasonable Objective Still Beyond Our Reach: Economics as an Empirically Disciplined Social Science

Giovanni Dosi

It is well in tune with the example of Herb Simon to pick sound intellectual controversies irrespective of prevailing academic doctrines, "self-evident" assumptions, and entrenched prejudices. I deeply believe that continuing to do so is a way of honoring his memory which he would have wholeheartedly encouraged. And this also what I shall try to do in the following.

My point of departure is the Mattioli Lectures (Simon 1997b), a recent sharp summary of good parts of his weltanschauung in the domain of economics (as we know, he has been a major maitre-à-penser also in a few other disciplines). And they entail the derived advantage of a somewhat "revisionist" critique by Ollie Williamson (2000a). I will still start from the latter and his succinct outline of the "Carnegie research program," arguing (i) that a good deal of what in my view went wrong since the early Simon's years has to do with the prevailing "ontology" of microeconomics agents, (ii) that an "empirically disciplined microeconomics" of the sort advocated by Simon requires a radical departure from such a representation of the ultimate drivers of behaviors, and (iii) that an evolutionary perspective is in a good position to undertake such a task.

Multiple, probably conflicting streams of research depart from the rich roots of Simon's Carnegie in the 1950s and the 1960s. Indeed, historians of economic thought are likely to identify the Carnegie Institute of Technology (later Carnegie-Mellon University), as well as the Cowles Commission, as major springs of ideas and methods developed thereafter into the core of contemporary economics (for all the good and all the bad that goes with it).

Such springs were so rich that many alternative rivers could have been notionally alimented. In my view, it is a cruel irony that the major river which emerged took a course deeply at odds with the research program of the founders. But so it went, notwithstanding Herb Simon's unending determination to work, first, "for the 'hardening' of the social sciences, so that they will better equipped with the tools they need for their difficult research tasks" (Simon 1997, p. 196) and, together, second, for solid empirical groundings of purported micro-behaviors, casual mechanisms, aggregate dynamics. Superficially, the former part went better than the most optimistic expectations half a century ago. In fact, things are a bit more complicated, and Simon kept screaming foul every time "hardening" simply meant proving theorems without the slightest reference to empirical phenomena.

On the latter point, the picture is mixed. An impressive work has been done on "bottom-up" empirical analysis concerning e.g. individual and organizational behaviors, innovation and technological change, industrial history, comparative institutional dynamics, etc. However, it is equally true that these diverse streams of empirical investigation and related theorizing did little to scratch the core of a paradigm which "omitted any serious testing of the validity of the assumptions of the model itself, even the kind of historical, experimental and anecdotal testing that we find in Smith and Marshall" (Simon 1997, p. 21).

Ultimately, such core of the neoclassical paradigm lingers upon the twin hypotheses of microeconomic rationality and collective equilibrium. True: many recent developments have tried to relax the former, but often they have done so in ways that would not pass any Simon-type check of empirical plausibility on how people actually behave, adapt, learn, etc.

At the same time, taken-for-granted assumptions on equilibrium most often continue to rest on the sheer faith in some unspecified process of adaptation and/or market selection.

This notwithstanding, ever simple exercises in (parsimonious!) "relaxation of rationality" together with a more explicit acknowledgment of institutions and organizations have yielded impressive fruits. One of them is the so-called New Institutional Economics. (For present purposes, see Williamson 2000a,b.)

But is that the only possible river flowing from Simon's Carnegie springs? Certainly not. There is at least another, more radical, river originating there which is explicitly *evolutionary* (in the sense given to the word by Richard Nelson, Sidney Winter, and many other like-minded scholars) and *institutionalist* (although in a meaning broader than that implied by "New Institutional Economics." (See below. For more details I am forced to refer to Dosi 2000, especially chapters 11, 12, and 23; to Dosi and Winter 2002; and to Nelson and Sampat 2001.)

In order to highlight overlappings, differences, and subsequent developments, I will follow part of the checklist of topics put forward in Williamson 2000a and compare the "Simon/Carnegie" perspective (SCP), transaction-cost economics (the central tenet of "New Institutionalism"), and what I shall call Post-Simonian Evolutionary Economics (PSEE). Williamson's points on transaction-cost economics (TCE) will be taken nearly verbatim, while I shall change every now and then according to my own views his reconstruction of SCP. The interpretation of PSEE is obviously my own.

In order to keep the controversy well alive, I will add scattered critical remarks on both orthodoxy and TCE. But I am sure that my friend Ollie Williamson will eagerly find a venue to reply.

Let me begin by focusing on some central, and diverse, underlying hypotheses from the different theories on "human nature."

Bounded Rationality

One does not need to say much about the fundamental contribution of SCP in this area: "Bounded rationality, a rationality that is consistent with our knowledge of actual human choice behavior, assumes that the decision maker much search for alternatives, has egregiously incomplete and inaccurate knowledge about the consequences of actions and chooses actions that are expected to be satisfactory (attain targets while satisfying constraints)." (Simon 1997, p. 17)

Conversely, TCE takes on board "bounded rationality" in much more homeopathic quantities and tends to reduce it to contract incompleteness (Williamson 2000a, p. 14). At the opposite extreme, PSEE fully subscribe the SCP perspective, and, if anything, it is even ready to abandon the notion of *procedural* rationality whenever the evidence on systematic cognitive biases warrants it. (For a more elaborate argument along these lines, see Dosi, Marengo, and Fagiolo 2003.) Indeed, there is a sense in which the very term "bounded rationality" might be misleading insofar as it hints at some notional benchmarks of "full" rationality—whatever that means. But in fact it means very little outside the simple "closed and small worlds" (paraphrasing classic Savage), made of simple decisions over a finite menu of known choices, to which forerunners like Savage himself were careful to confine their axiomatics of "rational choice."

All this, of course, applies if one agrees, as I do, with Herb Simon's teaching that any *descriptive* theory of deliberation (or lack of it) and behavior ought to be robustly nested into corresponding empirical generalizations from e.g. cognitive psychology, experimental economics, organizational studies, sociology, etc.

The other interpretation of rationality as an "objective" behavioral property of equilibrium—the "as ... if" assumption—has equally been target of the critiques of Simon and others, including prominently Sid Winter. In this spirit, just consider the following quotation:

... the objections (against profit maximization) rest on the assumption, much stronger than any in biological Darwinism, that only profit maximizers can survive. Again, it is clear that the issue has to be decided by empirical inquiry. In the biologic world at least, many organisms survive that are not maximizers but that operate as far less that the highest empirical efficiency. Their survival is not threatened as long as no other organisms has evolved that can challenge the possession of their specific niches. Analogously, since there is no reason to suppose that every business firm is challenged by an optimally efficient competitor, survival only requires meeting the competition. In a system in which there are innumerable rents, of a long-term and short-term duration, even egregious sub-optimality may permit survival.   (Simon 1997a, p. 283)

Incidentally, there is a widespread view that "bounded rationality" is theoretically sloppy and undisciplined since "anything goes," the adagio being that "there is one way of doing things right and an infinite number of ways of doing them wrong." What I think, in tune with Herb Simon, is quite the opposite: there is an infinite number of ways of setting up formally correct maximization problems, just exploiting the degrees of freedom on functional forms and choice of the arguments that the theory allows, which have little to do with evidence at hand while there are very few, hard to find, empirically sound generations.

Let me also try to avoid here some possible misunderstandings. Mainstream discipline has indeed produced a great deal of empirical microeconomics, some of which is admirable at the technical level and some of which is quite informative. Indeed, the latter tends to be true in proportion as the authors let the data speak (under moderate theoretical guidance) and do not overly encumber the empirical analysis with hyper-rationality assumptions about the agents. Relatedly, in my view, the fictive characters of the assumptions about the agents roughly appears in three genres of models and empirical exercises.

A first class involves micro "rationality" assumptions that are trivially common-sense and/or whose relaxation would in fact strengthen the qualitative conclusions of the model. On theoretical level, what comes immediately to mind are models à la Stiglitz and colleagues. Indeed,

I conjecture that the qualitative properties of the conclusions—on e.g. the implications of asymmetric information, etc.—would *a fortiori* hold if the (relatively undemanding) rationality assumptions were loosen up. (See my introduction to Dosi 2000.) I don't have much of a substantive argument against empirical investigations whose "micro-foundations" ultimately entail propositions of the kind "it is better to be rich than poor," "it is better being healthy than sick," "one generally chooses, other things being equal, more profitable rather than less profitable courses of actions," and so on. I most often find irritating the ways these propositions are wrapped up into an unnecessary baroque mathematical language (and too often by young scholars), but let it be it: they are generally innocent vis-à-vis the empirical findings.

A second class of empirical investigations is *prima facie* much less "innocent." The canonic format is aiming at "structural forms," possibly deriving reduced forms models and finally testing particular restrictions upon utility functions, productions functions and the like. As it happens, all these often more baroque efforts sometimes yield, fortunately, exercises not too different from the previous genre. That is, even if you left out the "micro-foundation efforts," the main qualitative results would nonetheless robustly hold. An example out of many: wouldn't most of Zvi Griliches's findings on the empirics of innovation, patenting, etc. apply even without the jingles and bells of standard production functions, maximizations of expected returns, etc.? I think they would, and they would even better shine out as genuine, newly discovered, "stylized facts."

Conversely, think of many of the efforts that have gone into estimating utility functions consistent with micro consumption data. Here, a sort of "pre-Copernican" epistemology comes fully into play: as you bind yourself to never question the core max $U(.,.,..)$ paradigm, you are driven to build as many epicycles as you need to accommodate the evidence.

In most respects, the third class of "empirical" (?) analyses is the horror version of the former. An archetype that I like to quote is an article from the 1980s, whose exact reference my unconscious repeatedly censured, set to show which type of utility functions American workers must have had in the 1930s. After all, everyone knows (?!) that (i) unvoluntary employment does *not* exist; (ii) people have rational forward-looking expectations; (iii) all empirical observations are equilibrium ones. Given that, it might have been quite rational for a good percentage of workers not to work, expecting the much higher wages after World War II (which of course everyone knew it was going to happen, with the Americans on the winning side). But, then, the puzzle is why so many Americans enjoyed so little of their idle time, preferring e.g. to queue for a bowl of stinking soup rather than borrowing against their future income and have fun in Monte Carlo.

Of course, this would be a bad joke about psychiatric disorders, were it not taken seriously by a good part of our discipline (and indeed by far too many macroeconomists).

Notice, in any case, the historical change in the relative frequencies of academic contributions and relative academic respectabilities of the different genres over the last century of economic thought. Major contributors to economic theory in the nineteenth, early-twentieth-century "orthodoxy," such as Marshall, deeply felt the challenge of "consonance with empirical data" as a criterion of theory evaluation. All that turned out to be increasingly rejected by later economic theorists as diverse as e.g. Samuelson and Hicks, among others, who saw microeconomic theory basically as a set of "tools" to be "applied" within a broader construction going from some axiomatic of micro behaviors to macro "laws of motions" and "predictions" (whatever that meant). At such a crucial divide, around the 1950s and the 1960s, just recall, amongst the most candid voices, Fritz Machlup claiming that microeconomic theory did *not* have anything to do with e.g. how firms went about making decisions, etc. and that genuine efforts ought to be put in "explaining away the data" insofar as they contradicted standard micro assumptions. In fact, things have not gotten much better since that time.

Motivations, Self-Interest, and, More Generally, the Underlying Anthropology

Ultimately, I believe, this is one of the crucial points that make the rest of any social theory turn one way or the other.

In the Christian Middle Ages the dominant anthropology—powerful, elegant and totally shielded from refutation—meant interpreting the ultimate driver of behaviors as the endless fight between sin and grace, temptation and salvation. Nowadays, it seems, one of the prominent weltanschauung is the familiar one—equally general and equally shielded from refutation—grounded on ubiquitous self-interest as the basic motivational force.

The SCP painstakingly began to investigate a multiplicity of motivational drivers which certainly include, yes, self-seeking ones, but also altruism, sheer acceptance of authority, and "docility in its sense of teachability or educability" (Simon 1997, p. 41).

Indeed, interpreting all that as "frailty of motive" (Williamson 2000a), as TCE appears to do is, in my view, missing the point. Together, the emphasis on opportunism—i.e., "self-interest with guile" (Williamson 1985)—places the anthropology of TCE rather too near orthodoxy for my personal tastes. Williamson puts it bluntly (2000a, p. 15): "opportunism ... takes us deep into the structure of contract and organization in ways that frailty of motive does not. Accordingly, even if frailty of motive describes day-to-day activity most of the time, candid reference to opportunism serves to uncover strategic issues that are ignored only at peril."

At the opposite extreme, the way I see, PSEE faces the urgent task of setting on firmer grounds its own breed of institutionalism whereby institutions themselves are a quasi-primitive concept of the theory rather than a derived one stemming from e.g. self-seeking rationality *cum* transaction-cost considerations. After all, we are all born with a sort of "ontological dependency" on institutions—initially the family, and later also larger social groups. We have all had our preferences and visions shaped by various authorities that we trusted or that were simply imposed upon us—parents, teachers, and others.

Relatedly, "most of that we know, most of what we are able to do, is acquired from our social environments from the time of birth on into adulthood. Among the 'facts' that we 'know,' or at least believe, there are very few that we have established ourselves and on the basis of evidence that we have ourselves and reasoning that we have carried out" (Simon 1997, p. 40).

"Docility" and (possibly imperfect) adaptation entail both a motivational component—the goals of organizations/institutions become at least in part our own—and a cognitive one—shaping the very identity of the actors. All this has led Jim March to suggest that humans a good deal of their time operate under a "logic of appropriateness" rather than a "logic of consequences." That is, our behaviors are driven by questions like "What would a good X (a father, a soldier, a priest, a Taliban) do in these circumstances?" rather than the more instrumental question "What would I gain according to the different courses of action?"

Of course, there is no clear-cut line between the domains of applicability of the two logics and in the overlappings always lingers the possibility of opportunism, "malicious strategizing," or even straightforwardly criminal behavior. Simply, I share with Herb Simon the skepticism about the notion that it is this shaded zone, where crooks and game theorists alike prosper, which justify the very existence of organizations (as opposed to "markets").

Two major points are worth emphasizing here.

First, following Sid Winter's comments on an earlier draft, I fully accept to weaken the earlier statement on "institutions as primitives" to the wilder one on "institutions as quasi-primitives." As Winter forcefully pointed out, over the longer run no entity is a true "primitive." All entities—including, of course, the writer and the readers of this paper, but also the institutions where we have all been nested—are "meta-stable" and bound to disappear with probability one as time goes to infinity (in most circumstances, well short of that), within a grand dynamical system where the candidates to be "primitive properties" might just be some properties of the long-run dynamic itself. Having acknowledged that, however, on shorter time scales—often corresponding to the scale of individual decisions, socio-economic interactions, institutional dynamics, etc.—the assumptions of institutions as *first-approximation* primitives generally holds. (In order to illustrate all this with some caricature examples, I will turn to support the opposite view entailing very "plastic" institutions subject to easy historical change whenever I will suddenly observe, e.g., the "representative" Afghan male respecting women's rights, modal voters of the current Italian prime minister paying taxes as a painful but dignifying duty, and American Protestants enjoying sex with innocent happiness.) In fact, over time scales that are typically longer than those over which most economic processes occur, a variety of institutions happen to be at the same time precious "social resources," path-dependent "carriers of history," and major determinants of individual and collective beliefs/ "cognitive frames"/expectations. (Within an enormous literature, see Nelson and Sampat 2001; David 1994; Dosi 2000, chapter 23; March 1994.)

Second, let me stress that "rationality" (or lack of it) bears complicated, still mostly unexplained, links with "deliberation." Certainly, *procedural efficiency* in problem solving often goes indeed together with *lack* of explicitly deliberation, with the development of *routinized action repertoires* and with the incremental refinements of routines themselves. (See Nelson and Winter 1982; Dosi and Egidi, reproduced in Dosi 2000; Cohen et al. 1996; Winter's chapter in this volume.[1])

Having said all that, I have no difficulty in admitting the persistent delays in operationalizing the foregoing ideas within PSEE.

However, I do believe, this is where one of the ultimate microfoundational challenges rest: and in its pursuit the conservatism of old researchers does not help in curbing the cowardice of most young ones.[2]

Processes Matter, in General, and Selection Processes, in Particular

That "processes matter" is a statement about which, *prima facie*, SCP, TCE, and PSEE agree. It is certainly a fundamental methodological maxim of PSEE: as is argued in Dosi and Winter 2002, if you need to explain why variable *x* has the value that it has at some time *t*, tell a convincing dynamic story on how it got such a value; if you need to explain why entity *a* became what it is, likewise, reconstruct the process through which it emerged and, possibly, how it was selected against competing entities.

It would also be fascinating to obtain particular organizational forms as results of explicit selection processes involving different governance arrangements, etc., whether the story is told in a qualitative or a formal mode. And, intuition suggests, this ought to be a field where TCE and PSEE have overlappings and synergies. Why is then that one find relatively few explicit *process stories*, even within TCE (let alone the rest of mainstream economics)?

My conjecture is that even TCE is too afraid of "rugged" selection landscape, endogeneity of selection criteria, multiple equilibria, path-dependencies, lock-ins, etc. Conversely, PSEE is generally inclined to assume that where the process will end up is neither clear to the agent nor to the analyst before one runs it through. On the contrary, TSE makes a lot of the foresight abilities of the agents. Indeed, if processes can be fully run *ex ante* through the heads of the agents (and agents have the *same* true models-of-the-world, and so on) you will never observe actual selection processes, since everyone will instantaneously converge to "rational expectation" equilibria of some kind. Certainly, TCE and PSEE agree that (at most!) selection operates in favor of some available (or feasible?) *fitter*, rather than an unconditional fittest, entities but the argument looses strength the more unbiased foresight one puts into the head of the agents themselves.

Foresight

One immediately detects here the same Carnegie root but two opposite branches. Very few social scientists, I believe, do not acknowledge the importance of motives and expectations (right or wrong) for the understanding of what individuals and organizations actually do. Hence also Herb Simon's repeated urge, since long time ago, to understand and model what goes on "in a people's heads." As it happened, one answer to that invitation has been the easy one: "Of course in people's heads runs the true model of the economy, precisely the same as the one I am presenting here in the model that follows." Conversely, a major disadvantage of those scientists searching for a different answer has been that they began to investigate what was *actually* going on in heads of people or in the metaphorical heads of organizations. And the search is still going on, slowly, with a lot of dead-ends, often under the scorn by respectable theorists who know the answer even before looking.[3]

In which camp does TCE belong?

In my view, quite a few of TCE ideas are likely to withhold genuinely "Simonesque" investigations. Relatedly, I cannot fully understand why TCE tends to overlook possible bridges with PSEE at both levels of analysis of micro cognition/behaviors, etc. (i.e. where units of analysis such as organizational routines rest) and of market-driven selection dynamics amongst competing organizational forms.

By the same token, I find quite dangerous the use of notions like that of (ir)remediability ("... if you observe a dominant organizational form, trust that it is the best *feasible* one. Otherwise, be sure someone would have seized the opportunity to construct more efficient governance alignment ..."). For my tastes, it is a notion far too near the Panglossian spirit of Chicago and surroundings, against which Herb

Simon restlessly fought: we do not live in the best possible world, and it might not be in the best use of our scientific abilities to assume that we do.

But let me go back to the issues of forecasts and expectations. Herb Simon was amongst the first to acknowledge the formidable tasks involved in the identification of a reasonable alternative to "rational" expectations, while fully aware of the crudeness of simple adaptive ones. I never asked him which of the extremes he would have chosen at gun-point. However, I believe that with a lot of qualifications he would have chosen the latter. This, of course, not because he believed that people were actually using e.g. devices like moving averages between yesterday and the day before in order to predict tomorrow, but rather as part of a general acknowledgment of the inertial features of our cognitive frames and information processing systems. And, indeed, the empirical properties of the latter turned out to be another field where Herb Simon gave path-breaking contributions.

Interestingly, Simon (1997) emphasizes also the pioneering works of George Katona, undertaken as early as the 1940s, painstakingly trying to identify empirical regularities in micro behavioral patterns (concerning consumption, saving, etc.) and expectation formation. It is a type of investigation that we should re-discover and refine, with a "bottom-up" respect for the evidence in tune with Katona's original investigations.

More generally, I do believe that an increasingly urgent task regards a much more systematic understanding of the links between evolutionary microfoundations and aggregate ("macro") regularities. In turn, all this requires also the identification of a few "stylized facts" on modal behaviors regarding e.g. corporate pricing and investments, consumers' patterns of demand, intertemporal choices, etc.

Some Conclusions

There are two major components, in my view, to the persisting lag between the "empirically based microeconomics" advocated by Herb

Simon, on one hand, and the achievement of the current state-of-the-art in economics, on the other—even in not-too-mainstream perspectives, such as transaction-cost economics (and the largely overlapping New Institutional Economics).

The first component is either a stubborn commitment to some postulated principle of microrationality, or, to the same effect, massive departures from it which however support set-ups whereby in equilibrium agents behave as if they were fully "rational" (cf. the widespread use in this vein of many evolutionary games models).

Together, second, all this goes hand in hand with a dramatic under-investment in humble, albeit theory-inspired, investigations into *what people and organizations actually do*, through a variety of methods, bridging across disciplinary boundaries to cognitive and social psychology, organization sciences, etc.

I have also advocated above that "Post-Simonian Evolutionary Economics" might be quite apt to face the challenges set out by Herb Simon. It does so insofar as, first, it embodies an "anthropology" quite richer than the running archetype of *Homo economicus*; second, it is fully committed to *process stories* about individual and collective learning, innovation and adaptation; and, third, it is genuinely committed to the empirics of cognition, decision making and behaviors rather than "armchair axiomatics."

Whether such a research program will succeed only time will tell. In any case, I can hardly accept a memory of Herb Simon just as a purported precursor of "quasi-rational" adaptation models. Rather, I prefer to hold him as a gigantic intellectual figure who relentlessly pursued scientific reason in the analysis of human behaviors and social organizations in an epoch where theorists found it particularly difficult to distant themselves from clumsy introspections of greedy shopkeepers (with no offense to the many shopkeepers who are indeed good-souled).

By the same token, I hold with a lot of pride that, few years ago, I and a couple of co-authors had a paper on industrial dynamics rejected by

Econometrica with one of the referees suggesting that publication there or anywhere else would have "brought back the discussion of industrial change to the Dark Ages of Herbert Simon." For sure, the integrity in the pursuit of knowledge has its costs: in any case, also on this ground, Herb Simon has been an example of total indifference to fashions and academic conformism.

Notes

1. Stan Metcalfe also signaled in his comments to an earlier draft of this paper the original contributions of G. Shackle on "bounded" rationality as a serendipitous, powerful, device to free us from the overwhelming tyranny of calculation, allowing humans to devote (at least in principle) some of their time to search and creativity.

2. Pernicious misunderstandings might stem from the overlapping appearance of diverse "evolutionary" labels in economics and social sciences at large. (For more detailed discussions, see Dosi 2000 and Dosi and Winter 2002.) For the purposes of this short work, let me just recall that "Post-Simonian Evolutionary Economics" (PSEE), as defined here, attempts to span well beyond the territory of "evolutionary games" and indeed tries to take on board essential insights from cognitive and social psychology, experimental economics, organizational sciences, etc. on how agents actually behave, learn, interact, etc. Conversely, it strikes me as rather bizarre that quite a few fashionable "evolutionary" approaches to socio-economic phenomena tend to entail rather Panglossian interpretations of the purported optimality of even the most backward characters of human behaviors and cultures.

3. Here I want to emphasize my nearly total ignorance of the early cultural and sociological history of the interaction with between Herb Simon, Muth, Lucas, etc. Historians of economic analysis are much more suited to the task. The only point I want to make is that, for sure, Herb Simon has been a major driver urging at least a couple of generation of economists to "take microfoundations seriously" including, of course, expectation formation.

References

Augier, M., and J. G. March. 2001. Conflict of interests in theories of organizations: Herbert Simon and Oliver Williamson. *Journal of Management and Governance* 5: 223–230.

Augier, M., and J. G. March, eds. 2002. *The Economics of Choice, Change and Organizations: Essays in Memory of Richard M. Cyert*. Elgar.

Cohen, M. D., R. Burkhart, G. Dosi, M. Egidi, L. Marengo, M. Warglien, and S. Winter. 1996. Routines and other recurring action patterns of organizations: contemporary research issues, *Industrial and Corporate Change* 5: 653–698.

David, Paul A. 1994. Why are institutions the "carriers of history"? Path dependence and the evolution of conventions, organizations and institutions. *Structural Change and Economic Dynamics* 5: 205–220.

Dosi, G. 2000. *Innovation, Organization and Economic Dynamics*. Elgar.

Dosi, G., L. Marengo, and G. Fagiolo. 2003. Learning in Evolutionary Environments. Forthcoming in K. Dopfer, ed., *Principles of Evolutionary Economics*. Cambridge University Press.

Dosi, G., and S. G. Winter. 2002. Interpreting economic change: Evolution, structures and games. In Augier and March 2002.

March, J. 1994. *A Primer on Decision-Making: How Decisions Happen*. Free Press.

Nelson, R. R., and B. Sampat. 2001. Making sense of institutions as a factor shaping economic performance. *Journal of Economic Behavior and Organization* 44: 31–54.

Nelson, R. R., and S. Winter. 1982. *An Evolutionary Theory of Economic Change*. Belknap.

Simon, H. A. 1997a. *Models of Bounded Rationality*, volume III. MIT Press.

Simon, H. A. 1997b. *An Empirically Based Microeconomics*. Cambridge University Press.

Williamson, O. E. 1985. *The Economic Institutions of Capitalism*. Free Press.

Williamson, O. E. 2000a. Empirical Microeconomics: Another Perspective. Working paper, Haas School of Business, Univeristy of California, Berkeley.

Williamson, O. E. 2000b. The new institutional economics: Taking stock, looking ahead. *Journal of Economic Literature* 38: 595–613.

Lessons I Learned from Herbert A. Simon and His Friends: A Reflection on My Years at the Graduate School of Industrial Administration

Julian Feldman

Herbert A. Simon, his friends, and their writings affected almost every major professional decision I made in the last fifty years. From them I learned many things about style and substance. I will always be grateful for their friendship and their efforts to educate me.

Detours Can Lead to a Better Path

Before World War II, Simon worked at the Bureau of Public Administration at the University of California at Berkeley. After he finished his work there, he had hoped to get a faculty appointment at Berkeley; but he wasn't offered a position. So he went on to Illinois Tech and Carnegie Tech and a Nobel Prize.

At a reception for new faculty members at Berkeley in the fall of 1959, the president of the university and several senior faculty members made comments about Simon when they found out that I had just graduated from Carnegie Tech. I still remember the comments of the long-time Dean of the School of Social Welfare who told me that the biggest mistake that Berkeley made during his lifetime was not offering Simon a junior faculty position.

One of Simon's collaborators influenced my own detour. I was an 18-year-old freshman physics major at the Illinois Institute of Technology. One day I arrived early for my morning class and stopped to listen at the open door of a classroom to a lecture in a class on American government.

The lecturer's recollections of actual government experience intrigued me. Whenever I arrived early that semester, I continued to eavesdrop on this lecturer. I didn't find out until later that the lecturer, Donald W. Smithburg, was a former colleague and collaborator of Simon and that Simon had been on the faculty at Illinois Tech.

I was having some difficulty with my choice of major even before I took a course in physics. And here was this political science lecturer making the study of government seem so attractive. When Illinois Tech didn't renew my freshman scholarship, I transferred to another school and became a political science major. Eventually I wound up in a master's program in political science at the University of Chicago.

Most of my courses in the M.A. program in political science were conventional political science: political theory, comparative government, public administration. One of my electives was a course in planning taught in the Committee on Planning. One of the readings in this course was in *Administrative Behavior*. I found the reading very interesting and an interesting contrast to the material in the traditional course in public administration I had taken in the political science department. I might have done some reading in *Public Administration* too. The material in *Administrative Behavior* and *Public Administration* must have impressed me a lot because when I decided to continue my graduate education to get out of the Army three months early, I only applied to one school—the one Simon was at.

Style

A Little Personal Attention Goes a Long Way
In the fall of 1956, my wife, my daughter, and I moved to Pittsburgh, and I started the Ph.D. program at the Graduate School of Industrial Administration (GSIA). My wife was happy that I was out of the Army, but she was unhappy about moving to Pittsburgh. So I told her that we would probably only stay in Pittsburgh for a year.

One of my classes in the fall of 1956 was Simon's class on organizations. The text was *Administrative Behavior*. Four weeks into the semester, Simon asked me to come to his office. I was not sure what he wanted to talk about. In the fall of 1956, GSIA had admitted four or five students into the Ph.D. program who had received master's degrees elsewhere. Until this time, virtually all of the doctoral students had received M.S. degrees at GSIA. Four weeks into the semester, all of these "master's degrees elsewhere" students had left except me. So Simon asked me if I was happy and if I was staying. I was flattered by the questions and his personal interest in me. I told him that I would stay. Actually I was afraid of what the Army would do to me if I left the program before completing at least a year.

The personal attention and support I received from Simon, Jim March, Dick Cyert, and Allen Newell were important factors in my decision to stay at GSIA beyond my one-year time horizon and to finish the program.

Enthusiastic Teachers Have a Major Impression on Students

What do I remember from the one class I took with Simon? Simon was a very enthusiastic teacher. He wanted your full commitment to the class. So he warned us to "come on time or don't come at all." He wanted us to take our reading seriously—anything worth reading is worth reading at least three times. While I do not remember anything specific about papers or exams, I clearly remember his enthusiasm and a couple of pithy pieces of advice.

Sometimes Simon got carried away, but his enthusiasm was an important part of his personality and an important part of his ability to attract converts to his ideas. The classic Simon over-enthusiasm story is an article on operations research written in the late 1950s in which Simon predicted that computer programs would become a chess champion, prove an interesting mathematical theorem, etc. These things happened. They just required more computing power, more money, and more effort than Simon imagined in the late 1950s.

Give Your Student Your Full Attention

I have never met anybody who could grasp the essence of a problem more quickly. I have never met anybody who could come up with so many very good suggestions about the problem more quickly. We cannot all be as insightful and profound as Simon, but we can give our students the same complete attention that Simon gave in every meeting with his students.

Whatever You Do, Do It Well, But Don't Overdo

Sometime during my 1956–1959 stay at Carnegie Tech, Simon was asked to serve as the outside member on a master's exam in studio art. So he took a week off and went to the library and read up on art. Was he concerned about being embarrassed? I think he just believed that whatever you do, you should do well. Like anything that's worth reading is worth reading three times.

The other side of the coin is "don't overdo." I was struggling to complete my thesis in the spring of 1959. One day, Simon asked me how I was doing, and I told him that I was struggling with some fine points of the argument. His advice was to wrap it up. It will not be the last piece of work you do. Finish it up and get out. Simon would never be satisfied with anything less than very good work. He thought that I had made my point, and he just didn't believe in overdoing.

Substance

The Value of Anecdotal Evidence in Gaining Adherents and in Studying the Behavior of Individuals, Groups, and Organizations

I found the anecdotes in *Administrative Behavior* to be memorable and important. For me the anecdotes were an easy way to remember important concepts.

From time to time, I continue to refer students, colleagues, and acquaintances to these anecdotes. For an example of the impact of role on decisions, I suggest they look at the Hetch Hetchy story: An administrator takes over his boss's job while the boss is away. In his new capacity the administrator turns down requests he had previously made with the comment that "from up here ... things don't look the same as they do from down there" (p. 214).

Another story from *Administrative Behavior* that I refer people to is the Ian Hamilton story (p. 237). This story is particularly appropriate when somebody is recruiting an assistant or a replacement for an assistant. Hamilton is the Deputy Quartermaster-General of the British Army in India. He works very hard alongside his boss. His boss is reassigned to Europe, and Hamilton is promoted to Quartermaster-General. But no funds are available for a deputy. Hamilton thinks he'll never be able to do the job alone, but he soon realized that most of his time as deputy was spent proposing and justifying choices to his boss. Now all he had to do was make decisions. No need for long memos considering alternatives and justifying choices.

The Importance of Experimental Data to the Study of Behavior

During my first semester at GSIA, I attended with Jim March and Ed Feigenbaum a one-evening-a-week tutorial on experimental psychology given by Lee Gregg, a faculty member in the Psychology Department. This was my introduction to experiments as a research vehicle in psychology. I think Simon arranged the tutorial.

In another semester or two, I took Jim March's course in experimental psychology. The goal here was to design an experiment, to execute the experiment, and to write it up. This course was my introduction to hands-on experimental psychology. The experiment I ran in this course morphed into the experiments I ran for my dissertation.

The Importance of "Thinking Aloud" Protocols, and Computer Programs as a Medium for Representing Complex Models

To try to obtain some insight into the behavior of subjects in my experiments, I adopted the technique that Newell and Simon were using to gain insight into the behavior of subjects solving logic problems. To provide Newell and Simon with information on the thought processes of the subjects, the experimenter asked the subjects to "think aloud" while they were solving the problem. These protocols provided the basis for the model of human behavior Newell and Simon proposed in the General Problem Solver.

Newell and Simon and their students used the protocols to obtain the information and used computer programs as the medium for construction of complex, realistic models of behavior.

Organizational Development

You Can Create a Distinguished Academic Unit in a Relatively Brief Period of Time ... but It Is Not Easy

G. L. Bach and Simon created a first-class business school in the Graduate School of Industrial Administration in the years 1947–1956.

Their accomplishment really impressed me. So when Jim March invited me to join him in 1964 to set up a new School of Social Sciences at the new campus of the University of California at Irvine, I thought it would be feasible and great fun to try to do what Bach and Simon had done at Carnegie Tech. But I was not a sufficiently careful observer of the process that created GSIA. I only realized after my experiences at UC Irvine that the creation of a new university with a new program in social sciences was a major, major effort. And that creating a new school within the context of an established university might be easier than creating a new school in the context of a new university. Maybe all's well that ends well. Social Sciences at UCI eventually became a very good and exciting school. And my other effort at school construction—Information and Computer Science at UCI—has also prospered. In retrospect, the development of both of these organizations required more time and more players than I anticipated.

Heuristics of Public Administration

Robert E. Goodin

In recalling his great theoretical contributions—to economics, to cognitive science, to organization theory and so on—we sometimes forget that Herb Simon's interests in all these fields grew out of some very practical experiences of public administration. His close-quarter observation of the Milwaukee city recreation department lay the groundwork for his classic study of administrative behavior (Simon 1947, 1999). From that Ur-text, all the rest of Simon's enormous corpus grew, often in highly technical and theoretical directions. But his theorizing was always empirically grounded, and his technical work always ultimately linked to some very practical concerns. Through it all, Simon's interest in public affairs remained undaunted.

Herb Simon was proud to describe himself, in his last address to the American Political Science Association, as having "treasonably defected to my political science origins, in order to defend our political institutions against the imperialism of utility maximization, competitive markets and privatization" (Simon 2000, p. 750). In honoring his memory, I want to return to that lecture (the last I heard him give) and expand upon its themes—often merely by recalling what Simon had himself said half a century or more before. Of course, to suggest that Simon forgot more than the rest of us know is a compliment Herb himself would not have accepted lightly, bristling as he doubtless would have at the suggestion that he had done any such thing!

Neoclassical economists, Simon's bête noir, tend to represent the contrast between markets and politics as a contrast between free-market exchange and command in hierarchical organizations. But that cannot be right. For, as Simon long emphasized, markets are replete with organizations, too. The real contrast between markets and politics is not between markets and organizations but, rather, between organizations public and private.

The differences between public and private organizations, in turn, lie in the "premises" or "maxims" upon which agents in those respective sorts of organizations act. Those are connected with the different "roles" in which public and private servants are acting, and the different considerations that are appropriate for occupants of each role to take into account. Simon (1947/1957, pp. xxx–xxxi) said as much in the preface to *Administrative Behavior*'s second edition. But those comments seem latterly to have been forgotten, perhaps even by Simon (1999, p. 118).

Linking Simon's earlier work on public administration to his later preoccupation with heuristics, I conclude by sketching some "heuristics of public administration" which might be appropriate decision premises in the public (but not private) sector. These could equally well be dubbed "maxims of public administration"—ironically, maxims of broadly the same sort that Simon so famously ridiculed in his 1946 *Public Administration Review* paper, destined to become ever-so-influential second chapter of *Administrative Behavior*.

The Difference between Politics and Markets

There are many ways of marking the difference between politics and markets: as a difference between imposed diktats and a spontaneous order; between centralized and decentralized information and control; between responding to political will rather than market forces, votes rather than dollars (Pigou 1932, part 2, chapter 20; Hayek 1944, 1945; Baumol 1952, chapter 12; Lindblom 1977; Esping-Andersen 1985).

Neoclassical economists and political scientists under their spell often tend to encapsulate all this by saying that the world of politics is the world of organized authority, whereas markets represent the world of voluntary exchange. The difference is one between "markets and hierarchy" (cf. Williamson 1973, 1975). Politics is the world of bureaucracy, governed by internal authority structures; and it is inevitably rigid, inefficient and unresponsive in consequence. Those "limits of organization" are what inevitably frustrate attempts to solve social problems through non-market—which is to say, political—means (Wolff 1988; cf. Arrow 1974).

Political economists apparently just cannot help setting up the basic problem in this way, even when they know it is not quite right. Consider, for example, Charles Lindblom's first stab at distinguishing between politics and markets:

Historically the alternative to governmentalization of a national politico-economic system has been the market. And just as hierarchical, bureaucratic, and governmental systems arise from the authority relation, so market systems arise from the simple exchange relation. (Lindblom 1977, p. 33. Cf. p. 11; Arrow 1974, p. 33)

As if to reemphasize the point, Lindblom (1977, p. 65) described the "characteristic incompetence" of authority systems as "strong thumbs, no fingers," thus coining a memorable phrase that has haunted public servants ever since.

Simon began his 2000 Gaus Lecture seemingly in the same vein. "Why," he asked (2000, p. 750), "in modern societies, do we have markets, and why do we have organizations, and what determines the boundary between these two mechanisms ...?" Undoubtedly, his audience—mostly of political scientists reared on the homilies just rehearsed—heard that as "Why markets, why politics, and what is the proper boundary between them?" But of course nothing could have been further from Simon's own intentions.

As Simon had long been wont to emphasize, and as he proceeded to reemphasize on that occasion, the notionally "market" sector is chockablock with organizations, too—so much so that "the economics of modern industrialized society can more appropriately be labeled organizational economies than market economies" (Simon 1991b, p. 42; 2000, p. 751). The organizations of the market are firms. They are governed by internal hierarchies and authority structures, just as are government bureaus; and that is a central rather than incidental feature of firms, as is clear from Coase's (1937, 1988) theory of the firm and from Simon's (1951) theory of the employment relation.

Given what "a large part of the behavior of the system now takes place inside the skins of firms," the central question for Simon (1991b, pp. 42, 26) had always been "What determines the make-or-buy decisions of firms, hence the boundaries between them and markets?" *Those*—the boundaries between organized authority within firms and market exchange between them, rather than the boundaries between market exchange and government authority—are what Simon's Gaus Lecture, like his earlier writings on the topic, was really all about.

This is not to say that Simon neglected the distinct and important role which government organizations must play, vis-à-vis those other market-oriented organizations. Not only are governments required to avoid concentrations of private power, to regulate externalities and to provide public goods. Even more basically,

Government organizations are needed, as they have always been needed, to enforce the rules of the game (including the rules of market contracting), to facilitate coordination of private organizations, and to perform services that are unlikely to be performed effectively by the private sector. The legal institutions must be vigorous and independent enough to curb corruptions of the rules of the game by bribery and other illegal activities. And the rules of the game themselves (e.g., rules for political campaign contributions) must themselves not enable influence buying.   (Simon 2000, p. 754)

Still, Simon supposes, organizations in the government sector are organizations like any other, and the same basic organizational theory should therefore apply to them all alike (Simon 1952, p. 1130; 1991a, p. 126; 1999, p. 116). At the macro level, that emphasis on iso-morphism pushes debates over "government versus the market" into discussions of alternative ways of organizing activities, where the options under discussion are actually shared across both spheres: "cen-tralization versus decentralization," in the case of the great "planning debate" of the 1940s (March and Simon 1958, p. 208), and again in the "reinventing government" debates of the 1990s (Osborne and Gaebler 1992; Osborne and Plastrik 1997). At the micro level, that isomorphism is sometimes taken to imply that it does not make much difference, "to either employee or consumer" (Lindblom 1977, p. 11), whether the activity is organized in the public or private sector.

Even in detailing the peculiarities of public administration, Simon, Smithburg, and Thompson (1950, p. 10) started out by emphasizing that "the similarities between governmental and non-governmental organizations are greater than is generally supposed." They went on to say that "some differences nonetheless exist." But the catalogue of fairly minor differences that followed that admission only served to reiterate the basic isomorphism.

Organizational Purpose and Identification

In the context of Simon's long-standing concern to emphasize that markets and politics are alike, in both being rife with organizations, it hardly suited his strategic purpose to dwell upon how public organi-zations actually differ from private ones. Yet clearly they must, in order for government organizations to play the regulatory role that Simon envisages for them. To do that they need to operate outside and above the ordinary system of market-oriented organizations; they need to be different, if not exactly "in kind" anyway "in orientation," from organizations in the market.

The key to differentiating public and private organizations presum-ably lies in their differing "organizational purposes," and the differing "organizational identifications" to which those give rise. The former points to the distinct aims that are adopted by different organizations or assigned to different sub-units. The latter points to the internalization of those organizational aims by individuals operating within those specific organizational sub-units. Simon had much to say on both scores, both separately and on their interconnections (Simon 1964).

In their classic text on organizations, March and Simon (1958, p. 152) told us that "the principal way to factor a problem" organizationally (as Newell and Simon's (1972) General Problem Solver does cognitively), is "to construct a means-end analysis. The means that are specified in this way become sub-goals which may be assigned to individual organizational [sub-]units. This kind of jurisdictional assignment is often called 'organization by purpose' or 'departmentalization by purpose.'" That is an effective way of achieving the larger goals of the organization overall, insofar as the problems are sufficiently decomposable and sub-unit tasks have actually been carved up in the right way (Simon 1947/1957, p. 218; 1969/1981, chapter 7; 2000, p. 753).

"Organization by purpose" gives rise administratively to the phenomenon that Simon, Smithburg, and Thompson (1950, pp. 543–544) dubbed the "bureau philosophy":

By this we mean the sum total of the group values, the accepted ways of doing things, that grow up in an administrative unit, and with which the members of the unit identify.

An agency working with a stable program over a long period of time develops a definite philosophy and point of view. It develops strong tendencies to harmonize its present decisions with past ones, and both present and past decisions with future ones. A body of rationalizing principles develops which reconciles past and present.... The philosophy tends to grow in the same way as does the common law....

A bureau philosophy tends to be self-maintaining. The agency tends to recruit and retain personnel in terms of their acceptance of the philosophy, and to subject its members to continual indoctrination in its values.

This phenomenon of "subgoal identification" was clearly manifest in the Milwaukee recreation department where Simon's work on all this began: "To the public works administrator, a playground was a physical facility, serving as a green oasis in the crowded gray city. To the recreation administrator, a playground was a social facility, where children could play together with adult help and guidance." (Simon 1979, p. 500; 1999, pp. 112–113)

Individuals' "identifying" in this way with the particular organization in which they are situated, and internalizing its aims as their own, is "a commonplace of organizational life" (Simon 1991b, p. 37; 1999, pp. 112–113; Dearborn and Simon 1958). Indeed, "it is the organizational identification of members, more than any other of their characteristics, that gives organizations their remarkable power to secure coordinated behavior of large numbers of people to accomplish organizational goals, thereby playing a major role during the past two centuries in the rise of modern organizations and their successful competition with traditional market mechanisms" (Simon 2000, p. 753).

It is a commonplace, not only within organization theory but also within political science, that "a person's organizational identification will shift with his or her position" (Simon 1991b, p. 37; 1999, pp. 112–113). The proposition that "where you stand depends on where you sit" is the key to understanding bureaucratic politics, quite generally (Allison 1971, p. 176; see also Tullock 1965; Downs 1967; Niskanen 1971). That explains, at one and the same time, why people in different bureaus have different aims and objectives from one another—and also why people in public organizations (government) have different aims and objectives from those in private organizations (firms in the market).

Premises as Heuristics

As I say, all that is very familiar, from both Simon and a great many others (e.g. Kaufman 1960, chapter 6; Wilson 1989, chapter 6). What I want to highlight is Simon's own distinctive and under-appreciated analysis of the way in which such "organizational identifications" and "bureau philosophies" work on the decision processes of individuals themselves. Sociologists would see all this as a matter of "role playing." Simon himself toyed with that terminology, in the preface to the second edition of *Administrative Behavior* (1947/1957) and for a while thereafter (Simon 1964, pp. 11 ff.; 1991a, pp. 126–127). For Simon (1947/1957, pp. xxx–xxxi), "a role consists in the specification of certain value and factual premises.... A role defined in terms of premises leaves room for rational calculation in behavior.... A role is a specification of some, but not all, of the premises that enter into an individual's decisions." (See also Hollis 1987, chapter 10.)

For Simon, rational action quite generally is "a conclusion reached from premises of two different kinds: value premises and factual premises." "Social influence" is exerted over people's action through "influence upon [those] decision premises" (Simon 1947/1957, pp. 223. p. xxx; 1944, p. 17). The process of defining "organizational purposes," and of inculcating identification with those purposes, is therefore largely a process of identifying the particular premises appropriate to occupants of a particular organizational role (Simon 1944, 1962).

"A bureau philosophy makes group decisions possible where otherwise anarchy would prevail ... by relating particular decisions to a coherent set of principles." (Simon, Smithburg, and Thompson 1950, p. 543) When working within organizations coordinated through sets of shared "premises" and "principles" of this sort, "doing the job well is not mainly a matter of responding to commands, but is much more a matter of taking initiative to advance organizational objectives. Commands do not usually specify concrete actions but, instead, define some of the premises that are to be used by employees in making the decisions for which they are responsible." (Simon 1991b, p. 32)

"A role is not a system of prescribed behaviors but a system of prescribed decision premises. Roles tell organization members how to reason about the problem and decisions that face them; where to look for appropriate and legitimate informational premises and goal (evaluative) premises, and what techniques to use in legitimating these premises." (Simon 1991a, pp. 126–127)

One crucial feature of the premises that guide organization members' behavior in this way is that they "involve a complex interweaving of affective and cognitive processes" (March and Simon 1958, p. 151). The affective and motivational aspects are typically at the fore of discussions of role-sociological discussions (Dahrendorf 1968). It is the cognitive aspects of the process that are more peculiar to, and more important from, Simon's point of view.

Given the cognitive limits under which we operate, we are all obliged to proceed on the basis of a "simplified 'model' of the real situation" which March and Simon (1958, p. 139) call "the chooser's ... 'definition of the situation.' The elements of the definition of the situation are ... themselves the outcome of psychological and sociological processes." First, there is the phenomenon of "selective perception": the individual's "frame of reference serves just as much to validate perceptions as the perceptions do to validate the frame of reference." Second is the phenomenon of "reinforcement" via "in-group communication" among people within an organization, "most of whom have frames of reference similar to our own." Third is the way in which "division of labor in the organization affects the information that various members receive," thus biasing "perceptions of the environment ... even before ... the filtering action of the frame of reference of the perceiver...." (March and Simon 1958, pp. 152–153).

A person's definition of the situation, organizationally shaped in that way, "represents a simplified, screened and biased model of the objective situation, and filtering affects all of the 'givens' that enter into the decision process: knowledge or assumptions about future events; knowledge of sets of alternatives available for action; knowledge of consequences attached to alternatives; goals and values" (March and Simon 1958, pp. 139, 154; Simon 1999, p. 115). All those important influences on perception and choice, note, are cognitive, not affective.

To adapt the standard political science aphorism of "where you stand depends on where you sit," it is not just a matter of "what you *want* depends on where you sit" but also one of "what you *see* depends on where you sit."

All this talk of decision "premises" in Simon's early and mid-career work in organization theory resonates with the talk of "heuristics" in his later work in cognitive science. Generically, Simon, Newell, and Shaw (1962/1979, p. 152) "use the term heuristic to denote any principle or device that contributes to the reduction in the average search to solution." More specifically, what they have in mind is this: "Even when the set [of possible solutions] P is large, as it usually is in complex problem solving, it is possible for the solution generator to consider at an early stage those parts of P that are likely to contain a solution and to avoid the parts that are most likely to be barren." That is the way the "Heuristic Compiler" works in the context of Simon's General Problem Solver, for example (Simon 1972).

Simon's own examples typically concern heuristics for playing chess or finding proofs of theorems in logic. For a more mundane example drawn from everyday social experience, however, we need go no further than the "maxims of conversation" proposed by Paul Grice (1975). Grice's central insight is that "communication" is an essentially cooperative enterprise: even when we are trying to dispute or criticize or insult one another, we nonetheless want our messages to be meaningful to one another. From that follows Grice's basic "Cooperative Principle: "Make your conversational contribution such as is required, at the stage at which it occurs, by the accepted purpose or direction of the task exchange in which you are engaged." That, in turn, resolves itself into four basic "maxims of conversation":

1. Quantity

- Make your contribution as informative as is required (for the current purposes of the exchange).

- Do not make your contribution more informative than is required.

2. Quality

- Do not say what you believe to be false.
- Do not say that for which you lack adequate evidence.

3. Relation

- Be relevant.

4. Manner

- Avoid obscurity of expression.
- Avoid ambiguity.
- Be brief (avoid unnecessary prolixity).
- Be orderly.

Maxims (heuristics, rules of thumb) of this sort are internalized, more or less imperfectly, by us all as we search for some appropriate thing to say in the course of ordinary conversations.

In the context of administrative decision making, even more certainly than in the context of interpersonal conversation, heuristics are amalgams of beliefs about facts and beliefs about values, in potentially unstable combinations. Heuristics are like Simon's decision "premises" not only in that respect but also in embodying partial, biased, and imperfect representations of the world. "In general, these heuristics are quite useful, but sometimes they lead to severe and systematic errors." (Tversky and Kahneman 1974, p. 1124) Furthermore, heuristics are often context-sensitive: '"Always protect your queen" might be a good heuristic for playing chess among amateurs, but in play among Grand Masters it is essential to be open to the occasional desirability of sacrificing one's queen (Simon 1972). Heuristics are undeniably limited in all these ways. Nonetheless, acting on such imperfect rules of thumb is often the best we can do, given the cognitive limits that characterize our human condition.

Insofar as people are trying to coordinate their actions with one another's, it would presumably be advantageous for them to assume common knowledge of the same heuristics—for the same reasons it

would presumably be advantageous for them to act on common decision premises. Different groups would presumably adopt different heuristics, for the same reasons given above for their adopting different
decision premises. In short, it is to be expected that "what *heuristics*
you use depends on where you sit," organizationally.

Heuristics of Public Administration

Piecing together these fragments suggests an analysis of the following sort. Different organizations occupy different niches in the social
system: they have different purposes and goals, different aims and
objectives. People working within those organizations differ, too: moti-
vationally, they internalize (at least partly) their respective organizations' differing goals; cognitively, they are subject to the (at least partly)
different informational inputs found in the different environments
of their respective organizations. These cognitive-and-motivational,
fact-and-value elements are blended into action premises and decision heuristics, which vary (at least in part) from one organization to
another.

Not only do they vary from one organization to another, however: they also vary from one *kind* of organization to another. Agents
of organizations in the public sector differ among themselves too, of
course, in what action premises and decision heuristics they employ.
Officials in Treasury inevitably see things differently—internalize different "bureau philosophies," action premises and decision heuristics—
than officials in Transportation or Health. Different though government organizations might be, one from another, however, they are
typically far more similar to one another than they are to profit-
maximizing firms in the market sector.

There are, I suggest, some standard "heuristics of public administration" which serve to differentiate organizations in the public government sector from organizations in the private market sector quite

generally. The status of these heuristics is normative, in both senses. That is to say, these heuristics constitute rules of thumb which public officials evaluatively should and sociologically do internalize. The evaluative "should," here, derives however not from some grand ethical theory but merely from mundane features of the internal logic of the place of officials and their organizations in the social division of labor, and what concerns are appropriate for people and organizations that occupy those positions.

Without any pretension of completeness, here is a sample of some such "heuristics of public administration":

1. Scope

- Attend to the needs of the whole, not just the interests of particular parts (Banfield 1955, pp. 322–329; Goodin 1996).

- Pursue the public interest, not private profit.

2. Time horizon

- Adopt a longer-term perspective (Eckstein 1961, pp. 457–459).

- Strive for sustainability of socio-economic practices (Brundtland 1987).

- Avoid irreversible decisions (Simon 1969/1981, p. 187).

3. Trusteeship

- Keep the capital intact (Pigou 1932, part 1, chapter 4; Barry 1989).

- Attend to the stock as well as the flow (Cohen 1985).

- "Leave the next generation ... with a better body of knowledge and a greater capacity for experience." (Simon 1969/1981, p. 187)

These heuristics are broad and general. But that is as it should be. After all, they are supposed to be heuristics applicable to any and all public functions; they are supposed to be open to interpretation, adaptation and application by very different public agencies to their peculiar activities in various different (possibly peculiar) ways.

Not only are the heuristics are indeterminate: they are also potentially in conflict with one another, in any given application. But that too is only to be expected. Among real-world decision makers, rules of thumb are starting points for reflection, not argument-stoppers. The way that real decision makers proceed, within themselves and among themselves, is by reflecting on the whole suite of rules of thumb that might be applicable, the whole range of perspectives from which they might look at the problem; and they then proceed to weigh the differing and possibly conflicting conclusions that those suggest, in coming to some overall judgment (Hollis 1987, chapter 6).

At the end of the day, one perspective (premise, heuristic) might prevail in respect of some particular decision. But it does so without eclipsing the countervailing claims of other considerations (premises, perspectives, heuristics), even in respect of the particular decision at hand, much less all future ones. That is the way courts seem to operate in applying the large suite of "principles of statutory interpretation" available to them, for example (Sunstein 1990, pp. 235–238). Presumably the same is true of public administrators more generally, confronted with the contradictory maxims of which Simon (1946; 1947, chapter 2) and his successors have made so much fun (Hood and Jackson 1991; Williams 2000).

What Would Simon Have Said?

Whether Simon would have accepted these analyses as "friendly amendments," broadly in keeping with the central thrust of his own larger theories, alas we will never know. The last time I tried attributing to him some cognate claims, he was definitely not buying (Goodin 1999; Simon 1999, p. 118); so perhaps my propositions should better be styled "after the fashion of Simon," rather than being attributed to Simon himself.

Still, the themes I have been developing clearly do grow out of, and resonate with, much that Simon wrote over half a century. Furthermore, I cannot see anything in the corpus (anyway, that subset of it with which I am competently acquainted) which would bar him from embracing my propositions as his own.

Clearly, my "heuristics of public administration" need to be given more concrete meaning, in specific contexts, to serve as any real guide to action. March and Simon (1958, p. 156) make that point forcefully, at the only place in Simon's large corpus I have been able to find any allusion to anything like one of my "heuristics of public administration":

The goal of "promoting the general welfare" is frequently a part of the definition of the situation in governmental policy-making. It is a non-operational goal because it does not provide (either *ex ante* or *ex post*) a measuring rod for comparing alternative policies, but can only be related to specific actions through the intervention of sub-goals. These sub-goals, whose connection with the broader "general welfare" goal is postulated but not testable, become the operational goals in the actual choice situation.

In his discussion of "designing without final goals" in *The Sciences of the Artificial*, however, Simon (1969/1981, pp. 185–187) was much more tolerant of amorphous goals. "How can we evaluate a design unless we have well-defined criteria against which to judge it, and how can the design process itself proceed without such criteria to guide it?" For a partial answer, Simon invited us to reflect upon "discovery processes," in which search processes "guided by only the most general heuristics of 'interestingness' or novelty" prove to be "a fully realizable activity." Simon went on to say the following:

This kind of search, which provides the mechanism for scientific discovery, may also provide the most suitable model of the social design process. . . . Exposure to new experience is almost certain to change the criteria of choice, and most human beings deliberately seek out such experiences.

A paradoxical, but perhaps realistic, view of design goals is that their function is to motivate activity which in turn will generate new goals. . . . The idea of final goals is inconsistent with our limited ability to foretell or determine the future. The real result of our actions is to establish initial conditions for the next succeeding stage of action.

That, too, could serve as an important "premise" for public administrators.

References

Allison, Graham T. 1971. *Essence of Decision*. Little, Brown.

Arrow, Kenneth J. 1974. *The Limits of Organization*. Norton.

Barry, Brian. 1989. *Democracy, Power and Justice*. Clarendon.

Baumol, William J. 1952. *Welfare Economics and the Theory of the State*. G. Bell and Sons.

Brundtland, Gro Harlem, chair. 1987. *Our Common Future. Report of the World Commission on Environment and Development*. Oxford University Press.

Coase, R. H. 1937. The nature of the firm. *Economica* 4: 386–405.

Coase, R. H. 1988. The nature of the firm: Influence. *Journal of Law, Economics and Organization* 4, no. 1: 33–47.

Cohen, Michael A. 1995. Stocks and flows: Making better use of metropolitan resources. *Brookings Review*, fall: 37–39.

Dahrendorf, Ralf. 1968. *Homo Sociologicus*. Routledge and Kegan Paul.

Dearborn, DeWitt C., and Herbert A. Simon. 1958. Selective perception: The identification of executives. *Sociometry* 21: 140–144. Reprinted in Simon 1947/1976.

Downs, Anthony. 1967. *Inside Bureaucracy*. Little, Brown.

Eckstein, Otto. 1961. A survey of the theory of public expenditure criteria. In National Bureau of Economic Research, ed., *Public Finances*. Princeton University Press.

Esping-Andersen, Gøsta. 1985. *Politics against Markets*. Princeton University Press.

Goodin, Robert E. 1996. Institutionalizing the public interest. *American Political Science Review* 90, no. 2: 331–343.

Goodin, Robert E. 1999. Rationality redux: Reflections on Herbert Simon's vision of politics. In J. Alt et al., eds., *Competition and Cooperation*. Russell Sage Foundation Press.

Grice, H. Paul. 1975. Logic and Conversation. In P. Cole and J. Morgan, eds., *Speech Acts*. Academic Press.

Hayek, Friedrich A. 1944. *The Road to Serfdom*. University of Chicago Press.

Hayek, Friedrich A. 1945. The use of knowledge in society. *American Economic Review* 35: 519–530.

Hollis, Martin. 1987. *The Cunning of Reason*. Cambridge University Press.

Hood, Christopher, and Michael Jackson. 1991. *Administrative Argument*. Dartmouth.

Kaufman, Herbert. 1960. *The Forest Ranger: A Study in Administrative Behavior*. Johns Hopkins University Press for Resources for the Future.

Lindblom, Charles E. 1977. *Politics and Markets*. Basic Books.

March, James G., and Herbert A. Simon, with Harold Gustzkow. *Organizations*. Wiley.

Newell, Allen, and Herbert A. Simon. 1972. *Human Problem Solving*. Prentice-Hall.

Niskanen, William A. 1971. *Bureaucracy and Representative Government*. Aldine-Atherton.

Osborne, David, and Ted Gaebler. 1992. *Reinventing Government*. Addison-Wesley.

Osborne, David, and Peter Plastrik. 1997. *Banishing Bureaucracy: The Five Strategies for Reinventing Government*. Addison-Wesley.

Pigou, A. C. 1932. *The Economics of Welfare*, fouth edition. Macmillan.

Simon, Herbert A. 1944. Decision-making and administrative organization. *Public Administration Review* 4: 16–25.

Simon, Herbert A. 1946. The proverbs of administration. *Public Administration Review* 6: 53–67. Reprinted in Simon 1947.

Simon, Herbert A. 1947. *Administrative Behavior*. Free Press. Second edition 1957; third edition 1976; fourth edition 1997.

Simon, Herbert A. 1951. A formal theory of the employment relationship. *Econometrica*, 19: 293–305.

Simon, Herbert A. 1952. Comments on the theory of organizations. *American Political Science Review* 46, no. 4: 1130–1139.

Simon, Herbert A. 1964. On the concept of organizational goal. *Administrative Science Quarterly* 9, no. 1: 1–22.

Simon, Herbert A. 1969/1981. *The Sciences of the Artificial*, second edition. MIT Press. Originally published in 1969.

Simon, Herbert A. 1972. The heuristic compiler. In H. Simon and L. Klóssy, eds., *Representation and Meaning*. Prentice-Hall.

Simon, Herbert A. 1979. Rational decision making in business organizations. *American Economic Review* 69, no. 4: 493–513.

Simon, Herbert A. 1991a. Bounded rationality and organizational learning. *Organizational Science* 2, no. 1: 125–134.

Simon, Herbert A. 1991b. Organizations and markets. *Journal of Economic Perspectives* 5, no. 2: 25–44.

Simon, Herbert A. 1999. The potlatch between economics and political science. In J. Alt et al., eds., *Competition and Cooperation*. Russell Sage Foundation Press.

Simon, Herbert A. 2000. Public administration in today's world of organizations and markets. *PS: Political Science and Politics* 33, no. 4: 749–756.

Simon, Herbert A., and Allen Newell. 1958. Heuristic problem solving. *Operations Research* 6: 1–10.

Simon, Herbert A., Allen Newell, and J. C. Shaw. 1962. The processes of creative thinking. Reprinted in Simon, *Models of Thought*, volume 1 (Yale University Press, 1979).

Simon, Herbert A., Donald W. Smithburg, and Victor A. Thompson. 1950. *Public Administration*. Knopf.

Sunstein, Cass R. 1990. *After the Rights Revolution*. Harvard University Press.

Tullock, Gordon. 1965. *The Politics of Bureaucracy*. Public Affairs Press.

Tversky, Amos, and Daniel Kahneman. 1974. Judgment under uncertainty: Heuristics and biases. *Science* 185: 1124–1131.

Tversky, Amos, and Daniel Kahneman. 1981. The framing of decisions and the psychology of choice. *Science* 211: 453–458. Reprinted in J. Elster, ed., *Rational Choice* (New York University Press, 1986).

Williams, Daniel W. 2000. Reinventing the proverbs of government. *Public Administration Review* 60, no. 6: 522–534.

Williamson, Oliver E. 1973. Markets and hierarchies: Some elementary considerations. *American Economic Review (Papers and Proceedings)* 63: 316–325.

Williamson, Oliver E. 1975. *Markets and Hierarchies*. Free Press.

Wilson, James Q. 1989. *Bureaucracy: What Government Agencies Do and Why They Do It*. Basic Books.

Wolf, Charles, Jr. 1988. *Markets or Governments: Choosing between Imperfect Alternatives*. MIT Press.

"Warmly Yours, Herb"

Harold Guetzkow

Herbert Simon supported the development of many scholars in the social sciences, and, of the many, I was one. The fact that he dedicated his 1957 book *Models of Man* to me (the book included two joint reports on our laboratory work at the Graduate School of Industrial Administration at Carnegie Tech (Simon and Guetzkow 1955a,b)) reflected the warmth and encouragement that Herb showered on me throughout our many decades together as colleagues and friends. Over the years, he generously sent me reprints of his many works, always inscribed "Warmly yours, Herb."

As Herb recorded in his autobiography *Models of My Life* (Simon 1991, p. 37), we met as incoming freshmen at the University of Chicago in 1933. My three years as an undergraduate were mind-opening to me, as Herb, others and I prepared ourselves for our "comprehensive" exams. As I think of Herb now, I recall the time when we suspended tables of geologic periods on the ceiling of our common shower stall as we crammed facts. By the end of our three years at Chicago, a strong camaraderie had developed. During "our frequent mealtime conversation and bull sessions" (ibid., p. 43), it seems that he never challenged my pre-college commitment to teaching at a high school and becoming a public school administrator, devoted to peace work. Herb always respected my need for autonomy, perhaps due to his own governmental involvements.

During my teenage years at Washington High School in Milwaukee (1930–1933), my anti-war thinking was enhanced by debates about the "Merchants of Death" (arms traders) and culminated in a spontaneous trek to Washington, led by my high school friend Richard Lippold in his Duesenberg, with the intention of having an evening at the residence of our isolationist, Wisconsin Senator Wiley, a Republican conservative. During my second year at college, classmate Stan Levy introduced me to the Quakers, who were active in the American Friends Service Committee. My anti-war posturing gradually expanded to include a pro-peace perspective. Even then, I wanted to do peace work as a teacher. Unfortunately, I did not engage my good friend Herb in these developments. This was, in retrospect, a most serious omission. When, along with Herb, I received my BA from the University of Chicago in 1936, I was able to join the faculty of Shorewood High School, an outstanding, campus-sited institution, located directly north of Milwaukee, at the grand salary of $900 for the academic year.

During my two years as a high school teacher, I remained in contact with Herb—and his new wife, Dorothea. It was my privilege to be invited to their wedding, a family affair in Herb's old home in Milwaukee, on December 25, 1937. Later, it became my custom to call Herb and Dorothea on Christmas to renew our warm ties. The two often returned to Milwaukee and helped me integrate into their so-called "Heretics" group at the local Congregational Church. At other times, I would revisit the Chicago University campus, so that I might enjoy a weekend in their apartment as their guest.

It had been my hope to eventually become a school administrator in order to teach peace. During my two years at Shorewood High, I reluctantly discovered that I did not know how to go about such an undertaking. I decided that it might be time to return to the University of Chicago to learn more, so that I could formulate my peace-minding plans while continuing my education as a social scientist. During my two years of graduate work in psychology (1936–1938) at the University of Chicago, I had frequent contact with Herb and Dorothea.

My studies with Psychology Professor Leon Thurstone and his newly appointed team, ones Dale Wofle, John Richardson, and Harold Gulliksen, centered on the creative use of factor analysis. It was exciting to share these developments with Herb—as well as to receive his encouragement to learn the calculus, along with the undergraduates at Chicago.

My desire to find a potential life partner, as well as interest in the structure of the intellect with respect to problem-solving, led me to want contact with the Gestaltists. I spent the summer of 1937 enrolled at the University of Michigan in Ann Arbor. Although I did not find a wife, I did gain contact with a number of the Gestaltists who later enticed me into doing my doctoral work with them, especially Norman F. D. Maier. Herb and Dorothea aided and abetted my move in the fall of 1938 to Michigan, Herb being especially interested in my work in problem solving.

Throughout the two years (1938–1940) in Ann Arbor, Herb "watched over me," as I completed my general doctoral exams in Psychology. Although Kurt Lewin died before occupying his new chair at Michigan, his MIT team moved to Ann Arbor, helping me to develop an interest in problem solving in groups. Herb reinforced this development. It was during these years that my peace interest matured into a conscientious objection. Three months before Pearl Harbor, I was assigned to "alternative service" in the U.S. Forest Service, which eventuated in 1943 to work in the laboratory of Ancel Keys at the University of Minnesota, serving as an assistant psychologist. It was most fortuitous that, while in alternative service, I was able to make a romantic match in the Twin Cities—and in September 1944 Herb and Dorothea provided a wedding breakfast for Lauris and me at their 57th Street apartment just before our Quaker-designed marriage in the 57th Street Meeting at the University of Chicago. Herb was supportive and warm, as always.

Being discharged from my alternative service at the end of World War II, Lauris and I returned to Michigan, so that I might complete my dissertation on the operation of "set" in group problem-solving (eventually published as Guetzkow 1947). The new chairman of the Department of Psychology, Don Marquis, wanted me to help teach the flood of GIs, but perhaps more importantly, guided me to seek funding for my interest in the study of decision-making conferences. Once or twice during my years as an Assistant Professor at Michigan, Herb accepted our invitation to serve as a consultant in our "Conference Research Project," in which I was ably associated with Roger ("Bob") W. Heyns. After these years, Herb and his colleagues invited me to join them in their new Graduate School of Industrial Administration (GSIA) at Carnegie Tech. Herb helped me in the transition from Ann Arbor to Pittsburgh, allowing me to complete our report on the Michigan project (Marquis, Guetzkow, and Heyns 1951).

My years at Carnegie Tech (1950–1956) were warmly supported by Herb, as he gave leadership to the behavioral components of the program at GSIA. Our arrival by car in Pittsburgh with our three young children late one night at the end of summer of 1950 was greeted by a spectacular view of the (soon to be closed) open-hearth, steel furnaces, as we slowly drove along the Monongahela River to our new home. Thanks to Herb and the brilliant colleagues he and Lee Bach (then GSIA director) had assembled, my growth as a social scientist was accelerated. In addition to my laboratory work on group decision making, I was included in such projects as the field study of accountants (Simon, Guetzkow, Kozmetsky, and Tyndall 1954). This interdisciplinary work with the economists enabled me to learn not only from the members of the team, but from such glorious GSIA associates as Charles Holt and Franco Modigliani. It was with reluctance that I bowed out of Herb's work on problem-solving with Al Newell (Newell and Simon 1972)—although Jim March and Herb involved me in their prepositional inventory, even giving me recognition for my contribution in their final product (March and Simon, with the assistance of Harold Guetzkow, 1958). My appreciation of the work was recorded in an essay on "Interaction Between Methods and Models in Social Psychology" almost immediately (Guetzkow 1958).

The years at GSIA were filled to the brim, all on top of classroom experience in teaching these developing ideas with our graduate student, Bill Dill, as well as with members of our Executive Program. In retrospect it is hard to believe there was time yet to work as a consultant to steel companies and steelworkers union, through Psychological Services of Pittsburgh, headed by Dora Capwell.

My interest in peace work continued to grow throughout my tenure at GSIA. There was an active chapter of the World Affairs Council in Pittsburgh. During three summers, thanks to Richard Van Wagenen, I was able to devote time to seminars on international affairs at Princeton University. It was my good fortune to be associated there with Karl Deutsch and his colleagues in the development of their theories and research, and particularly with Richard Snyder, who was developing his *Decision Making as an Approach to the Study of International Politics* (Snyder, Bruck, and Sapin 1954). Herb, as always, supported these extra-GSIA ventures.

In the spring of 1955, I received an invitation to be a Fellow at the newly founded Center for Advanced Study in the Behavioral Sciences, with the option of being there with Karl Deutsch and Richard Snyder, much to my delight. Lee and Herb gave me a leave of absence from GSIA, with the expectation that I would return to Carnegie upon completion of my fellowship. During the spring of 1956, my wife and I purchased a new home in a nearby suburb, so that our children could avoid making yet another change of schools upon our return from California.

Throughout the wonderful years at Carnegie Tech, Herb and "Dottie Pye" (Dorothea's nickname) helped to provide a rich family environment. Our children were of approximately the same age. Peter Simon and our son, Jim, hit it off, and I remember Peter availing himself of our TV hideaway in our basement in Squirrel Hill. There were family outings together during which there was much "shop talk," including findings from Dorothea's studies (Simon and Simon 1958). Some rainy Sundays, we would gather, listening to Herb's piano rendition of one of Beethoven's sonatas, discussing its structure with my wife Lauris, who was a composer in the making. Also, we Guetzkows joined the Simons' church. The climax of our inclusion into the Simons' extended family occurred on the celebration of the Simons' golden wedding anniversary, skillfully arranged by their daughter Katie. Lauris and I were among the friends and academics who convened in Pittsburgh to celebrate the occasion along with the Simon relatives. I remember that Herb chauffeured a myriad of "aunties" from the airport.

Herb's leadership in our GSIA projects energized everyone involved. He was remarkable in his intellectual depth and reach. Herb had a gift for clarity, even in his everyday discourse. When I read Herb's published material, I often have the illusion that I hear him talking. He seldom needed to make revisions of his first drafts of his manuscripts. When I served on doctoral examination committees with Herb, at times I would miss the "fatal flaw," later wondering about Herb's ability to so quickly perceive the key issues. Yet, with his ever-supportive warmth, both the candidate and this examiner left more determined than ever to increase our standards of rigor. Evermore, Herb helped one to do better.

Before taking off with the family for California in our convertible Nash Rambler at the end of the summer of 1956, there were a number of conversations with physicists at our faculty club as to whether it would be possible to create computer simulations of international affairs, similar to what they were doing in their explorations of nuclear processes, even though in Pittsburgh they had no direct access to laboratory work on such. I had long admired the work of Ray Cattell (1949) in attempting to describe international processes. These empirical findings provided starting points for my discussions at the Center for Advanced Study of the Behavioral Sciences with Richard Snyder and Karl Deutsch. It was feasible to include in our work group the participation of Charles McClelland, an historian, and Nate Maccoby, a media scholar. The five of us would meet at the Maccoby pool about once a week for an exchange of ideas. Given my background laboratory work in the operation of groups, it was not too surprising that the notion of developing a "Inter-Nation Simulation" soon seemed feasible, using humans decision makers, constrained by a structure of programs representing the international system, somewhat analogous to the all-computer simulations my colleagues in physics were using to study inaccessible nuclear processes. Before that time, it had seemed that such "gaming" theories would not be applicable to the problem of elite members of the world's decision-making community. My friend Herb was intrigued, even though he later wrote in his piece for my festschrift "My own research lies very far from the domain of international relations...." (Ward 1985, p. 535)

Although my family and I never lived in our intended home in the Pittsburgh suburb, having transferred directly from the Stanford Center to our new residence in Evanston, over the years at Northwestern it was possible to invite Herb to serve as a consultant in my work on the development of the Inter-Nation Simulation. In Evanston, on one occasion, to top all others, Herb presented a brilliant series of lectures on the social sciences. And, at times, it was feasible for me to stop in at Pittsburgh, as when Herb served as series editor for my work with Phil Kotler and Randy Schultz, *Simulation in Social Science: Readings*, which gathered the reports of my colleagues at Northwestern on their experiences in the use of simulations. Evermore, Herb warmly supported this venture, even though it was undertaken in my new and final academic home in Evanston.

The last time Herb supported me, ever so warmly, was when he made the day's round-trip trip from Pittsburgh to Chicago to honor me by joining a panel of the American Political Science Association. He was tired—and accepted my wife's invitation to rest in our hotel room before the event. That was my last meeting with Herb—but I had not realized then that such would be the way our rich interactions over the decades would come to their tragic end. When I learned of Herb's passing, I tried to call Dorothea to urge my condolences, but upon hearing his voice on the answering machine, I was devastated and wept uncontrollably.

What a supportive human being—what a warm friend—and what a skillful leader—and, especially, what a brain!

References

Cattell, R. B. 1949. The dimensions of culture patterns by factorization of national characters. *Journal of Abnormal and Social Psychology* 44: 443–469.

Guetzkow, Harold. 1958. Interaction between methods and models in social psychology. In R. Glaser et al., eds., *Current Trends in the Description and Analysis of Behavior.* University of Pittsburgh Press.

Guetzkow, Harold, and Anne E. Bowes. 1957. The development of organizations in a laboratory. *Management Science* 3, no. 4: 380–402.

Guetzkow, Harold, and William R. Dill. 1957. Factors in the organizational development of task-oriented groups. *Sociometry* 26, no. 3: 175–204.

March, James G., and H. A. Simon. 1958. *Organizations.* Blackwell.

Marquis, D. G., Harold Guetzkow, and R. W. Heyns. 1951. A social psychological study of the decision-making conference. In Harold Guetzkow, ed., *Groups, Leadership and Men.* Carnegie Press.

Newell, A., and H. A. Simon. 1972. *Human Problem Solving.* Prentice-Hall.

Simon, Dorothea P., and Herbert A. Simon. 1978. Individual differences in solving physics problems. In *Children's Thinking*, ed. R. Siegler. Erlbaum.

Simon, Herbert A. 1957. *Models of Man.* Wiley.

Simon, Herbert A. 1991. *Models of My Life.* Basic Books.

Simon, Herbert A., and Harold Guetzkow. 1955a. Mechanisms involved in group pressures on deviate-members. *British Journal of Statistical Psychology* 8, no. II: 93–101.

Simon, Herbert A., and Harold Guetzkow. 1955b. A model of short- and long-run mechanisms involved in pressures toward uniformity in groups. *Psychological Review* 62, no. 1: 56–68.

Simon, Herbert A., and Harold Guetzkow. 1955c. The impact of certain communication nets upon organization and performance in task-oriented groups. *Management Science* 1, no. 3–4: 233–250.

Simon, H. A., H. Guetzkow, G. Kozmetsky, and G. Tyndall. 1954. *Centralization and Decentralization in Organizing the Controller's Department.* Controllership Foundation.

Economics after Simon

Brian J. Loasby

Nothing is more fundamental in setting our research agenda and informing our research methods than our view of the nature of the human beings whose behavior we are studying.
—Herbert Simon (1985, p. 303)

What Bounds on Rationality?

All that most economists know about Herbert Simon is that he wrote about bounded rationality and organizational behavior. For most economists, the study of behavior is left to psychologists and sociologists; it is no more than an explanation of the error term in models of rational choice. Bounded rationality, however, has been seized on by others to explain the existence of firms in an analytical scheme which in its purest form, as an equilibrium allocation derived from a complete data set, has no use for them. The concept of equilibrium allocation is extended to the efficient allocation of the right to make decisions or to give orders, as a substantively rational response to narrowly conceived (but poorly specified) limitations on rationality: everyone can foresee the consequences of these limitations and deduces the optimal system for dealing with them.

The theory developed by Oliver Hart and his colleagues preserves the extreme version of methodological individualism, in which everyone optimizes from individual opportunity sets, but these opportunity sets are first redefined by the freely contracted reassignment of property rights which is prompted by correct foresight of the benefits to be obtained by this reassignment. Oliver Williamson, by contrast, insists on the importance of hierarchy, to which Simon gave much attention—but only as the post-contractual right to impose decisions on subordinates; the making of these decisions is apparently exempt from bounded rationality. Williamson's emphasis on efficiency keeps him clearly in the tradition of equilibria of optimizing agents; firms as organizations are no more than a defense against opportunism, an unfortunate consequence of human failure. It could hardly be otherwise against the standard theoretical background—especially when economists use this theoretical background to talk of 'markets' without deigning to provide any theoretical account of how markets come into existence and how they work.

All this is a very long way from Simon's ideas, and about as far from any functioning economy. In these models firms are not necessary for production, for all productive knowledge is available to all (Demsetz 1988, p. 150); they are incentive structures which ensure that the analysis of production remains part of equilibrium theory. Management does not exist, for there are no processes: post-contract control in Williamson's theoretical system is simply a set of instructions to subordinates which validate the rational expectations on which the governance system has been based. Thus, although Williamson (1996, p. 145) agrees with Simon that "the importance of intentional governance has been undervalued," he immediately and explicitly dissociates himself from Simon's (1991, p. 27) vision of an economy that is dominated by conscious organization: "That we appear to be subject to intentional governance structures everywhere we turn is misleading: the real action is largely invisible."

Such theorists seem more concerned to save the theory than to understand the phenomena of business organization; as we shall see this desire to preserve existing cognitive structures is a major influence on both individual and organizational behavior. Nicolai Foss (2001) has pointed out that even Williamson's account of intentional governance, which allows for superior-subordinate relationships that are not encompassed by principal-agent models, provides a very "thin" theory of organization, because it is based on a very "thin" notion of bounded rationality. He suggests that the abundant evidence supplied by psychologists of systematic patterns of behavior which violate the standard rationality assumptions in orthodox economics gives sufficient content to bounded rationality to permit much "thicker" theorizing about organizational problems and organizational remedies. In addition to respecting Simon's (1991, p. 43) call for "empirically sound theories," this proposal has the substantial merits of suggesting a continuing role for managers within a firm: the establishment of a firm is not the end but the beginning of analysis, as Simon wished.

In one important respect, however, Foss's proposal is still inadequate; it continues the established tradition of regarding firms as devices to protect against human inadequacies. If we wish to honor the memory of Herbert Simon (and also to improve our understanding of the working of economic systems and develop a better basis for policy recommendations) we should do better than that; and we should start, as Simon proposed, by taking a more careful look at the nature of human beings than most economists have been prepared to do in the past half-century. We may then observe that the systematic patterns of apparently non-rational behavior which Foss presents are pathologies of the particular evolved characteristics of human cognition, and that many features of economic and social organization may be explained as responses (often unintentional) to the potential as well as the pathology of this cognition.

Integral and Non-Integral Systems

In the same year in which Debreu published his definitive analysis of general equilibrium, Simon (1959, p. 272) observed of the choice-theoretic tradition in economics: "When perception and cognition intervene between the decision maker and his objective environment, this model no longer proves adequate. We need a description of the choice process that recognizes that alternatives are not given but must be sought; and a description that takes into account the arduous task of determining what consequences will follow on each alternative."

Jason Potts (2000) emphasized the fundamental difference between these two conceptions of analysis. General equilibrium exists in integral space, which ensures that every element in the system is directly connected to every other element; thus, every preference, resource, commodity, location, date, and contingency enters directly into the determination of the solution for the system being modeled. In integral space there is no room for dense clusters of connections, such as those that constitute firms or markets.

Equilibrium allocations are derived from the data, and do not depend on rational choice by anyone within the system. Indeed, the role of economic agents, however rational, is incompatible with the concept of a fully connected system; any interaction within a set of agents implies non-integral space and highly selective connections, and therefore requires a different category of analysis. Whether a multitude of such local interactions replicates the deduced allocation is a question which cannot be properly formulated within the conventions of general-equilibrium models, as Richardson (1960) demonstrated—not least because "time" as a period during which these interactions take place is categorically distinct from "time" as a dimension of all goods which is embodied in the specification of the general-equilibrium model.

Perception and cognition have no usable meaning in integral space, since their significance is defined by the selectivity of the connections by which they are constituted. In sharp contrast to the standard assumption that the information available to agents is always a partition of the full information set which corresponds precisely to the configuration of the economy, the selectivity of perception and cognition results from conjectures (rarely completely conscious) that are imposed on phenomena: it is not then surprising that "the decision-maker's information about his environment is much less than an approximation to the real environment" (Simon 1959, p. 272), especially when we recognize that the relevant "real environment" is nothing less than the total system, including its structure of connections.

Rational-choice theorists have preserved their conceptual system by endowing economic agents with "rational expectations" which are the equivalent of the analyst's integral model, and even allow the set of agents to be collapsed into a single representative agent, making organization undiscussable. The essential incompleteness of connections, which is the precondition of organization—including the organization of markets—and the essential incompleteness of knowledge both require an analytical foundation in non-integral space. Simon (1991, p. 27) argues for "the ubiquity of organizations." I suggest that we delete the final letter, and emphasize the ubiquity of organization, because perception, cognition, and decision processes, for individuals as well as firms, are organizational phenomena. Methodological individualism should begin, not with preference sets and possibility sets, but with evolving cognitive structures. Connections matter (Loasby 2001).

It is within non-integral space that we can begin to explore the implications of Marshall's (1920, p. 138) linked principles: "Knowledge is our most powerful engine of production.... Organization aids knowledge." (This passage dates from the fourth edition, dated 1898.) Simon's (1991, p. 28) suggestion that "organizational economy" is a more appropriate term than "market economy" is powerfully reinforced by the recognition of the intimate connection between organization and the knowledge on which an economy—especially a modern economy—depends. This connection also suggests that the familiar contrast between "firm" and "market" may be misleading; in addition to the variety of intermediate relationships to which Richardson (1972) drew attention, there are "market" elements within many firms, and "markets," like firms, rest on institutions and are often subject to management actions—which, of course, may have unintended consequences.

Why should organization aid knowledge? The essential point is that knowledge itself is organization: "Whatever we call reality, it is revealed to us only through the active construction in which we participate." (Prigogine and Stengers 1984, p. 293) As Simon (1959, p. 273) observes, if perception is a filter, then "the filtering is not merely a passive selection ... but an active process involving attention to a very small part of the whole and exclusion, from the outset, of almost all that is not within the scope of attention." The possibility of establishing "true knowledge" on an undisputable basis, either axiomatic or empirical, was conclusively refuted by David Hume (if not earlier); and Hume's friend Adam Smith (1980 [1795]) produced a remarkable psychological theory of the development of human, and eventually scientific, knowledge as a work of human imagination by which order was imposed on otherwise unaccountable phenomena through the invention of "connecting principles." Because, to use Karl Popper's term, all knowledge consists of conjectures, it is always liable to be confronted with anomalies; and a persistent failure to accommodate anomalies provides powerful psychological incentives to invent a new set of principles that will restore the comfort of understanding.

From Rationality to Cognition

I am afraid we must conclude that, in relation to conventional economics, "bounded rationality" is not a good label for the view of human nature on which Simon wished to base his analysis, because it has been interpreted as an exception to the norm of unbounded rationality which might be useful in resolving some awkward anomalies such as the existence of firms. Even Foss's proposal to make use of the evidence of psychologists seems to suggest that firms exist in order to cope with systematic departures from a norm of strictly rational behavior. But if the adjective is unfortunate, so is the noun; for once we accept that rationality is bounded, the economic concept of "rationality" is insufficient, and "optimality" is simply not good enough. Quite different cognitive skills are now required. Therefore instead of thinking of remedies for deficiencies of rationality we should turn our attention to the means of exploiting the remarkable human cognitive skills of classifying and connecting phenomena and ideas, which Adam Smith identified as the prime instruments of both scientific and economic progress. In a lecture on "mind in human affairs," printed as an appendix to *The Functions of the Executive*, Barnard (1938) emphasized the importance of such skills in the many situations in which there was no adequate basis for logical operations.

This switch from rationality to cognition entails, I believe, a shift of emphasis from symbol processing, on which Simon focused his attention, to pattern making and pattern using. Symbol processing has the dual virtues of directing our thoughts to how problems are handled and of reminding us that our mental processes necessarily take place in the space of representations, and not in the space of real-world phenomena: the correspondence between the two spaces (which Popper called World 3 and World 1) is problematic, and may be extraordinarily flimsy. Simon was well aware of the importance and the fallibility of representations, more aware than politicians, business strategists, and economists often seem to be. However, I suggest that the most promising approach to understanding representations is through the human facility for pattern making, by which representations are created (Hayek 1952) and the consequent importance of locally connected systems rather than a general processing capability. A recognition that all decisions are necessarily "framed" will allow us to understand Foss's examples as part of the pathology of a capability that can also be remarkably effective, and to incorporate Foss's proposal into a balanced appraisal of organizations as structures which may help to realize cognitive potential while combating cognitive error and opportunism. It will also allow us to keep in touch with neurophysiology, which seems to me desirable though not essential.

George Kelly's (1963) *Theory of Personality* is remarkably similar to Adam Smith's theory of science and to Shackle's (1967) reinvention of the latter. A "sense of order and consistency" (Shackle 1967, p. 286) is a psychological necessity, and this order must be created by the human imagination. Experience is not a sequence of events, but is constituted by the order that is imposed on them (Kelly 1963, pp. 72–74); thus, a sequence of events may result in different experiences for different observers. Change is fundamental; we make patterns of what we think might be viable subsystems, and use them as heuristics, both for action and for absorbing (or adapting) new knowledge. All heuristics are limited in their applicability, and these limitations carry the potential for systematic error. A substantial degree of decomposability, as Simon insisted, is essential, but decomposability tends to degrade with time, as Kelly and Marshall both recognized; and time is the ultimate bond— but emphatically not as domesticated in an Arrow-Debreu equilibrium. Local patterns provide local structures within which to think and act; but compatibility between patterns that may be juxtaposed is also a psychological need. The search for compatibility may be a major stimulus to the creation of new knowledge and new skills; but failure, at the level of the individual, may be disastrous, paralyzing action and even leading to mental breakdown, which was Kelly's professional concern. As we shall see, these human characteristics are significant in explaining the organization of economic activities.

Making patterns, in the form of grouping phenomena according to some principle of similarity while ignoring differences in other respects, was identified by Knight (1921, p. 206) as a condition of intelligent behavior in an uncertain world. Unlike Knight, Simon never sought to base his approach on fundamental uncertainty; he was content to rely on the interaction between complexity and human limitations to generate endogenous uncertainty. This allowed him to demonstrate that even in situations—notably when playing chess—for which it can be demonstrated that there is in principle a correct procedure, and therefore no intrinsic uncertainty in Knight's sense, there is nevertheless no possibility of formulating this correct procedure, and players must find their own guidelines. However, such "certainty in principle" invites representation as unqualified certainty, or well-defined risk, within a model which serves what Shackle (1967, p. 288) called "the chief service" of a theory in offering protection from "the uneasy consciousness of mystery and a threatening unknown." Following Simon's path, by contrast, entails a recognition that since there are no demonstrably correct procedures for making decisions, the decisions themselves cannot be predicted, and nor can the actions which they initiate. Individuals matter, because the individual organization of knowledge influences both actions and the development of knowledge. An inescapable consequence is that it is impossible to be certain about the decisions of others that may affect the outcome of a choice that one is about to make. Therefore organizations (of many kinds) and institutions matter, because they provide a (fallible) basis for securing compatibility between their members; as Knight (1921, p. 259) observes, coping with uncertainty merges into "the general problem of management," which in the end cannot be separated from enterprise.

Does this lead to the collapse of all theory? No; but it directs us towards two themes. The first is Simon's own theme of the ways in which decision making systems are organized, and the influences on the quality of the decisions that emerge from them, broadened to incorporate linkages between decision-making systems (for example, within networks of firms) and more generally to the role of institutions in channeling behavior. The second is much more clearly associated with George Shackle, though clearly foreshadowed by Knight's insight that uncertainty is the precondition of entrepreneurship—for opportunities as well as contingencies and interdependencies may be unknown. Shackle's contribution is the importance of imagination as the counterpart of uncertainty, though we should not forget the central role of imagination in Adam Smith's account of the growth of knowledge. Simon's own insistence that the range of alternatives between which people choose is a product of the decision process leaves ample scope for imagination; and people differ in their capacity for imagination and in the particular connections that they make. For a link between Shackle and Simon we cannot do better than to cite Shackle's (1969, p. 224) proposition: "The boundedness of uncertainty is essential to the possibility of decision." My own view is that "bounded uncertainty" rather than "bounded rationality" is the right end from which to start. Our systems of thought are not simplifications of known complexities; they have to be created by our own imagination.

The Epistemology of Science

Marshall (1994) and Hayek (1952) both devised psychological theories of knowledge as imposed connections before they turned to economics, and these theories left significant traces in their later work; but it is more relevant here to cite the accounts of scientific practice offered by the physicist John Ziman (1978, 2000). Ziman (2000, p. 289) argues that "the epistemology of science is inseparable from our natural faculty of cognition," for science relies on human "complex cognitive capabilities, such as recognizing patterns, defining similarity classes, constructing "maps" and mental models, and transforming these socially, through communication, into intersubjective representations" (Ziman 2000, p. 300). Certainty is unattainable, and the margins of scientific knowledge are particularly fallible; yet much scientific knowledge is highly reliable—though never certain—because of the process of generating, criticizing and testing conjectures within the particular institutional structures of science.

To use Simon's terms, the success of science, which satisfices because there is no criterion of optimality (Ziman 2000, p. 301), rests on procedural rather than substantive rationality, and these procedures are often discipline specific: potentially objective knowledge is produced by intersubjective means, which requires empathy (Ziman 2000, p. 303)—the equivalent of the "moral sentiments" that Smith (1976a [1759]) believed to be indispensable for a satisfactory human society. Rational-choice theory is an inadequate model for science: logical reasoning can be very helpful, notably in specifying the observable implications of a particular conjecture or in identifying inconsistencies between competing theories, both of which may suggest experiments; but it cannot control the process. Scientific truths cannot be deduced; nor can their truth be proved. As Hume showed long ago, the generation of new ideas, in science as in art or the economy, is necessarily a non-logical process. The organization of science aids the growth of scientific knowledge, which is itself an organized structure of relationships. (If economics is a science, all this is true of economics.)

Because contemporary science has evolved from the basic urge to make sense of our situation into a cluster of relatively well-ordered systems each focused on a particular area of knowledge, it is an illuminating special case from which to start our analysis of the organization of knowledge. What we may at once observe is that the progressive differentiation, and periodic recombination, of scientific disciplines illustrates the value, and the accompanying disadvantages, of the division of labor in improving knowledge, by specialization both on particular sets of phenomena and on particular premises and procedures for studying them. This indeed is an important theme of Smith's (1980 [1795]) own account of the emergence of science, leading to his subsequent emphasis on the dominant role of the division of labor in improving economic productivity (Smith 1976b [1776]). Smith's insistence on knowledge as the product of human imagination, which may subsequently be falsified, also serves to remind us that knowledge is constructed in the space of representations. However, these representations may themselves become the object of attention; indeed, Smith's observations about the aesthetic appeal of theoretical systems and the readiness of scholars "to give up the evidence of their senses in order to preserve the coherence of the ideas of their imagination" (Smith 1980 [1795]: 77) indicate how easily the representation may replace the phenomena that are ostensibly represented both as a subject of study and as a guide to action. Economics is a rich source of examples.

The progress of the sciences also reminds us of the importance of knowledge communities in fostering the institutional frameworks within which knowledge is structured, and suggests a means of explaining economic structures through their positive advantages, which derive from their patterns of connections, rather than as defense mechanisms. Firm-specific human capital relies on firm-specific connections. At the same time it suggests that we should not restrict our attention to firms, but consider the particular benefits which may be derived from other kinds of formal and informal arrangements. (Simon (1991) and Richardson (1972) have drawn attention to the importance of inter-firm connections for which prices are far from sufficient.) It may be helpful to recall that the proceedings of learned societies were often published under the title "Transactions"; knowledge exchange within each society is facilitated by a shared understanding of the procedural rationality of that society, and that is obviously true of any scientific, business, or even social community. Within a firm, this procedural rationality, which also depends on inter-subjectivity, may be partly shaped by the senior executives, but it also—and sometimes primarily—reflects the informal organization that develops within any formal organization; both of these elements receive due attention in Barnard's (1938) analysis of management.

Governance and Production

Penrose (1959, 1995) defined the firm as "a pool of resources the utilization of which is organized in an administrative framework." Simon's focus was on the administrative framework, and its effects on decision making; but a comprehensive understanding of economic organization and its effects must include the relationships between productive activities and the structure of both intra-firm and inter-firm relationships, for productive activities help to shape these relationships, and the relationships are major influences on the quality of these activities and their development. In Penrose's theory, firms grow because of the creation, selective retention, and application of resources, including managerial resources. Each resource, instead of constituting a well-defined input into a production function as in standard equilibrium theory, is a multi-specific asset the specific potential uses of which have to be discovered, invented, or imagined. Not all potentials are realized, either because they are not perceived or because the attempt to realize them is mismanaged; organizational design and decision-making procedures are both important.

Simon's insistence that perception is shaped by organizational structure and by the decision premises that arise or are imposed within it forms a natural connection with Penrose's theoretical system; and it is not difficult to extend Simon's analysis to include the perceptions and decisions which are part of normal productive operations, and the means by which new or modified resources emerge from these operations. Nelson and Winter (1982, pp. 15–17) followed Schumpeter (1934, pp. 20–21) in pointing out that decision making is a part of any productive activity, and though most decisions may simply serve to keep the activity within its intended bounds, a few may contribute to the growth of knowledge about some aspect of this activity or about one or more of the resources employed in it.

A firm is a sense-making system (Nooteboom 2001, p. 43); what sense it makes depends on how it separates and connects its ways of organizing, creating, and using knowledge, for different structures have different implications—not only for protecting against opportunism but more importantly for generating useful knowledge. Organization is an imposed order, which creates an environment for creating further order, both as predictable behavior and as new structures of knowledge. This is a path-dependent process, though not a path-determined one: movement is easiest to adjacent states, but there are typically many adjacent states (Potts 2000). Organizational design exists in the space of representations; it rests on conjectures (sometimes implicit) about similarity and complementarity (Richardson 1972), and it determines not only where problems will be worked on but how they will be defined and what will count as a solution. No organizational structure can be best for all the activities it is intended to encompass or for all the problems that might arise; for firms, industries, and economies, organization is a trial-and-error process, with a good deal of conscious design and a great many unintended consequences (harmful, beneficial or just unexpected). Some of the unintended consequences may stimulate organizational redesign, and sometimes a redefinition of the boundaries of firms. This never-ending process (most forcefully described in Young 1928), whose particular manifestations are unpredictable because they depend on knowledge that has not yet been created, means that efficiency, defined as the ability to adapt to or exploit future events, can at best be defined as a region (Potts 2000, p. 95) within which order may be maintained while permitting necessary and desirable change. Efficiency in this sense is a system property; as examples of relevant systems one might cite individual cognition, a firm, an industry, a cluster of firms (within a region or simply linked by knowledge complementarities), or an economy.

Decision Processes

Problem solving is a cognitive act—or, normally, a series of cognitive acts; in organizations it is frequently a cluster of cognitive acts by a group of people, acting sometimes in sequence and sometimes in parallel. These acts are necessarily governed by the characteristics of human cognition, moderated by the effects on human cognition of organizational structures and the institutions that have developed within those structures. These affect the distribution and the interpretation of information, what factors the participants in the decision process treat as externalities and which, if any, of these externalities are deemed relevant, the kinds of solutions that are sought, and the heuristics by which they are sought. In all these respects, human characteristics ensure that, except in simple and self-contained problems, the representations with which people work include only a small proportion of what would be required for a complete specification; and this proportion is not derived by a correct sampling procedure, since the relevant populations cannot be defined (Simon 1959, pp. 306–307).

When there are several decision makers, or when decisions are known to affect members of the organization who do not participate in the decision (and this includes situations in which people are commissioned to prepare viable options for senior management), it is necessary, as noted earlier, to have some means of enhancing coherence. Indeed, Simon (1982, p. 399) suggests that coherence may sometimes be more important than accuracy and observes that "the procedures for fact finding and for legitimating facts are themselves institutionalized." This is not only true of business organizations; as Ziman (2000) observes, similar institutionalization is to be found in science. (It is a very powerful force in economics; how else could so many economists be persuaded that modern economies can be satisfactorily represented by models of competitive equilibrium?) It is a major function of institutions to maintain coherence within groups by legitimating particular facts, interpretations, and decision premises, and individuals are generally predisposed to accept such legitimation as a scarcely dispensable aid to preserving the coherence of their own ideas and thought processes.

This powerful individual motivation explains why people are so often prepared to accept "a social prescription of some, but not all, of the premises that enter into an individual's choice of behaviors" (Simon 1982 [1963]: 345) as a natural consequence of taking a particular job in an organization; and the desire to stabilize expectations and to preserve procedures which seem satisfactory—or which at least are familiar and manageable—is a major support for organizational coalitions and organizational truce. An obvious opportunity cost is a strong tendency to inertia, even in the face of threats or opportunities, both of which may be denied for psychological and cognitive reasons. For those within the organization who perceive an opportunity that depends on a differently organized coherence of thought, and perhaps of relationships, such stability can be distinctly uncomfortable and may stimulate departure to create a new firm.

Process

"What Simon achieved ... was a theoretical dislocation of the agent from the field context" (Potts 2000, p. 113), and it is this dislocation that creates the degrees of freedom that allow agents to make decisions that may make a difference. But such decisions cannot be made by reinstating the field context, which is essential for rational-choice theory. Instead, as Simon insisted, the agent has to create a decision sub-space by setting boundaries and selecting connections between the elements within those boundaries. Because for complex decisions this can be a formidable task, it may be broken down into stages, as in Simon's distinction between intelligence, search, and choice, and also distributed between individuals, which requires a working agreement on the definition of the decision space and the procedures to be employed, including the procedures for constructing expectations and assigning values. Thus the creation of organizational arrangements—among which we should include arrangements for market transactions—is a natural consequence of intelligent behavior in the non-integral space of World 3. In order to cope with Knightian uncertainty, it is essential that these arrangements should take the form of contracts that are imperfectly specified—as Coase recognized in his original explanation of the firm: these imperfections provide the "organizational slack" that allows people to try something a little different.

It is clearly impossible to make such arrangements *de novo* for every decision (this was part of Coase's explanation for the creation of firms); as individuals we must therefore rely heavily, and often entirely, on pre-formulated decision spaces and decision procedures. For individual decisions, we draw on our own experience—which is an interpretation of a non-random sample—supplemented by conventions and rules that we have adopted from other people who seem to be skilled at making similar kinds of decisions, or conventions and rules that have become generalized into what we professionally call institutions. For joint decisions, we may enter into conscious arrangements of varying degrees of formality; prominent among these are firms, of many sizes and with many different orientations and structures. These were Simon's primary interest.

If knowledge and decision spaces have to be created, and the organizational structures to facilitate such creation have themselves to be created, there can be no procedure that would ensure that any of these creations are optimal—or even satisfactory. The analysis of any of these structures must therefore be embedded in time, in order to allow for many kinds of trial and error, with varying degrees of conscious direction. Change is fundamental; many of the consequences it reveals are unintended, and many of these may act as stimuli to further change. Though the distinction is fuzzy, it seems convenient to take separate account of management within stable structures, together with the maintenance of these structures, and of changes in these structures, whether deliberate or enforced by events. This distinction resembles that between detailed and architectural change in contemporary writing on strategy, not least in being applicable not only to individual firms but also to networks or clusters of firms. Both are also applicable to the organization of knowledge, and changes in the architecture of knowledge may lead to changes in the architecture of both firms and industries. Pharmaceuticals and telecommunications are prominent current examples.

Herbert Simon sought to organize our knowledge about the economy in a radically different way from that employed by most economists nowadays. His own system of analysis may be used to explain why it should have been either ignored or presented as a useful extension within a limited sphere, if kept under strict control. It would take another article to demonstrate how much Simon has in common with many other economists of the past and some of the present. He himself showed relatively little awareness of these connections; for example he seemed surprised to find an apparent relevance in Hayek's emphasis on dispersed and incomplete information. However, it would be in the spirit of Simon's recognition of the nature of human beings and of the effects of structures (mental, institutional, and organizational) on decision premises, procedures, and behavior to search for productive opportunities in the similarities and complementarities which are already in existence.

Simon insisted on process, not equilibrium; but he also insisted that process depended on some kinds of order. He rejected any restrictive categorization, but according to Steve Klepper (personal communication), who was a colleague for many years, he had "a strong belief in the appropriateness of evolutionary thinking/modeling to understand industrial competition," and evolutionary economists who recognize that change requires a stable ambiance can welcome his influence as well as his ideas and analysis. Human cognition and the organization of economic activity are essential to understanding both the generation of variety and the selection processes applied to that variety, and also for appraising policies intended to improve the quality of life and the many kinds of knowledge on which that quality of life depends. No one who is at all familiar with Simon's work could fail to recognize that productive organizations are knowledge communities, that all knowledge communities require shared assumptions (which remain problematic), that perpetual questioning of assumptions paralyses action while the avoidance of all questioning may lead to disaster, and that among the key questions for any economy are how much and what kind of variation should be encouraged and where should it be encouraged. Underlying all this is Potts's (2000, p. 80) question, which has also been Simon's question: "How do we, both as individuals and collectives, make good choices of the connections that build systems?"

References

Barnard, Chester I. 1938. *The Functions of the Executive.* Harvard University Press.

Demsetz, Harold. 1988. *Ownership, Control and the Firm.* Blackwell.

Foss, Nicolai J. 2001. The Problem with Bounded Rationality: On Behavioral Assumptions in the Theory of the Firm. DRUID discussion paper 01-15.

Hayek, Friedrich. 1952. *The Sensory Order.* University of Chicago Press.

Kelly, George A. 1963. *A Theory of Personality: The Psychology of Personal Constructs.* Norton.

Loasby, Brian J. 2001. Time, knowledge and evolutionary dynamics: Why connections matter. *Journal of Evolutionary Economics* 11: 393–412.

Marshall, Alfred. 1920. *Principles of Economics.* Macmillan.

Marshall, Alfred. 1994. Ye machine. *Research in the History of Economic Thought and Methodology*, Archival Supplement 4: 116–132.

Nelson, Richard R., and Winter, Sidney G. 1982. *An Evolutionary Theory of Economic Change.* Harvard University Press.

Nooteboom, Bart. 2001. From evolution to language and learning. In John Foster and J. Stanley Metcalfe, eds., *Frontiers of Evolutionary Economics: Competition.* Elgar.

Penrose, Edith T. 1959, 1995. *The Theory of the Growth of the Firm.* Blackwell, 1959; Oxford University Press, 1995.

Potts, Jason. 2000. *The New Evolutionary Microeconomics: Complexity, Competence and Adaptive Behavior.* Elgar.

Prigogine, Ilya, and Stengers, I. 1984. *Order out of Chaos: Man's New Dialogue with Nature.* Random House.

Richardson, George B. 1960. *Information and Investment.* Oxford University Press.

Richardson, George B. 1972. The organisation of industry. *Economic Journal* 82: 883–896.

Schumpeter, Joseph A. 1934. *The Theory of Economic Development.* Harvard University Press.

Shackle, George L. S. 1967. *The Years of High Theory: Invention and Tradition in Economic Thought 1926–1939.* Cambridge University Press.

Shackle, George L. S. 1969. *Decision Order and Time in Human Affairs,* second edition. Cambridge University Press.

Simon, Herbert A. 1959. Theories of decision-making in economics and behavioral science. *American Economic Review* 49: 253–283.

Simon, Herbert A. 1982 [1963]. Economics and psychology. In S. Koch, ed., *Psychology: A Study of a Science*, volume 6. McGraw-Hill. Reprinted in Herbert A. Simon, *Models of Bounded Rationality*, volume 2 (MIT Press).

Simon, Herbert A. 1982. The role of expectations in an adaptive or behavioristic model. In *Models of Bounded Rationality*, volume 2. MIT Press.

Simon, Herbert A. 1985. Human nature in politics. *American Political Science Review* 79: 293–304.

Simon, Herbert A. 1991. Organizations and markets. *Journal of Economic Perspectives* 5 (spring): 25–44.

Smith, Adam. 1976a [1759]. *The Theory of Moral Sentiments*. Oxford University Press.

Smith, Adam. 1976b [1776]. *An Inquiry into the Nature and Causes of the Wealth of Nations*. Oxford University Press.

Smith, Adam. 1980 [1795]. The principles which lead and direct philosophical inquiries: illustrated by the history of astronomy. In *Essays on Philosophical Subjects*. Oxford University Press.

Williamson, Oliver E. 1996. *The Mechanisms of Governance*. Oxford University Press.

Young, Allyn A. 1928. Increasing returns and economic progress. *Economic Journal* 38: 527–542.

Ziman, John. 1978. *Reliable Knowledge*. Cambridge University Press.

Ziman, John. 2000. *Real Science*. Cambridge University Press.

Clarence (left) and Herbert Simon, 1918.

Above: Herbert Simon at Evolution Basin in Sierra Nevada, 1941.

Opposite top: Herbert Simon at age 5, New Year's, 1922.

Opposite bottom: Herbert and Dorothea Simon after their wedding, 1937.

Left: Herbert Simon, 1948.

Below: Herbert Simon teaching at
GSIA, 1949.

GSIA faculty members and students, 1950. From right: Lee Bach, Elliott Dunlap Smith, Herbert Simon, William Cooper, six graduate students.

Herbert Simon (left) and James March, 1958.

Herbert Simon, 1960.

Herbert Simon contemplating the Tower of Hanoi puzzle, 1969.

William Chase (left) and Herbert Simon, 1973. In background: Neil Charness.

Herbert, Dorothea, Barbara, Katherine, and Peter Simon, Nobel week, 1978.

A committee of the National Research Council, 1982. Back row, from left: Gerald Debreu, Robert Solow, Herbert Simon, Gabriel Almond. Front row, from left: Julian Wolpert, William Estes, Mark Rosenzweig.

Allen Newell and Herbert Simon, 1985.

Edward Feigenbaum (left) and
Herbert Simon, 1985.

Herbert Simon, 1956.

Herbert Simon and Organization Theory: Lessons for the Theory of the Firm

Oliver E. Williamson

The theory of the firm was a recurrent interest of Herbert Simon's long and distinguished research career. Volume 2 of his collected papers on bounded rationality is organized around "a central theme: that organization theory, economics (especially the theory of the firm), and cognitive psychology are all basically concerned with the same phenomena. All three are theories of human decision making and problem solving processes; yet each of the three domains has developed in relative isolation from the other two." (Simon 1982, p. xv) It was Simon's view, first advanced in *Administrative Behavior* (1947), that this combined approach would illuminate organizational decision making processes and bring "organization theory closer to the classical theory of the firm by providing an economic rationale for important characteristics of organizations that have been observed empirically but not explained in theoretical terms" (1982, p. xv). Although his 1997 book *Empirically Based Microeconomics* ranges widely across a variety of economic topics, it deals especially with the joining of economics and organization theory as these relate to the theory of the firm.

I begin with some observations about Simon and Carnegie in the early 1960s. I then turn to what I take to be the chief lessons of organization theory for the theory of the firm. After sketching the rudiments of the governance structure approach to economic organization,

I conclude with some remarks about Simon and the Graduate School of Industrial Administration during its heyday.

Vast Influence

Certainly part of Simon's vast influence is because he was a renaissance man. One could not be in his company or read his work without being awed by the breadth and depth of his erudition. But there was more. Simon combined a brilliant and curious mind with enormous energy and missionary zeal. This last benefited from his exceptional expositional and argumentative skills. It was hard to be around Herb without becoming infected.

Simon was an interdisciplinary social scientist of the best kind: he combined interdisciplinary interests with extensive knowledge of the relevant literatures, a keen sense for important and underdeveloped issues, and exceptional modeling talents to pull these pieces together. He epitomized what I have referred to elsewhere as the Carnegie triple: be disciplined; be interdisciplinary; have an active mind (Williamson 1996, p. 25). Of the various fields that have claims to name him as one of their own—political science, economics, cognitive science, psychology, philosophy, organization theory—it is his contributions to organization theory from which I have learned the most. That, moreover, seems to be in agreement with Simon's self-image, in that he describes his entire scientific output as an "elaborate gloss" upon two interrelated ideas: "(1) human beings are able to achieve only a very bounded rationality, and (2) as one consequence of their cognitive limitations, they are prone to identify with subgoals" (1991b, p. 88). Both features make their appearance in *Administrative Behavior*.

Administrative Behavior was inspired by Chester Barnard's 1938 book *The Functions of the Executive*. Despite Barnard's grave skepticism about economics (pp. x–xi), his efforts to work out the logic of organization were very much of a rational spirit kind. Key contributions by Barnard—his theory of authority, his characterization of the employment relation, and the role of informal organization—all reflected an economizing orientation (Williamson 1996, pp. 32–35). But Barnard was writing as a businessman rather than a social scientist and many of his original and deep insights would have gone unnoticed but for Simon's and Philip Selznick's (1949, 1957) efforts to refine, extend, elaborate, and build upon them.

Simon simultaneously embraced Barnard and took issue with prevailing administrative theory, which was normative and based on "proverbs" (Simon 1947, chapter 2). Because I had previously taken an organization theory course (at Stanford) that was based on proverbs, I was able to relate immediately to this Simon critique. Indeed, as developed by Simon, Richard Cyert, James March, and others at Carnegie, I could see that organization theory truly was a scientific enterprise—even though many others (including some organization theorists) treated it otherwise. The selective joinder of organization theory with economics, as these two bear on the theory of the firm, is what motivated my dissertation (The Economics of Discretionary Behavior: Managerial Objectives in a Theory of the Firm, 1964) and describes much of what I have been up to since.

Like Yuji Ijiri (2002), I also benefited from taking Herb's course in Mathematical Social Science and having had Simon on my dissertation committee. Unlike Yuji, I never co-authored anything with Simon, but we did remain in correspondence. Because he thought me too deferential to economics, he frequently took exception with my work. Still, Herb was a pluralist. I was pleased that he described me as his student but not his disciple.

There is no question that I struck the balance between economics and organization theory in a way different from Simon and, for that matter, the exciting program in behavioral research that was in progress at Carnegie (Cyert and March 1963). Partly that can be attributed to the economics training that I had received previously at Stanford (where it had been my privilege to be in the classrooms of Kenneth Arrow, Bernard Haley, James Howell, Melvin Reder, and Hirofumi

Uzawa). But Jack Muth was also at Carnegie, and, in his quiet way, Jack had a subtle influence.

Perhaps the most overarching and important lesson that I can associate with economics is Arrow's unapologetic reference to the "rational spirit ... of the economist," whereupon he describes an economist as one who "by training thinks of himself as the guardian of rationality, the ascriber of rationality to others, and the prescriber of rationality to the social world" (1974, p. 16). To be sure, economists do not have a lock on rationality (Simon 1978). Indeed, the question might be put as one of degree: irrationality, nonrationality, myopia, bounded rationality, hyperrationality? The choice may well depend on the issue being addressed.

The degree of rationality that I have found instructive for studying economic organization falls short of hyperrationality yet invites social scientists to "push the logic to completion." Thus if organization theorists or others tell economists about a regularity that economists had hitherto neglected, the response is not simply to make note of this condition. The further step is to uncover the mechanisms and work out the ramifications for organizational design. Being around Jack Muth when I was at Carnegie brought this home to me repeatedly.

Jack was often one step ahead of those around him. Thus whenever I would discuss "managerial discretion" with him, he would always put it in a larger organizational design context: Might there be method to this madness? Was there an underlying rationale? Not only could I see the merit in such queries, but, consciously or otherwise, I began to pose such questions to myself.

To be sure, one can drift into hyperrationality constructions in this way—and some do. There is a tension, after all, between bounds on rationality on one hand and pushing the logic to completion on the other. Simon believed that I had the balance wrong—as witness his statement that, awaiting empirical research, the new institutional economics program with which I and others have been engaged was an "act of faith, or perhaps piety" (1991a, p. 27). And he subsequently remarked that "When we look at organizations in the real world, we find much more complexity than is hinted at in the theory of the firm, whether in its classical or its 'new institutional' versions" (1997, p. 38).

I have puzzled over these and related observations and decided in the spring of 2000 to respond to Simon's 1997 book *Empirically Based Microeconomics* in a paper titled "Empirical microeconomics: Another perspective."[1] I make the argument in this paper that not only is the TCE branch of the new institutional economics an empirical success story (there being over 600 empirical published papers on transaction-cost economics as of the year 2000),[2] but that the theory of the firm as governance structure differs significantly from the neoclassical theory of the firm. Thus whereas the latter works out of the resource allocation paradigm, is dismissive of organization theory, and views the firm as a production function (which is a technological construction), the former works out of the lens of contract, relies significantly on organization theory, and views the firm in comparative institutional terms as an alternative mode of governance (which is an organizational construction). So even if the theory of the firm as governance structure is neglectful of some of the complexities to which Simon refers, it nonetheless made serious efforts to move in Simon's direction.

To my surprise and delight, Simon seems to agree. I received an e-mail from Herb when that paper was still in middle-draft stages that reads in part as follows:

[I recently reread and was surprised] with what I found in your book [*The Economic Institutions of Capitalism*]. As you know, . . . I have been accusing you, from time to time, . . . of pouring the new bounded rationality wine into the old maximizing bottles. After rereading what you wrote, I can no longer say that, and must apologize for misinterpreting you . . . Furthermore, I was much impressed by your use of empirical evidence, especially historical evidence and case studies, to support your argument. I think we would both agree . . . that economics is necessarily a historical science, for human invention of new institutions and practices is one of its important processes.

Because, however, Simon's earlier views of my work were widely shared, I persevered with the work-in-progress and sent a copy to Herb inviting his comments. Alas, time ran out before he was able to get back to me. Had he replied, I am confident that our disagreements (albeit narrowed) would have continued. I am nevertheless pleased that he saw more merit in my work than he had previously; and I will be forever grateful for having been his student.

Organization Theory[3]

Richard Scott (1992) describes the leading schools of organization theory as rational, natural, and open systems. I focus on the contributions of the rational systems approach, with special emphasis on Simon. I begin with five lessons from organization theory that are central to the conception of the firm as governance structure.[4] Three follow-on lessons that accrue upon taking a comparative contractual approach to economic organization are discussed next.

Five Lessons

A first lesson from organization theory is to describe human actors in more realistic terms. Simon (1985, p. 303) is unequivocal: "Nothing is more fundamental in setting our research agenda and informing our research methods than our view of the nature of the human beings whose behavior we are studying." Social scientists are thus invited (challenged) to name the cognitive, self-interest, and other attributes of human actors on which their analyses rest.

Bounded rationality is the cognitive assumption to which Simon refers, by which he has reference to behavior that is intendedly rational but only limitedly so (1957a, p. xxiv). The main lesson for the science of choice[5] is to supplant maximizing by "satisficing" (1957b, p. 204)— the quest for an alternative that is "good enough."

Simon describes self-interest as "frailty of motive" (1985, p. 303), according to which most individuals will do what they say and some will do more. If they slip, it is a normal friction and often a matter of bemusement. Such benign and docile behavior is reinforced by describing organizations in terms of "routines."

Recall in this connection that the second of the two core ideas on which Simon's research agenda rested is that human beings are "prone to identify with subgoals" (1991b, p. 88). Such subgoal pursuit could be benign, in that individuals do the best they can with reference to the problem at hand (local goals) because global goals are too remote to engage in an operational way. But subgoal pursuit could also be strategic, in that individuals consciously pursue local goals that are in tension with larger global purposes. Agency problems would therein arise. Simon was loath to move in this direction, although he recognized the hazard (1947, pp. 40, 209).

A second lesson of organization theory is to be alert to all significant behavioral regularities whatsoever. For example, efforts by bosses to impose controls on workers have both intended *and* unintended consequences. In the event that workers are not passive contractual agents, naïve efforts to exercise control will be supplanted by more sophisticated mechanisms where consequences of both kinds are contemplated. More generally, the interest by organization theorists and sociologists in endogenous changes—that "organization has a life of its own" (Selznick 1950, p. 10)—serves to uncover regularities for which the student of governance should be alerted and thereafter factor into the organizational design calculus.

A third lesson of organization theory is that alternative modes of governance (markets, hybrids, firms, bureaus) differ in kind—which is to say, in discrete structural ways (Simon 1978, pp. 6–7). The usual marginal calculus out of which economics works gives way to a discrete structural examination of the strengths and weaknesses of each mode and an effort to align governance modes with the underlying attributes of transactions.

A fourth lesson of organization theory is that the action resides in the microanalytics. In that event, a unit of analysis that engages the microanalytics is needed. Simon proposes for this purpose that the "decision premise" be made the unit of analysis and avers that "Behavior can be predicted ... when the premises of the decision are known (or can be predicted) in sufficient detail" (1957a, p. xxx).

The fifth lesson of organization theory is the importance of cooperative adaptation. Interestingly, both Friedrich Hayek (1945) and the organization theorist Chester Barnard (1938) were in agreement that adaptation is the central problem of economic organization. But whereas Hayek (pp. 526–527) focused on the adaptations of autonomous economic actors who adjust spontaneously to changes in the market, mainly as signaled by changes in relative prices, Barnard emphasized the importance of coordinated adaptation among economic actors accomplished through administration (hierarchy). The latter is accomplished not spontaneously but in a "conscious, deliberate, purposeful" way (p. 4).

Three Follow-On Lessons

Examining economic organization through the lens of contract uncovers additional regularities to which governance ramifications accrue. Three such regularities are described here: the Fundamental Transformation, the impossibility of replication/selective intervention, and the idea of contract laws (plural).

The Fundamental Transformation is a manifestation of the proposition that contract also has a life of its own. Specifically, although many transactions have large numbers of qualified suppliers at the outset, some of these are transformed into what, in effect, are small numbers supply relations during contract execution and at the contract renewal interval. The key factor here is the characteristics of the assets. Transactions that are supported by generic assets are ones for which there are large numbers of actual and potential suppliers throughout. Because such assets can be redeployed to alternative uses and users with negligible loss in productive value, each party can go its own way with little cost to the other. Where, however, significant investments in transaction specific assets are put at risk, bilateral dependency sets in, whence continuity is important. In effect, the small numbers exchange relation described above takes effect. It is elementary that transactions of the latter kind pose contractual hazards if organized as simple market exchange.

The second follow-on lesson—the impossibility of replication/selective intervention—relates to the question of what is responsible for limits to firm size and illustrates the benefits of pushing the logic to completion. The obvious answer to that question was to invoke "diseconomies of large scale." But that is too facile. Wherein do these diseconomies reside? Satisfactory answers to the latter question were not forthcoming.

The governance structure approach serves to uncover the mechanisms by reformulating the basic question as follows: Why can't a large firm do everything that a collection of small firms can do and more? Were it that large firms could *replicate* a collection of small firms in all circumstances where small firms do well, then large firms would never do worse. If, moreover, large firms could *selectively intervene* to impose order wherever expected net gains can be projected, then large firms will sometimes do better. An examination of markets and hierarchies in a side-by-side fashion discloses that replication and selective intervention are both impossible (Williamson 1985, chapter 6)—which is consistent with Simon's view that alternative modes of governance differ in discrete structural ways. Specifically, replication and selective intervention break down because the internally consistent syndromes of incentive, control and contract law attributes that define markets and hierarchies differ (Williamson 1991).

Applying the lens of contract to the conventional assumption that there is a single, all-purpose law of contract is revealing. Is it really the case that market and internal transactions are identical in contract enforcement respects? Examination of the logic and practice of contract reveals that classical contract law of a *legalistic* kind applies to simple market transactions; contract as *framework*, which is a more elastic construction, applies as bilateral dependency sets in; and *for-bearance* law, according to which courts refuse to hear internal disputes, is the law of internal organization. The firm becomes its own court of ultimate appeal under forbearance law. Firms and markets differ in their access to fiat on this account.

The Firm as Governance Structure

Orthodox economics in general and the theory of the firm as production function in particular have been dismissive of the contributions of organization theory to the study of economic organization (Reder 1999, pp. 46–49, 122–124). That is because the reigning resource allocation paradigm, which views economics as "the science which studies human behavior as a relation between ends and scarce means which have alternative uses" (Robbins 1932, p. 16), is, in effect, a science of choice perspective. Utility maximization (by consumers) and profit maximization (by firms) are the main constructions. Economists who work out of such setups give emphasis to quantities as influenced by changes in relative prices and available resources.

A different—partly rival, partly complementary—science of contract perspective has been taking shape in economics over the past 30 years. The public ordering branch of the science of contract emphasizes collective organization (Buchanan and Tullock 1962; Buchanan 1987). The private ordering branch focuses on actions by the immediate parties to a transaction to perfect their contractual relationship. This branch divides into ex ante incentive alignment and ex post governance parts. The theory of the firm as governance structure is predominantly concerned with ex post governance (Williamson 2002a,b).

The issues have been worked out elsewhere. I merely sketch the ways in which the firm as governance structure relates to the lessons of organization theory set out above.

(1) Human actors. As against satisficing, the governance structure approach (GSA) to economic organization holds that the main lesson

of bounded rationality is that all complex contracts are incomplete. Also, as against frailty of motive, GSA describes self-interestedness as a combination of (nonstrategic) frailty of motive and (strategic) opportunism. Thus whereas routines describe what is going on "most of the time," much of what is interesting about human behavior in general and organizations in particular has reference not to routines but exceptions. Strategic considerations come into play when exceptions arise. To paraphrase Robert Michels on oligarchy (1962, p. 370), nothing but a serene and frank examination of the hazards of opportunism will enable us to mitigate these hazards. Attenuating the ex post hazards of opportunism through the discriminating alignment of transactions with governance structures is central to GSA.

(2) Intertemporal transformations. GSA takes a farsighted view of intertemporal transformations (including the Fundamental Transformation). Upon being advised that a particular intertemporal regularity is in prospect, GSA inquires into the mechanisms that are responsible for the regularity, works out the ramifications, and factors these back into the contractual/organizational design.

(3) Discrete structural. Not only does GSA view alternative modes of governance in a discrete structural way, but it takes the further step of identifying the crucial attributes with respect to which governance structures differ. These are incentive intensity, administrative controls, and contract law regime. Each generic mode of governance (market, hybrid, hierarchy, bureau) is described as an internally consistent syndrome of attributes, according to which each has distinctive strengths and weaknesses.

(4) Microanalytics. GSA concurs that the action resides in the microanalytics but nominates the transaction (rather than the decision premise) as the basic unit of analysis. This is broadly responsive to John R. Commons's advice (1932, p. 4) that "the ultimate unit of activity . . . must contain in itself the three principles of conflict, mutuality, and order. This unit is a transaction." Not only does GSA subscribe to the idea that the transaction is the basic unit of analysis, but governance is

an effort to infuse order, thereby to mitigate conflict and realize mutual gain. The key attributes of transactions that have governance structure ramifications are the condition of asset specificity (bilateral dependency), the disturbances to which transactions are subject, and the frequency with which they recur.

(5) Adaptation. GSA agrees that adaptation is the central purpose of economic organization and makes provision for both autonomous adaptation (in response to price signals in the market) and coordinated adaptation (of a purposeful kind within firms). The mix of adaptations to which governance is needed vary with the attributes of transactions.

There is no way that the theory of the firm as governance structure could have taken shape without these contributions from organization theory. Table 1 summarizes the foregoing.

The Heyday and Beyond

Though confident in his research agenda and research methods, Simon was also a pluralist, which befits anyone who holds that "the capacity of the human mind for formulating and solving complex problems is very small compared with the size of the problems whose solution is required" (Simon 1957b, p. 198). Faced with bewildering complexity, social scientists need to be open to alternative ways of addressing complex phenomena—subject only to the conditions that they address them in disciplined and plausible ways. So even though Simon often disagreed with those of us who, to his taste, were "too neoclassical," there was always an outside possibility that, in some degree, we might get parts of it right.

With the benefit of hindsight, the main differences between GSA and Simon-favored approaches to the theory of the firm are these: Simon was mainly concerned with the theory of choice whereas GSA works out of the lens of contract; Simon described self-interest in comparatively benign terms whereas GSA entertains the possibility of oppor-

Table 1
Lessons of organization theory for economics: Simon and GSA

	Simon	GSA
1. Human actors		
Cognition	Bounded rationality: satisficing	Bounded rationality: incompleteness
Self-interest	Frailty of motive: benign	Opportunism: strategic hazards
2. Organization has a life of its own	Uncover and be respectful of regularities	Plus: work out organizational design lessons
3. Discrete structural differences among modes	Marginal analysis gives way to discrete structural comparisons	Plus: uncover attributes to which discrete structural differences accrue (syndrome)
4. Unit of analysis	Decision premise Routine	Commons: "The ultimate unit of activity ... must contain in itself the three principles of conflict, mutuality, and order. This unit is the transaction."

5. Main purpose	Search for satisfactory outcome "Behavioral model of rational choice" (*QJE*, 1955a)	Adaptation
		  autonomous: Hayek
		  coordinated: Barnard

tunism; and whereas both subscribe to bounded rationality, each then goes off in different directions—Simon into satisficing and GSA into incomplete contracting. But GSA is only one of several lines of research on the theory of the firm that owe their origins to Simon. March and Simon's 1958 book on organizations was a precursor to *A Behavioral Theory of the Firm* (Cyert and March 1963), which in turn has had a huge influence on both evolutionary (Nelson and Winter 1982) and competence-based (Teece and Pisano 1994; Foss 1993; Hodgson 1998) perspectives.[6]

Jacques Dreze speaks for me and, I believe, for many others by summarizing his Carnegie experience as follows: "Never since have I experienced such intellectual excitement." (1995, p. 123) Doing inter-disciplinary research at Carnegie during the period 1950–1965 was both liberating and exhilarating. These years were the heyday (Augier and March 2001, pp. 21–25).[7]

At the center of the Carnegie project was Herbert Simon—with his extraordinary mind, his deep curiosity, and his prodigious energy. When, moreover, research at Carnegie came under criticism (which it did), everyone could take satisfaction that, should push come to shove, our guy (Simon) was smarter than your guy (X).

Although Simon did not realize all of his ambitions to reform eco-nomics, the influence of his intellectual contributions is vast and will continue to spin out "forever."

Acknowledgment

Helpful comments by James March are gratefully acknowledged.

Notes

1. This paper appears in Augier and March 2002.

2. For recent surveys of the empirical transaction-cost economics literature, see Shelanski and Klein 1995 and Boerner and Macher 2001.

3. This section is based on Williamson 2002b.

4. Simon made other contributions to which the theory of the firm as governance structure is less responsive. Thus, although the governance approach relates in part to Simon's insistence on the importance of identification, docility, and altruism (1991a), my treatments of the "economics of atmosphere" (Williamson 1975, 1993) are decidedly underdeveloped. Simon also took exception to the concept of the sur-vival of the fittest and speaks instead of the "survival of the fitter" (1983, p. 49). Governance deals always and everywhere with feasible (as against ideal) alternatives, but it is underdeveloped in evolutionary respects.

5. Choice was the subject of two of his best-known papers in economics: "A behav-ioral model of rational choice" (1955) and "Rational choice and the structure of the environment" (1956), which papers he describes as the "central core of [his] theory of choice," the object being to simplify "the choice problem to bring it within the powers of human computation" (Simon 1957b, p. 204). A third important paper is

"A formal theory of the employment relation" (1951). This last is a contractual construction and has been influential in subsequent work on the employment relation (Holmstrom 1999; Baron and Kreps 1999).

6. Although I have criticized this last as being vague and tautological (Williamson 1999), it is nonetheless true that competence based scholars are raising important issues and that, in combination with behavioral theory and evolutionary theory, have pushed others who work on the theory of the firm to address issues of intertemporal and of real time importance.

7. Studies by the Ford Foundation (Gordon and Howell 1958) and the Carnegie Foundation (Pierson 1959) record some of the programmatic successes. Augier and March report that "four members of the small cluster of faculty and doctoral students at GSIA in the 1950s and early 1960s have subsequently received Nobel Prizes in Economics; fifteen have subsequently been elected to the National Academy of Sciences" (2001, p. 21).

References

Arrow, K. J. 1974. *The Limits of Organization*. Norton.

Arrow, K. J. 1987. Reflections on the essays. In G. Feiwel, ed., *Arrow and the Foundations of the Theory of Economic Policy*. New York University Press.

Augier, M., and J. March. 2002. A model scholar: Herbert Simon (1916–2001). *Journal of Economic Behavior and Organization* 49: 1–17.

Augier, M., and J. March, eds. 2002. *The Economics of Choice, Change, and Organization*. Elgar.

Barnard, C. I. 1938. *The Functions of the Executive*. Harvard University Press.

Baron, J., and D. Kreps. 1999. *Strategic Human Resources: Frameworks for General Managers*. Wiley.

Boerner, C. S., and J. Macher. 2002. Transaction Cost Economics: A Review and Assessment of the Empirical Literature. Unpublished.

Buchanan, J. 1987. The constitution of economic policy. *American Economic Review* 77, June: 243–250.

Buchanan, J., and Tullock, G. 1962. *The Calculus of Consent*. University of Michigan Press.

Baron, J., and D. Kreps. 1999. *Strategic Human Resources: Frameworks for General Managers*. Wiley.

Cyert, R. M., and J. G. March. 1963. *A Behavioral Theory of the Firm*. Prentice-Hall.

Dreze, J. 1995. Forty years of public economics: A personal perspective. *Journal of Economic Perspectives* 9, no. 2: 111–130.

Foss, N. J. 1993. Theories of the firm: Contractual and competence based perspectives. *Journal of Monetary Economics* 3: 317–324.

Gordon, R. J., and J. Howell. 1958. *Higher Education for Business*. Columbia University Press.

Hayek, F. 1945. The use of knowledge in society. *American Economic Review* 35, September: 519–530.

Hodgson, G. 1998. Competence and contract in the theory of the firm. *Journal of Economic Behavior and Organization* 35, April: 179–201.

Holmstrom, B. 1999. The firm as a subeconomy. *Journal of Law, Economics, and Organization* 15, April: 74–102.

March, J. G., and H. Simon. 1958. *Organizations*. Wiley.

Michels, R. 1962. *Political Parties*. Free Press.

Nelson, R. R., and S. G. Winter. 1982. *An Evolutionary Theory of Economic Change*. Belknap.

Pierson, F. 1959. *The Education of American Businessmen: A Study of University-College Programs in Business Administration*. McGraw-Hill.

Reder, M. W. 1999. *The Culture of a Controversial Science*. University of Chicago Press.

Robbins, L. 1932. *An Essay on the Nature and Significance of Economic Science*. New York University Press.

Selznick, P. 1949. *TVA and the Grassroots: A Study of Politics and Organization*. University of California Press.

Selznick, P. 1957. *Leadership in Administration*. Harper and Row.

Shelanski, H., and P. Klein. 1995. Empirical research in transaction cost economics: A review and assessment. *Journal of Law, Economics, and Organization* 11, October: 335–361.

Simon, H. A. 1947. *Administrative Behavior*. Free Press.

Simon, H. A. 1951. A theory of the employment relation. *Econometrica* 19, July: 293–305.

Simon, H. A. 1955. A behavioral model of rational choice. *Quarterly Journal of Economics* 69: 99–118.

Simon, H. A. 1956. Rational choice and the structure of the environment. *Psychology Review* 63: 129–138.

Simon, H. A. 1957a. *Models of Man*. Wiley.

Simon, H. A. 1957b. *Administrative Behavior*, second edition. Macmillan.

Simon, H. A. 1978. Rationality as process and as product of thought. *American Economic Review* 68, May: 1–16.

Simon, H. A. 1982. *Models of Bounded Rationality*. MIT Press.

Simon, H. A. 1983. *Reason in Human Affairs*. Stanford University Press.

Simon, H. A. 1985. Human nature in politics: The dialogue of psychology with political science. *American Political Science Review* 79: 293–304.

Simon, H. A. 1991a. Organizations and markets. *Journal of Economic Perspectives* 5, spring: 25–44.

Simon, H. A. 1991b. *Models of My Life*. MIT Press.

Simon, H. A. 1997. *An Empirically Based Microeconomics*. Cambridge University Press.

Teece, D. J., and G. Pisano. 1994. The dynamic capabilities of firms: An introduction. *Industrial and Corporate Change* 3, no. 3: 537–556.

Williamson, O. E. 1964. *The Economics of Discretionary Behavior: Managerial Objectives in a Theory of the Firm*. Prentice-Hall.

Williamson, O. E. 1975. *Markets and Hierarchies*. Free Press.

Williamson, O. E. 1985. *The Economic Institutions of Capitalism*. Free Press.

Williamson, O. E. 1991. Comparative economic organization: The analysis of discrete structural alternatives. *Administrative Science Quarterly* 36, June: 269–296.

Williamson, O. E. 1996. *The Mechanisms of Governance*. Oxford University Press.

Williamson, O. E. 1999. Strategy research: Governance and competence perspectives. *Strategic Management Journal* 20, December: 1087–1108.

Williamson, O. E. 2002a. Empirical microeconomics: Another perspective. In M. Augier and J. March, eds., *The Economics of Choice, Change, and Organization*. Elgar.

Williamson, O. E. 2002b. The theory of the firm as a governance structure. *Journal of Economic Perspectives* 16, summer: 171–195.

The "Easy Problem" Problem[1]

Sidney G. Winter

Herb Simon was a highly influential critic of the rationality paradigm in economic theory. He believed that mainstream economists were on the wrong track when it came to rationality, and he expressed himself vigorously and frequently to that effect. The primary error he saw was not that economists relied too much on the assumption of rational behavior, but that they were incorrect in their understanding of what rational behavior *is*. By ignoring some of the constraints with which rational actors have to cope, economists *messed up* the analysis of this key concept. There is a characteristic note of reproach in much of Simon's commentary on rationality that is connected specifically to the perversity and persistence of this "messing up."

If—as Herb believed and I believe—the bounds of rationality are an important aspect of reality that mainstream economics ignores, a question arises as to the locus and extent of the scientific damage that results from this neglect. At least at first glance, it seems plausible to suppose that the damage is greatest where the discrepancy between the difficulty of the problem and the available resources for rational problem solving is the largest. Following that line of thought, one is led to consider example situations where full rationality seems clearly implausible because it would imply enormous calculation demands on the decision maker—demands that in all likelihood could not be met.

These situations then help to define the initial agenda for a modified theory that accepts some bounds to rationality.

A prominent example of this approach is Oliver Williamson's (1985) invocation of bounded rationality in the context of transaction-cost economics. A fully rational decision maker could envisage all the innumerable contingencies that might arise in the life of a contract, determine how action should unfold in each, and draft the contract accordingly. Williamson, however, makes the plausible judgment that this extravagant demand of rationality cannot be met, and proceeds to consider the governance options for transactions on the assumption that complete contracting is not among them.

In a similar spirit, some theorists have based the argument for bounded rationality on considerations of computational complexity ("NP-completeness"). If computation rises exponentially with problem size in some class of problems, it seems clear that realistic decision processes are necessarily overwhelmed at large problem sizes—and realistic problem sizes do get very large. (Of course, it could always be argued that the decision maker behaves "as if" capable of enormous computation—i.e., "as if" endowed with miraculous powers.)

In this discussion, I propose to explore the other end of the difficulty spectrum. Instead of considering situations where full rationality is *prima facie* implausible, I look at ones where it seems *prima facie* plausible and perhaps even compelling. At least, computational considerations alone do not seem to pose an obstacle to full rationality in these situations. More specifically, I ask whether there are problems that are "easy" in the sense that normal human intelligence should suffice to discover the right answer almost regardless of the attendant circumstances. To put it another way, is there a class of problems where the assumption of optimal behavior can considered robust? I call this the "easy problem" problem. Is there a set of problems that are easy in this sense, and if so how would one define its limits?

I posed this question to Herb Simon in 1983, when we were both attending a conference in Stockholm marking the hundredth anniversary of the birth of Joseph Schumpeter.[2] He responded by describing two example situations, which I would like to share with you today and discuss a bit. I might add that I do not recall that there was any request for clarification of the question, nor was there a noticeable computation lag, before Herb began expounding these two very relevant examples. Bounded rationality is ubiquitous but more apparent in some than in others.

In the first situation, our focal decision maker is seated at a circular table with five other symmetrically positioned participants. Approximately in the middle of the table, a reach and stretch away from the decision maker, a fifty dollar bill and a ten dollar bill repose side by side. At the word "Go," all participants are free to grab for one bill or the other, and may keep what they get. Which bill to grab for, that is the problem for our decision maker.

As Herb observed, at first glance this looks like an "easy problem" with the answer "grab for the 50." At second glance one sees the game-theoretic complexity: if the other participants get the easy answer and go for the 50, it might be better to go for the 10. Indeed, if grabs for the same bill result in ties that are resolved at random, going for the ten definitely has a higher expected value than completing a crowd of six going for the fifty. There is, of course, a Nash equilibrium in mixed strategies when all participants frame the problem in the obvious game-theoretic way and decide accordingly.[3]

Thus, while expressing the preference for the 50 over the 10 is an easy problem, the example embeds the choice in a context that makes the right decision problematic. There are in fact other aspects of the context, taken for granted in the account just given, that potentially have the same effect. What consequences should I anticipate, for example, if I don't wait for "Go" but just grab the 50 and smile benignly—or grab the 50 and bolt for the door? By positing that the "rules of the game" are respected, an element of simplicity is introduced that is often not present in real situations.

What the game theorist excludes by the posited rules is just the sort of rigged context by which the operator of a confidence game makes his profit. Confidence games invite victims to believe that they confront easy problems when they do not. Aware of that fact, potential victims often arm themselves with the protective heuristic "If something seems to be too good to be true, it probably is." But when that heuristic is being employed, even problems that are objectively easy become complex in the perception of the decision maker; situations in which the incentives are "overwhelmingly clear" are precisely the ones that warrant suspicion. That people are skeptical and often reluctant to respond straightforwardly in apparently simple choice situations is a point familiar to many sorts of experts, e.g., marketers, pollsters and experimentalists.

Herb's second example referred to problem-solving studies employing the Tower of Hanoi puzzle. That puzzle, you recall, involves a number of rings of graded size stacked on a small post, smaller rings toward the top. There are two other posts, one of which is the goal post. The problem is to move the stack of rings to the goal post, moving one ring at a time from post to post and never putting a larger ring on top of a smaller one.

For N rings, the problem is solved by the recursive scheme: move the top $N - 1$ rings to the third pillar, using the $N - 1$ ring solution. Move the bottom ring, the largest, to the goal pillar. Place the top $N - 1$ rings on top of it, using the $N - 1$ ring solution again. (The case $N = 2$ is, uh, easy.) In the experiments, subjects do this repeatedly and get better at it. They turn the necessary hand motions into a complex skill, no longer having to think about the logic of the solution.

Herb's remark about the Tower of Hanoi problem actually related to the consequences of a switch to "Upside-Down Tower of Hanoi"—same problem, only the rings are initially stacked with larger ones on top, and the rules prohibit putting smaller rings on top of larger ones. This problem is a simple logical isomorphism of the original one, and if the original has become easy through practice then the logical isomorph should be easy too—or so it might seem. In fact, however, a subject with a developed skill for the Tower of Hanoi puzzle has a lot of difficulty with the upside-down version. As I recall, Herb said that solution times initially increase 100 percent or more.[4]

This result is supported by many others relating to of transfer of learning. For example, in their experimental work on organizational routines Michael Cohen and Paul Bacdayan (1994) did a series of experiments in which two-person teams learned to function quickly and effectively in a two person game situation involving red and black playing cards. When trained teams were presented with the modified game in which the roles of red and black were simply reversed, they displayed large increases in solution times, which persisted over many trials.

The point here is that the simplicity of the logical connection between the two versions of the problem situation is no guide to "easiness" because logic has nothing to do with high performance in a repetitive task, specifically with high *speed* performance. In the skilled behavior of individuals or the routinized behavior of organizations, deliberative rationality is suppressed (as Dick Nelson and I emphasized in our 1982 book). The investment in learning is in large part an investment in suppressing rationality so that it doesn't interfere with performance. (Such interference is an aspect of what is commonly known as "clutching" in the context of skilled athletic performance.) Once suppressed, rationality does not automatically regain its influence when it is needed again.

Where does this leave us with respect to the "easy problem" problem? Herb's two examples direct us to the conclusion that the ease or difficulty of problem solution is shaped, first, by context, second and more specifically, by previous learning and practice. All problems have contexts, and no matter how they are stated, they still have *unstated* contexts. Thus, it will be very hard to meet the demand for a characterization of an easy problem that is robust in the sense that *it depends only the problem and not on the context.*

The conclusion about learning and practice has very fundamental implications. If previous learning can make problems either harder or easier, and if it involves the suppression of deliberative rationality, we are left with a picture of economic actors as heterogeneous even in their rationality. They are shaped in an irreversible, path-dependent way by their previous learning experiences. Further, these differences are particularly relevant to the domain of effective performance of repetitive tasks. Because competition drives performance toward high effectiveness, the nature of the connection between effectiveness and rationality is very important to the logic of economic activity. That high effectiveness comes partly at the expense of rationality is a point we should not forget.

Let me close with a view of the relationship between the bounded rationality that Herb Simon described and the full rationality that mainstream theory relies upon. The devices of the full rationality theory are indispensable tools for economic analysis, I have no doubt about that. That full rationality theory is indispensable does not mean, however, that it is fundamental. On the contrary, it is the bounded rationality perspective that is fundamental; it provides the general theory within which the true place of full rationality can be accurately seen. That is the point of the "easy problem" problem, and of Simon's answer to it.

Notes

1. This is a revised version of remarks delivered at the memorial session for Herbert Simon, meetings of the American Economic Association, Atlanta, January 6, 2002.

2. The proceedings of that conference, including discussions and papers by Simon and many others, were published as Day and Eliasson 1986.

3. A couple of months after writing these words, I saw the movie *A Beautiful Mind* and was amused at the portrayal of John Nash analyzing a real-life game that is structurally similar to the example Simon used—with "the blonde" in the role of the 50. What Nash offers in the movie is a cooperative solution of the form "we can all ignore the blonde and dance with the brunettes."

4. Unbeknownst to me, Simon was apparently much engaged with the issue of problem difficulty at about that time. See Kotovsky, Hayes, and Simon 1985 for a discussion of experimental results on several isomorphs of the Tower of Hanoi problem, one of which takes subjects 16 times as long to solve as the basic problem. The inversion of the basic problem is not discussed, but there is an analogous relationship between the "Acrobat" isomorph and "Reverse Acrobat"—in the latter, the

story line has large acrobats standing on the shoulders of smaller ones. Average solution time for Reverse Acrobat is almost 70% longer than for Acrobat itself (ibid., p. 252).

References

Cohen, M., and P. Bacdayan. 1994. Organizational routines are stored as procedural memory. *Organization Science* 5: 554–568.

Day, R. H., and G. Eliasson, eds. 1986. *The Dynamics of Market Economies*. Elsevier.

Kotovsky, K., J. R. Hayes, and H. A. Simon. 1985. Why are some problems hard? Evidence from the Tower of Hanoi. *Cognitive Psychology* 17: 248–294.

Nelson, R. R., and S. G. Winter. 1982. *An Evolutionary Theory of Economic Change*. Harvard University Press.

Williamson, O. 1985. *The Economic Institutions of Capitalism*. Free Press.

III   Modeling Systems

Causality, Decomposition, and Aggregation in Social Science Models

Albert Ando

In any empirical science, a structure or phenomenon in the real world which a scientist wishes to describe and analyze is almost always extremely complex and large, and its complete and detailed description is very difficult and often impossible. Even if it is possible, such a description is likely to be too complex to serve as the framework in which a scientist can gain some intuitive understanding of the problem at hand and design the strategy for a more formal analysis. Thus, a part of gaining an understanding of a structure or phenomenon in the real world always involves some procedure for simplification and approximation in its description. Even though the tremendous increase in the power of computers over the past fifty years has expanded our ability to analyze large and complex systems, I believe that the need for simplification and approximation will always remain as a part of most scientific inquiries.

The notion of causality is an important procedure for the approximate description of the structure that a scientist wishes to analyze. Because the word 'cause' has acquired some metaphysical, non-operational notions in the history of philosophy, it has been discredited in the literature of the methodology of science. The concept, however, has refused to disappear from the scientific literature because practicing scientists find the concept not only useful but almost indispensable.

In a series of papers (1947, 1952, 1953), Herbert Simon formalized the notion of causality as a special type of asymmetry in a given description of a structure. Thus, his notion of the causality is a feature of the scientist's description of the world, not an inherent nature of the world and therefore it is free of the philosophical controversy. Simon's formalization is easy to visualize when the structure is a system of linear non-homogeneous equations. Suppose that in a system of linear equations, denoted by A, we find a subset of equations, denoted by A', which contains the same number of equations and variables so that the variables in A' can be solved without reference to equations outside A'. It is convenient to define a set of non-homogeneous linear equations in which the number of variables is equal to the number of equations, like A', as a "self-contained" set. Let us denote the set of equations in A but not in A' by B. We can then first solve the equations in A', and then conditional on this solution, solve the remaining equations for the remaining variables. If this is possible, we then say that A' causes B, or variables in A' cause variables in B.

We can now look at the subsystem B and the repeat the process. If B contains a self-contained set, denoted by B', we designate the set of equations in B but not in B' as C. We can then solve B' conditional on the solution of A', and then solve C conditional in solutions of A' and B'. We then say that A' causes B', and that A' and B' cause C.

It is easy to see that this description can be generalized in several directions in a natural way. A may contain more than one self-contained sets, say A' and A''. In this case, we can view A' and A'' jointly to cause B. The causal structure can also be multi-layered. The concept can also be applied to a non-liner system of equations with some restrictions. The important point is that, if it is possible to identify the causal structure of the system, the task of analyzing the system can be greatly simplified. This is because we can analyze A' independent of the presence of B; B' without regard to the presence of C, and analyze C conditional on the solution of A' and B' rather than analyzing A as a whole. Furthermore, it is much easier to think of the functioning of the system A once a causal structure is identified. We have also understood that the presence of the causal structure is a necessary condition for the identification of the system for estimating its parameters. If the system is non-linear, then solution procedure for the value of variables that takes account of the causal structure of the system is far more efficient than those which do not.

It is also clear that the possibility of identifying the causal structure for a system depends on the pattern of zeros in the coefficient matrix.[1] Simon often asserted, somewhat facetiously, that most large structures representing social systems are almost empty, meaning that coefficient matrices of such systems contain many zero elements. He was fully aware, nevertheless, that we could not be sure that many of these elements were exactly zero. It is more likely that these elements are very close to zero in the sense that their order of magnitude is much smaller than genuinely non-zero elements. Even then, we can define the causal structure for such a system treating the near-zero elements as though they are exactly zero, and the solution of the system obtained by taking advantage of the causal structure would be approximately correct. This proposition can be made more precise and operational based on the property of the linear system that its solution is a continuous function of coefficients. If the system is non-linear, then an analogous constraint must be imposed on the system such as the differentiability of all functions with respect to their arguments. The role played by these small coefficients, however, is much more important than it appears in the statement in this paragraph, and it becomes much more apparent in a dynamic system. We therefore now focus our attention on a linear dynamic system. It is convenient to introduce a few equations.

$$x^*(t) = p^*x^*(t-1) \tag{1}$$

$$p^* = \begin{matrix} p^*_{11} & p^*_{12} \\ 0 & p^*_{22} \end{matrix} \tag{1a}$$

$$x^*_2(t) = p^*_{22}x^*_{22}(t-1) \tag{1b}$$

$$x_1^*(t) = p_{11}^* x_1^*(t-1) + p_{12}^* x_2^*(t-1) \tag{1c}$$

$$x(t) = px(t-1) \tag{2}$$

$$p = p^* + \varepsilon c = \begin{matrix} p_{11} & p_{12} \\ \varepsilon c_{21} & p_{22} \end{matrix} \tag{2a}$$

Let us first consider the system of the form (1), for which the transition matrix has the structure given by (1a). x^* is a column vector whose components, x_1^* and x_2^*, have dimensions n_1 and n_2. P^* is the transition matrix of the appropriate dimension. (1) can be viewed as a causal structure since its subsystem (1b) can be solved without reference to the remainder of the system (1c). (1c) can then be solved conditional on the solution of (1b). We assume that the largest root of P_{11}^*, λ_{11}^*, is larger than the largest root of P_{22}^*, λ_{22}^*. We also assume that all roots of P^* are strictly inside the unit circle for this exposition, though this assumption is not needed in general. We also consider a slightly modified system (2), with the transition matrix P given by (2a), where C is a matrix of constants whose row sums are all zero[2] and where ε is a small real number. The dimensions of (2) are identical to those of (1). Simon and Ando (1962) and Ando and Fisher (1963) then show that the dynamic behavior of the system (2) is characterized by the following features.

1. For a given ε and a required accuracy h_0, there will be a time period 0 to T_0 such that, for $t < T_0$,

$$|x_{i|I}(t) - x_{i|I}^*(t)| < h_0$$

for all i, where $x_{i|I}$ and $x_{i|I}^*$ are ith elements of x_I and x_I^*, $I = 1$ and 2. This phase may be called the short-run dynamics.

2. For a given ε and a required accuracy h_1, there will be a time period T_1 to T_2 in which the pattern of elements of x_1 is approximately equal to the pattern of the characteristic vector associated with the largest root of P_{11}^*, whereas the pattern of x_2 is approximately the same as the

pattern of the characteristic vector associated with the largest root of P_{22}^*. This phase may be called the short-run equilibrium.

3. For a given ε, there is a time T_3 such that for $t > T_3$ the pattern of $x(t)$ is defined by the characteristic vector associated with the largest root of P (which is equal to the largest root of P_{11}^* given our assumptions). We can refer to this phase as the long-run equilibrium.

4. For the time period from T_2 to T_3, x_1 and x_2 will each maintain the pattern described in item 2 above while approaching the long-run equilibrium. This phase can then be referred to as the long-run dynamics. In this phase, elements of x_1 move in parallel and so do elements of x_2, while two groups move toward the long-run equilibrium position. Therefore, for this phase of the dynamics, we can define indices for groups x_1 and x_2, and the dynamics of the system can be described as the dynamic interaction between two indices rather than the dynamics of all individual variables.

This understanding of a dynamic system like (2) makes its analysis greatly simplified and facilitates our intuitive understanding of its behavior. In the short run, we can treat the system as though it is a causal structure, even though not all elements of P_{21} are not exactly zero. In studying its long-run dynamics, we can define indices and deal with much small system, rather than working with a very large system. Furthermore, this formulation provides a natural framework in which we can estimate the degree of approximation involved in the short run by the decomposition of the system, and in the long run by the aggregation of the variables and equations in the system.[3]

Once this analytical framework is clearly understood, it is easy to see that it can be generalized in several directions. First, it is obvious that a system like (2) may have any number of subsystems rather than just two subsystems. Second, any of the subsystems may contain within itself a structure like the one described here. If so, it can itself be decomposed into a causal structure for a short-run analysis, or aggregated for a longer dynamics. Thus, we may have a whole hierarchy of structures, making it possible to gain a better intuitive understanding of a very large system and making the formal analysis greatly simplified and facilitated. Third, the stability condition that we have imposed for the exposition here is not strictly necessary, since we can always redefine the system in terms of deviations from trends generated by roots not strictly inside the unit circle. Fourth, the analysis can be extended to non-linear systems so long as such a system does not have serious discontinuities.

When I became a research assistant to Simon, he had just completed his work on the definition of causality and its relation to identifiability in the estimation of structural models, and was beginning to think about the generalization of his analysis to the dynamic context. He had an intuition that such an extention might have important implications on the feasibility of approximate aggregation of variables and equations in large complex systems. He thought that models of social structures that he often encountered had the pattern of zeros and near-zeros in their coefficients which may approximately satisfy the requirement of the causality. If this was the case, then the system should exhibit the features outlined above, and we should be able to gain better understanding of the behavior of the system by the decomposition of the system in the short run and the aggregation in the long run. He was particularly intrigued by the possibility of aggregation in an approximately, but not fully, dicomposable system, although such a structure did not play any role in the static equilibrium system in which his definition of causality was initially analyzed.

It was a remarkable intuition. I was an inexperienced graduate student when Simon put me on this project, and it took me some time to recognize the significance of the enterprise. It was my good fortune to have gained this fundamental insight into the nature of typical dynamic systems in social sciences[4] at the beginning of my career. Since then, I have often dealt with large models of economic systems, and I have always relied on the insight that I have gained from my work with Simon to organize problems, especially in the design, analysis and the use of the large-scale macroeconometric models of economies.

These models are complex and non-linear, and to solve these models involve serious computational challenge. The currently most powerful procedure for this purpose involves an identification of a self-contained set of variables and equations such that once they are isolated, the structure among other variables conditional on the solution of the first set of variables become much simpler. Such a set of variables in reality turns out to be relatively small even in a very large model. We then solve the first set of equations by a procedure that is guaranteed to be very accurate with good convergence properties while computationally quite heavy, and then solve the rest of the system by a cruder, computationally simpler procedure. This is an application of Simon's idea in a somewhat unexpected context. In designing the model, we begin with a description of the long-run dynamic model with plausible equilibrium properties in terms of relatively small number of aggregate variables. We then add short-run dynamics for sub-sectors in terms of more detailed variables.

In using this type of model for designing optimal policies, I have always taken account of the causal structure inherent in estimated model, and found that the control is much more effective when we do so. Thus, for the model of the U.S. economy, the causation roughly runs from output to employment to prices. We therefore define the target for the prices first, and then define the direct target for employment in terms its own ultimate target and its role as the control variable for prices. Finally, we define the direct target for output in terms of its own ultimate target and its role as the control variable for employment. We then control output directly, although by the nature of the scheme we control all three variables implicitly. Similarly, when I have participated in an attempt to model countries in the euro area, the design that recognizes the causal structure among countries turned out to be a good deal more successful than the one that treats all countries symmetrically.

Many of us now proceed to formulate our analysis following patterns like this without explicitly thinking about the intuition originally offered by Simon. Our younger colleagues are probably not even aware that it was a critical understanding of how to think about the social structures that were introduced into our discipline by Simon. I believe this is a major tribute to his contribution to the scientific methodology of which he was always very proud.

Notes

1. Our terminology refers to the linear case for simplicity of exposition. If equations are not linear, the elements of the matrix represent partial derivatives rather than coefficients themselves.

2. The restriction on the row sum is not necessary, but makes the property of the system much simpler.

3. The propositions in Simon and Ando 1961 and Ando and Fisher 1963 are existence theorems. Their operational counterparts were formulated and proved by Courtois (1977).

4. Similar types of structure appear often in physical sciences too. The vast literature on the subject in physics is perhaps best summarized in Wilson 1975.

References

Ando, Albert, and Fisher, Franklin M. 1963. "Near-Decomposability, Partition and Aggregation," and the Relevance of Stability Discussions. *International Economic Review* 4: 53–67.

Courtois, Pierre J. 1977. *Decomposability: Queuing and Computer System Applications.* Academic Press.

Fisher, Franklin M., and Ando, Albert. 1962. Two Theorems on Ceteribus Paribus in the Analysis of Dynamic Systems. *American Political Science Review* 56: 108–113.

Simon, Herbert A. 1947. The axioms of Newtonian fechanics. *Philosophical Magazine* 27: 888–905.

Simon, Herbert A. 1952. On the definition of the causal relation. *Journal of Philosophy* 49: 517–528.

Simon, Herbert A. 1953. Causal ordering and identifiability. In W. Hood and T. Koopmans, eds., *Studies in Econometric Method*. Wiley.

Simon, Herbert A., and Ando, Albert. 1961. Aggregation of variables in dynamic systems. *Econometrica* 29: 111–138.

Wilson, Kenneth G. 1975. Renormalization group methods. *Advances in Mathematics* 16: 170–186.

Bounded Rationality and Decomposability: The Basis for Integrating Cognitive and Evolutionary Economics

Peter E. Earl and Jason Potts

Here we explore the underlying unity of two of the concepts that we have most employed from Herb Simon's work, namely bounded rationality and decomposability, and how this unity provides the starting point for merging cognitively focused approaches to behavioral economics with evolutionary/institutional economics into a coherent single framework. Our interest in merging these programs can be traced back particularly to the formative influence of Brian Loasby, who first began to wrestle with both of Herb's concepts in his 1976 book *Choice, Complexity and Ignorance* and then used George Kelly's 1963 book *A Theory of Personality* to show just how much the cognitive strategies that people use for dealing with a complex world are dependent on that world's being at least partially decomposable. Once the two concepts were seen woven together at the level of the decision maker's mind, it gradually became apparent that this had relevance for consumer theory, for corporate strategy, and for public policy, and that institutions could be seen as devices for handling bounded rationality by partitioning the world into separable units. In the process of extending this line of thinking, we have increasingly moved from a cognitive focus to a focus on structural evolution in which the path taken by economic systems becomes seen as being shaped by increasing decomposition in some areas and by increasing interconnectedness in other areas, the changing mix of which affects the ability of decision makers to manage the system and its flexibility in the face of shocks. To solve problems, hybridization of modular elements is commonly employed, adding to the menu of elements on which further creative destruction may be founded.

To explore the unity of these concepts, and to illustrate the workings of a process of creative hybridization, we adopt a rather reflexive, and reflective, strategy, showing how our ideas developed with a blinkered focus on particular areas of the economic system considered separately before evolving a general system for making sense of the whole. It will become apparent that this is not simply our story of how Herb's work opened up a lifetime of research opportunities for us, but also a reflection of Herb's influence on Neil Kay, whose own Simon-inspired work has been a major ingredient of our research program.

Starting Point: The UK De-Industrialization Problem, 1975–1979

The point of view that we have reached is heavily inspired by the way in which we originally encountered Simon's work. Earl's first encounter with Simon (1959) and the idea of satisficing came as a Cambridge undergraduate via his tutor Ajit Singh, who subsequently prodded him further down the behavioral road by encouraging him to read Janos Kornai's *Anti-Equilibrium* (1971), a book that presents a very Simon-influenced view of the process of structural change in economic systems. These early encounters occurred at a time (1975–1977) when the de-industrialization of the United Kingdom in the face of competition from Europe and Japan was a major focus. Within the de-industrialization phenomenon lay a puzzle for satisficing theory to resolve: Why did successive major falls in the value of the pound not lead more UK consumers to substitutes back in favor of locally produced items and away from higher-quality, waiting-list-free imported products?

The poor standards of UK products might well be accounted for in terms of low aspiration levels on the part of UK firms, and poor labor relations might reflect the inability of boundedly rational managers to see a better way to interact with their workforces. Likewise, the willingness of UK consumers to turn elsewhere might well reflect the discovery of overseas offerings when strikes or over-zealous demand expansion (see the satisficing analysis in Mosley 1976) led to shortages of domestic products. But the emerging discussion of the importance of "non-price factors in international trade" seemed to imply something about the choice process that no one was articulating explicitly: the inapplicability of the axiom of gross substitution. It was as if, as was sometimes said in monetary theory lectures, there could "breaks in the chain of substitution," but since no alternatives to indifference analysis seemed to be on offer, Earl lacked a way of making sense of links between non-price factors and demand inelasticity.

In beginning his Ph.D. studies at Cambridge in 1977, Earl began with a broad vision of the workings of economies that combined cumulative causation and multiplier ideas from Myrdal and Keynes with a mixture of Simon/Kornai satisficing/threshold-of-adjustment ideas and Leijonhufvud's (1969, 1973) thinking in terms of liquidity buffers and corridors of stability within which orderly adjustment might normally occur. This was colored by acceptance of Shackle's (1967) emphasis on the scope for surprise and the difficulties of foreknowing the future, which seemed to complement Simon's notion of bounded rationality. Also on the agenda at this early stage was the idea that some decision makers might be resistant to changing their behavior in the face of changing external conditions, something that March and Simon (1958) explored at length in the organizational setting and which also seemed rather to apply to mainstream economists in the face of criticism from behavioralists. First on the list of books to read was Brian Loasby's *Choice, Complexity and Ignorance* (1976), which swiftly reinforced the idea that a synthesis of Simon and Shackle was in order. This book introduced Earl to Simon's (1962, 1969) notion of decomposability and pointed him in the direction of seeing that Kuhnian paradigms or Lakatosian research programs might be useful concepts for understanding how people in general, and not merely scientists, cope with bounded rationality. Having found it impossible to find a supervisor in

Cambridge who was both available and interested in behavioral economics, and with a lectureship offer from Stirling University in
Scotland, Earl headed north to work with Loasby, who agreed to serve
as an external Ph.D. supervisor.

The "Stirling School," 1979–1984

Initially the question of whether or not an economic system was
decomposable did not seem to be linked to the concept of bounded
rationality. Rather, its significance seemed to relate to the scope for
economic crises to occur. First, there was the question of the long-
run environmental impact of human actions. Long before discovering
Simon's work, Earl had read "A sound of thunder," Ray Bradbury's tale
of time-traveling dinosaur hunters. This fable opened up major questions about path dependence and the scope for "small" actions to have
major implications in interconnected systems over the long term. One
way that "small" actions might have small consequences was via the
system's having some kind of slack or buffering in it, such that any
shock waves would normally dissipate. Simon offered a different perspective: the overall system might be composed of modules such that
spillover effects only operated within a well-defined area, rather as if
confined to islands. He also argued that processes of evolution would
tend to select modular systems precisely because of their resilience
in the face of disturbances. But if we could take the "island" notion
only as a short-run approximation, scope for long-term ecological crisis
seemed considerable. The fate of wildlife on islands to which predators
were introduced indicated the hazards of specialization when a subsystem was not actually closed in the long run.

The idea that small changes might have dramatic long-term implications in systems with limited decomposability seemed to link with
bounded rationality in that the system might be impossible for mere
mortals to fathom, Already, possible links with what we now would
call chaos theory were being hinted at by Conrad Waddington in his

provocative 1977 book *Tools for Thought*. Earl began to feel that for understanding whether one could get away with non-historical, partial-equilibrium analysis, it would be essential to understand the extent of decomposability and how one event might lead to another. This theme has underlain our subsequent thinking on topics as diverse as buyer-seller chains in housing markets (Earl 1995, 1998) and browsing behavior in shopping malls (Earl and Potts 2000).

A second line of thinking came from having read Piero Sraffa's *Production of Commodities by Means of Commodities* (1960), which had introduced the notion of the "basic commodity," one that figures directly or indirectly, via the matrix of production, in the production of all items in the system. In 1979, when Earl arrived at the University of Stirling, the second OPEC oil shock had just been engineered, and despite Brian Loasby's commenting during a seminar that he could not think of any examples of a basic commodity, oil seemed a pretty good candidate for being thought of near enough as being one. That a rise in the price of oil could cause a crisis seemed to have something to with the sheer range of areas in which oil figures in the system. This is something that cannot be said for most products. For some products (say, sheet music of works by avant-garde composers), consumption and patterns of influence would be restricted to a very select circle. However, modern marketing techniques are increasingly recomposing the boundaries between products via complementary "product tie-ins" that generate and feed from brand ubiquity. This seems to produce highly skewed purchasing behavior compared with that which was observed in the much more decomposable consumer markets of not so long ago. (At the time of writing, *Harry Potter* is everywhere, with *Lord of the Rings* waiting in the wings.) There is much research waiting to be done linking bounded rationality's role in the significance of easily recognizable brands and superstars (Rosen 1981) to the managerial and industrial organization implications of the need to coordinate complementary activities aimed at capturing rents, quite often within short product life cycles.

Earl's first discussion of the significance of whether or not economic systems were decomposable was in the context of an analysis (in Dow and Earl 1982, pp. 145–166, originally written late in 1980) of Hyman Minsky's (1975) financial instability hypothesis. Not all financial crashes had the wide-ranging implications of the 1929 Wall Street crash, and in the lesser disasters particular pockets of the economy would suffer disproportionately. This theme was revisited rather more forcefully in Earl 1990, which included not only further Minskian case study work but also a chapter on bottlenecks and buffers that affect the stability of macroeconomic systems and the size of multiplier coefficients.

A crucial lead for taking Simon's ideas further came via Stirling alumnus Neil Kay, whose 1979 book *The Innovating Firm* Earl purchased a few weeks before moving to Stirling. Kay provided a strong critique of aggregative, "bottom-up," reductionist mainstream economic analysis in the context of the allocation of resources to corporate research and development. In its place he offered a hierarchical, "top-down" analysis of budgeting. Kay's critique of reductionism was influenced by the work of Arthur Koestler, who in his 1975 book *The Ghost in the Machine* had been an early adopter of ideas from "The Architecture of Complexity" (Simon 1962). Koestler had made Simon's thinking the basis for a systems-within-systems, Janus-faced (looking both ways) alternative to whole- or part-based, top-down or bottom-up modes of analysis. At the same time, Koestler (1975b) offered an analysis of the act of creation in which novelty entailed hitherto untried combinations of already-existing elements, a perspective similar to that offered by Shackle (1979) in his analysis of the imagination in terms of a capacity to make fresh combinations of existing alphabetic elements. New products could be seen as emergent systems within systems.

Kay (1982, 1984) was quick to offer in a pair of books an analysis of the kind of view of economic organization implied by the Simon/Koestler perspective. In a seminar titled "Diversification: Some Firms Do, Some Firms Don't" presented at Stirling in 1981, Kay gave a taste of what these books would contain: a striking synthesis of Ansoff's (1965) notion of synergy and Simon's decomposability perspective. Rather than focusing on the firm's activities as a set of product market involvements, he sought to reorient industrial economics to focus on linkages between product markets and the strategic strengths and vulnerabilities that came from them. Common technologies, markets and brand names give strength when times are good, enabling costs to be shared across different but related products. If the external environment changes as a result of new technology, government regulations, changes in fashion, and so on, the links become potentially dangerous: what is problematic for one product may prove problematic for products linked to it. Hence, firms that believe themselves to be operating in surprise-prone environments should avoid having too many linkages between their different products, so that if something goes wrong and causes the unexpected truncation of a product life cycle, they will still have other sources of cash flow.

An important aspect of Kay's 1982 work was his attempt to distinguish between system linkages at a point in time (synchronic) and linkages between things as time passes (diachronic): if a subsystem were subject to a shock, the structure of the former linkages could affect the set of events that then unfolded through time. In later work, Kay has increasingly looked at the implications of bounded rationality for industrial organization not merely in terms of decomposability of corporate activities but also in terms of the patterns of strategic alliances and networks that emerge as means of managing, simultaneously, strategic risk and the limits of what individual organizations can know and coordinate. (See Kay 1997.)

Earl set out to do for consumer behavior what Kay had been doing in the economics of industrial organization. Initially, he examined the organization of household spending in terms of top-down budgeting and the grouping of products into mental categories for comparison as a means of coping with bounded rationality. This seemed consistent with the design of real-world shopping environments, as with the division of supermarkets into separate sections for vegetables and fruit, dairy products, and so on. Simon-inspired work by James Bettman and others in marketing journals put Earl on to the trail of non-compensatory decision rules. These provided a means of making sense of consumer intolerance of products that would not meet particular standards, whether those of price (outside a budget range) or non-price factors. In other words, non-compensatory decision rules provided a basis for segmenting demand systems into approximately separate zones, where changes in one zone would have limited impacts on other zones. On this view, substitution in terms of price would come about because of the use of price as tie-breaking rule, or because a price cut repositioned a product within the budget ranges of buyers who previously would not have considered it; otherwise, choices would be based on relative abilities of products to match up with non-price standards of adequacy on consumers' checklists.

As a part of this checklist view of consumer choice, Earl developed a synthesis of Simon's work, George Shackle's (1979) theory of choice under non-probabilistic uncertainty, and the personal construct psychology of George Kelly (1963), to which Loasby had drawn his attention. Kelly's work presumes that people cope with the world by modeling it as if it is, in Simon's terms, decomposable; that they construct their view of the world in a hierarchical manner; and that they have limited dimensions in terms of which to see things. Consumers' checklists will be of finite length, dependent on their expertise and interest in the particular market. Where the performance of a product is uncertain in respect of a particular dimension, it will be deemed acceptable if a sufficiently good outcome seems sufficiently plausible in prospect and an unduly bad performance seem sufficiently implausible. (This is a kind of four-target/two-point test, rather than a simple aspiration level of the kind they would employ as a filter if not uncertain.) Earl (1983, 1984) explored these ideas at length, with a particular focus in the latter work on how non-compensatory decision rules related to the UK's de-industrialization problems.

The further Earl got into the clinical psychology literature associated with personal construct theory, the more it seemed that there were similarities with issues that Kay was raising in corporate strategy and that Kuhn and Lakatos had wrestled with in the philosophy of science. For Kelly, the development of a construct system, with some "core" constructs assigned a more significant, determining role, for compartmentalizing an integral universe was the way that people made life manageable. Those who got into a mess tended to have a lack of linking threads to bind their thoughts into some kind of order, or so many threads linking constructs to each other that they could not change one idea with producing massive change in their view of the world. For Kuhn and Lakatos, scientists seem to have certain key ideas, which they are very reluctant to change, on which they build their views of the world, and they are prepared to add in all manner of ad hoc notions to preserve their viewpoints if the latter seem at odds with evidence. In typically imposing hierarchical architectures that result in points of view that are vertically layered (with some ideas more to the periphery than to the core) as well as divided horizontally into subsystems, people are able to make the task of thinking about the world manageable. They also are not overwhelmed by the Duhem-Quine problem that asserts it is impossible to know when a particular idea is wrong because one is always testing a nested set of ideas.

For world views to be resilient and yet amenable to evolution, people must assign some firm spots on which to build their lives. They also need to segment their lives into different sections with limited spillover allowed between them. People who choose to build their entire lives around particular assumptions, such as the ongoing availability of a particular career path, person, or personal capability, will be devastated if these are falsified. For example, when Lee Iacocca lost his job at Ford, the disruption to his life was, until he was hired to revive Chrysler, every bit as problematic as Henry Ford had found car making decades before on the death of the Model T, to whose production the firm had become dedicated (Earl and Kay 1985; Earl 1986a). In a world of turbulence, people need partially decomposable ways of thinking and lifestyles, just as firms need to be diversified around a variety of business themes.

At the end of his time at Stirling (mid 1984), while finishing the final version of his Ph.D. dissertation, Earl began to see inelasticity of demand and the marketing notion of consumer "involvement" in relation to the extent of decomposability in consumers' world views and/or lifestyles. Even if choice involved some kind of more orthodox weighing of attractive and off-putting aspects of a product, resistance to change as price or non-price features were varied still seemed to be underpinned by the mental architecture people used to organize their thoughts. Crucial here were (i) the patterns of "implications" that particular changes were seen to entail and (ii) which thoughts about change were ruled out of court or unthinkable by higher-level constructs. Some changes are easy to make because their overall implications are limited; other have such dramatic negative implications that they are unthinkable (Earl 1986a, 1986b; see Laaksonen 1994 for a marketing perspective on involvement)). On this basis, what seem from the standpoint of onlookers with more decomposable points of view to be "minor changes" may cause people with highly interconnected points of view to get very hot under the collar.

Simon's general vision of the mind being usefully seen as a system of computer-like programs increasingly became a backdrop for Earl's thinking as he framed the nature of choice in the manner outlined above. There seemed to be a need for a limited set of rules that were hard-wired at birth, that would limit the kinds of ideas that decision makers could find acceptable as a basis for constructing further ideas, just as particular kinds of software will only run on particular kinds of computers. Some people simply will not buy some things or ideas. However, the hierarchy of ideas that a person employs might, like a constitutional system, include self-denying clauses that specified the conditions under which core notions would be abandoned and a radically new point of view taken on board. Put it another way: the mind's core is not simply like a computer operating system, but like a computer operating system that is open to upgrading in certain ways.

Just before leaving Stirling for the University of Tasmania, Earl got together with Kay, and together they mapped out their 1985 article employing many of the foregoing lines of thinking to argue that notions of hierarchy and decomposability provided a basis both for policy design and for replying to critics of subjectivist economists such as Shackle who emphasize the potential for kaleidic change in decision-making environments. Their core notions have not changed significantly since then. What has changed is the appreciation of what makes this kind of economics both different at its core and, in consequence, its breadth of scope. This heightened appreciation required a shift to the other side of the planet and the passage of ten years.

Complexity, and So On

Potts began his Ph.D. studies in 1995 at Lincoln University in New Zealand. He had been properly trained in neoclassical economics and therefore knew nothing of Herbert Simon or, for that matter, of anyone else mentioned above. But he was a great admirer of Veblen, he had read Robert Pirsig's *Lila* and Stuart Kauffman's *Origins of Order*, and he had dimly perceived how these ideas might apply to economics, if only economics could be interpreted in terms of evolutionary theory. He wanted to work on evolutionary economics, and with unabashed naiveté he presumed, post Veblen, that he was the first to ever think of this. He went looking for a supervisor. Through a random search he discovered Peter Earl, whom someone characterized en route as the only economist in New Zealand who did "that strange sort of economics." And an otherwise unlikely connection was made.

Potts thus came to Simon through Earl and thereby Loasby (1991). He already had a complex systems view of the nature of economic evolution in mind, and one of the first books he read was *The Sciences of the Artificial* and in particular the reprinted version of "The architecture of complexity."

In time, Potts's Ph.D. dissertation emerged as a high-level synthesis of complexity theory, evolutionary theory, computational theory, and economic theory. It was published in 2000 as *The New Evolutionary Microeconomics: Complexity, Competence and Adaptive Behavior*. At the heart of this book is the idea that an economic system is a complex system of complex systems. The agents are complex behavioral systems, composed of systems of decision rules, as Simon, Kelly and Earl had explained. Yet Potts soon realized, through reading Simon, Leijonhufvud, Richardson, Shackle, Loasby, and Kay, that firms, industries, and the entire macro system, including expectations, were also complex systems. There occurred an awakening in which the whole economic universe seemed to be made of complex systems and perhaps that was the key to a general framework. This was eventually synthesized with a graph-theoretic conception of the geometry of economic space (Potts 2000, chapter 2). This scheme was in direct contrast to the standard basis of microeconomics in field theory; instead it was based on an ontology of connections and the definition of a system as a set of elements connected in specific ways. A complex system was defined as a structure of connections with the property of partial decomposition. An economic system is then a complex system of complex systems and naturally an emergent product of boundedly rational agents. Economic evolution is a creative and destructive process of the dynamics of connection in systems, between systems, and sometimes between emerging new systems.

Potts's graph-theoretic superstructure further illuminated the relation between bounded rationality, decomposability and economic evolution as a growth-of-knowledge process. Bounded rationality is the dual statement that economic agents use systems of rules for thinking and that they are only partially connected to their environment. Most connections will be local. Some will be global. Sometimes changes will have dramatic effects. Sometimes large changes will have small effects.

Dynamics, in this view, are an express function of the geometry of connections. This is true at the level of the individual agent, as Earl had long realized, but it is also true throughout the economic system and the basis of its ability to evolve as a growth-of-knowledge process (Loasby 1999; Quine 1951). Evolution proceeds as systems attain and maintain complexity without losing coherence (too few connections) or freezing up (too many). This is how we both came to re-read Simon's views on the architecture of complexity. But now we had a framework that revealed the deep relation between bounded rationality and decomposability as a story about the evolutionary dynamics of partial connectivity in complex systems.

Research opportunities abound when everything is a complex system. One project is to synthesize evolutionary psychology with behavioral and evolutionary economics. Interestingly, this project has its roots in one point where Simon was wrong. He had argued for the idea of the mind as a general problem solver. Although seminal to artificial intelligence research, it has been rejected by evolutionary psychology, which has instead championed the notion of the mind as a massively modular system of *specialized* problem solving—as indeed Simon himself might have portrayed it if he had seen it in terms of his work on decomposability. These mind modules are adaptations to particular problems recurrent in the ancestral environment. The mind is then viewed as what the brain does, which is to coordinate these specialized competencies into a near-seamless complex parallel system of cognition: Simon was not so wrong after all. Earl and Potts (forthcoming) argue that his concept of bounded rationality would have been much better appreciated if he had made a distinction between inborn preferences and learned knowledge. If consumers can discover how the technologies of consumption impinge on the relatively limited set of high-level things that they desire, choice is relatively straightforward. Even when people know they face dilemmas, they are capable of jumping one way rather than another as their gut instincts dictate. Bounded rationality thus seems only to apply to information and knowledge that must be learned or acquired about contents of the set of feasible choices and the different implications of selecting any one of these options. We have come to see that this line of thinking has implications for the relation between information, knowledge, markets, and competence.

A second project is to explore the geometry of connections in economic systems, as the maps of associations, complementarities and in general of connections by which the whole is greater than the sum of the parts. At present, very little is known about the connective structure of an economic system. We do of course know a lot about resource flows (input-output tables) and spatial aspects of industry and factor markets. And we do know something about the inter-connective structure of corporations (Kay 1997). But we know little about the geometry of knowledge in economic systems, and in particular the structure of specialized knowledge as an ecology of expertise. There are many aspects to this, such as the bundling of commodities (store design, menu selection, product tie-ins, and so forth) and strategies (consultancy, marketing, management) and also the deep structure of knowledge that connects some industries more closely than others. What we might hope to learn from such analysis of the connective structure of economic systems is not just the architecture of consumer lifestyles and organizational competencies but also the spaces into which entrepreneurship moves by creating and destroying these connections. The direction this heading is toward a new evolutionary growth theory.

Post-Simon Economics in a World of Globalization

A third research task implied by our Simon-inspired approach to economic evolution is a thoroughgoing exploration of the relationship of globalization, decomposability, and bounded rationality. Our earlier comments regarding the analogy between systems of though that are open to change, and computer operating systems that can be upgraded, might strike some readers as rather similar to Thomas Friedman's popular writing on globalization. Friedman sees different nations as having different rules of operation and openness to change, which determine their relative performance in an increasingly interconnected global economic environment. Yet much of the best-selling writing of Friedman and others on globalization remains questionable when viewed from a post-Simon standpoint.

International labor mobility certainly becomes easier the more that firms operate in identical styles, lessening switching costs for boundedly rational workers and their colleagues. However, modern knowledge workers are often portrayed as moving in response to job opportunities regardless of any ties in terms of family and community links. Whether in the age of the Internet and cheap telecommunications such ties become much less significant is an open question: Are virtual relationships a close substitute for "being there"? (See Herb's Travel Theorem (Simon 1991, pp. 306–307).) If the ties continue to bind, the field perspective does not apply.

Likewise, with search engines and other Internet services, it may be possible to obtain excellent advice on what to choose and where to obtain supplies at the cheapest price, from anywhere on the planet. Yet running against this field perspective on markets is the possibility that demand will become increasingly driven by web links that enable specialized cells of demand to operate like never before. Within them, consumers may find a bewildering array of appealing items between which to choose, many of which they would otherwise have had little chance of discovering without great effort.

Finally, we return to the first policy area mentioned in relation to decomposability: financial markets. Perhaps the field conception of markets applies most strongly to the financial sector, at least in terms of that sector's ability to obtain information rapidly any time, anywhere. However, as far as the system's ability to operate in an orderly manner and promote real investment is concerned, it is the pattern of interconnectedness between balance sheets that is the crucial thing.

References

Ansoff, H. I. 1965. *Corporate Strategy*. Penguin.

Bradbury, R. 1953. A sound of thunder. In Bradbury, *Golden Apples of the Sun*. Rupert Hart-Davis.

Dow, S. C., and Earl, P. E. 1982. *Money Matters: A Keynesian Approach to Monetary Economics*. Barnes and Noble.

Earl, P. E. 1983. *The Economic Imagination*. M. E. Sharpe.

Earl, P. E. 1984. *The Corporate Imagination*. M. E. Sharpe.

Earl, P. E. 1986a. *Lifestyle Economics*. St. Martin's Press.

Earl, P. E. 1986b. A behavioral analysis of demand elasticities. *Journal of Economic Studies* 13: 20–37.

Earl, P. E. 1990. *Monetary Scenarios*. Elgar.

Earl, P. E. 1995. Liquidity preference, marketability and pricing. In Dow, S. C., and Hillard, J., eds., *Keynes, Knowledge and Uncertainty*. Elgar.

Earl, P. E. 1998. Information, coordination and macroeconomics. *Information Economics and Policy* 10: 331–342.

Earl, P. E., and Kay, N. M. 1985. How economists can accept Shackle's critique of economic doctrines without arguing themselves out of their jobs. *Journal of Economic Studies* 12: 34–48.

Earl, P. E., and Potts, J. 2000. Latent demand and the browsing shopper. *Managerial and Decision Economics* 21, no. 3–4: 11–22.

Earl, P. E., and Potts. J. Forthcoming. The market for preferences. *Cambridge Journal of Economics*.

Friedman, T. 1999. *The Lexus and the Olive Tree*. Farrar, Straus and Giroux.

Kauffman, S. 1993. *The Origins of Order: Self-organization and Selection in Evolution*. Oxford University Press.

Kay, N. M. 1979. *The Innovating Firm: A Behavioral Theory of Corporate R&D*. Macmillan.

Kay, N. M. 1982. *The Evolving Firm*. Macmillan.

Kay, N. M. 1984. *The Emergent Firm*. Macmillan.

Kay, N. M. 1997. *Pattern in Corporate Evolution*. Oxford University Press.

Kelly, G. A. 1963. *A Theory of Personality*. Norton.

Koestler, A. 1975a. *The Ghost in the Machine*. Pan.

Koestler, A. 1975b. *The Act of Creation*. Pan.

Kornai, J. 1971. *Anti-Equilibrium*. North-Holland.

Laaksonen, P. 1994. *Consumer Involvement*. Routledge.

Leijonhufvud, A. 1969. *Keynes and the Classics*. Institute of Economic Affairs.

Leijonhufvud, A. 1973. Effective demand failures. *Swedish Journal of Economics* 75: 27–48.

Loasby, B. J. 1976. *Choice, Complexity and Ignorance*. Cambridge University Press.

Loasby, B. J. 1991. *Equilibrium and Evolution: An Exploration of Connecting Principles in Economics*. Manchester University Press.

Loasby, B. J. 1999. *Knowledge, Institutions and Evolution in Economics*, Routledge.

March, J. G., and Simon, H. A. 1958. *Organizations*. Wiley.

Minsky, H. P. 1975. *John Maynard Keynes*. Columbia University Press.

Mosley, P. 1976. Towards a "satisficing" theory of economic policy. *Economic Journal* 86: 59–72.

Potts, J. 2000. *The New Evolutionary Microeconomics*. Elgar.

Quine, W. V. O. 1951. Two dogmas of empiricism. *Philosophical Review* 60: 20–43. Reprinted in Quine, *From a Logical Point of view* (Harper and Row, 1961).

Rosen, S. 1981. The economics of superstars. *American Economic Review* 71: 845–858.

Shackle, G. L. S. 1967. *The Years of High Theory*. Cambridge University Press.

Shackle, G. L. S. 1979. *Imagination and the Nature of Choice*. Edinburgh University Press.

Simon, H. A. 1959. Theories of decision-making in economics and behavioral science. *American Economic Review* 49: 253–283.

Simon, H. A. 1962. The architecture of complexity. *Proceedings of the American Philosophical Society* 106: 467–482.

Simon, H. A. 1969. *The Sciences of the Artificial*. MIT Press.

Simon, H. A. 1991. *Models of My Life*. Basic Books.

Sraffa, P. 1960. *Production of Commodities by Means of Commodities*. Cambridge University Press.

Waddington, C. H. 1977. *Tools for Thought*. Paladin.

Near-Decomposability, Organization, and Evolution: Some Notes on Herbert Simon's Contribution

Massimo Egidi and Luigi Marengo

Rationality within Economic Institutions: The Origins

One of the more illuminating ideas underlying bounded rationality is that the nature of organizations is deeply rooted in the limits of human intelligence and rationality. It is precisely because individual rationality and knowledge are limited that a social division of knowledge and competences is essential for human progress. This principle was stated clearly by the mathematician Alfred North Whitehead:

It is a profoundly erroneous truism, repeated by all copy-books and by eminent people when they are making speeches, that we should cultivate the habit of thinking what we are doing. The precise opposite is the case. Civilization advances by extending the number of important operations which we can perform without thinking about them.

Friedrich Hayek expressed similar ideas when he tried to explain the reasons of the economic institutions (1980: 50–51):

Clearly there is here a problem of *division of knowledge* which is quite analogous to, and at least as important as, the problem of the division of labour. But, while the latter has been one of the main subjects of investigation ever since the beginning of our science, the former has been as completely neglected, although it seems to me the really central problem of economics as a social science. The problem which we pretend to solve is how the spontaneous interaction of a number of people, each possessing only bits of knowledge, brings about a state of affairs in which prices correspond to costs, etc., and which could be brought about by deliberate decision only by somebody who possessed the combined knowledge of all those individuals.

In a conversation with one of the present writers, Herbert Simon acknowledged the close connection between the principle of bounded rationality and Hayekian assumptions on knowledge. It may thus be useful to focus here on the differences and the parallelisms between the two authors' views.

While both Simon and Hayek consider the analysis of institutions to be co-essential with a theory of the human mind, the main difference between them is that Hayek considered the market as the sole institution able to coordinate the decisions of distinct individuals endowed with fragments of knowledge, while Simon viewed the division of knowledge and the coordination as complementary processes that characterize the evolution of markets *and* of organizations.

The road to awareness that the human ability to solve problem with bounded rationality characterizes the nature of both markets and organizations was rugged and required many analytical steps.

In 1947, when Herbert Simon first published *Administrative Behavior*, organizational studies were considered to be a field of inquiry entirely distinct from microeconomics, and the scientific approach to the study of the internal mechanisms of organizations was not directly related to the rational behavior of economic agents.

Decision-making theory supposedly applied only to the behavior of independent agents in markets, and since people in organizations are by definition closely interdependent in their choice making, the study of human behavior within organizations was relegated to the sidelines.

Administrative Behavior opened up the "black box" of an organization's internal mechanisms. By radically criticizing the existing theories of administration, Simon identified decision making in conditions of uncertainty and interdependence as the basis on which administrative theory could be rebuilt, and thereby created the premises for a new vision of human activities within organizations.

This was a view that, by developing over many decades the idea of bounded rationality as problem solving activity, gave rise to a unified approach to economic behavior in markets and other economic institutions.

Bounded rationality and division of knowledge were the principles on which organizational studies had to be grounded and to which Simon devoted most of his research in the following decades. The former is certainly well known and underlies a much larger proportion of Simon's impressive scientific production, but Simon always considered equally important. Simon himself strongly emphasized in various letters and at a meeting with one of us just a year before his death that the twin notions of interdependence and decomposability related to the process of division of knowledge were not only a necessary complement to his theory of bounded rationality, human problem solving, and organizational behavior, but a sort of general unifying principle underlying all viable organized systems, human, biological, or artificial.

As we said, awareness that the two principles can lead to a unified approach required time: Simon built his theory of bounded rationality on close observation of the behavior of employees and managers in large organizations. During the 1950s and the early 1960s, he took part in numerous collaborations and research projects at the Graduate School of Industrial Administration at Carnegie Mellon, among them a study of decision making under uncertainty conducted jointly with Charles Holt, Franco Modigliani, and John Muth. The aim of the study was to develop mathematical tools to improve inventory-control systems for production planning at a plant of the Pittsburgh Plate Glass Company. It was in this context of the concrete study of empirical data that Simon developed his early notions of routines and satisficing.

But the milestone in the founding of organizational studies on bounded rationality was *Organizations*, written with James G. March and published in 1958. Here all the major issues connected with bounded rationality and its consequences in terms of adaptive and evolutionary economics were debated. That now-classic book moved forward from the notion of problem solving as individual activity to the notion of organizational problem solving, with clear recognition of the evolutionary processes of organizational adaptation and organizational learning within business corporations. Identification of these processes proceeded in parallel with the discoveries that the division of labor can be considered a problem solving activity and that the recursive division of problems into sub-problems is a property of both organizations and computer programs.

The development of a deeper theory of problem solving became crucial for explanation of organizational routines and procedures within business firms, and their evolution. Progress in one of the sciences of the artificial—the theory of computation—became of fundamental importance for progress in the other—the theory of organizational learning. It was probably for this reason that Simon's interests moved to computation theories as natural candidates for explanation of human problem solving and discovery.

From Decision Making to Cognition

About the time he was finishing his work on *Organizations*, Simon began his collaboration with Allen Newell, a celebrated founding father of Artificial Intelligence. The collaboration gave rise to the creation of new mathematical tools with which to model human problem solving and discovery processes. *Human Problem Solving*, published in 1972 with Newell, is a bridge between computation, artificial intelligence, and cognitive psychology. Here Simon went beyond the notion of "computation" as a human activity that relates means to ends, replacing it with the notion of *symbolic manipulation*. Simon's first studies on the limits of rationality, in fact, focused on the bounded ability of individuals to construct and explore their strategies for action, celebrated examples of which are the insurmountable obstacles encountered by the players of chess and other complex games. But as Simon's observations and field researches proceeded, he realized that beyond the limits on the human ability to "compute" a strategy in depth lay further limitations, and that these involved most of the cognitive activities connected with decision making. Therefore, when the limits to the human capacity for mental calculation were experimentally demonstrated, it became clear to him that this ability was an aspect—an important but not unique one—of the mind's more general capacity to *manipulate symbols* and to create *mental models* of reality.

The recognition that human decision making can be understood only if mental activity is viewed as symbolic manipulation reinforced the bridge with psychology. Simon's research thus shifted to a different version of the problem, subjecting the various mental abilities essential for explanation of human action—memorization, categorization, judgment, problem solving, induction—to increasingly intense experimental scrutiny. In parallel with this experimental work, Simon developed computational models of intelligence designed to explain the process of discovery. The BACON and DALTON programs (Langley et al. 1987), for example, simulate scientific discovery processes. After organizational theory and artificial intelligence, cognitive psychology became Simon's next fundamental area of inquiry as he developed his idea of the human solver and sought to clarify the shortcomings of the traditional theory of decision making within institutions.

The growth of experimental economics since the 1970s has been extraordinarily helpful in highlighting the importance of this line of research. The pioneering works by Allais on expected utility theory violations, and the subsequent discoveries by Kahneman and Tversky, have made it clear that Simon's claims about the scant realism of economic and organizational theories were solidly based.

Once again, and now with the precision of the experiments, the systematic discrepancy between the predictions of the traditional theory of decision making and real behavior became very apparent. Indeed, an enormous number of experiments conducted in recent years have shown that many types of human errors—defined as breaches of rationality—are systematic. Consequently, the benevolence still shown by the majority of economists toward the assumptions of decision theory can only be explained by the lack of a convincing alternative. Economists thus find themselves in the embarrassing situation that they have a largely falsified theory but can only offer fragments of alternative theories in its place.

Simon's insight that these discrepancies could be overcome by radically revising these theories, and by introducing closer concern with human activity so that systematic account could be taken of the limitations and richness of human intellectual activity, has accordingly become of crucial importance. Moreover, a large body of results from cognitive psychology and experimental economics has given further support to his view. We will cite only one of these developments of his views.

One of the profoundest of Simon's intuitions, namely that decision making is deeply rooted in learning activity, has been largely borne out by psychological research, and it gives us important directions for future inquiry. From the mid 1970s until their most recent study, *Choices, Values and Frames*, Tversky and Kahneman have investigated the psychological principles that govern the creation, the perception, and the evaluation of alternatives in decision-making processes. They find that preferences vary substantially according to the way in which the choice problem is presented ("framed"). Rather than being stable, preferences are constructed by individuals in the process itself of their elicitation; a clear demonstration of this process is provided by the well-known experiments in which different representations of the same choice generate a reversal of preferences. This suggests that the crucial aspect of the decision-making process is the ability to construct new representations of problems. This point was already present *in nuce* in Simon's empirical analysis of managerial decisions conducted in the 1950s. In 1956, Cyert, Simon, and Trow pointed out an apparent dualism in managerial behavior, which displays on the one hand coherent choices among alternatives and on the other hand a search for the knowledge necessary to define the choice context. Consequently, research into rationality shifted its focus from the coherence or incoherence of choices to the representation and editing of problems. How the mental models with which individuals and institutions frame problems are constructed is a crucial issue to be addressed by decision theory in the years to come, an issue that will yield better understanding of human innovative activities within institutions.

Here again an important parallelism emerges with Hayek's theory of the mind. Hayek's theory of institutions was based on a view of the workings of the human mind set out in *The Sensory Order* (1952). Published a few years after D. O. Hebb's celebrated book *The Organization of Behavior*, Hayek's book deals with ideas very similar to those expounded by the neurologist. The core of Hayek's approach is to consider brain activity as classificatory, thus developing a description closely related to the current theory of neural nets. This approach enabled Hayek to describe the process of learning as dynamic evolution of a neural net, and in this way to provide a first profound explanation of the typical features of learning: partial unawareness and unpredictability. Evidently, these characteristics are the conceptual pillars of Hayek's explanation of why the outcomes of the actions of individuals are only partially what they intended.

Thus, learning is a cornerstone of their theories. It would be easy to claim that Hayek can be considered a precursor of the connectionist approach to the study of learning and that Simon may be considered one of the founders of the symbolic approach. But this distinction, while useful, does not imply that the two approaches are necessarily opposite and incompatible. Some approaches, most notably John Holland's "classifiers systems" (Holland et al. 1986; Holland 1992), are indeed attempts to build a bridge between the connectionist and the symbolic approaches to learning, showing the complementarities between them. One important point made clear by the classifiers systems theory is that for both approaches—connectionist and symbolic—the representation of learning process is based on problem decomposability, as was understood well by Simon. In the following section we will briefly discuss this notion and examine some of its implications for the theory of organizations.

Decompositions and Near-Decompositions

In *The Sciences of the Artificial* Simon put forward the proposition that basically all viable systems, be they physical, social, biological, or artificial, share the property of having a near-decomposable architecture: they are organized into hierarchical layers of parts, parts of parts, parts of parts of parts, and so on, in such a way that interactions among elements belonging to the same parts are much more intense than interactions among elements belonging to different parts. By "intense" interaction is meant that the behavior of one component depends more closely on the behavior of other components belonging to the same part than on components belonging to other parts (i.e. the cross-derivatives are larger within a part), or that this influence happens on a shorter time scale (effects propagate faster within a part than among parts), or that the influence is more widespread (within a subunit almost all elements interact, whereas interactions among elements belonging to different subunits are more scarce). This kind of architecture can be found in business firms, where division of labor, divisionalization, and hierarchical decomposition of tasks are all elements that define a near-decomposable system: individuals within a hierarchical subunit have closer, more widespread, more intense, and more frequent interactions than individuals belonging to different subunits. But a very similar architecture can also be found in most complex artifacts (which are made by assembling parts and components, which in turn can be assemblies of other parts and components, and so on), in software (with the use of subroutines, and even more so in object-oriented programming).

Recently the near-decomposability hypothesis has been renamed the "modularity hypothesis" and is pervading diverse disciplines, ranging from software design (where the object-oriented programming paradigm is nothing but a prescription of a highly modular system) to management science (where largely the same principles are applied to the organization of firms and manufacturing systems—see Baldwin and Clark 2000).

In biology, modularity has been recognized as a fundamental design principle of both the RNA structure and genotype phenotype mapping. (See Wagner and Altenberg 1996 and Callebaut and Rasskin-Gutman, forthcoming.)

In cognitive science, Fodor (1983) is the main proponent of a modular theory of cognition. He argues that certain psychological processes are self contained, or modular. This is in contrast to the "Modern Cognitivist" positions which hold that nearly all psychological processes are interconnected and freely exchange information. Strangely enough, this is perhaps the field of inquiry where the modularity hypothesis is more controversial and strong empirical evidence has been gathered against it (to the point that Fodor himself has recently made his position less clear-cut).

Why should near-decomposability be such a general organizing principle characteristic of virtually all complex systems, as diverse as those just mentioned? Herbert Simon gives us a series of possible explanations, which provide food for thought for the various different disciplines connected with this hypothesis.

A first explanation refers to efficiency and is better cast in economic terms: it is basically the old Smithian argument for the efficiency of the division of labor. But we must note that *per se* this argument can at most explain the decomposition into modules, not the fact that such modules are organized into hierarchical systems. Moreover, it is not clear why there should be any limit to the division of labor, i.e., why we should not observe (not only in business firms but in all viable natural and artificial systems) an endless process of decomposition into finer and finer elements. In economics the importance of these puzzles has been understood and widely investigated: the former in particular has been the focus of, for instance, the literature of transaction costs.

(See, for instance, Williamson 1975, which heavily relies on Simon's bounded rationality theory.) As is well known, the transaction-costs explanation claims that the process of decomposition of economic activities is limited by the availability of coordination mechanisms that can efficiently coordinate sub-units. In the economic realm it is usually believed that competitive markets constitute such mechanisms, but the transaction-costs theory observes that under some circumstances markets cannot achieve their full efficiency.

Another explanation is more cognitive in nature and springs directly from Simon's work on problem solving and bounded rationality. (See especially Newell and Simon 1972.) Problem solvers faced with problems whose complexity outweighs their bounded computational capabilities are forced to work on conjectural decompositions of the problem into sub-problems. (See Egidi 1992.)

On the one hand such decompositions are necessary heuristics for computationally limited individuals, as they reduce to a collection of sub-problem of more manageable size problems whose complexity largely defeats their computational capabilities. Moreover, very often some of these sub-problems may already be familiar to the problem solvers or at least display some analogies with known problems. However, by treating sub-problems as independent or quasi-independent some existing interdependencies are almost inevitably ignored and sub-optimality, biases, and systematic mistakes are almost inevitably introduced. This is a fundamental source of suboptimality due to bounded rationality and computational constraints: it is a source that relates to limitations to bounds in the representational capabilities of individuals, organizations, and society and sets clear constraints on the efficiency of the division of labor and knowledge. In a world of interdependencies, the process of decomposition encounters an intrinsic (in the sense that it is not due to the quality of the coordination mechanisms) dynamic inefficiency, which arises from the inevitable separation of interdependent elements. In our view, transaction-cost economics does not recognize the importance of such a tradeoff because it does not consider that a given partition of activities between markets and hierarchical organizations embeds a particular "decomposition" of the "economic problem" and that, as a consequence, the features of this decomposition impinge on the efficiency of the system regardless the efficiency of markets themselves. (See Marengo et al., forthcoming.)

Biologists have a clearer view of the issues involved in a process of decomposition and modularization, and, as Simon (2000 and forthcoming) stresses, can teach interesting lessons to economists and organization scientists.

Indeed, sub-problem decomposition, complexity reduction and modular architecture also operate in the biological domain, where we observe modularity in the genotype-phenotype mapping and in the morphological properties of organisms. Thus modularity is a very important property that has evolved through selection. According to Wagner and Altenberg (1996), modularity may evolve through two opposite processes which they call, respectively, *integration* and *parcellation* in the genotype-phenotype mapping: integration means that genes acquire new pleiotropic effects phenotypic characteristics, while parcellation is the suppression of existing pleiotropic effects. Of course this applies also to social organizations and business firms, where sub-problem decomposition is indeed one aspect of the division of labor. This sub-problem decomposition theory suggests that two fundamental processes engender the dynamics of the "organizational architecture" of the economic system (and in particular the relative distribution of market and non-market coordination mechanisms): a process of deepening the sub-problem decomposition, with an endless division of problems and tasks into sub-problems and sub-tasks, and a process of recombining sub-problems and sub-tasks into modules.

Note that the transaction-cost argument is mainly restricted to consideration of the latter process, as it takes the division of labor to be given and looks for an explanation of the organizational structure of the economic system by establishing the conditions under which existing modules (organizations) cannot be efficiently coordinated by markets and must be combined hierarchically into higher order modules.

As Simon (forthcoming) observes, the latter process is likely to produce a near-decomposable system by agglomeration of parts, while the kind of near-decomposability we observe in the economic realm most often originates from the division of previously fully integrated parts.

That the process of integration should normally give rise to a near-decomposable system is stated clearly in Simon 1996 and even more clearly in Simon 2000. On p. 6 of the latter work, Simon claims:

> If we begin with a set of simple elements that, when they meet at random, are capable sometimes of forming stable combinations, and if the combined systems ... are themselves capable of combining into still larger systems, then the complex systems we will observe ... will almost all be near decomposable systems.

In Simon 1996 this proposition was exemplified by the parable of the two watchmakers, called Tempus and Hora. Both watchmakers are so successful that they receive many phone calls from potential clients which disrupt the production process. If the latter is organized as a unitary assembly chain, then after every disruption the watchmaker will have to start all over again. If instead the production process is organized into a hierarchical system of sub-assemblies of stable components, then a phone call will disrupt only the assembly of one component. Thus, systems that are nearly decomposable are much less vulnerable than systems that are not, as disturbances are more likely to remain confined to specific subcomponents: near-decomposable systems limit interactions and information flows among different parts of the system and thus are better able to keep damaging events confined to sub-parts. This argument is not limited to damaging events *stricto sensu*; it applies to all disturbances to the system that may feed adaptation and change. This point is very important: successful change and adaptation requires a great deal of trial and error. Every adaptive system must be able to bear a high rate of mistakes without losing its functionality. Variability is the driving engine of adaptation, but of course most of the variation produced amounts to error. The point has recently attracted the interest of computer scientists (mainly those working in the theory and application of evolutionary computation) and biologists, but it has enormous implications for the theory of economic organization, and once again one of the earliest illustrations of the point can be found in Simon 1965. Adaptation and evolution can work effectively only if variations are not too often very disruptive and not too rarely favorable. In computer science it is well understood that this depends crucially on how the task environment is coded (the so-called representation problem). By acting on the representation, we can make simple adaptive mechanisms such as mutation and recombination either very effective or totally ineffective. In biology a similar problem concerns the "evolvability" of organisms: if, as biologists claim, evolution is the result of the interplay between mutation and selection, then we must ask where these mutations come from, and in particular whether an evolvable genome is itself a product of evolution. A representation problem also arises in biology, because the crucial factor affecting "evolvability" is the genotype-phenotype map, which determines how variations at the genotypic level affect the phenotypic characteristics and thus the fitness of organisms. As mutations in the biological world are believed to be totally random, this randomness must be able to produce some improvement.

Again the likelihood of producing ordered and stable structures out of totally random events depends crucially on the representation: modularity and near-decomposability can be a way to solve the representation problem. (See Wagner and Altenberg 1996.) We can better understand this by asking whether there is some chance that a group of monkeys with their random actions are able to produce a verse of Shakespeare: if monkeys are simply given a piece of paper and a pencil they will probably draw signs which are no way similar to anything understandable, but if we give them a typewriter and let them play with its keyboard they will at least produce strings of letters, and the possibility that one of these strings is an English word (possibly also found in Shakespeare) is probably not so remote. If we give them tiles with English words and let them arrange them in sequences we might even get a short meaningful sentence from time to time. The likelihood of obtaining a verse of Shakespeare is probably still very low, but is certainly orders of magnitude higher than in the case in which we gave the monkeys only paper and pencil. What we are doing here is simply endowing monkeys with different representational systems; that is, different modules which they can recombine randomly. More structured representations involve higher-level modules which on the one hand greatly limit the space of possible variation (with pencil and paper monkeys could produce not only a verse of Shakespeare but also a drawing of Leonardo, while with a typewriter the latter is no longer possible), but they impose constraints upon variability which safeguard some kind of coherent structure.

We believe that it could be very fruitful to pursue a line of research in organizational economics that starts from the acknowledgment that the way in which economic activities are organized, and in particular their distribution between markets and hierarchies not only determines the static efficiency of the economic system but also, and more importantly and with inevitable tradeoffs, shapes the possible dynamic "morphological" paths the system can follow, its space of possibilities. (For an interesting formal characterization of the space of possibilities in biological evolution see Stadler et al. 2001.)

Final Remarks

Besides re-establishing close connection among economics, psychology, and the cognitive sciences, Simon's research suggests that the actions of decision makers in the real economic world should be studied, not merely in terms of rationality, but in the light of the capacity of the human mind to frame problems, and to represent reality in innovative ways, in an endeavor to reduce their uncertainty and ignorance. The "sciences of the artificial," namely organization theory, cognitive psychology, and artificial intelligence, are the new disciplines now investigating the classic yet still unresolved question of human creativity and learning, and their relationship with the evolution of institutions.

We have briefly elaborated on learning process, focusing the attention on near-decomposability, a notion that plays a very important role in Simon's theory of learning, organization, and complex systems. Simon's ideas with regard to near-decomposability are far from being exploited (and sometimes even from being understood) by current research in economics, and therefore by developing them (as biology is doing to a much greater extent) we could open new perspectives on important questions concerning the organization of economic activities and their distribution between market and non market coordination modes.

References

Baldwin, C. Y., and K. B. Clark. 2000. *Design Rules: The Power of Modularity*. MIT Press.

Callebaut, W., and D. Rasskin-Gutman. Forthcoming. *Modularity: Understanding the Development and Evolution of Natural Complex Systems*. MIT Press.

Cyert, R. M., H. A. Simon, and D. B. Trow. 1956. Observation of business decision. *Journal of Business* 29: 237–248.

Egidi, M. 1992. Organizational learning, problem solving and the division of labour. In H. Simon, ed., *Economics, Bounded Rationality and the Cognitive Revolution*. Elgar.

Fodor, J. 1983. *The Modularity of Mind*. MIT Press.

Hayek, F. A. 1952. *The Sensory Order*. University of Chicago Press.

Hayek, F. A. 1980 (reprint). *Individualism and Economic Order*. University of Chicago Press.

Holland, J. H. 1992. *Adaptation in Natural and Artificial Systems*. MIT Press.

Holland, J. H., K. J. Holyoak, R. E. Nisbett, and P. R. Thagard. 1986. *Induction: Processes of Inference, Learning and Discovery*. MIT Press.

Kahneman, D., and A. Tversky. 2000. *Choices, Values and Frames*, Cambridge University Press.

Langley, P., H. A. Simon, G. L. Bradshaw, and J. M. Zytkow. 1987. *Scientific Discovery: Computational Explorations of Creative Processes*. MIT Press.

March, J. G., and H. A. Simon. 1958. *Organizations*. Wiley.

Marengo, L., C. Pasquali, and M. Valente. Forthcoming. Decomposability and Modularity of Economic Interactions. In W. Callebaut and D. Rasskin-Gutman, eds., *Modularity: Understanding the Development and Evolution of Natural Complex Systems*. MIT Press.

Newell, A., and H. A. Simon. 1972. *Human Problem Solving*. Prentice-Hall.

Simon, H. A. 1947. *Administrative Behavior*. Macmillan.

Simon, H. A. 1965. The architecture of complexity. *General Systems* 10: 63–73.

Simon, H. A. 1996. *The Sciences of the Artificial*, third edition. MIT Press.

Simon, H. A. 2000. Near Decomposability and the Speed of Evolution. Working paper 549, Carnegie Mellon University.

Simon, H. A. Forthcoming. The structure of complexity in an evolving world: The role of near-decomposability. In W. Callebaut and D. Rasskin-Gutman, eds., *Modularity: Understanding the Development and Evolution of Natural Complex Systems*. MIT Press.

Stadler, B. M., P. F. Stadler, G. P. Wagner, and W. Fontana. 2001. The topology of the possible: Formal spaces underlying patterns of evolutionary change. *Journal of Theoretical Biology* 213: 241–274.

Wagner, G. P., and L. Altenberg. 1996. Complex adaptations and the evolution of evolvability. *Evolution* 50: 967–976.

Williamson, O. 1975. *Markets and Hierarchies: Analysis and Antitrust Implications*. Free Press.

Herb Simon

Axel Leijonhufvud

In the afternoon of the October day in 1978 that Herb's Nobel Prize had been announced, I received a phone call from a *Wall Street Journal* reporter who sounded pretty desperate. He had phoned around to his contacts in the economics profession, he explained, but had not been able to get anyone to comment on Herbert Simon's contributions. Someone had suggested that I might. I do not remember what I said but do remember a subsequent nice note of thanks from Herb.

Nobel and neglect. What a curious contradiction! The economics profession's schizophrenia with regard to Herbert Simon's work outlasted his long career. It has no parallel in any of the other fields to which he made notable contributions. I believe I know what the resolution of the contradiction will have to be. But how long will it last?

I have had a mild case myself. In 1960, an American-Scandinavian Foundation scholarship placed me as a research assistant in the Administrative Science Center of the University of Pittsburgh, of which James D. Thompson was then the Director but Herb Simon of Carnegie was the intellectual patron saint. There I read, and readily absorbed, *Administrative Behavior*. But *Models of Man* posed a problem. As a beginning graduate student in economics, not yet fully acculturated to the field, I was resistant to "satisficing" and prepared to argue that, with proper specification of constraints, it would reduce to optimization, thus saving an economist's notion of "rationality." Since that time, I have had to listen to that argument from generations of students, always with a twinge of embarrassment.

Herb was not in residence at Carnegie the year I spent in Pittsburgh, so I did not get to listen to him then. My first encounter with him had to wait until the Lakatos conference in Napflion in 1974, which Herb, John Hicks, and I have all independently testified to as the best conference we have ever attended. By that time, I had become aware of the spurious riddles produced in my own field of macroeconomics by dogmatic adherence to optimizing "as a necessary condition for the intelligibility of behavior" and made clear that I wanted to find an escape from this predicament. Herb took a kind interest in my talk and was very generous with his time in discussions with me afterward. I particularly remember several lunches with him and Dorothea and an afternoon wandering about Mycene in his company.

Despite all Herb's essays and forays in persuasion, the neoclassical economics of which he was already critical at an early stage gradually evolved over the span of his career into a doctrine much more dogmatic and claiming far wider scope. In the 1930s, it was still common to think of the optima for households or firms as the attractors of unspecified adaptive processes and as defined only over some limited, local region of commodity space. And, back then, economists took for granted that people make mistakes. Gradually, after the war, all this changed. Optimization came to be regarded as the way decisions were made. All behavior was to be interpreted as reflecting objectively optimal choice. The line between positive behavioral theory and normative operations research faded away. Cognitive limitations on obtaining information or on the capacity to process it were ruled out. Objective optimization by all agents was seen to imply a system always in equilibrium. With the addition of rational expectations, also non-existent markets were in equilibrium with agents optimizing over infinite-dimensional commodity spaces.

The macroeconomics built according to the rules of optimizing-equilibrium formalisms sees the economy's path through time as determined by "deep parameters" of preferences and technology. It has become the foundation of a new laissez faire doctrine, more rigid and unforgiving than the old. This economics is a rigorous discipline all right, but one without any sense of a "science of the artificial," of dealing with "systems that, given different circumstances, might be quite other than they are."

I cannot claim the long and close association with Herb that so many of the contributors to this volume have had (and which I envy). It is in large measure by living through the hardening of neoclassical orthodoxy over several decades, rather than by direct stimulus, that I have found myself coming around, step by step, to positions that he took long ago and consistently advocated ever since. Among those, the one that I would put foremost is his stress on procedure over solution, on process over end state. Among his other themes that fit under this umbrella are that economists must pay attention to how people actually make decisions, that institutions and organizational structure shape process, and that these structures tend also to reflect the cognitive limitations of the agents operating within them.

Herb agreed to come to the second Summer School of the four that Ned Phelps and I coordinated at Siena University's Certosa di Pontignano in the 1980s. The school dealt with Institutional Economics and featured rather an all-star cast, but in my memory Herb remains the dominant figure. He voiced his deep distrust of axiomatic theorizing in economics more than once, and it was a lesson to hear not just his insistence on empirical propositions but *the kind* of empirical knowledge that he considered to have some solidity. Taking derivatives on an *a priori* production function and running time-series regressions on it, for example, would not be Herb's way of studying production. His own paper memorably argued that in coordinating activities in an economy formal organizations are at least as important as markets. The priority given to the study of organizations over that of markets was a theme on which he elaborated later.

With time, I have come around more and more to Herb's way of thinking about economics and social science. I could have been a faster learner! But my own experience gives me some hope that economists in general will come around in the same way, and that the schizophrenia of Nobel and neglect will be resolved, as it ought to be, in favor of a deeper and more pervasive influence of the thought of Herbert Simon.

Trento is one center of learning where Herbert Simon will long be missed. He took a lively interest in the work done at the Computable and Experimental Economics Laboratory—in Massimo Egidi's experiments on individual cognition and cooperative problem solving, in Luigi Marengo and his collaborators' extensions of his ideas on near-decomposability as a key to understanding economic structures, and in Kumaraswamy Velupillai's development of a computable economics finally capable of meeting a challenge that Herb made long ago: "Rules of substantive rationality that are not backed by executable algorithms are a worthless currency" (*The Sciences of the Artificial*, second edition, MIT Press, 1985, p. 43). His generous encouragement meant a lot.

Rational Forecasting, Learning, and Decision Making

Charles C. Holt

This chapter tells the story of how the research team of Holt, Modigliani, Muth, and Simon worked together at GSIA in the 1950s to produce a very general and flexible business forecasting system that became the most popular in the United States even though the paper that developed the system never was published. The methods developed in that working paper played an important role in the Planning and Control of Industrial Operations project, and it generated more requests than any other project paper. Meeting my commitment to complete the manuscript for the "HMMS book" (C. Holt, F. Modigliani, J. Muth, and H. A. Simon, *Planning, Production, Inventories, and Work Force*, Prentice-Hall, 1960) before taking off for a year in England carried a higher priority than publishing the forecasting paper. An abbreviated version of the basic paper was included in the book, but the story of the team interactions that contributed to producing that forecasting system has not been told.

But this paper attempts to go further than just recapping research done fifty years ago. It briefly reexamines bounded rationality and rational expectations and argues that they are compliments—not substitutes. By drawing on the forecasting and decision-making research done by the HMMS team, it develops both empirical and mathematical support for that complimentarity.

Forecasting

Military and Engineering Uses of Exponentially Weighted Moving Averages

During World War II many anti-aircraft gun directors used exponential smoothing (EWMA) to damp the erratic fluctuations in predicted target positions. Using the EWMA principle, Charles Stark Draper at MIT designed a remarkably simple gyro-stabilized gunsight for the Navy's Bofors guns that was highly effective in anti-aircraft defense against Japanese attacks. In these systems simplicity in implementation was the great virtue of EWMA. Building on war experiences, Robert Brown wrote *Smoothing, Forecasting, and Prediction* (Prentice-Hall, 1963), which introduced extensions such as exponential averages of exponential averages. With a background in control engineering, I was fully aware of these developments, as were operations researchers at GSIA and elsewhere, so when the HMMS team needed for its research to generate economically a large number of accurate forecasts the EWMA approach was an obvious candidate for consideration.

Muth's Reverse Engineering of EWMA

Unfortunately, aside from simplicity and sensibly putting more weight on recent observations, little was known about the forecasting characteristics of EWMA formulas. Muth decided to reverse engineer the exponentially weighted moving average by posing the question "For what statistical world does the EWMA provide optimal solutions?" His answers, not easily obtained, were two:

(1) An EWMA would be optimal if in an independent random drawing each period had two effect: first a temporary impact lasting only one period, and second a small fraction of the random drawing that would permanently displace the expected value of the random distribution. The exponential rate of decay would depend on the relative sizes of the temporary and permanent components.

(2) Alternatively, an EWMA would be optimal if there were two independent random drawings each period, one with a temporary impact and the other with a permanent impact on the expected value of the temporary random distribution. The exponential rate would then depend on the ratio of the variances of the two distributions.

Each of these statistical models made good sense in terms of forecasting. For example, future values of sales data would follow a random walk that would gradually drift away from its starting level, the drift in the expected value depending on a small fraction of the temporary fluctuation or on a second distribution with a smaller variance. In both cases the temporary component does not persist, and the new expected value is the basis for forecasting next period sales. Muth's work offered insight into what one was assuming implicitly when one used an EWMA. That average could now be chosen for making forecasts for sound reasons—not simply because they are easy to calculate.

Recursive Modeling by the HMMS Team

About the time that the HMMS team was thinking about forecasting, Simon, Newell, and Shaw were exploring how bounded rationality might be modeled and simulated on a computer. Both teams found that simple recursive systems could often achieve unexpectedly powerful results that had significant implications for decision making. Those were heady times at GSIA, and all were excited by the potential implications of new operations research models and new psychological models. Specifically we were interested in whether simple recursive components such as EWMA could be extended to forecasting future sales in a more general context.

Making the Most of Bounded and Unbounded Rationality in Sales Forecasting

Even though simple exponentially weighted moving averages were being used increasingly to forecast sales and other business and economic variables, it was clear that they were subject to severe limitations.

Growth trends clearly are important for many companies, and they should not be ignored, as EWMA would do. Even more complex, spurts of growth often peter out and sales return to long-term trends. Also, monthly or other seasonals often are important components of sales. Trends and seasonals for some companies will be additive but for others will be multiplicative. For all of these considerations to be taken into account, at reasonable costs, it was clear that the structure of forecast relations would need to be flexible and highly adaptive.

One weekend it occurred to me that we might be able to forecast the exponential averages of these separate components recursively and then combine them. In this way we might be able to achieve the forecast flexibility and adaptability that we needed. A forecasting paper that seemed to combine bounded rationality and rational expectations quickly fell into place. This approach to forecast system design seemed interesting, even promising—but would such a system work. and how would its performance compare with available alternatives? The answer was far from obvious.

Testing System Performance

Peter Winters, then a graduate student, was tempted by the prospect of an easy publication. He programmed the system and tested it using samples of time-series data drawn from several fields. The system worked surprisingly well and was immediately built into the HMMS research system.

Other forecasting contests and tests compared the performances of alternative methods. Those tests have shown that the Holt-Winters system, as it has come to be called, is quite robust in its forecast accuracy and, while not quite as good as the Box-Jenkins method, it is almost as good and is much more easily administered.

Computer Forecasting

After completing the manuscript for the HMMS book, I set off for England to spend a year at the London School of Economics. Soon after arriving in London, I was contacted by three forecasters who worked for Imperial Chemical Industries Limited, one of Britain's largest companies. They had a copy of our forecasting paper and wanted to talk. It seems that ICI had bought not one but three of the new high-capacity electronic computers in order to see what potential computers might have for the chemical engineering business. One of the computers was assigned to the three forecasters, who were to see how well the computer could do in competition with the forecasting department, which had a staff of 200 professionals. The three forecasters had easily programmed our system and had found that it could substantially outperform the forecasting department. Now they had a problem. It was clear that a lot of forecasters might lose their jobs, and the forecasting department had plenty of political clout. If some were to be fired, the three computerized forecasters weren't at all sure who would get the axe: the three with their computer or the 200 professionals. I never did hear how that forecast challenge worked out.

Forecasting with Bounded Rationality and Rational Expectations

Herb Simon had long been concerned that economists tended to overemphasize rational behavior and to pay too little attention to important limitations inherent in data, analysis, and computation. The tension between these two approaches is often expressed as a choice between Simon's bounded rationality and Muth's rational expectations. I argue that such a choice is not necessary, and that the two approaches are complimentary—not mutually exclusive. The HMMS forecast model serves as an illustrative example of my position, but first I will have to describe that model a bit more fully.

Muth's analysis of an exponentially weighted moving average showed that it could be viewed as a feedback system in which the expected value forecast is adjusted in response to the forecast error—the adjustment being a certain fraction of the error. That is a pretty crude forecasting model, and one quite consistent with Simon's bounded rationality. If your data, your analysis, and your computation are severely limited, you can at least adjust your forecast of variable level in response to the forecast error that you have just experienced. That is the starting point of the forecast model. However, any rational consideration of the forecast problem immediately suggests that the forecasted variable has multiple components—not just level but often trend and seasonal as well. Why not apply the error feedback adjustment to each of the components, and then combine them into an integrated forecast? Because this model is still so crude, we could easily make the seasonal either multiplicative or additive, and the strength of the feedbacks could differ for the different components. There you have the HMMS forecast system—partially crude and bounded-rational, and partially rational-expectational based on an analysis of components. The surprising outcome of this mixed system design was that it produced forecasts that were hard to beat. The results were robust in not being sensitive to the system parameters, so crude parameter estimates would suffice.

Such partial rational forecasts might perform quite well and have low administrative costs. If that proved to be the case, the mix of bounded rationality and rational expectations could offer interesting new options for forecasting.

Box and Jenkins later developed an elegant and powerful statistical forecasting model that could be rigorously fitted to past data, but the fitting process was somewhat complex and problematic. Their forecasting model can be viewed as rational expectational.

Decision Making with Partial Rationality

A major thrust of the HMMS research was discovering how to jointly optimize decisions on production, workforce, overtime, idle time, inventory, and stockouts both at the aggregate and at the individual product levels. To solve that problem we needed to develop a new mathematical decision model. We used a quadratic function and linear equality constraints to approximate the cost structure. The solution of that optimization problem gave us a deep understanding of a large and general class of decision problems. It is interesting and significant that understanding offers clear examples of both bounded rationality and rational explanations.

The optimal decisions in a period were found to depend on the known past values of factory sales and on the unknown future values of sales, the exogenous variables. The relevant time series were infinite, running backward and forward in time. The known past time series were readily accessible and so were consistent with bounded rationality, and the future time series to be forecast called for rational expectations. Because the first order conditions were linear, past sales and forecasts of future sales entered simply as weighted averages.

Setting up the full optimization problem and solving it not only gave a rigorous example of the two versions of rationality, bounded and rational expectations; it also indicated how the probabilities in the distribution of the inevitable random forecast errors should be weighted. Herb Simon showed that this decision analysis produced a clear and rigorous concept of certainty equivalence for dynamic uncertainty.

That decision analysis offers a clear example in which bounded rationality and rational expectations are complimentary—not substitutes. In the forecasting model we have an empirical example of complimentarity, and in the production planning decision model we have a mathematical example. Now we have a sample of two.

Learning with Partial Rationality

Since forecasting relationships are special cases of the general class of predictive relationships, the potential of partial rationality may well apply to learning about relationships generally. Servomechanisms and state-space control systems operate using feedback exclusively, with no attempt to use feedforward (anticipation). Adding a rational-expectations dimension may well improve learning about relationships generally. While the prospect of such improvements in research and learning admittedly is speculative, the HMMS research on forecasting and on decision making supports that conclusion.

Summary Conclusion on Rationality

The arts of forecasting, research learning, and decision making may be improved by utilizing two versions of rationality. The first recognizes the limitations on data, analysis, and computation, and utilizes models of the world that are crude but robust. The second seeks to tap the power of more refined theoretical methods and relationships, but at some risk to common sense and loss of robustness. By drawing on these two approaches to the rational investigation of real-world relationships, research performance could be improved. The research done by the team of Holt, Modigliani, Muth, and Simon seems to offer both empirical and mathematical support for that speculative conclusion.

What Are the Morals of This Tale?

The first is to pay honor to a beloved colleague, Herb Simon, who touched many lives by contributing to the fun and intellectual stimulation of a great many researchers. The second is to illustrate the importance of teams in research productivity. In these forecasting and operations research examples we can see how the varied backgrounds and talents of five researchers interacted with, and complimented, each other. Those interactions between Holt, Modigliani, Muth, Simon, and Winters were subtle, complex, and highly relevant to research productivity. The third is to recognize how important is Simon's continuing contribution. Learning more about the mechanisms that make the human brain so powerful and flexible will make computerized thinking machines ever more productive. And that will feed back to augment human capabilities and to interact with them.

I would love to get Herb's take on the potential complimentarity between bounded rationality and rational expectations that was developed above. We had the data on forecasting and decision making in our faces, but we may have missed their important implications. Perhaps Muth or Modigliani will pick up on this argument and rebut it or develop it further.

It is too bad that Herb will not be around to enjoy the fun and the stimulating intellectual work that lie ahead. He would certainly enjoy seeing economics move in his direction. But this is a time for celebration, not regrets, for he contributed more in his lifetime than few could ever aspire to. His rationality may have been bounded, but his bound was astronomically high. Not only did forecasting, operations research, and psychology benefit from his influence, but a great many other fields have benefited from Herb's having been here. We will miss him.

Herbert Simon: Intellectual Magnet

Michael C. Lovell

I first became aware of Herbert Simon on reading a chapter in *Models of Man*, which was assigned by Wassily Leontief to students in his second-year graduate theory course. Later, when I was teaching at Yale, a succession of young visitors from Carnegie-Mellon—Andrew Winston, Edward Mansfield, and John Muth—described in glowing terms the sharp intellectual atmosphere at Carnegie-Mellon's Graduate School of Industrial Organization, stressing the pivotal role of Herbert Simon. So it was with great excitement that I eagerly accepted an offer to join the faculty at GSIA in the fall of 1963.

I arrived at Carnegie-Mellon at the same time as Morton Kamien from Purdue, Lester Lave from Harvard, and Robert Lucas from Chicago. Leonard Rapping had arrived from Chicago via RAND the year before. We constituted a new wave of economists at GSIA, but we were obviously not a homogeneous group. I think a common factor in drawing us to GSIA was that we had in large measure been attracted by the intellectual magnetism of the legendary Herbert Simon.

By the time I arrived at Carnegie-Mellon, Simon's main interests had shifted from economics to psychology. But he was still a commanding intellectual presence at GSIA. When one got to sit at Herb's table at lunch in the Skibo faculty cafeteria, one could count on an exciting intellectual encounter. Herb would draw out the conversation with a series of thoughtful questions, often focusing on the area of specialized expertise of one or another of the participants. While Herb's questions were designed to elicit information, it would quickly become apparent that he was extremely well versed in the subject and often knew as much if not more about it than anyone else at the table. And this would be so regardless of the topic of the day.

My first year at Carnegie, Herb Simon, Bob Lucas, and I served as members of the board of a mock corporation run by second-year MBA students—this was the Carnegie Tech Management Game (Cohen et al. 1964). The Management Game was a pioneering computer-aided instruction program in which teams of students serving as officers of the firm would submit their decisions for production scheduling, employment practices, advertising strategy, pricing, and so forth to be run as a batch job on the IBM 650, a wonder for its day with 2,000 words of storage. The computer would digest this information along with the decision of the other competing student firms and respond with information about the market outcome. Herb was chairman of the board of our firm, and he did a masterful job at playing that role. Lucas and I would sit quietly while Herb would sharply question the officers of the firm about the reasons for their decisions and their plans for the future. I am sure that the students found these encounters the high point of their GSIA educational experience.

Herb Simon had a special attraction for me. Before coming to Carnegie, both as a graduate student at Harvard and later at Yale, I had been conducting an intensive empirical investigation of the determinants of inventory investment based on a flexible accelerator model. My defense against the charge that this was an *ad hoc* model lacking appropriate micro foundations rested on Simon's analysis (1956) of certainty equivalence. At Carnegie I continued working with this inventory model and undertook with Albert Hirsch of the Department of Commerce a related book project involving the empirical testing of several models of expectations, including Muth's model of rational expectations. At the time I did not fully appreciate the link between Simon's certainty equivalence result and Muth's concept of rational expectations. As was recently shown by Young and Garity (2001), antecedents for Muth's concept of rational expectations may be discerned in the works of Modigliani and Simon, but as I will demonstrate in what follows, it turns out that Simon's certainty equivalence result requires that the forecasts must be rational in the sense of Muth.

In his classic paper, Simon explained (1956, p. 74):

> ... I shall show that, when the criterion function is quadratic, the planning problem for the case of uncertainty can be reduced to the problem for the case of certainty simply by replacing, in the computation of the optimal first-period action, the "certain" future value of variables by their unconditional expectations. In this sense, the unconditional expected values of these variables may be regarded as a set of ... "certainty equivalents."

In that paper, Simon focused on an inventory scheduling model in which the firm's future sales were not known with certainty. In a follow-up paper, Theil (1957) referred to a macro application where unemployment is influenced by government expenditure.

Let us look at the simplest possible single-period example of certainty equivalence. We start by considering the case of certainty: Let y denote the variable we are interested in controlling (say, a firm's inventory or a nation's unemployment) and suppose that it is determined by the equation

$$y = ax + bz, \tag{1}$$

where x is an exogenous forcing variable (e.g., private investment or a firm's sales) and z is a policy or control variable (e.g., government spending or a firm's production).

Suppose that our objective is to minimize the loss function

$$L = (y - T)^2, \tag{2}$$

where T denotes the target value of Y.

Substituting (1) into (2) yields

$$L = (ax + bz - T)^2. \tag{3}$$

To find the optimal value of z, we differentiate, obtaining

$$\frac{\partial L}{\partial z} = 2(ax + bz - T)b = 0, \tag{4}$$

or

$$z = (T - ax)/b, \tag{5}$$

and we enjoy zero loss in the case of certainty.

Now suppose that the exogenous variable x is not observed precisely at the point in time when the policy maker must set the value of z. Specifically, suppose that $\hat{x}$ is the forecast or predicted value of x and ε is the prediction error:

$$x - \hat{x} = \varepsilon, \tag{6}$$

where we assume that $E(\varepsilon) = 0$; i.e., the forecast is unbiased. To use $\hat{x}$ as the "certainty equivalent" of x, we simply substitute it into the policy equation (5),

$$z = (T - a\hat{x})/b, \tag{7}$$

which results in

$$y = T + a(x - \hat{x}). \tag{8}$$

Since $y - T = a(x - \hat{x}) = a\varepsilon$, our expected loss is

$$E(L) = E(y - T)^2 = a^2 \sigma_\varepsilon^2. \tag{9}$$

Although the certainty equivalence procedure seems simplistic, the remarkable result of Simon is that under certain circumstances it is the optimal way to proceed, and the validity of policy rule is independent of the magnitude of σ_ε^2, although the magnitude of the minimum obtainable loss is obviously affected. Furthermore, the certainty equivalent procedure is interesting because it holds true with much richer linear in the variable models that involve maximizing over an extended horizon with complicating lag structures.

Simon's certainty equivalence result has attracted much attention, earning more than 170 citations in the *Social Science Citation Index*. His result is surprising in part because it contrasts with the classical analysis of portfolio selection by Markowitz (1952) and Tobin (1958). While both models involve a quadratic loss function, the portfolio model yields a diversified portfolio under uncertainty rather than certainty equivalence. The difference arises because in the portfolio model the decision maker's actions affect the variance of the outcome while in Simon's certainty equivalence model the variance is a constant independent of x. If the Simon model is enriched by allowing for uncertainty in the model's parameters, certainty equivalence no longer goes through (Brainard 1967). Prescott analyzed the implications of sequentially re-estimating the model's parameters by adding to the data set the new observation that becomes available at the end of each decision period (1971).

The optimality of the certainty equivalence procedure requires that the forecast error, ε in equation 6, must be distributed independently of forecast $\hat{x}$. This is the case of rational expectations, analyzed by Muth (1961a,b). The condition would be satisfied if the forecast $\hat{x}$ is calculated with a correctly specified econometric model with parameters that are known, perhaps by divine revelation or because they have been estimated with a sufficiently large data sample. The certainty equivalence solution is not optimal, however, if ε is distributed independently of realization x. Expectations of this type, called "implicit expectations" by Edwin Mills (1957), would arise if the prediction of $\hat{x}$, a firm's expected sales say, was based on a random sample survey of customers. Furthermore, the "errors in the variable expectations model," developed by Muth (1985) because he observed that expectations are not fully rational, also fails to satisfy the independence condition required for certainty equivalence.

To see that we can do better than use the certainty equivalent strategy in the case of Mills's implicit expectations, consider the alternative to certainty equivalent (7):

$$z^* = \left\{ T - a \left[\left(\frac{\sigma_x^2}{\sigma_x^2 + \sigma_\varepsilon^2} \right) (\hat{x} - \bar{x}) + \bar{x} \right] \right\} \Big/ b. \tag{10}$$

With this alternative, the policy reaction is less sensitive to movements in expectations than when it was used as a certainty equivalent in (7).

As a first step toward verifying that alternative control variable z^* yields a smaller loss, note that the equivalent expression is obtained if we replace the implicit forecast $\hat{x}$ in (7) with the corrected value

$$\hat{x}^c = \gamma_0 + \gamma_1 \hat{x}, \tag{11}$$

where the coefficients are obtained from the least squares regression of the realized x on the predicted value $\hat{x}$ and we again assume that our sample is large enough to make sampling error negligible; i.e.,

$$x = \gamma_0 + \gamma_1 \hat{x} + e. \tag{12}$$

For this regression $\gamma_1 = \mathrm{cov}(x, \hat{x})/\sigma_{\hat{x}}^2$, $\gamma_0 = \bar{x} - \gamma_1 \bar{\hat{x}}$, and $\sigma_e^2 = \sigma_x^2 - \gamma_1^2 \sigma_{\hat{x}}^2$. With Mills's implicit expectation assumption that ε is distributed independently of x with $\mathrm{E}(\varepsilon) = 0$ we have $\bar{x} = \bar{\hat{x}}$, $\sigma_{\hat{x}}^2 = \sigma_x^2 + \sigma_\varepsilon^2$ and $\mathrm{cov}(x, \hat{x}) = \sigma_x^2$; therefore,

$$0 < \gamma_1 = \sigma_x^2/\sigma_{\hat{x}}^2 = \sigma_x^2/(\sigma_x^2 + \sigma_\varepsilon^2) < 1$$

and

$$\gamma_0 = \bar{x} - \gamma_1 \bar{\hat{x}} = (1 - \gamma_1)\bar{x}.$$

We have as the $\hat{x}^c$ analogue of (7)

$$z^* = (T - a\hat{x}^c)/b, \tag{13}$$

yielding

$$y^* = T + a(x - \hat{x}^c) \tag{14}$$

with expected loss

$$\mathrm{E}(L^*) = \mathrm{E}(y^* - T)^2 = a^2 \sigma_{x - \hat{x}^c}^2 = a^2 \sigma_e^2. \tag{15}$$

To verify that $\mathrm{E}(L^*) < \mathrm{E}(L)$, we find from regression (12) with Mills's assumptions that

$$\sigma_e^2 = \sigma_x^2 - \gamma_1^2 \sigma_{\hat{x}}^2 = \gamma_1 \sigma_{\hat{x}}^2 + \gamma_1(\sigma_x^2/\sigma_{\hat{x}}^2 \sigma_{\hat{x}}^2) = \gamma_1(\sigma_{\hat{x}}^2 - \sigma_x^2) = \gamma_1 \sigma_\varepsilon^2. \tag{16}$$

Therefore, a comparison of (9) with (15) reveals that the relative gain from using the corrected forecast is

$$\mathrm{E}(L^*)/\mathrm{E}(L) = \sigma_e^2/\sigma_\varepsilon^2 = \gamma_1 = \sigma_x^2/(\sigma_x^2 + \sigma_\varepsilon^2) < 1. \tag{17}$$

This means that a forecast should be used as the certainty equivalent, even in the simplest possible case of a single endogenous variable with no lags, only if it is rational in the sense that the forecast error is uncorrelated with the prediction. When, as with Mills implicit expectations (e.g. sample survey information), this requirement is not satisfied, either the certainty policy equation must be modified, as in (10), or the raw expectation must be corrected with (11) prior to its use as a certainty equivalent. Note that corrected forecast $\hat{x}^c$ is a blend of two types of information: It combines the survey evidence $\hat{x}$ with $\bar{x}$, the average value of x, which might be the best forecast if $\hat{x}$ were not available. Also, it discounts the evidence provided by $\hat{x}$ when it is far away from $\bar{x}$. The correction reduces the excessive variance of the forecast relative to the realization.

Simon's certainty equivalence theorem requires that the outcomes be randomly distributed around their predicted values, conditional on the information that is available at the time the forecast is made. This is what Simon meant by his terse statement that "the 'certain' future values of variables [are replaced] with their unconditional expectations." In this limited sense, his paper on certainty equivalence was ahead of its time because he was implicitly invoking Muth's assumption of rational expectations. However, Simon himself did not refer to certainty equivalence in 1991–92 correspondence with Warren Young and William Darity about the antecedents of rational expectations. (Warren Young and William Darity Jr. kindly allowed me to review the full text of their correspondence with Herbert Simon that is partially quoted in their 2001 paper.) It seems reasonable to conclude that Simon invoked his *ad hoc* independence assumption in order to make his theorem go through without thinking about its economic significance. Muth's concept of rational expectations places Simon's independence assumption on strong micro foundations by justifying it in terms of maximizing behavior.

References

Brainard, William. 1967. Uncertainty and the effectiveness of policy. *American Economic Review* 57, May: 411–425.

Cohen, Kalman J., William R. Dill, Alfred A. Kuehn, and Peter R. Winters. 1964. *The Carnegie Tech Management Game: An Experiment in Business Education*. Irwin.

Markowitz, Harry. 1952. Portfolio selection. *Journal of Finance* 6, March: 77–91.

Mills, Edwin S. 1957. The theory of inventory decisions. *Econometrica* 25, April: 222–328.

Muth, John F. 1961. Optimal properties of exponentially weighted forecasts of time series with permanent and transitory components. *Journal of the American Statistical Association* 55, June: 299–306.

Muth, John F. 1961. Rational expectations and the theory of price movements. *Econometrica* 29, July: 315–335.

Muth, John F. 1985. Properties of some short-run business forecasts. *Eastern Economic Journal* 11, September: 200–210.

Prescott, Edward. 1971. Adaptive decision rules for macroeconomic planning. *Western Economic Journal* 4, December: 369–378.

Simon, Herbert A. 1956. Dynamic programming under uncertainty with a quadratic criterion function. *Econometrica* 24, January: 74–81.

Theil, H. 1957. A note on certainty equivalence in dynamic planning. *Econometrica* 25, April: 346–349.

Tobin, James. 1958. Liquidity preference as behavior toward risk. *Review of Economic Studies* 25, February: 65–86.

Young, Warren, and William Darity Jr. 2001. The early history of rational and implicit expectations. *History of Political Economy* 33, winter: 773–813.

Herbert Simon: Some Cherished Memories

Franco Modigliani

The loss of Herbert Simon was for me a hard, unexpected blow. Since I first met him, a little over 50 years ago when we were both attending seminars at the Cowles Commission in Chicago, I have considered him a very special kind of human being—a genius. Somehow, I had come to assume that a genius, being perfect in nearly all respects, would not die—at least before me. Unfortunately, my assumption was wrong, or maybe Destiny is not able to recognize genius.

So, I have had to reconcile myself to the loss of a man whom I not only admired but also regarded as a wonderful friend. Though much of it was at a distance, the relationship that Serena and I had for so many decades with Herbert and Dorothea was a very warm and rewarding one. It added measurably to the quality of our lives. Herb and I had a great deal in common. We shared similar views and values about the world, particularly politics and both he and I posed, for our wives, similar problems of workaholism—a syndrome that Herb so well encapsulated in the saying "it is not so much the case that men have ideas but that ideas have men!"

To be sure, Herb sometimes liked to poke a little fun at me. He hinted at my being one of those thickheaded economists who was not prepared to use the "satisficing" instead of the "maximizing" hypothesis as a guide to understand human economic decisions. But, I think he understood my reasons for that, just as I think I understood and appreciated the grounds for his criticism. In any event, these small differences did not interfere with our constructive and enjoyable collaboration in projects such as a book on production scheduling, jointly authored by Herb, Holt, Muth, and me or the restructuring of business school curricula.

Memories of our long relationship fill me with anecdotes. There are a few I would like to share with you. The first I particularly love because it shows how Herb applied the "satisficing" precept to his own life. To understand the story you must remember that Herb thought of "satisficing" as a way of cutting down on decision time in a world that required too many decisions relative to available time. During our frequent lunches, we observed that Herb always ordered the same lunch: American cheese on white. To satisfy our curiosity, he explained that he had adopted a rule for lunch: when faced with a choice, he would always request American cheese on white. This order, he explained, avoided time-consuming decisions about what to choose and could certainly be executed anywhere in the United States. Though the outcome might not be the most refined dish available, it was "good enough" (satisficing.)

Another classic story involves Herb and Serena. He once declared at a social occasion that he avoided traveling abroad because it was a sheer waste of time. "Anything worth knowing about a foreign country," he insisted, "you can surely find in a good library." At this point Serena objected: "You are wrong Herb!" Said Herb: "Tell me, Serena, what is there that you cannot find in the library?" Serena's reply left Herb open-mouthed: "Smells, Herb." Whether for this reason or others, Herb took a trip around the world the very next year!

One last anecdote shows that though Herb had great foresight, he also had some lapses. One fall day in the early 1950s, when Herb was up to his head in work on artificial intelligence, we invited the new faculty recruits to lunch. They were all carefully selected and full of promise. Once we were seated, Herb said, rather mischievously, that, with great regret, he felt obliged to tell them they had chosen the wrong career. In the near future, they would surely be replaced by computers capable of teaching. It was hard to advise, he said, what alternative career they should try, because he could not think of a pursuit that the computer could not perform better than humans. After scratching his head, he added: "Come to think of it, there is one thing that computers don't seem to be good at, namely walking. Perhaps you should think of preparing yourself for a career as postmen!" Proud owners of hard-won degrees, the young faculty members were dumbfounded. Perhaps they should not have been. Soon enough, computers would be delivering mail from office to office, unimpaired by the inability to walk. Herbert's foresight about the power of computers at the very dawn of their existence, though understated, was typical of his genius. Herbert has passed, but, even in his absence, that genius—his academic contributions and his wit—will continue to warm our minds and hearts.

Herbert Simon and Production Scheduling

John F. Muth

I first met Herbert Simon in the fall of 1952, while a green graduate student. It was at a conference of the research team on the Planning and Control of Industrial Operations project. Others at the meeting included Charles Holt and Franco Modigliani. All were approachable, friendly, and dedicated to whatever problem was at hand. Working for and with them was an incredible experience.

The project was organized with support from the Office of Naval Research. Holt was an electrical engineer and economist from MIT. Modigliani was an economist, from Illinois, who had studied economics in Italy and the New School for Social Research. Simon, in his own words, was a card-carrying political scientist from Chicago. He was also a organizational theorist, a cognitive scientist, and an economist.

It was a time when many standard tools of operations research were just being developed, including queuing theory, linear programming, and game theory. The standard calculating device was a desktop machine with less power, and much slower, than an inexpensive hand-held calculator of today.

The researchers were able to bring a fresh view to the problem of production and inventory control. Textbooks at the time focused on the EOQ formula, Gantt chart displays, punched card systems for dispatching, moving average forecasts, and that's about it.

When the project started, engineers sought only good or optimal steady-state behavior of processes, with stable adjustment to errors or disturbances. In fact, we discussed the matter with engineers but learned nothing. Pontryagin's maximum principle may have been devised, but it was unknown in engineering circles. Richard Bellman's dynamic programming was under development, but models had been solved only for toy problems.

Economic theory was in about the same state. The idea of optimum dynamic response was unknown, although the mathematician G. C. Evans and others had considered problems involving time under certainty.

Controllability and its dual, observability, were just being developed. It also emerged in economics. Until that time, full employment and price stability were regarded as incompatible goals. Paul Samuelson—of all people—pointed out that this is not necessarily the case.

Simon had already studied the dynamics of inventory feedback on production rates (1952). Standard stability and frequency-response analyses could be carried out. Up to that time, inventory-cycle models in economics hypothesized a complete attempted inventory correction each time period.

Holt and Simon then compared the costs of various decision rules for such adjustment. I believe the comparison involved a servomechanism model and a calculus of variations solution with various plausible forecasting rules.

In the process they discovered significant computational problems. Computational instability of the optimal decision led Simon to believe that optimal behavior was dynamically unstable (1955). Hence business must rely on rules of thumb. He later believed in the significance of corrective error feedback in achieving stability.

I was involved primarily on the aggregate scheduling problem and inventory models. Aggregate scheduling included the formulation of first-order conditions for minimization of quadratic production, inventory storage, and employment costs. Holt was primarily responsible for formulating this model. Two problems remained, however:

1. Computational instability. Rounding errors gradually dominate the solution obtained with ordinary numerical methods. Modigliani first solved the problem analytically, a method I later simplified (Muth 1956).

2. Appropriateness under uncertainty. Simon showed that expected value forecasts lead to optimal solutions as long as the costs are quadratic and the residual variance is independent of the decisions (1956).

Simon's 1956 paper was to me his most important, but it was merely a sidelight of his career. The paper showed optimal decisions with a quadratic objective function may be based on scalar "certainty equivalents." Furthermore, this certainty equivalent is the mathematical expected value as long as the residual error variance is independent of the expected value. In other contexts, the entire probability distribution is relevant. This paper is fundamental to the relevance of point expectations in decision problems. It was a foundation of my paper on rational expectations (Muth 1961).

It is worth noting that Simon's paper on certainty equivalence clashes with his overall views of human behavior. On the other hand, we should recognize that my 1961 rational expectations model allows for both cognitive limits and cognitive biases.

Inventory control under uncertainty was concerned with order quantities and buffer stocks. Modigliani was primarily responsible for this phase of the project, with feeble assistance from me. We addressed three major problems:

1. Uncertainty with reorder point or reorder period regimes. This had recently been studied by T. M. Whitin with discrete demands.

2. Reconciliation of item decisions with desired aggregate inventory levels, solved by Holt with Lagrange multipliers.

3. Demand forecasting aspects of the project introduced me to statistical methods of forecasting, which played an important part of my rational expectations model.

Norbert Wiener's work on forecasting time series was published as a classified document during the 1940s. (Because it was bound in yellow covers, it came to be known as the "Yellow Peril.") Kalman filters had not yet been devised.

The practical forecasting problem fizzled when it was learned that most of the demand fluctuations were induced by the firm's own distribution system. Final demand was relatively flat.

In later years, I became interested in artificial intelligence, not from the standpoint of cognitive behavior, but for obtaining good solutions to problems in production management such as balancing assembly lines, programming numerically controlled machine tools, and scheduling job shops.

Many lives, including my own, have been enriched by Herbert Simon and his work.

References

Holt, C. C., F. Modigliani, and J. F. Muth. 1956. Derivation of a linear decision rule for production and employment. *Management Science* 2: 159–170.

Holt, C. C., F. Modigliani, J. F. Muth, and H. A. Simon. 1960. Planning production, inventories, and work force. Prentice-Hall.

Holt, C. C., F. Modigliani, and H. A. Simon. 1956. A linear decision rule for production and employment scheduling. *Management Science* 2: 1–1–30.

Muth, John F. 1961. Rational expectations and the theory of price movements. *Econometrica* 29: 315–335.

Simon, H. A. 1952. On the application of servomechanism theory in the study of production control. *Econometrica* 20, April: 247–268.

Simon, H. A. 1955. Some Properties of Optimal Linear Filters. *Quarterly of Applied Mathematics* 12: 438–440.

Simon, H. A. 1956. Dynamic programming under uncertainty with a quadratic criterion function. *Econometrica* 24: 74–81.

IV   *Minds and Machines*

"On a Different Plane"

Edward A. Feigenbaum

Before Christmas of 2001, the San Francisco Symphony performed the Bach Christmas Oratorio. As a choral singer, I attended, score in hand, trying to be as much a student of Bach as a concert listener.

This work of Bach's is especially wonderful, magical. In one dimension, the music is elegantly simple and beautiful. But in another dimension, there is a complex, intricate, and surprising harmonic structure that inspires awe and opens the mind to possibilities. The student in me asks over and over: "How could Bach have thought of that?" So beautifully simple, yet so profoundly complex.

Later I had an exchange of messages with Stanford's professor of choral music about this. He admitted that teaching and conducting Bach was difficult for him. "Bach," he said, is "on a different plane of existence."

Simon operated on a "different plane of existence" from me, and probably from most of us. His theories of behavior—he would call them models—are simple and beautiful, indeed beautifully simple. Yet they are deeply insightful and full of possibilities. Simon's development of these models in depth, with his mathematical and computer tools, or with his powers of reasoning in the social sciences and philosophy, was often complex and surprising, expanding one's concept of what it means to model and explain human behavior.

Profoundly Simple: Satisficing

The concept of satisficing is an elegantly simple insight. Yet it brought forward many possibilities, including an empirically valid basis for economic theory and administrative theory, a grounding concept for a theory of problem solving, and a key mechanism for artificial intelligence programs.

The Unified Theory

Simon was a unifier. He would say of the observation I just made that surely this was no surprise; that underlying economic and administrative theories is a theory of human decision making. He would say that decision making *is* problem solving, that the essence of problem solving *is* decision making. He would go on to say that human problem solving is but an instance of a general information processing theory of problem solving that is as valid for artifacts (like computers) as for people.

Depth in a Working Model

The striking thing about Simon's unity of concepts and models is that he made this unity work. Simon's great abstractions could indeed be realized in fine detail; and when they were, they *worked*. Though he wrote several important papers in the philosophy of science, Herb Simon was not a philosopher. He was a scientist, even an engineer at times.

Profoundly Simple: The Ant on the Beach

The concept of how the complex environment of a decision maker (problem solver) can shape behavior and give rise to unfathomably intricate behavior patterns is made real for us by Simon's metaphor of "the ant on the beach." The ant is obeying simple goal-seeking rules, but the pattern of the grains of sand give the behavioral path its intricacy.

This concept is fundamental to all the work on intelligent problem solving computer programs. The "environment" for such programs is a knowledge environment. An entire sub-field of AI has developed to deal with the problem of (internal) representation of the knowledge environment. Most of any high-performance AI program is in its knowledge base. Its "behavioral engine," like the ant's, is relatively simple, usually some kind of search procedure or rule-based reasoner.

A Simple Architecture of Complexity

Complex systems have so many internal interactions that it is difficult to think about them, to analyze them, or to predict their behavior. But Simon, with his drive toward simplicity, would say: "Not so. Not if they are nearly decomposable. Then they can be readily understood. Here is the method for determining near-decomposability. There is a simple architecture with which to understand system complexity." And the concept of near-decomposability *worked*. Other scientists could build upon it.

The Art of Essential Simplification

What Simon did so masterfully was "essential simplification"— simplify to the essence of the matter, but not further. Choose behavioral phenomena that contain the essential kernel of what needs to be understood and modeled. Avoid the clutter of secondary phenomena. Go to the heart of the matter. How to see the heart of the matter, how to choose the essential behavior and the key mechanisms that were simple yet central, is art, not science. Or maybe it is the art in the science. I have seen it in the thought of two other great scientists with whom I had the privilege and good fortune to collaborate, Joshua

Lederberg and Carl Djerassi. Seeing it in action, knowing how hard it is to do, has sometimes made me feel like I was Salieri observing Mozart in the play *Amadeus*.

Profoundly Simple: Heuristic Problem Solving

I saw it early, in my first week as a graduate student at Carnegie Tech's Graduate School of Industrial Administration. Simon and Newell were rapidly creating the intellectual and technical basis for the computational modeling of cognition. For an environment in which to study problem solving phenomena, they had chosen as their essential simplification: proving theorems in propositional logic. That was a superb choice because it disentangled the essentials of the problem solving method using heuristic search from the complexities of the semantics of symbols (which AI and cognitive science have yet to fully unravel). The p's and q's of propositional calculus were pure symbols—they had no meaning, no semantics.

Profoundly Simple: Verbal Learning and EPAM

Simon was seeking the same essential simplification for the phenomena of human symbolic learning. He looked to memorization and to recognition. For memorization, he thought of connecting to the vast literature in psychology that experimented with "nonsense" materials. The phenomena associated with these experiments were (again) unlikely to be cluttered with the complexities of semantics. As with problem solving, he saw the basic nature of a fundamental act of cognition, that of recognition, as being essentially decision making.

From those insights was born the EPAM model of human verbal learning behavior. This acronym stands for Elementary Perceiver And Memorizer. For my dissertation work, with Herb's supervision, I worked out the details of the model and its validation and collaborated with

Herb on extensions for several years. Herb continued to extend EPAM to other cognitive phenomena, in collaboration with several students (particularly Howard Richman), until his death.

At the Right Place, at the Right Time

I was lucky. I was lucky to have found an orbit around Herb Simon while I was an undergraduate student, and to have had the good sense to stay parked in that orbit for my graduate work. I was lucky to have encountered Simon and Newell at just the magical moment when AI and computational models of cognition were being born. In fact, I am often cited as the source of the oft-quoted sentence that Simon uttered in our classroom in January 1956: "Over the Christmas vacation, Al Newell and I invented a thinking machine." That sentence, and what followed, changed my life.

The Most Important Thing I Learned

What I learned at these earliest moments of my scientific career is what some scientists take years to learn and most never learn: the art, the beauty, and the power of essential simplification. This is the most important thing I learned from Herb Simon, and I was fortunate to learn it again from Lederberg and Djerassi.

Radical Simplification

Over the years of a long career that now seems so short, I mentored many graduate students, always with Herb Simon as my model of a mentor. It was hard to teach technical details to the best and the brightest Stanford graduate students who came my way. Each grasped the details and invented new technical arcana faster than I could get the thoughts out of my head. But what I could usefully teach to each student, or more accurately lead each student toward, was essential simplification. To make the idea vivid and to emphasize the pattern of thought one needed to do it, I reworded the idea as *radical simplification.*

Simon's "Christmas Oratorio"

And from my bookshelf I pulled a small volume for her to read, one of Simon's works of beautiful and elegant simplicity, of deep insight, rich and full of possibilities, perhaps Simon's own "Christmas Oratorio," *The Sciences of the Artificial.*

Striking a Blow for Sanity in Theories of Rationality

Gerd Gigerenzer

I took the title of this chapter from an email Herbert A. Simon sent me in May 1999. In this email, he wrote a statement for the back cover of *Simple Heuristics That Make Us Smart* in which he commented: "I think the book strikes a great blow for sanity in the approach to rationality [and shows] why more than minor tampering with existing optimization theory is called for." But Herb wouldn't be Herb if he hadn't added "and you wouldn't believe I had ever skimmed the volume if I didn't find SOMETHING to disagree with." And so he continued, pointing out that he hadn't found the expert/novice topic treated, that scientific discovery would have been a great example for ill-structured domains....

Bringing sanity into theories of rationality was a major guideline in Herbert Simon's scientific life. However, as he himself was prepared to admit, sanity in rationality entered his thinking as a negatively defined concept, a kind of black box that contained everything that was not optimization. What he opposed has various names: full rationality, substantial rationality, maximization of expected utility, *Homo economicus*, or simply optimization. What he proposed had its seeds in his revised dissertation, *Administrative Behavior* (1947), and eventually became termed bounded rationality, satisficing, or procedural rationality. Because of its initial vague definition, bounded rationality, however, came to mean many things to many people.

Bounded Rationality in the Plural

Simon's (1955, 1956) concept of bounded rationality has been claimed by three different programs. One of these Simon opposed, one he tolerated, and one he embraced. I will call the three programs optimization under constraints, cognitive illusions and anomalies, and ecological rationality, although I am not sure that Herb always wanted to distinguish the latter two programs the way I do.

What Bounded Rationality Is Not: Optimization under Constraints

In models of full rationality, all relevant information is assumed to be available to *Homo economicus* at no cost. This classical version of *Homo economicus* has a distinctive Christian flavor: he is created in the image of an omniscient God. Real humans, however, need to search for information first. In an attempt to render economic theory more realistic, Stigler (1961) introduced constraints on full rationality, such as costs of information search. The idea of optimization under constraints is to propose one or a few constraints (too many would make the mathematics too hard or even intractable) while retaining the ideal of optimization. In this view, for instance, a person who wants to buy a used car of a certain brand stops search when the costs of further search—direct costs and opportunity costs—exceed those of its benefits. Introducing real constraints does make the approach more realistic, but maintaining the ideal of optimization, that is, calculating an optimal stopping point, does not. Such an ideal of optimization invokes new kinds of omniscience, that is, foreseeing the benefits and costs of further information search (Conlisk 1996). This is little evidence that humans make decisions this way.

Lack of psychological reality was an objection Herb made time and again. The argument against his and others' concern with omniscience and psychological evidence has been the "as if" conjecture: The question is not whether people actually optimize, with or without constraints, but whether they *act as if* they were doing so. As long as optimization predicts behavior, one need not be concerned with the actual motivations, emotions, and reasoning of people (Friedman 1953). In this view, the bounds in bounded rationality are just another name for constraints, and bounded rationality is merely a case of optimizing under constraints. Despite Herb's vehement protests, this message has become the doctrine. But this doctrine comes at a price: retaining the ideal of optimization can make models of optimization under constraints more demanding than models of full rationality, both mathematically and psychologically. In the words of Thomas Sargent, a proponent of the view that bounded rationality means optimization under constraints: "Ironically, when we economists make the people in our models more 'bounded' in their rationality . . . *we* must be smarter, because our models become larger and more demanding mathematically and econometrically." (Sargent 1993, p. 2) In optimization under constraints, agents are recreated in the image of econometricians, one step above the gods. In personal conversation, Herb once remarked with a mixture of humor and anger that he had considered suing those authors who misuse his term of bounded rationality to construct ever more psychologically unrealistic models of human decision making.

Optimization, with or without constraints, has also spread beyond economics. Psychologists often propose models of cognition that assume almost unlimited memory, storage capacities, and computational power. That is, many psychologists also build "as if" models of behavior. Over lunch, I once asked Herb about his impact on psychology and got one of his straightforward responses:

GG: Do you think you had much effect on psychologists with "bounded rationality?"

HS: Yes. There is an abundant literature on recognition and search, for instance, in Newell and Simon's *Human Problem Solving*.

GG: But what about exemplar models of categorization and the many other Laplacean demon models of cognition?

HS: Oh, these are of no relevance.

Why should we listen to Herb rather than building "as if" models of optimization under constraints? Is there a problem with the program of making right predictions from wrong assumptions?

Optimization is impossible in most natural situations. The ideals of "as if" optimization is obviously limited because, in most natural situations, optimization is computationally intractable in any implementation, whether machine or neural (Michalewicz and Fogel 2000). In computer science, these situations are called NP-complete; that is, the solution cannot be computed in polynomial time. For instance, no mind or computer can apply Bayes's rule to a large number of variables that are mutually dependent, because the number of computations increases exponentially with the number of variables. In such situations, a fully rational Bayesian cannot exist. Even for games with simple and well-defined rules, such as chess and Go, we do not know the optimal strategy. Nevertheless, we know what a good outcome is. In these situations, "as if" optimization can only be achieved when the real situation is changed and simplified in a mathematically convenient way so that optimization is possible. Thus, the choice is between finding a good heuristic solution for a game where no optimal one is known, and finding an optimal solution for a game with modified rules. That may mean abandoning our study of chess in favor of tic-tac-toe.

Optimization is unfeasible when problems are unfamiliar and time is scarce. In situations where optimization is in principle possible (unlike those under the first point), a practical issue remains. Selten (2001) distinguishes between familiar and unfamiliar problems. In the case of a familiar problem, the decision maker knows the optimal solution. This may be due to prior training or because the problem is simple enough. In the case of an unfamiliar problem, however, the decision maker cannot simply execute a known method that leads to the best result because that method must first be discovered. In other words, the agent has to solve two tasks: level 1, executing a method that leads to a solution, and level 2, finding this method. Thus, two questions arise.

What is the optimal method to be chosen? And what is the optimal approach to discovering that method? (There may be an infinite regress: level 3, finding a method for level 2, and so on.) At each level, time must be spent. Although Selten's argument concerning unfamiliar problems has not yet been cast into mathematical form, as the previous issue of combinatorial explosion has been, it strongly suggests that an optimizing approach to unfamiliar problems is rarely feasible when decision time is scarce.

Optimization does not imply an optimal outcome. Some economists, biologists, and cognitive scientists seem to believe that a theory of bounded rationality must rely on optimization in order to promise optimal decisions. No optimization, no good decision. But this does not follow. Optimization needs to be distinguished from an optimal outcome. Note that the term optimization refers to a mathematical process—computing the maximum or minimum of a function—which does *not* guarantee optimal outcomes in the real world. The reason is that one has to make assumptions about the world in order to be able to optimize. These assumptions are typically selected by mathematical convenience, based on simplifications, and rarely grounded in psychological reality. If they are wrong, one has built the optimization castle on sand, and optimization will not necessarily lead to optimal results. This is one reason why models of bounded rationality that do not involve optimization often can make predictions at least as good as those made by models that do involve optimization (Gigerenzer and Selten 2001a; Selten 1998; March 1978).

A good fit, per se, is not an empirical validation of the model. Friedman's (1953) argument in favor of "as if" models was this: What counts is not descriptive accuracy, that is, the psychological validity of the axioms and assumptions, but rather the accuracy of the predictions a model makes. Despite Friedman's introductory example of the law of falling bodies, this explicit disinterest in a proper description of the underlying mechanisms would be unusual in physics, molecular biology, or genetics. (This does not mean that "as if" models are never used; optimal foraging models in animal biology are an example.) The point I want to make here is that one needs to be careful in distinguishing between two kinds of statistical tests that have both been labeled "predictions." One is *data fitting*, that is, "explanations" of existing data; the other is *ex ante prediction*, that is, predictions of *new* observations.

In cognitive science and economics, the validity of a model is often reported in terms of its fit with *given* observations, such as what proportion of the variance a model explains. However, the belief that a good fit between model and data would provide empirical evidence for the model is unfounded if the model has numerous free parameters (Roberts and Pashler 2000). For instance, introducing more and more relevant constraints into models of optimization increases the number of adjustable parameters, which can make the resulting model too "powerful" to allow for falsification by empirical data. In these situations, a model can fit almost all possible data, including data produced by two logically inconsistent theories. Here, a good fit is a mathematical truism, not an empirical result. Utility maximization models often have many adjustable parameters—such as the utilities and utility functions in each particular case (Simon 1986; Arrow 1986). This problem of "overfitting" is not specific to optimization models, but rather occurs in any statistical model that has a relatively large number of adjustable parameters, including neural networks (Geman, Bienenstock, and Doursat 1992). If smart enough, one can always find parameters so that the model fits a given situation. The problem of overfitting becomes particularly stringent in the "as if" philosophy because the only empirical test for a model concerns its predictive power. Models of bounded rationality such as fast and frugal heuristics (Gigerenzer and Selten 2001a) that dispense with optimization and also, for the most part, with utilities and probabilities, reduce this validation problem in two ways. First, they model the underlying mechanisms of choice and inference, and thereby provide a second source for testing their validity (process and outcome). Second, they are simple and robust so that their predictions show consistently less overfitting than optimizing models (Gigerenzer, Todd, and ABC Research Group 1999).

These four issues highlight some limits of "as if" optimization. There are other well-known problems, such as the "infinite regress" problem of determining how much information to gather in order to determine the cost of information. These issues indicate that optimization under constraints is not the last word, despite its mathematical beauty. Bounded rationality needs a different intellectual home. But which?

What Bounded Rationality Is Not: Cognitive Illusions and Anomalies

Optimization with decision costs taken into account is one misreading of Herb's concept of bounded rationality. It is not the only one. Many psychologists and some economists assume that the study of bounded rationality is the study of cognitive limitations and systematic errors in judgment and decision making (e.g., Camerer 1998; Rabin 1998). Surprisingly, this second meaning amounts to something like the converse of the first. The cognitive illusions program aims at demonstrating that people's judgments and decisions do not follow the predictions of "as if" optimization.

For instance, in his article "Bounded rationality in individual decision making," Camerer (1998, p. 179) reviews anomalies in decisions and errors in judgments and calls this the "exploration of procedural (bounded) rationality of individuals." Kaufman (1999, p. 141) gives the example of a gay man who practiced unsafe sex with multiple partners and "is now HIV positive and admits to his bounded rationality." This view that the study of bounded rationality is the study of systematic errors in judgment and decision making has spread from psychology into economics and law, shaping new research areas such as behavioral economics (e.g., Camerer 1995) and behavioral law and economics (e.g., Jolls, Sunstein, and Thaler 1998). In Camerer's words, "the goal is to test whether normative rules are *systematically* violated and to

propose alternative theories to explain any observed violations"
(p. 588). The products of this research are well known: a list of cognitive biases such as base rate neglect, overconfidence bias, and the sunk-cost effect.

This program assumes that the meaning of bounded rationality is that humans have cognitive limitations, which express themselves in errors in judgment and decision making; therefore, the study of errors is the study of bounded rationality. Compared to optimization under constraints, this second interpretation of bounded rationality is a relatively new one. The origin of this interpretation seems to be a mentioning of Simon's work on bounded rationality in the preface of Kahneman, Slovic, and Tversky's 1982 anthology. Since there are no citations at all to Simon in the early influential papers of Kahneman and Tversky, which are reprinted in this anthology, this mentioning was probably more an acknowledgement to a distinguished figure than an intellectual debt (Lopes 1992). Nevertheless, the notion that bounded rationality is the study of cognitive illusions has since become widespread.

Herb applauded the demonstrations of systematic deviations from expected utility by Kahneman, Tversky, and others. But what did he think when the followers of Kahneman and Tversky labeled these demonstrations the study of "bounded rationality?" I asked him once, and his response was "That's rhetoric. But Kahneman and Tversky have decisively disproved economists' rationality model." Herb was surprised to hear that I held their notion of cognitive illusions and biases to be inconsistent with his concept of bounded rationality. I think he liked their results so much that he tended to overlook that these experimenters accepted as normative the very optimization theories that Herb so fought against, at least when the results were interpreted as cognitive illusions. A true theory of bounded rationality does not rely on optimization theories, neither as descriptions nor as norms of behavior. (I gave reasons for the normative limits in the previous section.) We once discussed this issue on a walk through the beautiful

Carnegie Mellon campus in the spring of 1997. A systematic deviation from an "insane" standard should not automatically be called a judgmental error, should it? "I hadn't thought about it in this way," Herb replied.

Why is bounded rationality not the same as irrationality? Herb has given the answer in the form of an analogy. Bounded rationality is like a pair of scissors: the mind is one blade, and the structure of the environment is the other. To understand behavior, one has to look at both, at how they fit. In other words, to evaluate cognitive strategies as rational or irrational, one also needs to analyze the environment, because a strategy is rational or irrational only with respect to an environment, physical or social (Simon 1990). The study of cognitive illusions and errors, however, studies only the cognitive blade, and compares it with laws of probability rather than with the structure of the environment. One blade alone does not cut well.

As a consequence, apparently stable cognitive illusions can be made to disappear and reappear by varying crucial structures of the environment. For instance, Gigerenzer, Hoffrage, and Kleinbölting (1991) theoretically derived and experimentally demonstrated that two apparently stable cognitive illusions, the overconfidence bias and the hard-easy effect, disappear when the underlying questions are randomly sampled from an environment rather than systematically selected. Juslin, Winman, and Olsson (2000) confirmed this initial demonstration in a quantitative analysis of all 130 extant studies. Other research has pointed to the ecological reasons for people's difficulty in following Bayes's rule when reasoning with probabilities. Bayesian reasoning can be strongly improved when the information is not presented in probabilities but rather in natural frequencies, which correspond to the environmental input that humans have received during most of their evolution (Gigerenzer and Hoffrage 1995, 1999). Meanwhile, this method has been proven to help physicians and patients, judges and law students alike to understand the uncertainties in HIV tests, DNA fingerprinting, and other technologies (e.g., Gigerenzer 2002; Hoffrage and Gigerenzer 1998; Hoffrage, Lindsay, Hertwig, and Gigerenzer 2000; Koehler 1996). An analysis of environmental structures—such as sampling type, sample size, representation, degree of predictability, and social rules—helps to understand how the cognitive blade and the environmental blade work together (Fiedler 2000; Gigerenzer 2000).

The confusion between bounded rationality and the study of cognitive illusions and irrationality is the second misunderstanding of Herb's idea of sanity in theories of rationality. Bounded rationality is not merely an attack on the assumptions underlying optimizing models; it is a positive program to replace optimization—when it is unrealistic—with something better.

What Bounded Rationality Is: Ecological Rationality (the Adaptive Toolbox)

Let me illustrate a fast and frugal heuristic from the adaptive toolbox with an example from sports (Gigerenzer and Selten 2001b). In cricket, baseball, and soccer, players need to catch balls that come in high. A company wants to design a robot that can catch the ball. This is a thought experiment; no such robot exists as yet. For the sake of simplicity, we consider only the case where a ball comes in high, behind or in front of a player, but not to his left or right.

One team of engineers, which I call the optimizing team, proceeds by programming the family of parabolas into the robot's brain (in theory, balls fly in parabolas). To select the proper parabola, the robot needs to be equipped with instruments that can measure the distance from where the ball was thrown or shot, as well as its initial velocity and projection angle. Yet in a real game, due to air resistance and wind, balls do not fly in parabolas. Thus, the robot would need further instruments that can measure the speed and direction of the wind at each point of the ball's flight in order to compute the resulting path. In addition, there are further factors, such as spin, that affect the flight of the ball. The optimizing team eventually succeeds in producing a lengthy equation that specifies the trajectory of the flight and the spot where the ball will land, given all these measurements. Note that this equation is an "as if" model—the team is not concerned with the actual mechanisms that real players or robots use—and, consequently, the equation does not inform us how to actually build a robot. The optimizing team responds that their task is not "robot psychology," that is, to understand how a robot actually does, or could do, the job. Their claim is that the model will predict the point to which real players and robots would run to catch the ball.

A subgroup within the optimizing team objects that there is no time for the robot to make the proposed measurements and computations, given that the ball is only in the air for a few seconds. A fully rational robot would just sit on the field, measuring and calculating, and thus missing every ball. The more precise the measurements are, the longer they take, and the less time the robot has left to run to the spot where the ball is supposed to land. The real constraint, they argue, is not money but time. Instead of trying to model an omniscient robot, the team proposes to build one that optimizes under constraints. After some deliberation, the subgroup puts forward a number of constraints concerning the robot's ability for information search. Finally, the members of this subgroup design a sophisticated formula that optimizes the outcome under the given constraints, a mathematical masterpiece. The hard-core members of the optimizing team, however, object that this formula is even more complex than the first one, and that the robot will sit even longer on the field measuring and calculating. So what's the point?

A second team enters the field and argues that you need to understand the cognitive processes in order to find out what players do in order to eventually design a robot. One should experimentally study real players, and create situations in which they systematically demonstrate judgmental errors, that is, deviations from the optimizing model. These errors will be the window for the underlying cognitive processes. This team calls itself the "cognitive illusions team." After a phase of trial and error, the team has found a task in which the players show a bias. A player is positioned on a fixed point in the field, a ball is shot in high, and the player is asked to predict how many yards in front of or behind his position the ball will hit the ground. The surprising result is that the players don't predict very well: they consistently underestimate the distance between their position and the point where the ball will land. This systematic error is called the "optimistic bias" in baseball, cricket, and soccer—because underestimating the distance suggests to players that they might actually get the ball even when they can't. A debate opens on whether this judgmental error could be adaptive, because not trying to run for a ball that actually could have been reached is a more costly error in a real game than trying without success. The cognitive illusions team claims that the model of the optimizing team has been descriptively disproved; actual players show systematic errors whereas the optimizing model doesn't predict any. The optimization team responds that they will nevertheless maintain their model, because a model that can at least approximately predict the data is better than no model. After all, they argue, the notion of an "optimistic bias" is only a redescription of the data; the bias team hasn't put forward any alternative model of the underlying cognitive mechanisms, nor of how to build the robot.

A third team is called in. This team agrees with the second team that humans may not be able to compute the point where the ball will land. However, they argue that the negative goal of disproving the optimization team's predictions does not directly lead to positive models of the underlying cognitive processes. For instance, the notion of an "optimistic bias" does not describe how a player actually catches a ball, but only how his judgment deviates from the actual landing point. The third team proposes to unpack what they call the adaptive toolbox of human behavior and cognition, that is, the smart cognitive and social heuristics as well as the building blocks from which the heuristics are constructed. What do players actually do in order to catch a ball, given that they do not seem to perform the measurements and calculations that the optimization team proposes? Are there fast and frugal heuristics that players use? Experiments show that there are. One of these is the "gaze heuristic." When a ball is high in the air, an experienced player visually fixates the ball and starts running. The heuristic is to adjust the running speed so that the angle of gaze—the angle between the eye and the ball—remains constant (or within a certain range—see McLeod and Dienes 1996). Assuming the player can run fast enough, this gaze heuristic will take him to the spot where the ball will land. The gaze heuristic is fast and frugal: It pays attention to only one cue, the angle of gaze. It does not attempt to acquire the relevant information concerning initial distance, velocity, wind, spin, or other causal variables, nor does it try to calculate the resulting path given this information. All the relevant information is contained in one variable: the angle of gaze. I call this *one-reason decision making*. The gaze heuristic creates an environment that the player can easily exploit. In place of the complicated trajectory of the ball's flight—which the optimizing team has worked out—the gaze heuristic creates a linear relation between the player's eye and the ball. The rationale behind the gaze heuristic is an instance of ecological rationality.

The optimizing team responds that it may be very interesting to know how actual players do the job, but that it is not really relevant. The successful player will run exactly to the same point that can be calculated from our equations, the team maintains, and so the player acts "as if" he were optimizing. Not exactly, the adaptive toolbox team replies, for there are two advantages to realistic process models. First, the omniscient, optimizing player exists only "as if" and therefore does not lead to instructions on how to build a robot, or how to teach human beginners. The information and computation necessary will likely lead to computational explosion, that is, the model is impossible to implement in any hardware, human or computer. In contrast, the gaze heuristic can be taught to inexperienced players, and we may eventually succeed in building a robot that uses it. Second, with a good model of the heuristic a person uses, one can make much more precise predictions than with an "as if" model, including behaviors that an "as if" model cannot foresee. For instance, the gaze heuristic predicts that the player will catch the ball *while running*. This is an experimentally testable prediction, and in fact, players do not move to the spot where they think the ball will land and then wait there; rather, they catch the ball while running. The reason is in the environment: the trajectory of the ball is not linear, and thus the player has to move in order to keep the angle of gaze constant. Optimization models would not predict this behavior. Similarly, knowing the heuristics players use helps to predict what players cannot do. Remember that the cognitive illusions team had shown that even experienced players cannot correctly predict where the ball will land. Knowing the heuristic, we understand why this is in fact not necessary for successfully catching a ball. The gaze heuristic succeeds without this ability. A player using the gaze heuristic does not calculate where the ball will land; the heuristic takes him where the ball lands. Thus, what looks like a serious judgmental bias in need of de-biasing turns out to be irrelevant for good ball catching.

Homo heuristicus

This thought experiment illustrates the program of ecological rationality: to study (i) the heuristics people actually use to solve a class of tasks, (ii) the structure of the task environment, and (iii) what environmental structure a heuristic can exploit. The corresponding methodologies used to investigate these issues are experimental research, analytical proofs, and computer simulations. The aim of such research is to establish a "periodic system" of heuristics and their building blocks, as well as a conceptual language to describe the structures of relevant real-world environments. This program develops Simon's ideas: to study the rational principles that underlie the behavior of real people, who do not optimize and, for the most part, do not calculate utilities and probabilities. Recall that this program differs from the optimizing program in that it analyzes the actual process—the heuristics—rather than constructing "as if" models based on a convenient mathematical structure. Unlike the cognitive illusions program, it directly analyzes the decision process rather than trying to demonstrate violations of the assumptions underlying "as if" models. I have used a heuristic from sports, because sports are a "neutral" topic for most economists and cognitive scientists and are unlikely to invoke strong emotional a priori beliefs. Most of the heuristics studied, however, deal with consumer choice, treatment allocation, risk estimation, social games, and other forms of judgment under limited time and knowledge. The various heuristics in the adaptive toolbox consist of a small number of building blocks, including rules for information search, stopping, and decision. The program is described in detail in Gigerenzer et al. 1999 and in Gigerenzer and Selten 2001a.

In *Bounded Rationality: The Adaptive Toolbox*, Reinhard Selten and I start out with this goal: "to promote bounded rationality as the key to understanding how actual people make decisions without utilities and probabilities." The adaptive toolbox signifies a radical departure from the classical "repair program" of adjusting theories of rational behavior, where one variable, such as regret, is added to the expected utility calculus, or where one tinkers with the functions for probabilities or utilities, as in prospect theory. We start, in contrast, from the empirically rooted knowledge about the human mind and its capabilities (Todd and Gigerenzer 2000). Quantitative probabilities, utilities, and optimization appear to play little role in the actual capabilities of the human mind, whereas fast and frugal processes, such as name recognition, aspiration levels, imitation learning, sequential search, stopping rules, and one-reason decision making, do. The models of heuristics typically have zero adjustable parameters, which makes it easier to empirically test and falsify them. In statistical terms, heuristics err on the side of "bias" rather than "variance" (Geman et al. 1992). This work on the adaptive toolbox and on ecological rationality will, I hope, provide a positive alternative to the investigation of rational choice: the study of how *Homo heuristicus* makes decisions in an uncertain world.

The question of the rationality of *Homo heuristicus* concerns the question of ecological rationality. A heuristic is not good or bad, rational or irrational, in itself, but only relative to an environment, just as adaptations are context bound. Heuristics can exploit regularities in the environment—this is the meaning of ecological rationality. In the ball example, the regularity is that a constant angle of gaze will cause a collision between the ball and the player, or between any two moving objects. Just like human organs, heuristics are domain-specific, that is, designed for a class of problems, rather than for general strategies. For instance, the gaze heuristic is useful in situations where one wants to generate a collision between two moving objects, as described before, but also for avoiding collisions. If you learn to fly a plane, for instance, you will be taught a version of the gaze heuristic: when another plane is approaching, look at a scratch in your windshield and see whether the other plane moves relative to that scratch. If it does not, dive away quickly.

The study of heuristics illustrates that, contrary to conventional wisdom, limitations of knowledge, memory, and computational capability need *not* be a disadvantage. The gaze heuristic, for instance, ignores all the causally relevant information; it cannot predict where the ball will land but solves the problem of catching the ball anyway. More information is not always better. Goldstein and Gigerenzer (2002) specify the conditions under which intermediate levels of knowledge lead to systematically more correct predictions than higher levels of knowledge—the "less is more" effect. Computer simulations indicate that memory limitations actually enable a child to learn its first language, while a fully developed memory would in fact prevent language learning (Elman 1993). Relying on only one good reason can lead to better predictions of demographic and economic variables—such as homeless and school drop-out rates—than can regression analysis with many variables (Czerlinski, Gigerenzer, and Goldstein 1999). The working memory limitation of "7 plus minus 2" seems to improve the detection of covariances in the environment (Kareev 2000). Investment portfolios based on pedestrians' brand name recognition have outperformed the market and major mutual funds (Borges, Goldstein, Ortmann, and Gigerenzer 1999). For further examples of situations in which limited knowledge or cognitive capacities can speed up learning and promote successful problem solving, see Bjorklund and Green 1992 and Todd 2001. This is not to say that heuristics are foolproof or that limitations are always good, for again the interesting question concerns ecological rationality: to specify the tasks or environmental structures that a heuristic can exploit and those where it will fail.

The term "adaptive toolbox" is not Herb's, although it is in his spirit. The rationality of the adaptive toolbox is not logical, but ecological. It refers to the match between a heuristic and the structure of an environment, which is the essence of Simon's analogy of a pair of scissors. For instance, one can specify a class of environmental structures and mathematically prove that a heuristic that simply relies on the best reason while ignoring the rest—such as Take The Best (Gigerenzer and Goldstein 1999)—is at least as accurate as any linear model with any number of predictors (Martignon and Hoffrage 1999). In these circumstances, heuristics are not just faster and more frugal than optimization models, but they are also at least as accurate. (Here I mean accuracy in prediction, not in fitting.) When heuristics can exploit the structure of environments, they can avoid a tradeoff between accuracy and effort. Whereas in Stigler's classical example the used-car buyer typically does not get the best buy, because information search costs limit his attempt at an exhaustive search, there exist situations in which a smart heuristic can solve a task perfectly, as illustrated by the gaze heuristic. Studying ecological rationality—the match between heuristics and environments—is important for freeing the concept of heuristics from the flavor of always being the second-best solution. The issue can be posed with a different twist. If one has a good model of the mechanism, what is the additional value of an "as if" model? "As if" may well turn out to be the second-best solution.

Epilogue

Herb is no longer among us. But his spirit is. His struggle with the concept of bounded rationality will stay with us, and I believe that if he could see how it is being developed, he would be enthusiastic. Let me end with his own words:

Dear Gerd:

I have never thought of either bounded rationality or satisficing as precisely defined technical terms, but rather as signals to economists that they needed to pay attention to reality, and a suggestion of some ways in which they might. But I do agree that I have used bounded rationality as the generic term, to refer to all of the limits that make a human being's problem spaces something quite different from the corresponding task environments: knowledge limits, computational limits, incomparability of component goals. I have used satisficing to refer to choice of "good enough" alternatives (perhaps defined by an aspiration level mechanism) or "best-so-far" alternatives to terminate selective search among alternatives—the latter usually not being given in advance, but generated sequentially. So one might apply "satisficing" to the "good-enough criterion" or to any heuristic search that uses such a criterion to make its choice.

Final remark on this point, going from most general to most specific, we have bounded rationality, then heuristic search, then satisficing. Further, on the same level as heuristic search, we have a second class of methods, very important in the theory of expertise: problem solution by recognition. Currently, that is my taxonomy of decision and problem solution methods. You can decide better than I can where you want to place fast-and-frugal in this rough classification. I would tend to regard it as a class of heuristics, hence on the same level as satisficing.

I guess a major reason for my using somewhat vague terms—like bounded rationality—is that I did not want to give the impression that I thought I had "solved" the problem of creating an empirically grounded theory of economic phenomena. What I was trying to do was to call attention to the need for such a theory—and the accompanying body of empirical work to establish it—and to provide some examples of a few mechanisms that might appear in it, which already had some evidential base. There still lies before us an enormous job of studying the actual decision making processes that take place in corporations and other economic settings....

End of sermon—which you and Reinhard [Selten] don't need. I am preaching to believers.

Cordially,
Herb

References

Arrow, K. J. 1986. Rationality of self and others in an economic system. *Journal of Business* 59: 385–399.

Bjorklund, D. F., and Green, B. L. 1992. The adaptive nature of cognitive immaturity. *American Psychologist* 47: 46–54.

Borges, B., Goldstein, D. G., Ortmann, A., and Gigerenzer, G. 1999. Can ignorance beat the stock market? In G. Gigerenzer et al., *Simple Heuristics That Make Us Smart*. Oxford University Press.

Camerer, C. 1995. Individual decision making. In J. H. Kagel and A. E. Roth, eds., *The Handbook of Experimental Economics*. Princeton University Press.

Camerer, C. 1998. Bounded rationality in individual decision making. *Experimental Economics* 1: 16–18.

Conlisk, J. 1996. Why bounded rationality? *Journal of Economic Literature* 34: 669–700.

Czerlinski, J., Gigerenzer, G., and Goldstein, D. G. 1999. How good are simple heuristics? In G. Gigerenzer et al., *Simple Heuristics That Make Us Smart*. Oxford University Press.

Elman, J. 1993. Learning and development in neural networks: The importance of starting small. *Cognition* 48: 71–99.

Fiedler, K. 2000. Beware of samples! A cognitive-ecological sampling approach to judgmental biases. *Psychological Review* 107: 659–676.

Friedman, M. 1953. *Essays in Positive Economics*. University of Chicago Press.

Geman, S. E., Bienenstock, E., and Doursat, R. 1992. Neural networks and the bias/variance dilemma. *Neural Computation* 4: 1–58.

Gigerenzer, G. 2000. *Adaptive Thinking: Rationality in the Real World*. Oxford University Press.

Gigerenzer, G. 2002. *Calculated Risks: How to Know When Numbers Deceive You*. Simon and Schuster.

Gigerenzer, G., and Goldstein, D. G. 1999. The recognition heuristic: How ignorance makes us smart. In G. Gigerenzer et al., *Simple Heuristics That Make Us Smart*. Oxford University Press.

Gigerenzer, G., and Hoffrage, U. 1995. How to improve Bayesian reasoning without instruction: Frequency formats. *Psychological Review* 102: 684–704.

Gigerenzer, G., and Hoffrage, U. 1999. Overcoming difficulties in Bayesian reasoning: A reply to Lewis and Keren and Mellers and McGraw. *Psychological Review* 106: 425–430.

Gigerenzer, G., Hoffrage, U., and Kleinbölting, H. 1991. Probabilistic mental models: A Brunswikian theory of confidence. *Psychological Review* 98: 506–528.

Gigerenzer, G., and Selten, R., eds. 2001a. *Bounded Rationality: The Adaptive Toolbox.* MIT Press.

Gigerenzer, G., and Selten, R. 2001b. Rethinking rationality. In Gigerenzer, G., and Selten, R., eds., *Bounded Rationality.* MIT Press.

Gigerenzer, G., Todd, P. M., and ABC Research Group. 1999. *Simple Heuristics That Make Us Smart.* Oxford University Press.

Goldstein, D. G., and Gigerenzer, G. 2002. Models of ecological rationality: The recognition heuristics. *Psychological Review* 109: 75–90.

Hoffrage, U., and Gigerenzer, G. 1998. Using natural frequencies to improve diagnostic inferences. *Academic Medicine* 73: 538–540.

Hoffrage, U., Lindsay, S., Hertwig, R., and Gigerenzer, G. 2000. Communicating statistical information. *Science* 290: 2261–2262.

Jolls, C., Sunstein, C. R., and Thaler, R. 1998. A behavioral approach to law and economics. *Stanford Law Review* 50: 1471–1550.

Juslin, P., Winman, A., and Olsson, H. 2000. Naive empiricism and dogmatism in confidence research: A critical examination of the hard-easy effect. *Psychological Review* 107: 384–396.

Kahneman, D., Slovic, P., and Tversky, A., eds. 1982. *Judgment under Uncertainty: Heuristics and Biases.* Cambridge University Press.

Kareev, Y. 2000. Seven (indeed, plus or minus two) and the detection of correlations. *Psychological Review* 107: 397–402.

Kaufman, B. E. 1999. Emotional arousal as a source of bounded rationality. *Journal of Economic Behaviour and Organization* 38: 135–144.

Koehler, J. J. 1996. On conveying the probative value of DNA evidence: Frequencies, likelihood ratios, and error rates. *University of Colorado Law Review* 67: 859–886.

Lopes, L. L. 1992. Three misleading assumptions in the customary rhetoric of the bias literature. *Theory and Psychology* 2: 231–236.

March, J. G. 1978. Bounded rationality, ambiguity, and the engineering of choice. *Bell Journal of Economics* 9: 587–608.

Martignon, L., and Hoffrage, U. 1999. Why does one-reason decision making work? A case study in ecological rationality. In G. Gigerenzer et al., eds., *Simple Heuristics That Make Us Smart.* Oxford University Press.

McLeod, P., and Dienes, Z. 1996. Do fielders know where to go to catch the ball or only how to get there? *Journal of Experimental Psychology: Human Perception and Performance* 22: 531–543.

Michalewicz, Z., and Fogel, D. B. 2000. *How to Solve It: Modern Heuristics*. Springer.

Newell, A., and Simon, H. A. 1972. *Human Problem Solving*. Prentice-Hall.

Rabin, M. 1998. Psychology and economics. *Journal of Economic Literature* 36: 11–46.

Roberts, S., and Pashler, H. 2000. How persuasive is a good fit? A comment on theory testing. *Psychological Review* 107: 358–367.

Sargent, T. J. 1993. *Bounded Rationality in Macroeconomics*. Oxford University Press.

Selten, R. 1998. Aspiration adaptation theory. *Journal of Mathematical Psychology* 42: 191–214.

Selten, R. 2001. What is bounded rationality. In G. Gigerenzer and R. Selten, eds., *Bounded Rationality*. MIT Press.

Simon, H. A. 1947. *Administrative Behavior*. Macmillan.

Simon, H. A. 1955. A behavioral model of rational choice. *Quarterly Journal of Economics* 69: 99–118.

Simon, H. A. 1956. Rational choice and the structure of the environment. *Psychological Review* 63: 129–138.

Simon, H. A. 1986. Rationality in psychology and economics. In R. Hogarth and M. Reder, eds., *Rational Choice*. University of Chicago Press.

Simon, H. A. 1990. Invariants of human behavior. *Annual Review of Psychology* 41: 1–19.

Stigler, G. J. 1961. The economics of information. *Journal of Political Economy* 69: 213–225.

Todd, P. M. 2001. Fast and frugal heuristics for environmentally bounded minds. In G. Gigerenzer and R. Selten, eds., *Bounded Rationality*. MIT Press.

Todd, P. M., and Gigerenzer, G. 2000. Precis of simple heuristics that make us smart. *Behavioral and Brain Sciences* 23: 727–780.

Tsotsos, J. K. 1991. Computational resources do constrain behavior. *Behavioral and Brain Sciences* 14: 506–507.

Attribute Substitution in Intuitive Judgment

Daniel Kahneman and Shane Frederick

Simon's first contribution to social science was a study of how public officials in Milwaukee allocated funds between playground maintenance and playground supervision (Simon 1935). From his economic training, Simon initially assumed that they equated the returns of a marginal dollar spent on those two uses. However, when he looked for evidence that the public officials actually performed such a calculation, he found none. He concluded that they must be doing something else instead.

This issue would occupy Simon for the next half-century: How could humans actually reach decisions when they had no prospect of applying the maximizing models of neoclassical economic theory? How did humans choose when they could not consider every alternative, were unable to specify the consequences of these alternatives, or lacked a general and consistent utility function for comparing heterogeneous options?

Simon proposed that individuals made choices by examining a limited set of promising options until they found one that was satisfactory. This view of "bounded rationality" was less ambitious than the neoclassical conception of rationality it was intended to replace. Once the assumption of utility maximization was abandoned, choices could no longer be explained in terms of a single powerful theoretical principle. Nor could choices be predicted solely from a description of the "external" world (e.g., price vectors, budget constraints). Instead, any descriptively adequate account of human decision making now appeared to require detailed understanding of the panoply of imperfect cognitive devices and procedures on which boundedly rational agents must rely.

One of the lines of research within the broad Simonian umbrella sought to identify the "heuristics" people use to simplify choice—the procedures they use to limit the amount of information that is processed or the complexity of the ways it is combined. On the basis of process tracing methods, verbal protocols, introspection, and theory, many different choice heuristics have been postulated. (For reviews, see Payne, Bettman, and Johnson 1993 and Gigerenzer et al. 1999.) These heuristics of choice—"elimination by aspects" is an example (Tversky 1972)—are conscious strategies that are intentionally designed to simplify the task of decision.

Another program of research, which became defined by the conjunction "heuristics and biases" (Tversky and Kahneman 1974) was concerned with the related question of how people make judgments on the basis of incomplete and imperfect information. However, unlike the research on choice heuristics, which focused on deliberate strategies, the "heuristics and biases" research program focused on automatic, perception-like processes. Like perceptual processes, these heuristic judgmental operations appear to produce illusions—judgments that reflect inappropriate use of available information. As with perceptual illusions, the errors created by cognitive illusions are not easily detected, but could, in principle, be avoided by the proper use of readily available information.

We now see that such cognitive illusions reflect the joint failure of two different systems: a basic system of rapid and effortless perception-like intuitive operations (which Stanovich and West (2002) call "system 1"), and more deliberate and effortful operations that could correct the erroneous intuitive judgment (which Stanovich and West (ibid.) call "system 2").

In the context of such a dual-system view, errors of intuitive judgment raise two questions: (1) "What features of system 1 created the error?" and (2) "Why was the error not detected and corrected by system 2?" (cf. Kahneman and Tversky 1982). This duality was not fully appreciated at the outset. Thus, Tversky and Kahneman (1974) and Kahneman, Slovic, and Tversky (1982) focused exclusively on the first question when they introduced the notion of heuristics and biases:

The subjective assessment of probability resembles the subjective assessment of physical quantities such as distance or size. These judgments are all based on data of limited validity, which are processed according to heuristic rules. For example, the apparent distance of an object is determined in part by its clarity. The more sharply the object is seen, the closer it appears to be. This rule has some validity, because in any given scene the more distant objects are seen less sharply than nearer objects. However, the reliance on this rule leads to systematic errors in the estimation of distance. Specifically, distances are often overestimated when visibility is poor because the contours of objects are blurred. On the other hand, distances are often underestimated when visibility is good because the objects are seen sharply. Thus the reliance on clarity as an indication leads to common biases. Such biases are also found in intuitive judgments of probability.

This statement was intended to extend Brunswik's 1943 analysis of the perception of distance to the domain of intuitive thinking and to provide a rationale for using biases to diagnose heuristics. However, the analysis of the effect of haze is flawed: It neglects the fact that an observer looking at a distant mountain possesses two relevant cues, not one. The first cue is the blur of the contours of the target mountain, which is positively correlated with its distance, when all else is equal. This cue should be given positive weight in a judgment of distance, and it is. The second relevant cue, which the observer can readily assess by looking around, is the ambient or general haziness. In an optimal regression model for estimating distance, general haziness is a suppressor variable, which must be weighted negatively because it contributes to blur but is uncorrelated with distance. Contrary to the argument made in 1974, using blur as a cue does not inevitably lead to bias in the judgment of distance—the illusion could just as well be described as a failure to assign adequate negative weight to ambient haze. The effect of haziness on impressions of distance is a failing of system 1: the perceptual system is not designed to correct for this variable. The effect of haziness on judgments of distance is a separate failure of system 2. Although people can easily be trained to correct their impressions of distance for the effects of ambient haze, they rarely do so on their own. A similar analysis applies to some of the judgmental biases we discuss later, in which errors and biases only occur when both systems fail.

In the particular dual-process model we assume, system 1 quickly proposes intuitive answers to judgment problems as they arise, and system 2 monitors the quality of these proposals, which it may endorse, correct or override. The judgments that are eventually expressed are called intuitive if they retain the hypothesized initial proposal without much modification. The roles of the two systems in determining stated judgments depend on features of the task and of the individual, including the time available for deliberation (Finucane et al. 2000), the respondent's mood (Isen, Nygren, and Ashby 1988; Bless et al. 1996), intelligence (Stanovich and West 2002), and exposure to statistical thinking (Nisbett et al. 1983; Agnoli and Krantz 1989; Agnoli 1991). We assume that system 1 and system 2 can be active concurrently, that automatic and controlled cognitive operations compete for the control of overt responses, and that deliberate judgments are likely to remain anchored on initial impressions. Our views in these regards are similar to the "correction model" proposed by Gilbert and colleagues (1989, 1991) and to other dual-process models (Epstein 1994; Hammond 1996; Sloman 1996).

Although system 1 is more primitive than system 2, it is not necessarily less capable. On the contrary, complex cognitive operations eventually migrate from system 2 to system 1 as proficiency and skill are acquired. A striking demonstration of the intelligence of system 1 is the ability of chess masters to instantly perceive the strength or weakness of chess positions. For those experts, pattern matching has replaced effortful serial processing. Similarly, prolonged cultural exposure eventually produces a facility for social judgments—e.g., an ability to recognize quickly that "a man whose dull writing is occasionally enlivened by corny puns" is more similar to a stereotypical computer programmer than to a stereotypical accountant. Contrary to a common misunderstanding, an interest in the biases of intuitive thinking implies no lack of respect for its extraordinary skills.

Attribute Substitution

Early research on the representativeness and availability heuristics was guided by a simple and general hypothesis: when confronted with a difficult question people often answer an easier one instead, usually without being aware of the substitution. A person who is asked "What proportion of long-distance relationships break up within a year?" may answer as if she had been asked "Do instances of swift breakups of long-distance relationships come readily to mind?" This would be an application of the availability heuristic. A professor who has heard a candidate's job talk and now considers the question "How likely is it that this candidate could be tenured in our department?" may answer the much easier question: "How impressive was the talk?" This would be an example of the representativeness heuristic.

The heuristics and biases research program has focused primarily on representativeness and availability—two versatile attributes that are automatically computed and can serve as candidate answers to many different questions. It has also focused on thinking under uncertainty. However, the restriction to particular heuristics and to a specific context is largely arbitrary. We will say that judgment is mediated by a heuristic when an individual assesses a specified target attribute of a judgment object by substituting another property of that object— the heuristic attribute—which comes more readily to mind. Many judgments are made by this process of attribute substitution. For an example, consider the well-known study (Strack, Martin, and Schwarz 1988) in which college students answered a survey that included these two questions: "How happy are you with your life in general?" and "How many dates did you have last month?" The correlation between the two questions was negligible when they occurred in the order shown, but it rose to 0.66 when the dating question was asked first. We suggest that thinking about the dating question automatically evokes an evaluation of one's satisfaction in that domain of life, which lingers to become the heuristic attribute when the happiness question is subsequently encountered.

Biases

Because the target attribute and the heuristic attribute are different, the substitution of one for the other inevitably introduces systematic biases. In this chapter we are mostly concerned with weighting biases, which arise when cues available to the judge are given either too much or too little weight. Criteria for determining optimal weights can be drawn from several sources. In the classic lens model, the optimal weights associated with different cues are the regression weights that optimize the prediction of an external criterion, such as physical distance or the GPA that a college applicant will attain (Brunswik 1943; Hammond 1955). Our analysis of weighting biases applies to such cases, but it also extends to attributes for which no objective criterion is available, such as an individual's overall happiness or the probability that a particular patient will survive surgery. Normative standards for these attributes must be drawn from the constraints of ordinary language, and they are often imprecise. For example, the conventional meaning of overall happiness does not specify how much weight ought to be given to various life domains. However, it certainly does require that substantial weight be given to every important domain of life, and that no weight at all be given to the current weather, or to the recent consumption of a cookie. Similar rules of common sense apply to judgments of probability. For example, the statement "John is more likely to survive a week than a month" is a true statement in ordinary usage, which implies a rule that people would wish their probability judgments to follow. Accordingly, neglect of duration in assessments of survival probabilities would be properly described as a weighting bias, even if there is no way to establish a normative probability for individual cases (Kahneman and Tversky 1996).

For some judgmental tasks, information that could serve to supplement or correct the heuristic is not neglected or underweighted, but simply lacking. If asked to judge the relative frequency of words beginning with K or R (Tversky and Kahneman 1973) or to compare the population of a familiar foreign city with one that is unfamiliar (Gigerenzer and Goldstein 1996), respondents have little recourse but to base their judgments on ease of retrieval or recognition. The necessary reliance on these heuristic attributes renders such judgments susceptible to biasing factors (e.g., the amount of media coverage). However, unlike weighting biases, such biases of insufficient information cannot be described as errors of judgment, because there is no way to avoid them.

Accessibility and Substitution

The intent to judge a target attribute initiates a search for a reasonable value. Sometimes this search terminates almost immediately because the required value can be read from a stored memory (e.g., the question "How tall are you?") or current experience ("How much do you like this cake?"). For other judgments, however, the target attribute does not come to mind immediately, but the search for it evokes other attributes that are conceptually or associatively related (e.g., a question about overall happiness may retrieve the answer to a related question about satisfaction with a particular domain of life). Attribute substitution occurs when the target attribute is assessed by mapping the value of another attribute on the target scale. This process will control judgment when three conditions are satisfied: (1) the target attribute is relatively inaccessible; (2) a conceptually or associatively related candidate attribute is highly accessible; and (3) the substitution of the heuristic attribute in the judgment is not rejected by the critical operations of system 2.

Some attributes are permanent candidates for the heuristic role because they are routinely evaluated as part of perception and comprehension, and therefore always accessible (Tversky and Kahneman 1983). These natural assessments include physical properties such as size and distance, and more abstract properties such as similarity (e.g., Tversky and Kahneman 1983), cognitive fluency in perception and memory (e.g., Jacoby and Dallas 1981; Schwarz and Vaughn 2002; Tversky and Kahneman 1973), causal propensity (Heider 1944; Kahneman and Varey 1990; Michotte 1963), surprisingness (Kahneman and Miller 1986), affective valence (e.g., Bargh 1997; Cacioppo, Priester, and Berntson 1993; Kahneman, Ritov, and Schkade 1999; Slovic et al. 2002; Zajonc 1980), and mood (Schwarz and Clore 1983). Other attributes are accessible only if they have been recently evoked or primed (see e.g. Bargh et al. 1986; Higgins and Brendl 1995). The "romantic satisfaction heuristic" for judging happiness illustrates the effect of temporary accessibility. The same mechanism of attribute substitution is involved, whether the heuristic attribute is accessible chronically or only temporarily.

System 2: The Supervision of Intuitive Judgments

Our model assumes that an intuitive judgment is expressed overtly only if it is endorsed by system 2. The Stroop task illustrates this two-system structure. Observers who are instructed to report the color in which words are printed tend to stumble when the word is the name of another color (e.g., the word BLUE printed in green). The difficulty arises because the word is automatically read, and activates a response ("blue" in this case) that competes with the required response. Errors are rare in the Stroop test, indicating generally successful monitoring and control of the overt response, but the conflict produces delays and hesitations. The successful suppression of erroneous responses is effortful, and its efficacy is reduced by stress and distraction.

Gilbert (1989) described a correction model in which initial impulses are often wrong and normally overridden. He argues that people initially believe whatever they are told (e.g., "Whitefish love grapes") and that it takes some time and mental effort to "unbelieve" such dubious statements. Here again, cognitive load disrupts the controlling operations of system 2, increasing the rate of errors and revealing aspects of intuitive thinking that are normally suppressed. In an ingenious extension of this approach, Bodenhausen (1990) exploited natural temporal variability in alertness. He found that "morning people" were substantially more susceptible to a judgment bias (the conjunction fallacy) in the evening and that "evening people" were more likely to commit the fallacy in the morning.

Because system 2 is relatively slow, its operations can be disrupted by time pressure. Finucane et al. (2000) reported a study in which respondents judged the risks and benefits of various products and technologies (e.g., nuclear power, chemical plants, cellular phones). When participants were forced to respond within 5 seconds, the correlations between their judgments of risks and their judgments of benefits were strongly negative. The negative correlations were much weaker (although still pronounced) when respondents were given more time to ponder a response. When time is short, the same affective evaluation apparently serves as a heuristic attribute for assessments of both benefits and risks. Respondents can move beyond this simple strategy, but they need more than 5 seconds to do so. As this example illustrates, judgment by heuristic often yields simplistic assessments, which system 2 sometimes corrects by bringing additional considerations to bear.

Schwarz (1996) and Clore (1983) have shown that attribute substitution can be prevented by alerting respondents to the possibility that their judgment could be contaminated by an irrelevant variable. For example, sunny or rainy weather typically affects reports of well-being, but Schwarz and Clore (1983) found that merely asking respondents about the weather just before the well-being question eliminates the effect—apparently by reminding respondents that their current mood (a candidate heuristic attribute) is influenced by a factor (current weather) that is obviously irrelevant to the requested target attribute (overall well-being). Schwarz (1996) also found that the weight of any aspect of life on judgments of happiness is actually reduced by asking people to describe their satisfaction with that particular aspect of life just before the global question. As these examples illustrate, the effects of a variable on judgment are normally increased by priming (a system 1 effect), but can be reduced by an explicit reminder that brings the self-critical operations of system 2 into play.

We suspect that system 2 endorsements of intuitive judgments are granted quite casually under normal circumstances. Consider the puzzle "A bat and a ball cost $1.10 in total. The bat costs $1 more than the ball. How much does the ball cost?" Almost everyone we ask reports an initial tendency to answer "10 cents" because the sum $1.10 separates naturally into $1 and 10 cents, and 10 cents is about the right magnitude. Many people yield to this immediate impulse. The surprisingly high rate of errors in this easy problem illustrates how lightly system 2 monitors the output of system 1: people are not accustomed to thinking hard, and are often content to trust a plausible judgment that quickly comes to mind.

The ball and bat problem elicits many errors, although it is not really difficult and certainly not ambiguous. A moral of this example is that people often make quick intuitive judgments to which they are not deeply committed. A related moral is that we should be suspicious of analyses that explain apparent errors by attributing to respondents a bizarre interpretation of the question. Consider someone who answers a question about happiness by reporting her satisfaction with her romantic life. The respondent is surely not committed to the absurdly narrow interpretation of happiness that her response seemingly implies. More likely, at the time of answering she thinks that she is reporting happiness: a judgment comes quickly to mind and is not obviously mistaken; end of story. Similarly, we propose that respondents who judge probability by representativeness do not seriously believe that the questions, "How likely is X to be a Y?" and "How much does X resemble the stereotype of Y?" are synonymous. People who make a casual intuitive judgment normally know little about how their judgment came about, and know even less about its logical entailments. Thus, attempts to reconstruct the meaning of intuitive judgments by interviewing respondents (see e.g., Hertwig and Gigerenzer 1999) are unlikely to succeed, because such probes require better introspective access and more coherent beliefs than people normally muster.

Heuristics: Deliberate or Automatic?

So far, we have described judgment by heuristic as an intuitive and unintentional process of attribute substitution, which we attribute to system 1. However, attribute substitution can also be a deliberate system 2 strategy, as when a voter decides to evaluate candidates solely by their stance on a particular issue. In other cases, a heuristic is both initiated spontaneously by system 1 and deliberately adopted by system 2. The recognition heuristic proposed by Gigerenzer and his colleagues appears to fall in that class.

Experiments described by Gigerenzer and Goldstein (1996) show that respondents rely on feelings of familiarity and unfamiliarity to compare uncertain quantities, such as the relative size of two cities. (See also Gigerenzer et al. 1999.) For example, 78 percent of a sample of German students recognized San Diego as an American city, but only 4 percent recognized San Antonio, and every student who recognized San Diego but not San Antonio concluded (correctly) that San Diego is larger. Though far from perfect (the correlation between actual population and recognition was only 0.60 in that experiment), the recognition heuristic is surely a reasonable strategy for that task. Indeed, when students were given pairs of the 22 most populous cities in the United States or Germany, Americans slightly outperformed Germans when comparing the size of German cities, and Germans did slightly better than Americans when judging American cities (Gigerenzer and Goldstein 1996).

Gigerenzer and his colleagues have described the recognition heuristic as a deliberate strategy, which in our terms is an operation of system 2. This description seems highly plausible. In addition, however, we have proposed that familiarity is an attribute that system 1 evaluates routinely, regardless of the current judgment goal. On this view, the recognition heuristic has an automatic component, which could be studied by varying tasks and by measuring reaction times. Imagine a reaction-time study in which respondents on each trial see a question such as "Which city name is printed in larger font?" or "Which city name contains more vowels?," immediately followed by a pair of cities that differ in familiarity. Research on conceptual Stroop effects (e.g., Keysar 1989) suggests that the more familiar city name will be the favored answer to any question that is associatively related to prominence, size or quantity. On this hypothesis, errors will be systematic, and response times will be faster for compatible than for incompatible responses. An even more radical possibility, arising from the work of Gilbert (1989), Begg (see e.g. Begg and Armour 1991; Begg, Anas, and Farinacci 1992), and Mandler (see e.g. Mandler, Hamson, and Dorfman 1990) is that there will be a bias favoring the familiar item as an answer to any question—perhaps even "Which city is smaller?" or "Which city has fewer dentists?" If either of these hypotheses is correct, the recognition heuristic belongs to the family of heuristics that we consider here. Like many other members of that family, the recognition heuristic for judging city sizes (i) draws on a "natural assessment" of recognition or familiarity, (ii) may be endorsed as a deliberate strategy, (iii) makes people look smart under some conditions, and (iv) will produce systematic errors and biases, because impressions of familiarity and recognition are systematically correlated with factors other than city size, such as number of mentions in the media.

The Representativeness Controversy

Many of the original demonstrations of the representativeness heuristic and its concomitant biases (neglect of base rates and conjunction errors) used a "subtle" design: participants had enough information to avoid the error, but no effort was made to call their attention to all of the relevant information. For example, in one experiment (Kahneman and Tversky 1973; p. 127 in Kahenman, Slovic, and Tversky 1982), respondents read a personality summary of "Tom W."—a fictitious graduate student who was described as having, among other things, "a need for order and clarity." They then ranked the likelihood that Tom specialized in each of nine different academic fields. Although respondents knew that the base rates of these fields differed greatly (as the judgments of a separate group confirmed), base rates were not explicitly mentioned in the problem. Similarly, in a separate experiment (Tversky and Kahneman 1983; pp. 91–96 in Kahneman, Slovic, and Tversky 1982), respondents read about "Linda"—a fictitious 31 year old woman who was described as being "single, outspoken, very bright" and who had, as a student, "participated in antinuclear demonstrations" and been "deeply concerned with issues of discrimination." Respondents were then asked to rank the likelihood that Linda was a member of one of eight categories (e.g., elementary school teacher, psychiatric social worker, bank teller, insurance salesperson). Although the two critical items—#6 (bank teller) and #8 (bank teller and active in the feminist movement) were both included, they were embedded among six other "filler" items, so that respondents were not compelled to directly compare them. Thus, in both of these studies, system 2 was given a chance to correct the judgment, but was not prompted to do so.

In view of the confusing controversy that followed, it is perhaps unfortunate that the articles documenting base-rate neglect and conjunction errors did not stop with these subtle tests. Each article also contained an experimental flourish—a demonstration in which the error occurred in spite of a manipulation that called participants' attention to the critical variable. The engineer-lawyer problem

(Kahneman and Tversky 1973) included special instructions to ensure that respondents would notice the base rates of the outcomes. The brief personality descriptions shown to respondents were reported to have been drawn from a set containing descriptions of 30 lawyers and 70 engineers (or vice versa), and respondents were asked, "What is the probability that this description belongs to one of the 30 lawyers in the sample of 100?" To the authors' surprise, base rates were largely neglected in the responses, despite their salience in the instructions. Similarly, the authors were later shocked to discover that more than 80 percent of undergraduates committed a conjunction error even when asked point-blank whether Linda was more likely to be "a bank teller" or "a bank teller who is active in the feminist movement" (Tversky and Kahneman 1983). The novelty of these additional direct or "transparent" tests was the finding that respondents continued to show the biases associated with representativeness even in the presence of strong cues pointing to the normative response.

These experimental flourishes were in many ways irrelevant to the authors' central claims about intuitive prediction. These claims did not deny the possibility that system 2 could intervene to modify or override intuitive predictions of system 1. Thus, the articles would have been substantially the same, though less provocative, if transparent tests had led respondents to overcome base-rate neglect and conjunction errors. Nevertheless, the direct conjunction fallacy and the engineer-lawyer problem have been the object of nearly all the critical attention directed to the heuristics and biases research program.

To appreciate why the strong forms of base-rate neglect and the conjunction fallacy sparked so much controversy, it is useful to distinguish two conceptions of human rationality (Kahneman 2000). Coherence rationality is the strict conception, which requires the agent's entire system of beliefs and preferences to be internally consistent, and immune to effects of framing and context. For example, an individual's probability p("Linda is a bank teller") should be the sum of the probabilities p("Linda is a bank teller and is a feminist"), and

p("Linda is a bank teller and not a feminist"). A subtle test of coherence rationality could be conducted by asking individuals to assess these three probabilities on separate occasions under circumstances that minimize recall. Coherence can also be tested in a between-groups design. Assuming random assignment, the sum of the average probabilities assigned to the two component events should equal the average judged probability of "Linda is a bank teller." If this prediction fails, then at least some individuals are incoherent. Demonstrations of incoherence present a significant challenge to important models of decision theory and economics, which attribute to agents a very strict form of rationality (Tversky and Kahneman 1986). Failures of perfect coherence are less provocative to psychologists, who have a more realistic view of human capabilities.

A more lenient conception, reasoning rationality, only requires an ability to reason correctly about the information currently at hand, without demanding perfect consistency among beliefs that are not simultaneously evoked. The best-known violation of reasoning rationality is the famous four-card problem (Wason 1960), in which respondents are presented with four, two-sided cards bearing the letter "A", the letter "K", the number "4", and the number "7" and asked which card(s) must be turned over to test whether the following rule is true of those four cards: *"If there is a vowel on one side of the card, then there is an even number on the other."* The normative response ("A" and "7") is very rare. The failure of intelligent adults to reason their way through this problem is surprising because the problem is "easy," in the sense of being easily understood once explained. What everyone learns, when first told that intelligent people fail to solve the four-card problem, is that one's expectations about human reasoning abilities had not been adequately calibrated. There is, of course, no well-defined metric of reasoning rationality, but whatever metric one uses, the Wason problem calls for a downward adjustment. The surprising results of the Linda and engineer-lawyer problems led Tversky and Kahneman to a similar realization: The reasoning of their subjects was less proficient than they had anticipated. Many readers of the work shared this conclusion, but many others strongly resisted it.

The implicit challenge to reasoning rationality was met by numerous attempts to dismiss the findings of the engineer-lawyer and the Linda studies as artifacts of ambiguous language, confusing instructions, conversational norms, or inappropriate normative standards. Doubts have been raised about the proper interpretation of almost every word in the conjunction problem, including 'bank teller', 'probability', and even 'and' (see e.g. Dulany and Hilton 1991; Hilton and Slugoski 2001). We do not scrutinize these claims here, though we suspect that they are generally valid—that these critics have identified features that amplified the effects in the engineer-lawyer study and in particular versions of the Linda problem. However, all these objections share one significant weakness: They provide no explanation of the essentially perfect consistency of the judgments observed in direct tests of the conjunction rule and in three other types of experiments: (1) subtle comparisons, (2) between-subjects comparisons, and, most importantly, (3) judgments of representativeness (see Kahneman and Tversky 1973; Bar-Hillel and Neter 1993). For example, interpreting the conjunction fallacy as an artifact of experimental instructions effectively implies that the nearly perfect (0.99) correlation between judgments of probability and judgments of representativeness is merely a coincidence.

Demonstrations that people can avoid the conjunction fallacy in direct tests, or use explicit base-rate information when its relevance is emphasized, led some scholars to the blanket conclusion that judgment biases are artificial and fragile, and that there is no need for judgment heuristics to explain them. This position was promoted most vigorously by Gigerenzer (1991). Kahneman and Tversky (1996) argued in response that the heuristics and biases position does not preclude the possibility of people performing flawlessly in particular variants of the Linda and of the lawyer-engineer problems. Because lay-people readily acknowledge the validity of the conjunction rule and the relevance of base-rate information, the fact that they sometimes obey these principles is neither a surprise nor an argument against the role of representativeness in routine intuitive prediction. However, the study of conditions under which errors are avoided can help us understand the capabilities and limitations of system 2. We assume that the persistence or disappearance of biases primarily reflects the efficacy of these corrective operations, which may depend both on cognitive skills (education, intelligence) and on the extent to which the particular formulations increase the saliency of a relevant factor or the apparent applicability of a relevant rule.

The controversy about heuristics and biases has sometimes been heated, although there is little substance to it (Kahneman and Tversky 1996). The debate has sometimes appeared to be driven by the question of whether people are intelligent or stupid—a question that is emotionally arousing but intellectually empty. The basic findings of the heuristics and biases approach have not been challenged empirically. The challengers have principally shown that the correction of erroneous impressions can be facilitated—a possibility that was never denied. There is broad agreement that mental operations exist along a continuum, ranging from rapid, automatic, perception-like impressions to deliberate computations that apply explicit rules or external aids (see Hammond 1996). The basic notion of a judgment heuristic—that people often respond to a difficult question by answering an easier one instead—is even championed by the program's best-known critic (see e.g. Gigerenzer et al. 1999). Elsewhere, we argue that the process of attribute substitution accounts for a much broader set of judgments than were contemplated in the early discussions of judgment under uncertainty (Kahneman and Frederick 2002). However, attribute substitution is surely not the only process on which people rely to make judgments, and assigning values to attributes is just one class of mental operations. A boundedly rational mind may exploit many different mechanisms, of which some may be specialized for certain classes of problems (as Cosmides and Tooby 1996 have argued), whereas others—including attribute substitution, we believe—may be quite general in their function. No single idea will fully illuminate the vast intellectual territory defined by Simon's concept of bounded rationality.

Acknowledgment

This chapter is an abridged version of Kahneman and Frederick 2002. It also draws on Frederick 2002.

References

Agnoli, F. 1991. Development of judgmental heuristics and logical reasoning: Training counteracts the representativeness heuristic. *Cognitive Development* 6: 195–217.

Agnoli, F., and Krantz, D. H. 1989. Suppressing natural heuristics by formal instruction: The case of the conjunction fallacy. *Cognitive Psychology* 21: 515–550.

Bargh, J. A. 1997. The automaticity of everyday life. *Advances in Social Cognition* 10: 1–61.

Bargh, J. A., Bond, R. N., Lombardi, W. J., and Tota, M. E. 1986. The additive nature of chronic and temporary sources of construct accessibility. *Journal of Personality and Social Psychology* 50, no. 5: 869–878.

Bar-Hillel, M., and Neter, E. 1993. How alike is it versus how likely is it: A disjunction fallacy in probability judgments. *Journal of Personality and Social Psychology* 65, no. 6: 1119–1131.

Begg, I., Anas, A., and Farinacci, S. 1992. Dissociation of processes in belief: Source recollection, statement familiarity, and the illusion of truth. *Journal of Experimental Psychology: General* 121, no. 4: 446–458.

Begg, I., and Armour, V. 1991. Repetition and the ring of truth: Biasing comments. *Canadian Journal of Behavioural Science* 23: 195–213.

Bless, H., Clore, G. L., Schwarz, N., Golisano, V., Rabe, C., and Wolk, M. 1996. Mood and the use of scripts: Does a happy mood really lead to mindlessness? *Journal of Personality and Social Psychology* 71, no. 4: 665–679.

Bodenhausen, G. V. 1990. Stereotypes as judgmental heuristics: Evidence of circadian variations in discrimination. *Psychological Science* 1, no. 5: 319–322.

Brunswik, E. 1943. Organismic achievement and environmental probability. *Psychological Review* 50: 255–272.

Cacioppo, J. T., Priester, J. R., and Berntson, G. G. 1993. Rudimentary determinants of attitudes: II. Arm flexion and extension have differential effects on attitudes. *Journal of Personality and Social Psychology* 65: 5–17.

Cosmides, L., and Tooby, J. 1996. Are humans good intuitive statisticians after all? Rethinking some conclusions from the literature on judgment under uncertainty. *Cognition* 58, no. 1: 1–73.

Dulany, D. E., and Hilton, D. J. 1991. Conversational implicature, conscious representation, and the conjunction fallacy. *Social Cognition* 9: 85–110.

Epstein, S. 1994. Integration of the cognitive and the psychodynamic unconscious. *American Psychologist* 49, no. 8: 709–724.

Finucane, M. L., Alhakami, A., Slovic, P., and Johnson, S. M. 2000. The affect heuristic in judgments of risks and benefits. *Journal of Behavioral Decision Making* 13: 1–17.

Frederick, S. W. 2002. Automated choice heuristics. In T. Gilovich, D. Griffin, and D. Kahneman, eds., *Heuristics of Intuitive Judgment*. Cambridge University Press.

Gigerenzer, G. 1991. How to make cognitive illusions disappear: Beyond "heuristics and biases." *European Review of Social Psychology* 2: 83–115.

Gigerenzer, G., and Goldstein, D. G. 1996. Reasoning the fast and frugal way: Models of bounded rationality. *Psychological Review* 103, no. 4: 650–669.

Gigerenzer, G., Todd, P. M., and the ABC Group. 1999. *Simple Heuristics That Make Us Smart*. Oxford University Press.

Gilbert, D. 1989. Thinking lightly about others: Automatic components of the social inference process. In J. Uleman and J. A. Bargh, eds., *Unintended Thought*. Guilford.

Gilbert, D. 1991. How mental systems believe. *American Psychologist* 46, no. 2: 107–119.

Hammond, K. R. 1955. Probabilistic functioning and the clinical method. *Psychological Review* 62: 255–262.

Hammond, K. R. 1996. *Human Judgment and Social Policy*. Oxford University Press.

Heider, F. 1944. Social perception and phenomenal causality. *Psychological Review* 51: 358–374.

Hertwig, R., and Gigerenzer, G. 1999. The 'conjunction fallacy' revisited: How intelligent inferences look like reasoning errors. *Journal of Behavioral Decision Making* 12, no. 4: 275–305.

Higgins, E. T., and Brendl, C. M. 1995. Accessibility and applicability: Some "activation rules" influencing judgment. *Journal of Experimental Social Psychology* 31: 218–243.

Hilton, D. J., and Slugoski, B. R. 2001. Conversational processes in reasoning and explanation. In A. Tesser and N. Schwarz, eds., *Blackwell Handbook of Social Psychology*, volume 1. Blackwell.

Isen, A. M., Nygren, T. E., and Ashby, F. G. 1988. Influence of positive affect on the subjective utility of gains and losses—it is just not worth the risk. *Journal of Personality and Social Psychology* 55, no. 5: 710–717.

Jacoby, L. L., and Dallas, M. 1981. On the relationship between autobiographical memory and perceptual learning. *Journal of Experimental Psychology: General* 3: 306–340.

Kahneman, D. 2000. A psychological point of view: Violations of rational rules as a diagnostic of mental processes (Commentary on Stanovich and West). *Behavioral and Brain Sciences* 23: 681–683.

Kahneman, D., and Frederick, S. 2002. Representativeness revisited: Attribute substitution in intuitive judgment. Forthcoming in T. Gilovich, D. Griffin, and D. Kahneman, eds., *Heuristics of Intuitive Judgment*. Cambridge University Press.

Kahneman, D., and Miller, D. T. 1986. Norm theory: Comparing reality with its alternatives. *Psychological Review* 93: 136–153.

Kahneman, D., Ritov, I., and Schkade, D. 1999. Economic preferences or attitude expressions? An analysis of dollar responses to public issues. *Journal of Risk and Uncertainty* 19: 203–235.

Kahneman, D., Slovic, P., and Tversky, A. E. 1982. *Judgment under Uncertainty: Heuristics and Biases*. Cambridge University Press.

Kahneman, D., and Tversky, A. 1973. On the psychology of prediction. *Psychological Review* 80: 237–251.

Kahneman, D., and Tversky, A. 1982. On the study of statistical intuitions. *Cognition* 11: 123–141.

Kahneman, D., and Tversky, A. 1996. On the reality of cognitive illusions: A reply to Gigerenzer's critique. *Psychological Review* 103: 582–591.

Kahneman, D., and Varey, C. A. 1990. Propensities and counterfactuals: The loser that almost won. *Journal of Personality and Social Psychology* 59, no. 6: 1101–1110.

Keysar, B. 1989. On the functional equivalence of literal and metaphorical interpretations in discourse. *Journal of Memory and Language* 28: 375–385.

Mandler, G., Hamson, C., and Dorfman, J. 1990. Tests of dual process theory—word priming and recognition. *Quarterly Journal of Experimental Psychology* 42, no. 4: 713–739.

Michotte, A. 1963. *The Perception of Causality*. Basic Books.

Nisbett, R. E., Krantz, D. H., Jepson, C., and Kunda, Z. 1983. The use of statistical heuristics in everyday inductive reasoning. *Psychological Review* 90, no. 4: 339–363.

Payne, J., Bettman, J., and Johnson, E. 1993. *The Adaptive Decision Maker*. Cambridge University Press.

Schwarz, N. 1996. *Cognition and Communication: Judgmental Biases, Research Methods, and the Logic of Conversation*. Erlbaum.

Schwarz, N., and Clore, G. L. 1983. Mood, misattribution, and judgments of well-being: Informative and directive functions of affective states. *Journal of Personality and Social Psychology* 45, no. 3: 513–523.

Schwarz, N., and Vaughn, L. A. 2002. The availability heuristic revisited: Ease of recall and content of recall as distinct sources of information. In T. Gilovich, D. Griffin, and D. Kahneman, eds., *Heuristics of Intuitive Judgment*. Cambridge University Press.

Simon, H. A. 1935. Administration of Public Recreational Facilities in Milwaukee. Unpublished manuscript.

Sloman, S. A. 1996. The empirical case for two systems of reasoning. *Psychological Bulletin* 119: 3–22.

Slovic, P., Finucane, M., Peters, E., and MacGregor, D. G. 2002. The affect heuristic. In T. Gilovich, D. Griffin, and D. Kahneman, eds., *Heuristics of Intuitive Judgment*. Cambridge University Press.

Stanovich, K. E., and West, R. 2002. Individual differences in reasoning: Implications for the rationality debate. In T. Gilovich, D. Griffin, and D. Kahneman, eds., *Heuristics of Intuitive Judgment*. Cambridge University Press.

Strack, F., Martin, L. L., and Schwarz, N. 1988. Priming and communication: The social determinants of information use in judgments of life-satisfaction. *European Journal of Social Psychology* 18: 429–442.

Tversky, A. 1972. Elimination by aspects: A theory of choice. *Psychological Review* 79: 281–299.

Tversky, A., and Kahneman, D. 1973. Availability: A heuristic for judging frequency and probability. *Cognitive Psychology* 5, no. 2: 207–232.

Tversky, A., and Kahneman, D. 1974. Judgment under uncertainty: Heuristics and biases. *Science* 185, no. 4157: 1124–1131.

Tversky, A., and Kahneman, D. 1983. Extensional vs. intuitive reasoning: The conjunction fallacy in probability judgment. *Psychological Review* 90: 293–315.

Tversky, A., and Kahneman, D. 1986. Rational choice and the framing of decisions. *Journal of Business* 59: S251–S278.

Wason, P. C. 1960. On the failure to eliminate hypotheses in a conceptual task. *Quarterly Journal of Experimental Psychology* 12: 129–140.

Zajonc, R. B. 1980. Feeling and thinking: preferences need no inferences. *American Psychologist* 35, no. 2: 151–175.

Encounters with the Force of Herbert A. Simon

David Klahr

In high-energy physics, one standard method for determining the properties of a particle is to examine its influence on other particles, whether through attraction, repulsion, absorption, deflection, fission, or fusion. Analogously, in the domain of human interactions, it is possible to infer some of the characteristics of a man by examining the nature of his impact on those who felt the force of his mind and his character.

As evidenced by the volume you hold in your hands, Herb Simon's diverse, profound, and multi-faceted interactions with the authors of these chapters, as well as with hundreds of other people, produced life trajectories vastly different from what they would have been otherwise. Herb's influence came in a variety of forms: personal, scientific, intellectual, institutional, and political. In some chapters, the account of Herb's impact is either implicit or abstract. In this chapter, the story will be explicit, direct, and personal. This approach is not without its hazards, because it could be construed as inappropriately self-centered in a volume intended to honor and acclaim one of the most important thinkers of the twentieth century. Let me acknowledge at the outset then, that while I gratefully acknowledge Herb's immense influence on me, I am humbled by realizing what a small fraction of his attention or energy it consumed.

Action at a Distance

Herb's first influence on me could be viewed as "action at a distance." I had been advised, as an undergraduate engineer with an interest in computers, to read some recent (in 1959) papers in a new area called "heuristic problem solving" (Newell and Simon 1956; Newell, Shaw, and Simon 1958; Simon and Newell 1958) in order to get some ideas on how to advance my senior thesis project aimed at creating a FORTRAN program that learned how to play a game. This was my first encounter with what would eventually be called "cognitive science" and with the (then) startling proposal that thinking was a process of symbolic computation.

Attraction

A few years later, I decided that, although I enjoyed working with computers, I wanted to get an MBA. I was advised that the only B-school in the world that could also teach me something about "thinking machines" was the Graduate School of Industrial Administration (GSIA) at (then) Carnegie Tech. Thus, Herb's second influence was to attract not only my attention, but also my physical presence to the center of the intellectual webs he was beginning to spin at Carnegie Tech.

In 1962, when I arrived, GSIA was a powerhouse of exciting new ideas in economics,[1] organization theory, managerial decision making, AI, and cognitive psychology. I was dazzled by Herb's work on mathematical social psychology (recasting classic propositions about economic decision making, group interaction, etc. in terms of simultaneous differential equations). I was also exposed to the innovative approaches of March and Simon (1958) and Cyert and March (1963) to the area of Organizations and Social Behavior (as it was called within GSIA at the time). I was excited to find that the same mathematics that I had learned in my undergraduate engineering courses could be applied to the formulation of models of human behavior. Determined to sit at the foot of the throne, within a year I had transferred from the Masters program to the Ph.D. program and persuaded Herb to be my dissertation advisor.

Charged States

Sometimes the smallest action by one actor in a dynamic system has an enormous influence on another actor. In my case, the little action with a huge impact occurred when Herb asked me, during one of our weekly meetings, to take a look at a paper that he was preparing on problem representation. After reading it carefully, I returned a few days later—not without some trepidation—to show Herb my comments. I was relieved when he seemed quite pleased (well, maybe not "quite pleased," but at least not annoyed) with my suggestions, and I was delighted, several months later, when I saw the final version of the manuscript, in which he included my name in the acknowledgments section (Paige and Simon 1966).[2] My name in print! And in the same footnote with Allen Newell! So here was a new idea: you could be formally and publicly recognized for your ideas. This was a rush for me. As academics, we forget that we have a unique system of credit assignment, quite unlike the systems in other disciplines. Herb's simple courtesy of acknowledging, in print, my small improvements to his paper revealed a new source of satisfaction in life: the public attribution of one's intellectual contributions.

Redirections and Deflections

Curiously, Herb did not have a major influence on my dissertation, beyond the usual support, encouragement, and scholarly advice that one gets from a well-established mentor. The dissertation examined the decision-making structure used by CMU admissions officers. Although my analysis was based in part on some ideas from March and Simon's

organizations book (March and Simon 1958), the main contribution was to use the newly developed technique of non-metric multi-
dimensional scaling (Kruskal 1964) for describing the admissions
officers' decision space and how they searched it (Klahr 1969).

However, Herb did play an influential role in a major choice I faced
at the end of my graduate years: where to go for my first job. I had
narrowed several offers down to two. One was from a top-notch, well-
established, research business school: the Graduate School of Business
at the University of Chicago. The other was from a college of social
science in an exciting, innovative, unconventional, and untested new
university: UC Irvine (where, ironically, Jim March had recently moved
to build a new Social Science program). Herb helped me to frame my
decision in terms of a recently developed thesis that posited two types
of academic careers: "cosmopolitans" and "locals" (Gouldner 1957).
Under this dichotomy, cosmopolitans make their contributions and
achieve their fame through their research, as well as through their
activity in national and international professional organizations.
Locals, by contrast, tend to be known for their contributions to their
own university, through outstanding teaching, program and institutional development, high-level administrative service, and so on. As
Herb described it to me, the choice of career type—cosmopolitan or
local—had relatively clear consequences and different types of payoffs.

This was typical of Herb: to view theoretical constructs in the behavioral sciences not simply as abstract notions but as useful tools for
guiding decision making. For the first time, I saw how such "academic"
ideas could produce not only journal articles, but also important life
choices. And in characteristic fashion, having structured the decision
for me, Herb refused to make a recommendation one way or the other.[3]

But here, I must note that on this point Herb Simon failed to take his
own advice; he never chose between being a cosmopolitan or a local
because he had the energy and intellectual power to achieve overwhelming success as both. The cosmopolitan record is nothing short of
astonishing. For starters there is the Nobel Prize in Economic Sciences,

the National Medal of Science, and membership in the National Academy of Science. In addition, Herb received honorary degrees from two dozen universities around the world, as well as the top research contributions awards from the American Psychological Association, the American Psychological Foundation, the American Psychological Society, the Association for Computing Machinery, the American Economic Association, the American Society of Public Administration, the Academy of Management, the American Political Science Association, the Operations Research Society of America, and the Institute of Management Science. Moreover, he was a member of the Chinese Academy of Sciences and the Automation Hall of Fame at the Chicago Museum of Science and Technology, and an honorary member of the Institute of Electrical and Electronic Engineers. He was also the first social scientist appointed to the President's Science Advisory Committee.[4]

Herb's record as a "local" who came to Carnegie Mellon[5] in 1949 and never left is equally impressive. During the same extended period during which he published the nearly 1,000 articles that made him so famous, he exerted a profound, long-lasting, and intentional influence on his home institution. Herb was both a University Professor—our highest academic honor—and a Life Trustee of the University. In the pursuit of his intellectual goals, Herb created, rearranged, sacked, supported, and integrated many organizational elements within Carnegie Mellon University. As a result, the list of CMU departments that bear his irrevocable and indelible stamp includes not only the Department of Psychology but also the Department of Philosophy, the Department of Social and Decision Sciences, the Graduate School of Industrial Administration, the Heinz School of Public Policy and Management, the School of Computer Science, and, yes, even the Physics Department. Not only do each of these individual units bear the stamp of Herb Simon's creative vision and administrative determination, but also the ethos and nature of the entire university reflect his vision and commitment.

Reactions

The next example of Herb's influence on me falls into the category of intellectual and scientific influence, rather than personal influence. Via a complex path not worth describing here, my research focus changed, early in my career, to the investigation of cognitive processes in young children. I had begun to collaborate with my colleague Iain Wallace on a project that aimed to characterize young children's thought processes by using the same general approach to cognition as had been developed at CMU by Simon and Newell. One could summarize our research program as an attempt to revisit the questions proposed by Piaget (1968) in terms of the constructs and methods used by Newell and Simon (1972). This required that we move beyond the type of tasks and form of analysis commonly used in developmental psychology.

The work that had immense influence on us was the landmark paper on letter series completion (or rule induction) by Simon and Kotovsky (1963).[6] An important innovation in their approach was to propose several different strategies (implemented as programs) that participants might have used to solve the problems, and then to see which strategies best matched human performance. We took the same general approach with 5-year-old problem solvers. I would have chosen neither this type of problem nor this type of analysis had I not been familiar with the Simon and Kotovsky work.

After working on the project for a while, I noticed a few weaknesses in their paper which I described in an early draft that I sent to Herb. His response was characteristically gracious; he acknowledged that our critiques were valid, but he wondered why they had such an adversarial tone. (Neither Herb nor I would even touch the idea of anything Oedipal going on here!) "Science is cumulative," he wrote in what would have been—from a lesser person—an angry putdown, "and your paper would be stronger if you pointed out how your approach differed from ours and how each approach had specific shortcomings yet to be remedied." Of course we did what he suggested, and thus produced our first paper in the area of cognitive development (Klahr and Wallace 1970). Having learned the rules of academic protocol from the Master, I was happy to acknowledge Herb's contribution to our paper in a footnote, although in what now strikes me as an unnecessarily ungracious way: "We are most grateful to Professor H. A. Simon," our footnote said, "for his critical comments on an earlier version of this paper, not all of which we have heeded." (Perhaps I can excuse the unmannerly tone here by blaming it on my having been around too many economists during my graduate school days.)

Reabsorption

Shortly thereafter, I received an invitation to return to GSIA to work on problems of applying cognitive psychology principles to the GSIA education process. Herb had convinced Richard Cyert (then the Dean of GSIA) that cognitive psychology had reached the point where it could be applied to the design of more effective managerial instruction and had convinced the Ford Foundation to support the effort lavishly. The main attraction for me was the chance to have Simon and Newell as colleagues, and to return to an intellectual environment that was unique in the world and precisely suited to my needs and interests.

Like many of Herb's ideas, the concept of a "learning engineer"—someone who could translate basic principles from the science of cognitive psychology to the creation of more effective instructional systems—was well ahead of its time.[7] After I returned to GSIA in 1969, the idea was instantiated in what now look like quite mundane activities such as the creation of instructional video tapes, teacher evaluation instruments, and well-defined cognitive objectives for courses. But I was excited at the idea of becoming the "point man" for such an idea, and flattered to be invited back to Cognitive Mecca by two of the icons of my graduate school days: Cyert and Simon.

Nevertheless, at the time, I couldn't see how the "learning engineering" had much relevance to my increasing interest in information processing models of children's thinking, so we arranged a some-what unusual effort allocation. My work on the GSIA teaching issues would comprise my teaching load and I would be free to pursue my developmental interests as my research agenda. I would also have an appointment in the psychology department, where Herb had recently taken up permanent residence, after moving his office out of GSIA.

Equilibrium

I will condense the next 25 years by posing a question: How can a young investigator carve out an independent scientific career when in the same department with a prior mentor who maintains a vigorous, prolific, and highly visible world-class research program well into his eighties? My answer was to create a comfortable distance from Herb by situating my work in a niche in cognitive psychology into which Herb had never bothered to wander: cognitive development.[8] For many years I continued to work on information processing models of cognitive development (Klahr and Wallace 1976; Klahr 1992). But this too was a dynamic equilibrium, with the need for distance countered by the obvious relevance of the work of Simon and Newell, and of Herb's specific interest in the psychology of scientific discovery. Only when I was beyond my own 60th birthday did I feel secure enough in my own expertise to finally collaborate with Herb on a paper that reviewed the area representing the intersection of our mutual interest in scientific thinking in adults and children (Klahr and Simon 1999). Although this collaboration was one of the most satisfying experiences of my career, it saddens me still to recall that, on the day that the proofs for a brief report on that project (Klahr and Simon 2001) appeared in my mail-box, I learned that Herb had died.

This need to find an equilibrium position with respect to Herb's ideas and influence was also manifest during the 10 years that I served as head of the Department of Psychology (1983–1993). From the outset, I felt that my responsibility was to treat each faculty member and each area in the department with equal respect and consideration, rather than to implement Herb's agenda. Thus, before accepting the position, I met with Herb and told him that if I became head of the department, I would not continue the regular private meetings with him that previous department heads had held to discuss departmental business. Once again, Herb's grace, civility, and sense of fair play prevailed. He just game me a mischievous smile and said that would leave him even more time for his research meetings.

This is not to suggest that, either during the period of my headship or for the nine years thereafter, Herb suspended his vigorous promotion of the ideas and decisions that he thought were the right ones for the department. Quite the contrary, for he remained an active participant in departmental decisions up to the end. Herb was strong willed, brilliant, tenacious, and aggressive when he wanted to be, but he was a "mensch" at all times, and he knew what fair play, decency, and integrity meant.

Having said that, I must acknowledge my uneasiness at praising Herb Simon's character! I'm sure it would embarrass and perhaps annoy him to read the many plaudits in this chapter and this volume. He was uncomfortable around groupies and acolytes. He once dismissed his seemingly endless list of awards and honorary degrees by telling me that "after a while the criterion for getting an honor is to have been awarded a lot of other honors." And so it must have seemed to him as he garnered dozens of awards, any one of which would have been cherished by most of us.

For Herb, the real rewards were in the discovery, the solved problem, the novel idea, the deep insight, the published paper, the citation, and the work that his work spawned. What he didn't like was being told, directly, that he was one hell of a guy. The following story, taken from the introduction to a Simon festschrift that Ken Kotovsky and I organized, illustrates the point:

Early in our careers, both of us had the privilege of having Herb as our dissertation advisor, and we are both deeply indebted to him for the kind of values, skills, and attitudes that such an apprenticeship inculcates. Another thing we both learned long ago was to respect the dual-edged sword of Herb's rapid insight and equally rapid impatience with poor ideas.... Thus, even two decades beyond our graduate student days, it was with some trepidation that we approached him with our plan for this volume. Would the whole idea strike him as tangential to the real business of science?... his general reaction was supportive, but he had two requests. First, he would not be a passive participant in his own Festschrift; at the age of 71, as always, the research was his focus and priority: and he wanted to present a paper on his current research program at the symposium. Of course, we were delighted with that idea, and we agreed. Second, he wanted us to instruct the other participants to "avoid hagiography." We agreed to that too. And so we left his office with his blessings, and without the slightest idea about what 'hagiography' meant.[9] (It was not the first time that we had left his office concealing our ignorance and scurrying off to remedy it.)   (Klahr and Kotovsky 1989, p. xvi)

Although Herb was always uncomfortable with acolytes, he was certainly not a distant, cool person. He could write as eloquently about love and meaning as about goals and problem spaces. As he put it (1965, p. 110):

Man is a problem-solving, skill-using, social animal. Once he has satisfied his hunger, two main kinds of experiences are significant to him. One of his deepest needs is to apply his skills, whatever they be, to challenging tasks—to feel the exhilaration of the well-struck ball or the well-solved problem. The other need is to find meaningful and warm relations with a few other human beings—to love and be loved, to share experience, to respect and be respected, to work in common tasks.

Over the years, his colleagues in the department made it very clear to him that he was indeed in the company of those who shared experience with him, who respected him and valued his respect, and who worked on common tasks. One particularly warm occasion was on Herb's seventieth birthday. I was head of the department at the time, and I decided to create a design for his birthday cake that could somehow represent one of his contributions to the field. I labored for a few hours and came up with "Herb's EPAM birthday cake." EPAM (Elementary Perceiver And Memorizer) was a pioneering computational model of memory and retrieval that Herb developed with Ed Feigenbaum (Simon and Feigenbaum 1964); he continued to extend

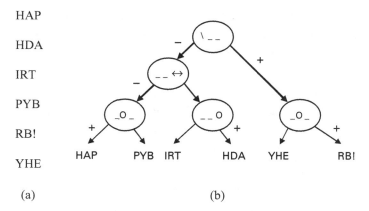

HAP

HDA

IRT

PYB

RB!

YHE

(a)   (b)

Figure 1
An EPAM discrimination net for sorting letter triads for Herbert Simon's 70th-birthday greeting. (a) Letter triads. (b) Discrimination net.

and develop it to the end of his life (Gobet, Richman, Staszewski, and Simon 1997; Richman, Staszewski, and Simon 1995). The design on the cake was an EPAM discrimination net that sorted the letters of the birthday greeting down to the terminal nodes. The tests were for features of letters in specific positions of a set of letter triads. For example, the node _O_ tests a triad for a closed curve in the letter in the center position, and _ _ ↔ tests for symmetry in the right-most letter in the triad. The triads are shown, in alphabetical order on the left of figure 1, and the EPAM tree is shown on the right. Designing this cake is the kind of project that my teenage children would call "dorky," but Herb's cheerful reception made it clear that he appreciated the fondness with which it was offered.

High Energy

I have yet to convey the energy that emanated from this man. You couldn't escape it: in the intensity with which he listened to your ideas, in the excitement with which he described his own most active project, or in the way he attacked even the most mundane everyday puzzles.

Let me illustrate with an example from the last category. About 25 years ago, Herb and I and a few other colleagues were returning from a conference that had concluded in a late spring snowstorm that led to several muddled airline connections. At the end of it all, we wound up flying from Denver to Cleveland, and then driving to Pittsburgh at 1 A.M. I was at the wheel. (I thought Herb was too old to drive at that late hour, but he was younger then than I am now!) It had been a long day, and we were all tired. Conversation waned. I muttered something about how the roads were pretty deserted. Oops, that did it.

"Hmmm," said Herb: "I wonder what the density of cars on the interstates is right now. How many cars in the US? What proportion might be on the road at 1 A.M.? Well, let's see: How many linear miles of interstate? Assume the US is a rectangle 2,500 miles long by 1,200 miles wide. Estimate that there the interstates are distributed on a grid, with the east-west routes approximately every 200 miles apart and the north-south routes approximately 300 miles apart." And so it went. I did *not* fall asleep at the wheel. The man never stopped thinking. Ideas were his passion.

Binding Forces

I have attempted to summarize the dynamics of more than 40 years of interaction with Herb Simon, from a distant intellectual attraction to a close colleagueship. By the time I had approached my sixties and Herb his eighties, I had become sufficiently close to him and confident of our relationship to converse comfortably about personal as well as professional issues. In one particularly revealing episode, we were exchanging e-mail messages about a book by Calvin Trillin that I had given to Herb during his recuperation from heart surgery. Trillin (1996) describes his experiences as an assimilated Jew growing up in the Midwest, as well as his attempt to figure out what kind of "messages" about life his father attempted to convey to him. The book, and his recovery, led Herb to talk about two things he had never mentioned to me before and about which he had only written briefly in his autobiography: his father and his Judaism.

I'll let Herb close this chapter in his own words, so characteristically intelligent, articulate, curious, funny, honest, and humane:

Feb. 20 1998

Dear Dave,

On medical matters, angina sooner or later ends in a heart attack (if the blood flow is blocked) or a stroke (if the blood pressure gets too high before the flow stops entirely). My angina having reached the point where I could no longer walk comfortably back and forth to school, I had the appropriate x-rays made (I have a great picture of the coronary artery and its branches; looks just like an EPAM net) and, on the basis of the evidence, decided that it was time to act. There are two kinds of by-pass, depending on where the blockage is. In the first, they have to actually stop the heart and pump blood artificially during much of the operation. That isn't a great idea for people at age 81, and frequently fatal. In the second, which fortunately was my case, the blockage was located so that they could make the graft (from the mammary artery!) without stopping the heart—not terribly dangerous at all. I feel great (far better than before the operation), and everything seems to be continuing smoothly.

That's your medical lesson for today.

Thank you very much for the Trillin book, which I have read, and found very moving. Dot is reading it at present. Reading such a book invites comparison with one's own life. My father, like Trillin's, was a very private person, and if he had any ambitions for me, he never communicated them, nor did I discover before he died (when I was about 32) whether I had followed a path he expected—although he seemed quite satisfied with my academic career, and the facts that I kept out of jail and paid my bills without too much dependence on him. If he secretly wanted me (or my brother) to be an engineer or a farmer, or any more esoteric thing that he himself aspired to, I never had any inkling, although I myself found my approach toward engineering (during my Operations Research days) to bring me closer to him in an unexpected way.

The other interesting theme of the book was the gradual assimilation of a Jewish family. In my case, it had happened a generation earlier, for both my father and my mother had lost any religious attachment to Judaism. Yet the Jewish background of my family on both sides made me identify with those origins and influenced me in very deep ways.

Dot and I, as devoted *New Yorker* readers (until the new regime came along five or ten years ago), read a number of Trillin's tales about midwestern towns, but somehow, his name never stuck in our minds, or had somehow been washed away, until you sent the book.

Thanks very much. It was a great way to keep my mind off my troubles when I came home from the hospital a week ago. (Although I must confess that I have had almost zero troubles, including no pain or complications, and an immediate relief from the angina whose progress had gradually convinced me, over the past several years, that this plumbing job was necessary.)

I'm going to indulge myself in another three weeks or so of house arrest, and then I'll be back to roam the Baker Halls in my usual way.

Warm regards,
Herb

Herb Simon died three years later from surgical complications unrelated to his successful bypass operation. The Force is gone, but not the forces. His monumental intellectual achievements will continue to shape not only the dozens of fields to which he directed his attention, but also the paths of many hundreds of colleagues who were fortunate enough to interact with him, and through them, thousands of others. I hope that in my own small way, I can influence the personal, professional and scientific trajectories of a few others in the way that Herb Simon influenced mine. I owe him that, at the least.

Notes

1. It has a reasonable claim on four Nobel laureates in economics—including Herb—who started their careers there. The others are Franco Modigliani, Merton Miller, and Robert Lucas.

2. This paper appeared in the first Carnegie Symposium on Cognition. This first volume on problem solving (Kleinmuntz 1966) includes, in addition to the CMU participants, chapters by B. F. Skinner, R. Gagné, and D. E. Berlyne, among others.

3. Although I was quite tempted by the unorthodox organization of the new university, I decided to take the more conservative route.

4. A more complete record of Herb's awards and accomplishments is available at http://www.psy.cmu.edu. His own description of his remarkable life can be found in his autobiography (Simon 1991). For a fascinating account of his role in the "cognitive revolution," see McCorduck 1979.

5. More precisely, to the Carnegie Institute of Technology (CIT). Carnegie Mellon University founded in 1965 with the merger of CIT and the Mellon Institute.

6. This paper is of historical as well as scientific interest because it was the first ever to create a computational model for a high level cognitive task and compare the model's performance to human behavior.

7. I believe that only in the past dozen years or so has this idea been realized through the creation of theoretically grounded and widely disseminated cognitive tutors (cf. Corbett, Anderson, and Patterson 1990; Koedinger, Anderson, Hadley, and Mark 1997; Singley, Anderson, Gevins, and Hoffman 1989).

8. An overstatement, I must admit. Herb had, in fact, written one extremely insightful paper about the relationship between issues in cognitive development and the emerging area of information processing psychology (Simon 1962). Lucky for me, he chose not to do any further work in the area.

9. It means the writing and critical study of the lives of the saints.

References

Corbett, A. T., Anderson, J. R., and Patterson, E. G. 1990. Student modeling and tutoring flexibility in the LISP intelligent tutoring system. In C. Frasson and G. Gauthier, eds., *Intelligent Tutoring Systems*. Ablex.

Cyert, R. M., and March, J. G. 1963. *A Behavioral Theory of the Firm*. Prentice-Hall.

Gobet, F., Richman, H. B., Staszewski, J. J., and Simon, H. A. 1997. Goals, representations and strategies in a concept attainment task: The EPAM model. *Psychology of Learning and Motivation* 37: 265–290.

Gouldner, A. W. 1957. Cosmopolitans and Locals: Toward an Analysis of Latent Social Roles—I. *Administrative Science Quarterly* 2, no. 3: 281–306.

Klahr, D. 1969. Decision making in a complex environment. *Management Science* 15: 595–618.

Klahr, D. 1992. Information processing approaches to cognitive development. In M. Bornstein and M. Lamb, eds., *Developmental Psychology*, third edition. Erlbaum.

Klahr, D., and Kotovsky, K., eds. 1989. *Complex Information Processing: The Impact of Herbert A. Simon*. Erlbaum.

Klahr, D., and Simon, H. A. 1999. Studies of scientific discovery: Complementary approaches and convergent findings. *Psychological Bulletin* 125, no. 5: 524–543.

Klahr, D., and Simon, H. A. 2001. What have psychologists (and others) discovered about the psychology of scientific discovery? *Current Directions in Psychological Science* 10, no. 3: 75–83.

Klahr, D., and Wallace, J. G. 1970. The development of serial completion strategies: An information processing analysis. *British Journal of Psychology* 61: 243–257.

Klahr, D., and Wallace, J. G. 1976. *Cognitive Development: An Information Processing View*. Erlbaum.

Kleinmuntz, B., ed. 1966. *Problem Solving: Research, Method and Theory*. Wiley.

Koedinger, K. R., Anderson, J. R., Hadley, W. H., and Mark, M. 1997. Intelligent tutoring goes to school in the big city. *International Journal of Artificial Intelligence in Education* 8: 30–43.

Kruskal, J. B. 1964. Multidimensional scaling by optimizing goodness of fit to a nonmetric hypothesis. *Psychometrika* 29: 1–27.

March, J. G., and Simon, H. A. 1958. *Organizations*. Wiley.

McCorduck, P. 1979. *Machines Who Think*. Freeman.

Newell, A., and Simon, H. A. 1956. The logic theory machine. *IRE Transactions on Information Theory* IT-2(3): 61–79.

Newell, A., and Simon, H. A. 1972. *Human Problem Solving*. Prentice-Hall.

Newell, A., Shaw, J. C., and Simon, H. A. 1958. Elements of a theory of human problem solving. *Psychological Review* 65: 151–166.

Paige, J. M., and Simon, H. A. 1966. Cognitive processes in solving algebra word problems. In B. Kleinmuntz, ed., *Problem Solving*. Wiley.

Piaget, J. 1968. Quantification, conservation and nativism. *Science* 162: 976–979.

Richman, H. B., Staszewski, J. J., and Simon, H. A. 1995. Simulation of expert memory using EPAM IV. *Psychological Review* 102, no. 2: 305–330.

Simon, H. A. 1962. An information processing theory of intellectual development. In W. Kessen and C. Kuhlman, eds., *Thought in the Young Child*. Monographs of the Society for Research in Child Development, serial no. 83.

Simon, H. A. 1965. *The Shape of Automation for Men and Management*. Harper and Row.

Simon, H. A. 1991. *Models of My Life*. Basic Books.

Simon, H. A., and Feigenbaum, E. A. 1964. An information-processing theory of some effects of similarity, familiarization, and meaningfulness in verbal learning. *Journal of Verbal Learning and Verbal Behavior* 3: 385–396.

Simon, H. A., and Kotovksy, K. 1963. Human acquisition of concepts for sequential patterns. *Psychological Review* 70: 534–546.

Simon, H. A., and Newell, A. 1958. Heuristic problem solving: The next advance in operations research. *Operations Research* 6: 1–10.

Singley, M. K., Anderson, J. R., Gevins, J. S., and Hoffman, D. 1989. The algebra word problem tutor. In D. Bierman et al., eds, *Artificial Intelligence: Synthesis and Reflection.* IOS.

Trillin, C. 1996. *Messages from My Father.* Farrar, Straus and Giroux.

Strong Ideas

Kenneth Kotovsky

Over the past forty years or so, I have been a graduate student, colleague, collaborator, and friend of Herb Simon. Although it hasn't always been obvious to me, I find myself increasingly realizing that I often look at the world through his eyes, examine it from his perspective and think about it with thoughts that are engendered by his strong ideas, ideas that more and more have come to feel like my own. I hope that, at least some of the time, I am able to act in it with some approximation of his values. It wasn't always that way, but now that he is gone his continued presence is even more obvious to me and even more treasured.

My name is Kenneth Kotovsky and I first met Herb when I showed up at Carnegie Mellon (then the Carnegie Institute of Technology) to be his graduate student (I think I hold something of a record for longevity in that role). We did a good deal of scientific work together, but there is a public record of that elsewhere, so I will focus more on another, somewhat less obvious way in which I feel strongly influenced by him; his enduring interest in education and the values he expressed through that interest. I must admit it took a while for me to fully appreciate who he was—I was very young when we first met and very impressionable, and he was more than one.

In fact, I think there have always been two Herb Simons for me. It started in 1961, the morning of my first day as a young graduate student. when I first saw him—it was in a large Masters class in organizations consisting of a hundred or more students. Herb entered wearing a suit and tie and his first words were "put down the pencils and notebooks; there's no longer a need to copy out your own textbook, the printing press has been around for a long time. I want you to listen and think." It was the first of many pedagogical theories I heard him articulate—he thought a lot about teaching and learning and had strong and forcefully stated ideas about the process—no surprise there! It was a big class taught with a lot of authority and control, and I was pretty intimidated in thinking that I would be working for that brilliant but tough guy who stood in front of the class—actually, I was scared stiff. That afternoon though, I showed up at another class of his, a small doctoral-level class in Mathematical Models in the Social Sciences. It was an absolute delight. He showed up in an old sweater, very relaxed, and threw out dozens of wonderful ideas—the discussions were intellectually exciting, creative, wide-ranging and invigorating, it was the very ideal of a graduate class. I loved it and couldn't wait to start working on research with him, but then, a couple days later, it was morning again and the scary Herb was back. I think I resolved the emotional dilemma by finally dropping the organizations class!

Even as a faculty colleague there were two Herbs for me. When I was away from CMU and encountered people who knew of him I'd be reminded of what a towering figure of international reputation he was—and I would be absolutely awestruck; but here at CMU in our everyday interactions, he was just that wonderful guy whose office was down the hall … the guy who once playfully informed me that his greatest accomplishment in the past year was getting a new towel dispenser placed in the men's bathroom on our floor! Shortly thereafter, following a meeting with a third colleague, Jonathan Cagan, where we were working on a chapter arguing for computational and cognitive similarities between creative design and scientific discovery (Cagan,

Kotovsky, and Simon 2001), the three of us happened to all meet again in the men's bathroom, where I promptly broke the handle on the new towel dispenser and somewhat desperately tried to fix it. I finally gave up and left, but Herb took over and kept at it for some time. I remember commenting to Jon, as we walked out, that we'd just left a Nobel laureate working on the towel dispenser, but of course we shouldn't have been surprised, after all, there was a problem to be solved!

This little example also typifies another of Herb's; qualities; he really believed in doing his share of the work. A collaboration with him, whether as a faculty colleague or as a graduate student, was a true collaboration with both parties getting their hands dirty. I have a distinct memory of one argument we had about authorship when I was a graduate student. Herb, Dick Hayes, and I had been working on a project and I felt that it was really their project that I had joined late, that they had done most of the work and one of them should be first author. We argued long and hard, and I saved myself from defeat only by saying "Let's settle it at our next meeting" so I could come prepared with better arguments. I did, and I still "lost." (The lethal blow was Herb's assertion that "the only thing that matters is the intellectual contribution"—a value that he lived by.) It was, to put it mildly, not the typical dispute about authorship that many graduate students relate! Herb didn't just consult or advise on the intellectual projects he was involved with, he was a person who did the work. Another revelatory anecdote comes from a former student and recent collaborator of Herb's, Jim Staszewski. Jim relates an encounter that occurred just before Herb's death:

Late one afternoon this past November, Herb and I were meeting to discuss how to present a very complex set of findings on human category learning. Our research group had been struggling to extract these findings from a massive body of qualitative and quantitative data, truly labyrinthine in its complexity. Herb had saved the day, of course, having invested possibly more than 80 hours alone in analysis, after our group had spent easily 10 times that without success. After he summarized the findings, we paused for moment as his presentation and my comprehension took all available capacity. He smiled and remarked with his eyes twinkling brightly that he "had not had as much fun in a long time." "I will forever cherish his words and these moments—and so many more. I feel immeasurably grateful to have been so incredibly privileged to work with this wonderful man. (as quoted in Klahr and Kotovsky 2001)

Being Herb's graduate student meant you were treated as an intellectual colleague with the accompanying assumption that you shared his values about the importance and the joy of doing such work. One other very strong value I learned during that period of our work together was his willingness to pursue ideas and scientific truth wherever it took him. One of the discoveries we made then was that problem difficulty depended on factors other than the size of the problem space that had to be searched.[1] It was the continuation of a line of work that Herb and Dick Hayes had started with their work on problem isomorphs, and when I realized that it was contradicting an assumption implicit in the Newell-Simon view of the centrality of problem space search. I wrote it up but was a bit muted in presenting the conclusions that were at variance with the size of search space view, in that it would involve Herb in publishing work that at least implicitly seemed to contradict an aspect of his own earlier work. On reading it, he immediately saw through the soft pedaling and said, with a broad smile, "Look, we have to be stronger in presenting this—be direct, just say those old guys were totally wrong on this" ... where he was one of "those old guys"! The truth had to be pursued, wherever it led.

Herb created a place of magic in my life—and I'm sure in the lives of many—a place of unbounded scientific curiosity, of intellectual intensity, a place where any and all ideas could be explored and played with, and new insights attained. It usually occurred in a deliberately un-air-conditioned office where, when you settled down into one of those old red leather chairs that graced his office, you knew you were about to begin an intellectual adventure; a place where you were sure to have a great discussion that usually went well beyond the issue that brought you there. An interaction with Herb was always a feast of ideas—a feast made even more savory by the flattery of the usually unwarranted assumption that you understood the tangents that inevitably came up, that you of course knew about Krebs's metabolic discoveries, or special relativity, or embryology or Faraday's work on electromagnetism ... that you could somehow follow where that great mind soared. Talking with Herb there was an adventure, an adventure that was often accompanied by an almost impish delight and playfulness. An illustration of his wonderful humor is contained in an email exchange he had with Dick Hayes, who related this exchange about some bugs that were devouring his tomatoes:

Forwarded Message: Date: Wed, Oct 18 2000 9:50 AM −0400
From: Herb Simon ⟨Herb_Simon@v.gp.cs.cmu.edu⟩
To: jh50@andrew.cmu.edu
Subject: Tomatoes

Dear Dr. Hayes:

I submit herewith the entomological report you requested concerning the insects that are obtaining nutriment from your tomatoes.

The insects in question, from your brief description of their larvae, almost certainly belong to the order Lepidoptera, which includes the moths and butterflies. There are three highly likely candidates as the criminals (criminals, that is, from your particular, and not disinterested, standpoint); Phlegethontius carolina or P. celeus, well-known Sphinx Moths and Heliothis armiger, which belongs to the family Noctuidae. The former have larvae (caterpillars) about three inches long, with light diagonal markings on the (grayish brown?) abdomen. They will be glad to eat your potatoes or tobacco when they run out of tomatoes. In all cases, I believe they will eat the leaves as well as the fruit.

H. armiger, sometimes called the Tomato Fruit-worm, has a larva little more than an inch long. The larvae are light green, reddish brown, or almost black; spotted, striped or plain. There are two annual generations in the North. When feeding on tomatoes, they prefer the green or just ripening fruit. They will also be pleased to inhabit your corn, cotton, and tobacco plants in various ways. In the North, winter plowing kills many of the pupa, which hibernate, but, my source suggests that "the best plan with this, as with other insect pests, is to send an SOS to your State Entomologist or to the United States Department of Agriculture for special information and help. It is for this, among other things, that you pay your taxes." I must add that, in connection with a recent investigation of black-eyed peas (really beans!), and other exotic Southern varieties of beans, I discovered that the Web has tons of information on these matters provided by various state departments of agriculture and the USDA, and suggest that might be a fruitful source of additional information about your visitors. Google is the best search engine.

You may make out your check for my consulting services to Herbert A. Simon, 128 N. Craig St., Apt. 504, Pittsburgh, PA. Wormy tomatoes are not accepted as payment in kind.

Your servant,
Herbert A. Simon

He created a place of real magic and invited so many of us in to share that place with him. Another former student of Herb's has eloquently attested to this:

Many graduate advisers in the sciences teach their students how to write. Mine taught me what to read and how to read it. My first and every conversation with Herb turned out to be the kind I had read about in C. P. Snow's novels about life at Cambridge: civil conversations with a tutor who gave you a great deal of stuff to read, discuss and write about week after week, year after year. I was nudged to read Theory of Oscillations by Andronow and Chaikin ("Have you had any nonlinear differential equations?") and the Federalist Papers ("They were modeling and building a whole new society, can you imagine what they would have done with computer simulations?"). Over the next three years, I was encouraged to read the classics in an astonishing range of subjects: general equilibrium theory in economics, real analysis, operations research, mathematical logic, the infant science of computer networks, cognitive psychology, and the philosophy of knowledge. I was made to read. Few human beings, including my classmates, have received the quantity and quality of educational attention I received in those years. I simply enjoyed myself, insufficiently realizing the responsibility that comes with such an education." (Ramamoorthi Bhaskar, personal communication, as quoted in Klahr and Kotovsky 2001)

I had my real Bar Mitzvah in that magical place. When Herb was in a passionate argument about some idea, a not infrequent occurrence, and felt the need to take the gloves off and set someone straight he would often preface a killer argument with the words "look friend" as if to control his intensity and insure his interlocutor that it was the idea and not the person or the relationship he was about to demolish. However, I noticed that he never used the phrase with students—with his students he wasn't the tough adversarial Herb, but the nurturing supportive Herb. So that memorable day many years past the age of 13, when he first said "Look, friend, . . ." to me, I felt that I had finally entered adulthood—at least in his eyes, and those of course were the eyes that counted.

Herb was the ultimate academic—his devotion to exploring ideas and doing research was paramount. Whatever position he was offered or whatever honors he had received—evidenced by the array of medals and citations strewn haphazardly over the top of his file cabinet—his singular focus was on furthering knowledge. The honors and power and influence he attained were not distractions but were used only in support of higher level goals—either to make a contribution to one of his many communities—this lifelong New Dealer had a strong social conscience and commitment—or to insure that the research environment he created at Carnegie Mellon was a good and supportive one. He never accepted a position that took him away from his research and teaching. Pittsburgh is a place where community matters and people stay. Herb stayed and built a research and teaching community at Carnegie Mellon that supported his launching of an intellectual revolution. His devotion to his scientific work and his love of discussing ideas, pouring over new data and exploring intellectual issues never wavered, and it didn't matter if you were a colleague, a graduate student or an undergraduate.

I still remember him sitting on the floor of a dormitory lounge a couple years ago; he was probably 83 years old at the time. It was in a very well-appointed room with some beautiful tables and chairs, but he was on floor—that's where the students were—eating extremely inelegant submarine sandwiches with a group of freshmen who had invited him to talk. Well past the announced ending time, I offered to drive him home and he said "We're doing fine here—I'll just walk." . . . after all there were minds to be enriched and ideas to be explored. In another instance, Ken Kwok, his graduate teaching assistant for the last course that Herb taught, relates how, in that very popular course on cognition that drew graduate and advanced undergraduate students from all reaches of the university, Herb did a sizable portion of the TA's job himself; he insisted on reading the student's progress reports on their term projects because they were so exciting! The clarity and strength of his values is also evident in his words at one of the last department meetings he attended. Our department was discussing with some trepidation whether to allow a sudden doubling in the size of our graduate core class by taking in an extra group of students from another department. Herb settled the matter by saying "you know, when people come to you and want to learn—you should teach them"! He lived that view. His devotion to teaching and learning, his absolute devotion to academic pursuits is a model for the life of the mind, but there was a heart there as well as a head—and a wonderful value system and a deep pride in and love of family ... and the way he lived his life up to the end was also a model for the life of a man.

An example: At the end, there was an issue of how invasive the attempts to prolong his life should be. His daughter Kathie has related how he finally told her it was time for him to go. He told her, about a day before his passing, that life has a beginning a middle and an end, that he'd had a wonderful life and career, that there were no projects that he'd started that he was essential for, and that it was time for the end. The decision of a clear, powerful and wise decision maker demonstrating his rationality right up to the end. (Katherine Simon Frank, personal communication)

When giants walk on the earth they can trample on others or they can uplift those around them. Herb was an uplifter. He certainly lifted me up at many points in my life and in many ways. My colleagues in social psychology tell me that relationships are important—that they help determine the quality and richness of our lives, and even our health. Well they play another role as well; we define ourselves by the important relationships in our lives. And so in saying goodbye to Herb we also are saying goodbye to a part of ourselves.... for me, one of the best parts. But as I write this on a Saturday afternoon in an office about ten yards up the hall from where his was for so many years I can feel his presence. It is how he spent his Saturdays, doing his intellectual work throughout his long and fruitful career. So I have to say in concluding that as much as I miss him, there are still two Herbs—the Herb that is gone and the Herb that goes on ... through the institution that is built around his ideas, through his monumental contributions to so many disciplines, through the loving family he has left behind, and for me, through his teaching—when I hear myself say things and suddenly recognize the words as his, or find myself thinking about a phenomenon and realize I'm doing it in ways he's taught me. His teaching goes on with every memory, and for that I am thankful and hopeful, hopeful that my own teaching reflects some of the strong ideas and perhaps even some of the strong values that his exemplified.... and ultimately, for the privilege and joy of knowing and working with this man, words just don't suffice.

Note

1. We found that the differences in performance across problem isomorphs was due not to search space size but to differences in the cognitive load imposed by the various isomorphs interacting with the limited immediate memory capacity people brought to the task (Kotovsky, Hayes, and Simon 1989). I remember coming to the sudden realization that the central issue in that work, the limited immediate memory capacity available for formulating moves and plans for making moves in the problem space was the same issue that I'd worked on with Herb starting with our first paper in 1963 (Simon and Kotovsky 1963) and in much subsequent work as well (Kotovsky and Simon 1973, 1990). The feeling I had was that I was only capable of working on one idea, but it was of course one manifestation of a very strong idea of Herb's, that of bounded rationality, and thus well worth it.

References

Cagan, J., Kotovsky, K., and Simon, H. A. 2001. Scientific Discovery and Inventive Engineering Design: Cognitive and Computational Similarities. In Antonsin, E., and Cagan, J., eds., *Formal Engineering Design Synthesis*. Cambridge University Press.

Klahr, D., and Kotovsky, K. 2001. A life of the mind: Remembering Herb Simon. *APS Observer* 14, no. 4: 14–33.

Kotovsky, K., Hayes, J. R., and Simon, H. A. 1985. Why are some problems hard? Evidence from Tower of Hanoi. *Cognitive Psychology* 17: 248–294. Reprinted in Simon, H. A., *Models of Thought*, volume 2 (Yale University Press, 1989).

Kotovsky, K., and Simon, H. A. 1973. Empirical tests of a theory of human acquisition of concepts for sequential patterns. *Cognitive Psychology* 4: 399–424. Reprinted in Simon, H. A., *Models of Thought* (Yale University Press, 1979).

Kotovsky, K., and Simon, H. A. 1990. Why are some problems really hard? Explorations in the problem space of difficulty. *Cognitive Psychology* 22: 143–183.

Simon, H. A., and Kotovsky, K. 1963. Human acquisition of concepts for sequential patterns. *Psychological Review* 70: 534–546. Reprinted in Simon, H. A., *Models of Thought* (Yale University Press, 1979).

Heuristics for Scientific Discovery:
The Legacy of Herbert Simon

Pat Langley

I had the good fortune to interact with Herb Simon on a regular basis between 1975 and 1984, initially as a graduate student in the psychology department at Carnegie Mellon University and later as a collaborator in extensions to my dissertation research. During the latter period, we were joined by Gary Bradshaw, another Carnegie Mellon Ph.D. student, and Jan Zytkow, a visiting researcher with background in the philosophy of science.

My presence at CMU was not accidental, as I had come there specifically to work with Herb Simon. During my undergraduate days at Texas Christian University, I had an odd, recurring experience. For every topic that drew my interest—human cognition, artificial intelligence, philosophy of science, econometric models—it seemed that Simon had published one or more seminal papers, and I decided that I needed to study with this many-faceted scientist. Of course, after arriving in Pittsburgh, I learned that I had seen only the tip of the iceberg, since he had contributed significantly to other fields as well.

Clearly, Herb Simon was fascinated by many phenomena, but in this essay I will focus on only two of them. One concerns the heuristic nature of human decision making and problem solving. Heuristics are rules of thumb that let one simplify a decision task or problem to make it more tractable. Their use typically does not guarantee that one will find the optimal solution, or even any solution at all, but they can make practical the achievement of many tasks that would otherwise fall beyond the reach of human memory and cognition.

On another front, Herb Simon was intrigued with science itself as an instance of complex cognitive activity. He showed a special interest in the creative aspects of science that lead to the discovery of laws, the formation of explanatory theories, and the design of experiments. He was committed to moving beyond vague accounts of discovery processes to characterize them in terms of cognitive mechanisms. Naturally, the notion of heuristics figured centrally in his work on scientific discovery, as it did in his studies of problem solving and other aspects of human thought (e.g., Newell and Simon 1972).

Thus, it seems appropriate to review Herb Simon's career in terms of his personal heuristics for scientific research, both because it will illuminate many aspects of his scientific style and because it may hold useful ideas that others can incorporate into their own work. Moreover, it makes sense to illustrate these rules of thumb with examples taken from Simon's work on discovery processes. Fortunately, I was in a good position to collect these examples, since our collaborations over the years centered on just this topic.

Be Audacious

Herb Simon was audacious in that he was willing to tackle imposing problems which others had been reluctant to face or even admit might be solvable. Not only did this heuristic increase his chances of making large-scale advances, but it took him regularly into more interesting, less explored territories than other researchers. One early problem, which he pursued well before my time, focused on building the first computer to prove theorems in logic and, arguably, the first to emulate human thought processes (Newell and Simon 1956).

A second important pursuit, which I was lucky enough to partly witness, involved uncovering the cognitive and computational mechanisms that support the processes of scientific discovery. In 1966, Herb Simon published a chapter, "Scientific Discovery and the Psychology of Problem Solving," in which he had the audacity to suggest that one could explain and model scientific discovery, which often involved some creative insight, in terms of normal cognitive processes, using the same mechanisms that underlie everyday human problem solving and decision making.

We can only understand the radical nature of this claim by reviewing the intellectual climate of the time. Philosophers of science were focused almost entirely on the logic of verification, by which one evaluates models and theories in terms of evidence. Indeed, some prominent philosophers, including Popper (1961), rejected even the possibility of a logic of discovery. In other circles, there was a general air of mysticism about scientific discovery, which supposedly relied on unfathomable intuitions or creative sparks. Herb Simon's position stood in stark contrast to these neo-vitalists, and his radical chapter set both the agenda and the tone for research on cognitive and computational studies of scientific discovery for the next 35 years. Challenging problems of this sort do not fall to a single blow of trumpets, however piercing, but we will see later that Simon responded to the complexity of science by drawing on additional heuristics.

However, I should note the contrast between Herb Simon's audacity as a scientist and his humility as an individual. Meetings in his Baker Hall office, despite the books lining its walls, the papers stacked on its tables, and the expressions on its slate blackboard, felt less like visiting an academic's office than coming to the living room in the house of an older, valued friend. Herb sat in an easy chair, with no intervening desk, and he treated even the least experienced student as a colleague. He was always interested in your ideas and, though he might disagree with you, he never seemed to judge. As a result, the physical space that he engendered was friendly but fully professional, challenging but always respectful, and comforting but genuinely creative. Despite his many scientific breakthroughs, Herb maintained that he was nothing special, just a normal human engaging in everyday problem solving, and he reflected that attitude in his style of interaction. I count my visits to Herb Simon's office, and my meetings with him and colleagues there, as the most memorable, enjoyable, and important times of my life.

Ignore Discipline Boundaries

Another heuristic that Herb Simon applied repeatedly was to ignore traditional boundaries between disciplines. For any given research problem, he became familiar with the work done in every relevant field and incorporated the best ideas from each one into his own approach to the task. This strategy provided him not only with a rich source of metaphors and methods; it also imposed constraints that narrowed his search for a solution.

In his research on scientific discovery, Herb Simon borrowed concepts from a variety of disciplines. Naturally, he took advantage of his earlier ideas, and those of his collaborators, on the nature of human problem solving, especially the notion that this activity involves constrained search through a problem space. He also incorporated techniques from artificial intelligence, many of which he co-developed, to implement the search metaphor in running computer programs. In addition, he read widely in the philosophy of science, borrowing ideas about what constitutes a legitimate theory, and in the history of science, from which he collected phenomena to explain with his computational models.

During our research meetings on scientific discovery, Herb frequently suggested papers or books that were relevant to our current discussion. These might come from the literatures on cognitive psychology, artificial intelligence, philosophy, or history, and we could never predict in advance from which discipline he would draw. Herb Simon had an incredibly dense semantic network that indexed ideas not by their field of origin, but rather by their relevance to problems that interested him.

Of course, we were able to read only a fraction of the items that he suggested, as we found it difficult to match his pace and scope.

Moreover, Herb Simon's Renaissance scholarship was bi-directional, in that he made his research results accessible to members of the communities on whose earlier ideas he built. Thus, he published his contributions on scientific discovery in the literature on cognitive science (e.g., Qin and Simon 1990), artificial intelligence (e.g., Valdes-Perez, Zytkow, and Simon 1993), and philosophy of science (e.g., Simon, Langley, and Bradshaw 1981), and he kept in touch with historians whose analyses he had used. He also authored works designed to make contact simultaneously with all of these communities (e.g., Langley, Simon, Bradshaw, and Zytkow 1987). In each field, Simon's papers gradually convinced many that discovery was a topic suitable for scientific study, and his work gained a respectable following therein.

Use a Secret Weapon

A third heuristic that appeared in Herb Simon's research was his repeated use of "secret weapons"—methods and metaphors that he had mastered but that were not yet widely available to the broader community. These intellectual tools let him solve problems more rapidly, and with less effort, than most other scientists, and their use accounts, at least partly, for his great research productivity. Herb Simon was quite aware of this strategy, and I have borrowed the epigram "use a secret weapon" directly from his advice to students.

In his research on scientific discovery, Simon drew repeatedly on two frameworks that had been developed at Carnegie Mellon to model cognitive processes in humans. The first was the idea, mentioned earlier, that problem solving involves heuristic search through a problem space. Adopting this view requires one to specify the initial state, operators for generating new states, heuristics for selecting among alternatives, and some halting criterion. The second innovation concerned the use of production systems to model cognition. A production system consists of a long-term memory, stated as a set of condition-action rules, and a short-term memory that contains a set of goals or beliefs. On each cycle, the system matches the conditions of each rule against the contents of short-term memory, selects one or more matching rules, and executes their actions, which change these contents.

Both frameworks suggested mechanisms that we used in our models of scientific discovery, but they also supplied constraints on the systems we developed. They constituted secret weapons because they provided powerful metaphors, along with associated computational techniques, that had not yet been adopted by the research communities in either cognitive psychology or artificial intelligence, although Simon and his colleagues had been using both for some time. Ironically, Herb's secret weapons were never truly secret, in that he was willing to share his metaphors and methods with whoever was willing to adopt them. Over the years, he did much to popularize the notions of problem space search and production systems across different research communities, both in his papers and in his talks, and both in the context of specific models and in more general terms.

Balance Theory and Data

Yet another aspect of Herb Simon's research that we can characterize as a heuristic was his balance between theory and data. He realized that scientific models must explain observations, as this is a major criterion by which one judges their success. But he also understood the need for these models to remain connected with existing knowledge that had previously explained other, equally important, phenomena. When constructing models of cognition, he utilized effectively the constraints imposed by both data and knowledge to guide his efforts.

Herb Simon's work on computational models of scientific discovery exhibited this balance between theory and data. In this case, the phenomena involved episodes from the history of science, ranging from the discovery of descriptive relations, such as Kepler's third law of planetary motion and the chemical behavior of acids and alkalis, to the formation of explanatory models, such as structural models of chemical compounds and biochemical pathways in organisms. These were important events that should be handled by any complete account of the scientific process. At the same time, such an account should be constrained by established knowledge about human cognition, including the heuristic nature of problem solving, and connect to useful theoretical formalisms, such as production systems.

However, although Simon always operated within a clear theoretical framework, he was willing to expand upon and revise it when the need arose. For example, many ideas from our early work on the discovery of numeric equations (like Kepler's law) proved transferable to modeling the construction of qualitative laws (like those about acids and alkalis), but they were less relevant to modeling the formation of structural or process models (like the molecular model of water). In this case, he introduced new state representations and new operators to handle the novel aspects of these problems, though the models were still cast within the broader frameworks of heuristic search and production systems, which were consistent with these discovery phenomena.

Satisfice

One of Herb Simon's central contributions, made well before he delved into either cognitive simulation or artificial intelligence, was the observation that humans seldom find optimal solutions to the problems that confront them. Rather, they *satisfice* by finding solutions that are good enough for their purposes but that they can obtain with the limited cognitive resources they have available. Although developed originally to explain aspects of human decision making, Simon and his colleagues also applied this idea profitably to their development of artificial cognitive systems.

However, Herb Simon treated the notion of satisficing as more than a useful theoretical construct; he also invoked it regularly as a heuristic in his own research. Our initial work on scientific discovery addressed a number of challenging problems, but we also idealized these tasks enough to make them tractable. For instance, we quite consciously focused on episodes from the early history of science, where relatively simple and general methods had sufficed to make important discoveries. Moreover, we deliberately ignored issues of problem formulation, variable selection, design of measuring instruments, and other aspects of scientific reasoning.

These idealizations were a source of continuing criticism of our discovery work for many years, but Herb's response reflected his approach to research. He pointed out that science operates in incremental steps, not by producing completed theories that emerge fully grown from the scientist's brow. Our work, he claimed, constituted progress in that it provided partial computational accounts of scientific phenomena where none had existed before. Nevertheless, he also acknowledged the limits of our idealizations and the need for additional research on this important topic.

On a related note, I have always been something of a perfectionist, which has often led me to take longer in finishing papers than might be desirable. One of Herb's favorite lines was "Anything worth doing is worth doing badly," which he used to encourage me and, I suspect, many others. It took me years to realize that he meant this as more than just practical advice, and that it followed directly from the theory of satisficing and bounded rationality that was the cornerstone of his intellectual career. However, to my knowledge, Herb Simon never wrote a bad paper in his long and productive life. But then many of us have long suspected that his rationality was somewhat less bounded than our own.

Persevere

The gradual nature of science means that major advances seldom occur overnight. For this reason, Herb Simon combined his satisficing strategy with another, complementary, one. His research program involved persevering over extended periods of time, letting him build incrementally on his previous results and extend his models to cover ever more phenomena. He was realistic about the time and energy that true progress in science demands, even when taking advantage of his other heuristics, and he was willing to devote the effort required.

Herb Simon's research on computational models of scientific discovery provides a clear example of such perseverance. Not even counting his early essays on the topic, he worked steadily in this area for well over 20 years. Most of this research involved collaboration with others, but none except Herb had the sheer staying power to continue working actively on the topic throughout this period. The result was a substantial body of results on the nature of scientific discovery, cast in cognitive and computational terms that made clear contact with other knowledge about human behavior.

Moreover, Herb Simon and his colleagues incorporated the notion of perseverance in research to their work on the scientific process itself. Our early efforts had focused on isolated discoveries from the history of science, despite the clear evidence that research often involves a lengthy sequence of interconnected steps. Later, in joint work with Deepak Kulkarni, Simon developed a computational model of extended episodes in science, such as Krebs's discovery of the urea cycle. Their account (Kulkarni and Simon 1988) combined heuristics for designing experiments, formulating qualitative relations, and specifying new problems based on surprising results, all of which are evident in Simon's own career.

One additional benefit of perseverance, less obvious at first glance, is the accumulation of knowledge in the form of domain-specific chunks. This knowledge not only makes the research process itself more effective, but can aid in the communication of results. Herb Simon told a story about sitting down to write a paper and, with little effort, completing the introductory paragraph. But then he noticed the text seemed very familiar. He turned to his filing cabinets and, after some search, uncovered another paper, written over a decade earlier, with nearly the same introduction, word for word. We all acquire chunks from experience but, as usual, Herb did things in a bigger way than most of us.

A Research Challenge

Although Herb Simon is no longer with us, he would certainly have wanted us to carry on the research program he started so many years ago. And despite his many achievements, he would acknowledge that our understanding of scientific discovery remains incomplete, and that we should continue to study this diverse activity and extend our computational models of its operation. In our efforts, we should take advantage of the heuristics he utilized in his own research career, along with any others that aid us in addressing this complex task.

In this context, I will suggest a research problem that would stretch our abilities and shed further light on the nature of science. I propose that we attempt to model the behavior of a scientist who, over the course of his career, formulated the notion of satisficing in human decision making, co-invented list processing and heuristic search on computers, co-developed computational theories of human memory and problem solving, used these theories to model scientific discovery and other key phenomena, and fostered a new field—cognitive science—that knows no discipline boundaries. We have already seen some of this scientist's strategies, and we have detailed records of his many accomplishments. The task of modeling his wide-ranging behavior seems challenging, but that would not have daunted Herb Simon, and, armed with the legacy of his heuristics, we know how to proceed.

References

Kulkarni, D., and Simon, H. A. 1988. The processes of scientific discovery: The strategy of experimentation. *Cognitive Science* 12: 139–176.

Langley, P., Simon, H. A., Bradshaw, G. L., and Zytkow, J. M. 1987. *Scientific Discovery: Computational Explorations of the Creative Processes*. MIT Press.

Newell, A., and Simon, H. A. 1956. The logic theory machine. *IRE Transactions on Information Theory* IT-2: 61–79.

Newell, A., and Simon, H. A. 1972. *Human Problem Solving*. Prentice-Hall.

Popper, K. R. 1961. *The Logic of Scientific Discovery*. Science Editions.

Qin, Y., and Simon, H. A. 1990. Laboratory replication of scientific discovery processes. *Cognitive Science* 14: 281–312.

Simon, H. A. 1966. Scientific discovery and the psychology of problem solving. In R. G. Colodny, ed., *Mind and Cosmos*. University of Pittsburgh Press.

Simon, H. A., Langley, P., and Bradshaw, G. 1981. Scientific discovery as problem solving. *Synthese* 47: 1–27.

Valdes-Perez, R., Zytkow, J. M., and Simon, H. A. 1993. Scientific model-building as search in matrix spaces. In *Proceedings of the Eleventh National Conference on Artificial Intelligence*. AAAI Press.

Herb Simon: A Recollection

Pamela McCorduck

His name was everywhere. He popped up as required reading in under-graduate courses on municipal governance, and in graduate courses on theory of the firm. His books were assigned in courses about admin-istrative behavior, and in courses exploring list-processing computer programming. In the basement of South Hall, a Victorian jumble of bricks which housed the business school at Berkeley in the late 1950s, a snooty young English major, working her way through college by typ-ing course outlines and exams, suspected that the ubiquity of that name meant only one thing. Academically speaking, business was a pretty thin field. After all, you didn't see the same name in every course in English lit.

A year or two later, Ed Feigenbaum and Julian Feldman, two recently hired assistant professors of business, invited me to be their gofer for an anthology they were putting together, *Computers and Thought*, the first book of readings ever about something called artificial intelligence. (I said yes before I knew what the term meant.) There it was again, that ever-present name, Herbert A. Simon. By now I was a bit more respect-ful. By now I'd begun to see that the field wasn't thin, the prodigy was—well, prodigious. Even if I hadn't seen that, the deep respect and affection for their teacher and mentor that Ed and Julian always showed would have convinced me. If this Simon was their demi-god, that was good enough for me.

It was nearly ten more years until I actually met him. My husband, Joseph Traub, had been appointed head of the computer science department at Carnegie-Mellon in 1971, and the department held a welcoming party at Allen and Noël Newell's house one early September evening, with all faculty, their spouses, and the graduate students. I was aware of the stature of many of those people, and was suitably awed.

But Herb Simon—Herb Simon was a different proposition altogether. I'd read some Simon, beginning with the articles he'd written in collaboration with Allen Newell and Cliff Shaw at RAND on early AI problems, and surely by then I'd read *The Sciences of the Artificial*. Thirty years later I can still feel the accelerating pulse, remember the voice that simply stopped in my throat at coming face to face at last with a legend. Some people thought of him, I knew, as remote, overly intellectual, even cold. He could be slashing, they said, if he was crossed. But that evening, Herb grinned his crooked Simonian smile, held out his hand, and I was won completely.

Herb and his wife Dorothea took more interest in me than I had any right to expect, and since my first novel had been published just before we moved to Pittsburgh, they soon arranged a dinner with the city's most eminent writer, the historical novelist Gladys Schmitt. It was a splendid occasion, full of good talk and laughter, and the beginning of many more good talks and much laughter around a congenial table. At these gatherings I learned about Herb's penchant for the outrageous fib. "I never read newspapers," he declared. "It's just a waste of time." True, as far as it went. He and Dorothea subscribed to the *Post-Gazette* so that over the breakfast table, she could read the news and he could read the comics, which he loved. "You can learn just as much about a place in a good library as you can by visiting it," he loved to say. "Travel is just a waste of time." But he and Dorothea were off to China soon after we arrived in Pittsburgh, as part of the first group of Western visitors after Nixon broke the ice. They traveled, and sometimes stayed, in China often after that. Moreover, Herb was an indefatigable missionary on behalf of AI, and dutifully traveled to the remotest, the least interesting and insignificant destinations, if there was a chance of making converts.

A few years after we arrived in Pittsburgh, Joe and I bought a house on Northumberland Street, which, it emerged, was on Herb's route home. My study faced the front garden and sidewalk. I'd see Herb striding purposefully home each late afternoon, slightly hunched, decidedly grim-looking, wearing his beloved black beret if the weather were the least bit cool, or his Peruvian *chu'ulla*, a kind of knit helmet, bright and betasseled, in the snow. By then he'd been making that walk for a quarter-century, a couple of round trips to California, he calculated.

But at my hedge he'd glance sideways; see me at work; grin and wave. If I were just putting the cover on my typewriter, I'd open the front door and invite him in for a sherry. I treasured these hours with him: it was the end of the day for both of us, and grim visage notwithstanding, Herb was always in a fine mood, full of fun (and gossip, which he also claimed to disdain). That walk to and from work was his cud chewing time, he told me, and I recorded his thoughts about it in *Machines Who Think*. "I try to think about things when I'm walking, but I'm a terrible daydreamer. I seldom can keep a coherent line of thought, and going from one block to the next, I go off to thinking about something else. Still, I find the cud chewing just an important part of mental activity for one's research. So I guess an awful lot of cud chewing gets done, but usually in short spurts—you see things on the street, or you think of something else, and there's nothing to get you back in context again. Maybe if I carried a sign in front of me saying *This morning I'm thinking about X*." A pause. A grin. "I'm willing to have my crotchets, but I'd feel a little self-conscious about doing that."

In *Machines Who Think*, I also described the difference between Herb's demeanor when he spoke publicly, which was imposing, always beautifully organized with facts in persuasive abundance (he'd been a high school debater and the uses of rhetoric never left him) and his private conversation. In private he was always soft-spoken and unemphatic, almost shy. Most striking, he insisted on a response: at least a nod or a smile, but best if you spoke up and made it a genuine dialogue. He had a wonderful gift for making you believe that he regarded your mind seriously, and not until you parted did the intellectual glow diminish, did you remember that the Mendelian shuffle had not dealt you brains that came anywhere near his.

One afternoon he said with great gravity: "I simply don't understand English humor. You're an English girl. Can you explain the curate's egg?" I'd never heard of the curate's egg, and so in measured Simonian cadences he told me the old joke, the poor young curate describing his terrible soft-boiled egg to the bishop at breakfast as "excellent in parts." I collapsed. I dissolved. I thought it was priceless. I *was* an English girl; I understood it perfectly but couldn't explain it, even if I'd been able to stop laughing. He finished his sherry, put on his beret, shook his head, and left as puzzled as he'd arrived "I have something to confess," he said another time. Delicious dish on a fellow CMU trustee? A scientific scandal? I leaned forward. "I never outline before I write. I just write, and outline after." He looked at me doubtfully. I burst out laughing. I was a professional writer and never outlined until afterwards either. It seemed to relieve him immensely.

In those sunset hours I was exceptionally fortunate to continue my tutorial in artificial intelligence, a tutorial that had begun with Ed Feigenbaum. Deliberately, perhaps, Herb made sure I felt viscerally what I appreciated intellectually. Once, we were at dinner with Hans Berliner, a chess grandmaster who'd designed one of the most successful chess programs of its time, and Hans and Herb were speculating about other areas AI might succeed at. "Novel-writing?" Hans said wickedly. "Why not?" Herb said deadpan, Herb who loved novels and was the only person in my acquaintance to have read *A la recherche du temps perdu*— in the original—twice. Lots of reasons why not for a long time to come, but I remember that sudden clutch in my soul as an important part of my education in AI.

Perhaps in those late afternoon talks the seed was planted to record the story of early efforts in artificial intelligence, for the conscious decision came about during a summer in 1975 at Stanford, a decision that had Ed Feigenbaum's strong encouragement. When I returned to Pittsburgh that fall and tried the idea out on Herb, he was delighted. What a splendid project! He'd certainly help me. He did help generously (as did other Carnegie faculty, Allen Newell and Raj Reddy), consulting his copious contemporary notes, patiently taking me through not only history, but revealing what he and his colleagues thought they were doing at the time, why they did it, their disappointments, their false starts, their successes, but above all, the grand and glorious exhilaration of those days of the mid 1950s at RAND and at Carnegie, when, in endowing a machine with rudimentary intelligence, they felt they'd stumbled on one of the greatest enterprises science had ever taken up. Once, as he explained the steps in developing the General Problem Solver (done in a matter of weeks), I said, you must hardly have slept. He laughed. "I never slept better in my life."

After interviews were finished and I'd written, I asked him to read a late draft of my history of AI, by then already titled *Machines Who Think*. He wrote meticulous marginalia, again consulting his own notes (others had relied on their none too dependable memories) to make sure issues were clear, and more important, accurately reported. I must have done two or three subsequent drafts of the story of how the Logic Theorist was announced to the world (at an MIT conference) cross-checking with those who were there and who remembered, before each of us was satisfied. Thirty years later, just a few months before he died, he wrote email trying to persuade me to put down the project I was working on and instead revise my old chestnut. "Pamela: Do consider what might be done about bringing *Machines Who Think* back into print. More machines are thinking every day, and I would expect that every one of them would want to buy a copy. Soccer robots alone should account for a first printing."

During the time I was writing *Machines*, I was teaching at the University of Pittsburgh, and over one of those late afternoon sherries, I complained to Herb that although my students sat around discussing the Great Issues, all my colleagues and I ever talked about was the tedious minutiae of academic life. For a moment he said nothing. "When we were at the University of Chicago, Dot and I had a kind of salon on Sunday nights. Everybody knew it was for serious talk, not chitchat. You could do something like that."

Thus was born what I privately called The Squirrel Hill Sages, named after the neighborhood where we all lived. Herb suggested the rules: the group should be small, a topic should be announced in advance, and we'd better not let ourselves get distracted by dinners, or somebody would end up in the kitchen and miss the fun. The group comprised Herb and Dorothea, Allen and Noël Newell, the novelist Mark Harris and his wife Josephine, also a writer, and Joe and me. We began to meet monthly after dinner, and took turns choosing topics.

The topics ranged all over, to suit our fancy. The Newells once proposed we talk about what a civilization should do when it had sufficient surplus: was building pyramids (or their twentieth-century equivalent) a good idea? Had we Americans arrived at that point? If so, what should our pyramids be? We examined the Two Cultures problem, a juicy bone for a group that straddled the two (or as Allen Newell insisted, the many) cultures. I'd been much taken with Robert Pirsig's *Zen and the Art of Motorcycle Maintenance*, and one night proposed we talk about the concept of *arête*, which translates roughly as "excellence."

One occasion stands out, however. At the Harrises' one evening, the topic was "criticism." We'd all been subject to it, beginning with our parents, peers and teachers; some of us in the group had dealt with professional critics who took on, in public, our published work. It was a fraught subject, and we did some thrashing until Herb, in his typical way, cut straight to the heart of the matter. He began with an elegant distinction between criticism as appreciation of a work, and criticism as an evaluation of it. He admitted that, for his part, he'd seen plenty of both. Even if it hurt, the fair criticism was helpful, he claimed; the unfair criticism was inevitable and not worth bothering about. We took this up and more, offering personal experiences, some funny, some painful. I began to sense that Herb too was as engaged emotionally as he was intellectually.

Curious, I asked him. "Who do you write for?"

He was quiet for a moment. "Not many people, really. Maybe ten, fifteen people at the most."

"Who?" I persisted.

"They're not all living."

"Who?"

The room was still. We sensed we'd somehow penetrated to an essential part of Herb, were about to behold a revelation. A strange look came over his face, part sheepish smile, part struggle to confess. "Well. Aristotle, for one." Then he roared with laughter, that we shouldn't take him seriously, and that of course we must.

When, at the end of the 1970s, Joe and I left Pittsburgh, the Squirrel Hill Sages disbanded. I kept in touch with Herb for many reasons, and after he won the Nobel Prize, I proposed to write his biography. At first he demurred, but eventually he agreed. With a contract from Columbia University Press, I began the research. I came across references to his work in Robert Venturi's *Complexity and Contradiction in Architecture*. In a chance conversation, George Cowan, the founding director of the Santa Fe Institute, told me how much Herb's metaphor of a clock made up of simple parts that produces complex behavior had clarified and influenced his own beginning thoughts about complexity.

The scholarly issues were clear enough. Herb himself was known to say that everything he did was a kind of gloss on that evergreen idea of his called bounded rationality. The facts of the life were also clear. I sat up on the top floor of the Simons' house going through old documents and photograph albums (the breathtaking beauty of the 22-year-old Dorothea! No wonder he fell in love at first sight). I was guided by Herb or left alone by him, as I wished.

But something was amiss. After a few months of work, it came to me that a biographer has many purposes, and among them (as Herb had once said of criticism) is evaluation as well as appreciation. I only wanted to write a valentine. I felt too close, too admiring, to write anything else.

Somehow I let Herb know I was backing out. I returned the advance the Columbia University Press had given me (and was so upset I forget to tell the IRS, so still paid income tax on it). Herb was very gracious, only teasing me now and then with a mock grumpy, "If you won't write it, I suppose I'll have to write it myself." Which he did. The draft arrived a few years later, and when I read it, I was glad I'd been wise enough to leave the project to him.

References

Feigenbaum, Edward A., and Julian Feldman. 1961. *Computers and Thought*. McGraw-Hill.

McCorduck, Pamela. 1979. *Machines Who Think*. Freeman.

Simon, Herbert A. 1969. *The Sciences of the Artificial*. MIT Press.

Venturi, Robert. 1966, 1977. *Complexity and Contradiction in Architecture*. Museum of Modern Art.

Letter to Herb Simon

George Miller

Dear Herb,

News of your death hit me hard. You have so long been a fixture in my intellectual world that it seemed a part of me died with you. Then a letter from March and Augier offered a chance to enjoy that intellectual world a little longer.

I don't think I ever thanked you for your contributions to psychology. American psychologists today, even experimental psychologists, don't believe me when I describe our field before World War II. You were an enormous help in what I like to call the cognitive counter-revolution—the re-introduction of mental processes into psychology. And even after you won a Nobel you continued to call yourself, among other things, a psychologist. And to publish in psychological journals. You shed your respectability over the whole field. You must have known I was grateful. I hope so. But I should have told you.

Why do I remember best our arguments? Perhaps because you taught me that two friends could disagree violently, could shout at each other, and still be friends. I can't recall winning an argument with you, not one that mattered, even when I was right. Your absurd ideas about Zipf's Law, for example—you simply would not concede that it is only a random process. Nobody won that one. We just quit talking about it.

Sometimes we fought toe to toe, sometimes shoulder to shoulder. The matter of simulation, for example. In 1958 you got me excited about simulating cognitive processes because I thought a good simulation had a chance to become a good neurophysiological theory some day. Of course, a good simulation had to make the same kind of mistakes that people make. AI was our enemy. They saw no point in writing programs to make mistakes.

I recall a breakfast at the Cosmos Club in 1964, I think, when you tried to tell me about a chess-playing program. How well does it work, I asked. Fine, you said. Have you written a program to play chess that way? No, not yet. Then how do you know it works? Oh, you said, I use it when I play chess and it works very well, better than when I don't use it. Is that simulation? Sure. Breakfast ended while I was still trying to visualize you simulating yourself simulating yourself playing chess. What a brain!

Eventually you and George Baylor did write that program. It looked for forced-mating combinations. At the time you took its speed in finding such combinations as "a tribute to the advantages of selectivity over machine brute force." I liked that. It meant simulation was still alive and well and living in Pittsburgh.

But in the long run, of course, machine brute force won out. Your famous prediction about chess-playing machines did come true, although not until Big Blue had the raw power to compute everything. So much for simulation. I thought we lost that argument. But you still deserve credit for a bold prediction.

I'm glad I knew you. I was lucky you were willing to argue with me. And I am going to miss you terribly.

Sincerely,
George A. Miller

Herbert Simon, David Hume, and the Science of Man: Some Philosophical Implications of Models

Joseph C. Pitt

In the preface to his 1957 collection of essays *Models of Man*, Herbert Simon discusses his objective in collecting these particular essays together:

For when these essays are viewed in juxtaposition, it can be seen that all of them are concerned with laying foundations for a science of man that will accommodate comfortably his dual nature as a social and rational animal. (p. vii)

The papers concern a variety of fields: political science, social psychology, sociology, statistics, logic, learning theory, and more. It is in the orientation from first one social science and then another that we see the sense in which these papers present *models* of man. There is the model that deals with issues in political science, the model that deals with issues in psychology, the model that deals with issues is sociology, etc. Simon goes on to say that he has resisted any attempt to rewrite these papers, turning them into a systematic treatise, because he wants readers from different fields to be able to relate to them in their own way. That comment points to two different but equally interesting observations: (1) the variety of possible models of man suggest a variable object of analysis that, like a chameleon, takes on the coloring of the closest object, in this case, the color of the field of analysis and (2) the difficulty of articulating a genuine and unified science of man.

The variable character of human beings has been noted for some time. It is, in part, the source of philosophical reflection, poetic inspiration, and sometimes total frustration. What are we? Why is it so difficult to pin us down? And despite his desire to lay the foundation for a science of man, even Simon is forced to settle for something that allows for our dual nature, as social and rational. This suggests that he therefore will need at least two models, not one. But one model is what a science of man calls for. For if there are two, questions will remain. There is, for example, the problem of hierarchy, for surely both models cannot provide an equally valid explanatory framework. How, for example, would you determine when one model is more appropriate than the other? In addition to the two models we would require a decision procedure for when to apply one or the other. But to produce such a decision procedure we must already know the nature of man, thereby begging the question.

In his concern to construct a science of man, Simon is in good company. The eighteenth-century Scottish philosopher David Hume had that same goal in his *Treatise of Human Nature* (1743). Hume was primarily concerned with what he called moral philosophy, which in the eighteenth century did not mean what it means today. "Moral Philosophy" encompassed all the social sciences, including politics, morality, economics, and political theory. Hume (1743, p. xix) saw them all dependent on our understanding of the kind of creature man is:

'Tis evident, that all the sciences have a relation, greater or less, to human nature; and that however wide any of them may seem to run from it, they still return back by one passage or another. Even Mathematics, Natural Philosophy, and Natural Religion, are in some measure dependent on the science of Man; since they lie under the cognizance of men, and are judged by their powers and their faculties.

Like Simon, Hume also saw that same dual nature of man, only for him the two sides were represented by the rational and the passionate or natural. Unlike Simon, Hume saw that one of two sides had to be primary. Interestingly, he did not see the duality of man in conflict.

But, contrary to what one would expect from the greatest philosopher of the Enlightenment, Hume (ibid., p. 413) placed the passions in the primary role, not reason:

> Nothing is more usual in philosophy, and even in common life, than to talk of the combat of passions and reason, to give the preference to reason, and to assert that men are only so far virtuous as they conform themselves to its dictates. Every rational creature, 'tis said. Is oblig'd to regulate his actions by reason; and if other motive or principle challenge the direction of his conduct, he ought to oppose it, 'till it be entirely subdu'd, or at least brought to a conformity with that superior principle.... In order to shew the fallacy of all this philosophy, I shall endeavour to prove first, that reason alone can never be a motive to any action of the will; and secondly, that it can never oppose passion in the direction of the will.

In his proof, Hume first analyzes the two main operations of reason: giving deductive proofs, and reasoning from cause and effect. He argues that giving a deductive proof in and of itself provides no motivation to act. The relation between reason and action is a standard problem for all theories of action even today. From the fact that one has reasoned well to a conclusion such as "One ought to do X" nothing follows with respect to how it comes to be the case that one in fact does X. In fact, this may be the major problem for philosophy—what is the connection between reason and action? The Enlightenment enthusiasm for the powers of reason is not enough to overcome this logical divide.

When Hume turns to cause and effect, he quickly rehearses the results of his famous attack on causation in Book 1. Since all knowledge is formed from judgments relating ideas derived from direct experience, and since we never directly experience a cause as such, we have no knowledge of cause and effect, only of constant conjunction. Hence we cannot be motivated to act on the basis of cause-and-effect knowledge:

> Since reason alone can never produce any action, or give rise to volition, I infer, that the same faculty is as incapable of preventing volition, or of disputing the preference with any passion or emotion.... But if reason has no original influence, 'tis impossible it can withstand any principle, which has such an efficacy,.... (ibid., pp. 414–415)

Hume concludes that "reason is and ought only to be the slave of the passions, and can never pretend to any other office than to serve and obey them" (ibid., p. 415). It therefore follows that there is no conflict between reason and the passions.

Herbert Simon did not have Hume's inclination toward the superior role of the passions in mind when he spoke of the dual nature of man. Despite his aversion to universal models of rational decision making, he had more than a certain fondness for rationality, especially bounded rationality. Simon (1957, p. 1) also thought that Humean-like theories were "inadequate for predicting and explaining human behavior in organizations." Simon (ibid.) sees it this way: "What is required for organization theory—and more broadly, for a workable 'theory of action'—is a framework that makes appropriate provision for both rational and non-rational aspects of human behavior." I want to look closely at Simon's proposed solution to the problem dealing with both the rational and the non-rational, concentrating on these early papers because they have a freshness to them even today, almost fifty years after they were written. I will not presume to extend my conclusions to his later work at this time. Herbert Simon was a towering intellect. Like all towering intellects he never ceased growing. It is, thus, unfair to impose on the body of his work the illusion of a stultifying sameness.

What Is a Model?

There is a vast literature on models. It is to be found in many disciplines: philosophy, economics, statistics, mathematics, physics, biology, and the list goes on. Only one thing can be gleaned from that literature—there is no agreement on what constitutes a model or what role it should play in our investigations. Thus, we can ask:

1. Is a model normative or descriptive?

2. Is a model an abstraction?

3. Is a model an idealization?

4. Are models representations of reality or merely instrumental?

5. Must a model be expressed in the language of mathematics?

6. Etc.

And, given the range of questions, one can expect as many answers as there are researchers.

Hume did not talk about models—although it might have helped him make his case, or at least explicate his strategy in Book 1 of his *Treatise*. Here is what I have in mind. Following Simon's strategy in *Models of Man*, where the models he develops represent various disciplinary concerns, Hume could have avoided some confusion by explaining that he was offering two models of how the mind works in Book 1. The first is a philosophical model based on the then-popular "theory of ideas." The second is a psychological model for which he was primarily responsible. Hume's famous skepticism was directed at the philosophical model. It fails to provide us with an account of how we can have knowledge of the world. Nevertheless we do think we know certain things and we generally are reasonably successful in making our way around. How the mind works so as to make this success possible is accounted for by the psychological model. Using Simon's multiple model approach Hume could have avoided the charge of extreme skepticism and also be credited with offering a positive account as well. This is not the place to work this out, but it is but one example of how using multiple models could be very useful. Now back to Simon.

The first question we need to answer for Simon is "What does he mean by 'model' in *Models of Man*?" It turns out that he doesn't offer one. He gives a formal definition of a linear model that is dependent on an assumed understanding of what a model is. But that doesn't help. However, we can find a definition of sorts if we look elsewhere. In a 1956 paper co-authored with Allen Newell, "Models: Their uses and limitations,"[1] Simon claims that "in contemporary usage, the term 'model' is, I think, simply a synonym for 'theory'." He goes on shortly thereafter to amplify slightly by noting that a model is a "mathematical theory." He considers mathematics a language and the one best suited to the sciences as it avoids ambiguities and permits the most precise explication of the concepts and claims of scientific theories.

Theories have content:

> By the content (or total content) of a theory I shall mean the totality of the empirical statements that the theory makes, explicitly or implicitly, about the real world phenomena to which it refers. That is, the content of a theory is comprised of all the assertions about the world, whether true or not, that are explicitly stated by the theory or that can logically be inferred from the statements of theory.

We now have four things:

i. a mathematical model that is a theory

ii. the content of the theory

iii. real-world phenomena

iv. the relation of "about" between the theory and the world.

Simon continues:

> Consider now some body of phenomena, and imagine that there is a theory that tells the truth, the whole truth, and nothing but the truth about these phenomena. By this I mean that any statement that is true of the phenomena is stated in or derivable from the theory; and that any factual statement contained in or derivable from the theory is true of the phenomena. Then we may define the content of the body of the phenomena as identical with the total content of this particular theory.

In short, imagine a situation in which we have a theory that completely accounts for a domain of phenomena and all its actual and possible statements about those phenomena are true. We would then have a true theory about the world. But, says Simon,

> the particular theory I have just mentioned is, or course, non-existent for any actual body of phenomena. The theories that actually occur do not have the same content as the phenomena to which they refer. They do not tell the truth—or at least they do not tell the whole truth and nothing but the truth.

Thus, Simon has effectively concluded that it is not possible to have a true theory about the world—either theories say too little, in which case their content is not co-extensive with theory world, or they say too much, in which case they say false things. But he does allow us to compare theories, provided they refer to the same phenomena, or provided we can set up a correspondence between their variables. What comes next is interesting:

If two theories have the same variables (or variables that can be put in one-to-one correspondence), and if the first tells nothing but the truth, but not the whole truth, about the second, then we will call the first a simplification of the second.

The reason it is interesting is that here Simon moves to a meta-level. We can now add a fifth and a sixth item to Simon's account of a model:

v. Theories can say true and false things about the world.

vi. Simplification of a model by another model yields only true statements about another model.

This leaves us in a very interesting situation. First, we can have an ascending order of simplifications, leaving us with a model with only one variable at the end of the series. Second, truth is not exclusively a property of the relation of "about" between theory and real-world phenomena, now it is also a property of the simplification of a model. Finally, we cannot have an exhaustively true theory about a domain of phenomena. We conclude that, logically speaking, for Simon it is not possible to have a true theory/model/science of man. Let us consider some of this in greater detail.

According to Simon, if a model, B, is a simplification of another model, A, it tells the truth but not the whole truth about A. This appears to me to be a difficult move to make because, despite what Simon says, model B is not about model A. Simon initiates his discussion here by establishing a correlation between the *variables* of the two theories. For Simon the relation between A and B is this: B contains a subset of the true claims of A. B is not about A; it is about the world, since the variables of A are about the world, in some sense of "about," only less of the world than is described by A. Thus the ascending order of simplifications is not an ascending order of models about models, it is an ascending order in which less and less of the content of the models is about the world until the final model says only one true thing about the world. This does make more sense since the simplification of a theory is generally conceived to be a reduction in its content or a reduction in the number of fundamental axioms.

But it is troubling because there is no constraint on which variables to reduce. Not all truths about the world are equally important. More importantly, just because two variables are correlated, it does not follow that they designate the same thing.

The problem is a function of what the variables are supposed to point to in the world. (Here I would direct the reader to Quine's (1953) discussion of underdetermination in chapter 2.) Another way to put this is to note that simplifications contain fewer truths. But, variables are not true or false. For a variable to carry a truth value it has to be interpreted; it has to obtain a meaning. The meanings of variables in theories are determined by the way in which they are used in a theory. Their meanings are contextualized. Another way to put this is as follows: The meaning of a variable is a function of the number of possible inferences in which it can play a role. If you simplify the theory, you reduce the number of possible inferences, hence you change the meaning.

Another unhappy consequence of the realization that the meanings of the terms of a model are a function of the way they are used in the model is that it makes it impossible for Simon to use the variety of models he delineates in *Models of Man* to give us a science of man. The point follows naturally. If the meanings of the terms of the model are contextually defined, then it cannot be shown that each model is about the same thing in the world without begging the question.

The even more troubling point is that Simon appears to have ruled out of court from the start the possibility of a unified theory of man. This conclusion derives from his claim that there are no theories in which the content exhaustively maps one on one onto the phenomena. This is not the weaker claim that every theory is restricted in the number of variables it can manipulate. It is the stronger claim that no theories completely map the phenomena in their domain. Although asserted as a description of what is alleged to be the case, the suggestion is that not only is it now the case, but it must always be the case. Since no theory can exhaustively map onto its phenomena, no complete theory of man is possible. But no explanation is given for the bald assertion that no theory can exhaustively map onto its phenomena.

To overcome this *a priori* restriction of the content of a theory we need to do two things. First, we need to look into further Simon's view of the dual nature of man. Second, we need to examine the plausibility of Simon's claim that no theory completely maps onto its domain.

The Dual Nature of Man

It is unfortunate that Simon gives no defense of his claim that man has this dual nature. In the introduction to *Models of Man* it is taken as a premise. If there is a defense, it comes in the form of Simon's taxonomy of theories of human nature (1957, p. 1):

Theories of human behavior tend to go to one or another extremes in their treatments of rationality. At the one extreme we have theories, advanced principally by economists, that attribute to man a high degree of rationality in his behavior. At the other extreme we have theories, chiefly psychological, that are preoccupied with motivations, emotions, and other aspects of affect in human behavior; and theories, sociological and anthropological, that seek to explain human behavior in terms of the culture in which it is embedded.

As Simon notes, these are extremes. Their main fault lies in their inability to explain and predict "human behavior in organizations." He continues:

What is required for organizational theory—and more broadly, for a workable "theory of action"—is a framework that makes appropriate provision for both rational and non-rational aspects of human behavior."

So the duality is built into the analysis. Man's dual nature is a given. But is Simon's duality the only way to go? He has parsed the various theories of human behavior this way, but can they be restructured so as to avoid the duality? Or, if they cannot, is there perhaps something wrong with the initial categories? I believe there is and it falls in the category of rationality.

One of the most seductive parts of Simon's view on rationality is his insistence of its contextualized nature. Because organizations form the foundations for contemporary social and economic structure, his question is "what does it take to be rational in an organization?" Once framed in that way, the answer seems clear: find out what the organizational goals are and act so as to maximize those goals while minimizing your own losses. Your rational maximizing behavior is bounded by the goals and values of the organization in which you have chosen to work. That is a crude account, but it will suffice for now. Two key points: First, rationality remains a property of an individual. Second, individuals are always restricted in their actions by the circumstances in which they find themselves. If those circumstances are membership in an organization, some of the parameters are more readily acted upon than others. This picture makes sense—up to a point.

Simon's account places him squarely in the Western tradition in which man's most prized attribute is his rationality. For millennia thinkers have been obsessed by this idea: that man is rational. But what does it mean to say that man is rational? The primary effort has been to isolate those universal features of human reasoning that capture this unique property of rationality. For Kant, it was rational to act in accord with one's duty. But most of the rest of the West saw rational thought as somehow tied to systematically achieving one's goals. As the tradition matured and as the theory of rationality has been appropriated by economics, political economy, etc. there has been a bit of slippage between two intertwined notions: reason and rationality. And, to be blunt, from the fact that man can *reason* it does not follow that man is *rational*, if we mean by rational something akin to what is proposed in economic theories of rationality, even bounded theories of rationality. Let us call these the *Homo economicus* models. Man the economic creature—man the maximizer, however constrained.

The problem is this: All the maximizing theories of rationality and their variations, i.e., theories about what it is to decide rationality, have two things in common: (1) They assume that man is rational—what this means needs exploration. (2) They assume that to be rational one must succeed. To put it another way: If one is rational, one will succeed. Being rational and being successful are taken as synonymous. But surely, one can be rational and fail. Let's pursue this thought for a moment.

Very simply, it ought to be the case that one can reason through a situation very well and still fail to achieve one's goals none-the-less. The fact that one is reasoning well does not mean one will succeed. The slip from (1) having the capacity to reason to (2) the twin state of being rational and being successful has the inherent problem of explaining failure. We know the standard moves here: one appeals to having incorrect information, to unforeseen catastrophes, to possessing the wrong value structure, to projecting unrealistic goals, etc. But the need for these so-called explanations comes from the fact that, as Simon himself puts it (1957, p. 3), theories "very much in the general tradition of economics, require of rational man powers of prescience and capacities for computation resembling those we usually attribute to God." Taking "seriously the limits of human capacity for calculation" leads him to his own account, which effectively reduces the number and variety of variables.

Even here Simon recognizes the limits of rational man. But to speak of rational man is already to infer from the fact that man can reason that man is rational. However, I would suggest, these are two different things. That man has the capacity to reason does not entail that he is rational in any important sense. And surely there is something odd about speaking of the *limits* of rational man. It might be the case that man could be deemed to have done a *rational thing* if he followed one or another model of rationality, for it is individual acts of reason that can be anointed "rational," but surely not the species *Homo sapiens*, especially in the light of so much irrationality on its part.

My frustration comes in several stages: first, to speak of rational man as opposed to something else is to already accord to human beings something that may not be possible, i.e., rationality. It is, on the one hand, one thing to say of human beings that they have a property, i.e., being rational, and, on the other hand, to say they only have that property when they act in certain ways, i.e., as maximizers. Second, in fact human beings are not rational, under any definition, all the time. Third, because humans are not rational all the time, to speak of the dual nature of man as rational and social creates a false dichotomy, either we are one or the other. But what if we are neither and both?

In *Thinking about Technology* I addressed this problem to a certain degree, urging that we consider a different approach. I proposed that we start, if you will, at the other end. That is, that we take our clue from an example of an irrational decision. Here is a pretty clear cut case of irrationality: you make a decision to do A, assuming that in doing A you will achieve goal X. You do A and you fail. You then continue to repeat yourself, making no modifications in your assumptions, in your value structure, etc. and you continue to fail. That is one example of acting irrationally.

What would it take to act rationally in those circumstances? What if you reassessed your assumptions and decided that what you thought you knew to be the case wasn't, then, having adjusted your assumption in the light of that reconsideration, you try again, and fail again. The failure isn't the important point, the readjustment is. Consider a third attempt. This third time you adjust something else and try again and this time you succeed. The act of reconsidering your assumptions, your knowledge base, factoring in what you learned from your failure and readjusting the parameters in that light, is the very mark of acting rationally. Further, this method of reconsidering what you thought you knew, your values, your goals, your fears, your desires, is how we account for not being omniscient—not being God-like in our powers of computation. I call it using common sense, and it is the basis for what I call the *common sense principle of rationality* (CPR), which states "Learn from experience."

Note, you can learn from experience and still fail to achieve your goal. After all, your goal might be crazy. Consider: what if you desired to fly, not in a plane, but like Icarus. So you manufacture some wings, using all the information at your hands on bird wing structure. When completed you get on the roof of your house, flap your wings madly and jump, fall, and break an arm. So, having failed, apply CPR, readjust in the light of the experience and try again, and again, and again. Given that bones take time to heal, you have the opportunity to contemplate what has gone wrong as you recuperate and you decide that maybe the goal is what is wrong—see: learn from experience. Take up bike riding.

The main difference in the approach I am urging is that, unlike the *Homo economicus* view, being rational involves a complicated process involving knowledge, values, goals, assessment procedures, and a feed back loop—all that without a guarantee of success. Moreover, making rational decisions only occurs on specific occasions under specific circumstances. One is not rational when asleep, or when driving a car. On my account, being rational involves steps that allow for analysis, but which in practice are often not noted. The resulting picture of the individual is, in effect, a blend of the social, the animal, and the reasoning parts of human beings to form a whole. The emphasis here is on the process—to the extent that people are rational, the person is rational in this instance if, when a decision is called for, he or she engages in this process. And if, after engaging in this process, he or she fails, they are irrational only if they fail to learn from their failure. That they have learned from the experience is manifested in their behavior. Furthermore, when not engaged in making decisions, the person is not being rational, but more importantly, he or she is not being irrational. Rationality is a property of acts or decisions, not people *tout court*.

Using CPR as an account of rationality has the following advantages—it does not from the start assume that man is rational or not. It says nothing about the appropriateness of values and goals. And it does not assume that one acts either rationally or socially—but, rather, I claim that these factors are all involved in any decision making.

Consider the other pole of the dichotomy: the social. If there is truly a dual nature to man, one would assume, Jeckyll-and-Hyde-like, one is one or the other at any given time. But what would it mean to be social and not rational? We have placed all our emphasis on what it is to be rational—but what does it mean to be social *simpliciter*? I do not think it means acting as an unthinking beast. I happen to own some beasts and they are very much thinking when being social. It is always fascinating for me to watch any two of my wolfhounds at play—they chase each other round and round in a very sophisticated came of tag and in that game they are very calculating as to what to do next to head the other off and catch him. In play, and what could be more social than play, they are very much thinking things. In the human arena, one is not "merely" social—I don't even know what that means, to be *merely* social. For in social circumstances one is engaging other human beings and one is thinking about what to say or how to behave, even as one is trying to disengage, perhaps. For this reason and for other reasons, I want to urge the view that we are neither rational nor social, but human. In being human we act and we interact with other human beings, with nature, and our built environment. How we respond in these situations is a function of a variety of things, all of which we possess, but by none of which are we permanently tainted. They include, reason, desires, goals, values, knowledge, needs, and the capacity for reevaluation and readjusting our perspective. We do not employ all of these features at once, nor is having one or another taken singly or in pairs the mark of being human. It is the whole, taken in snap shots, that gives us the final picture.

I have been arguing that to have a science of man we have to conceive of man as one thing and not as even two parts of one thing. One cannot be social without employing reason. To do otherwise would be to reduce man to some kind of beast at the very bottom of the great chain of being—for any social beast reasons (not insects—for I doubt the attribution of sociality to insects, despite the fact that their behavior appears to be structured). One also employs reason in a social context—no one is isolated from the world. So the assumption of a dual nature for man seems to be wrong-headed. How did Simon get there? I think innocently enough. It is apparent that Simon wanted to concentrate on the rational dimension of human activity and to do so he had to differentiate it from something else, let's call it the social. The mistake was to reify the two domains.

Final Theories

The final problem I wish to address is the possibility of developing a model that completely captures its domain. This is the sort of complete theory Simon thinks is impossible. In this I think he is right.

The issue here concerns the nature of the growth of knowledge. The problem is threefold, at least. First, to assume that a theory or a model can completely capture its domain we must assume that the entities and processes of nature the theory is about, in some sense of "about," are static. That is, we must assume that nature is not continually changing—which it is. Even if we could map a domain completely today, there is no reason to assume the domain will remain the same tomorrow, therefore, whatever truth can be claimed for the theory is useless as soon as it is completed. Second, there is the problem of securing the domain. That is, how does one know what the domain is without trivializing it? If one narrows the domain too much, one will necessarily exclude relevant factors. If one expands the domain to try and take account of all possible factors, one runs into Simon's omniscience problem. Third, the key concepts we employ around theories are in constant flux. The key concepts I have in mind are such things as the nature of evidence, the relation between theories and their evidence, explanation and prediction, observation, etc. One uses a theory to offer explanations and to make predictions, but what counts as an explanation changes. In the pre-Copernican world, Aristotelian explanations often referred to the intrinsic nature of things. Today we demand some subsumption of individual events under generalities and laws of nature. What counts as a legitimate prediction also changes. Prophesies were once considered predictions. Today, in a scientific context, they are not. Likewise, what counts as an observation changes, and what counts as an experiment or a test, etc. The point here is this: even if one had a theory that completely accounted for a domain, how one used that theory would vary depending on what one understood these meta-level concepts to mean. And surely the use of a theory is part of its meaning and significance.

These factors all impinge on the quest for a general science of man. If the objective of a science of man is to develop a model/theory that completely captures the domain, then look at the problem we face: is the thing we call man static or changing? I have argued elsewhere that we are own best technology. If you buy the definition of technology I offer in *Thinking about Technology*, where technology is defined as Humanity at Work, humanity is our own best example of a technology. We have created what we are by selective breeding, and we are continuing to modify the result, the next step comes out of the human genome project. To look for a final theory of man is to assume we are some static thing, when in fact we are a constantly changing phenomenon. Moreover, the issue here goes beyond the biological. What we mean when we talk of the human is also changing—and it changes as our capacities change, and our capacities change as our technologies change—opening new doors and presenting new possibilities.

So, the domain is changing, the problem of what to include as human is underdetermined, and the concepts we use to characterize the objects of the domain are in flux. Where does that leave us? It leaves us in the same position as any other science. For this is true of all the sciences.

The science of man is in no better or worse shape as far as its possibility goes than physics. But unlike physics, we have yet to figure out what we want from our science of man. The objective of physics is a systematic explanation of how the physical universe works. Is that what we want from a science of man, i.e., a systematic explanation of how human beings work? I don't think Herbert Simon really wanted that kind of a science of man. He wanted a science of the rational and that is fine. We should not, however, confuse the science of the rational with a science of man. Hume, on the other hand, wanted a science of man that would tell him what motivates people to act as they do, for he was first and foremost a political theorist and the control of man is at the heart of that enterprise.

In closing I would like to examine the proposition that we already have a science of man and that it is the domain of philosophy. The various sub-fields of philosophy all deal with different aspects of the human enterprise, all under the guise of trying to make sense of man in the world. The history of philosophy is the history of our attempts to make sense of man in the world. Logic is the science of reasoning, metaphysics is the science of making sense of the real, epistemology is the science of knowing, etc. The subject matter is always some aspect of human interaction with the world and our reaction to that exchange. What philosophy does not give us as a science of man is the ability to predict with accuracy what human being will do in the future. But in this respect philosophy is no worse off than those sciences that deal with less global issues, sciences such as economics, sociology, political science, i.e., all the other sciences of man. They are all very bad at prediction. But not all the physical sciences have good records with respect to prediction either, e.g. atmospherics. One major flaw in this account is that philosophy is a normative activity. Except for the history of philosophy, it is primarily concerned with how we *ought* to consider these various dimensions of human activity. But then again, in this respect it is no different from physics that deals with idealizations of physical phenomena. The constructs for physics are not real—they are created in a framework of perfect interactions.

Where does this leave us? May I suggest that if we want a science of man other than philosophy, then we need to ask ourselves what else we want from it. What, for example, ought its subject matter to be beyond questions of who we ought to be in the contexts in which we find ourselves? I would appreciate an answer.

Note

1. I thank Mie Augier for bringing this paper to my attention.

References

Hume, D. 1743. *A Treatise of Human Nature*. Oxford University Press.

Pitt, Joseph C. 2000. *Thinking about Technology*. Seven Bridges Press.

Quine, W. V. O. 1953. *Word and Object*. MIT Press.

Simon, H. 1956. "Models: Their uses and limitations." In *The State of the Social Sciences*, ed. L. White. University of Chicago Press.

Simon, H. 1957. *Models of Man*. Wiley.

Markets as Artifacts: Aggregate Efficiency from Zero-Intelligence Traders

Shyam Sunder

... the possibility of building a mathematical theory of a system or of simulating that system does not depend on having an adequate microtheory of the natural laws that govern the system components. Such a microtheory might indeed be simply irrelevant.
—Herbert A. Simon, *The Sciences of the Artificial*

Three phenomena—the disparity between the assumed and observed attributes of economic man, the link between nature and artifacts, and the use of computers as a source of knowledge—fascinated Herbert A. Simon. He built a new paradigm for each field—bounded rationality to deal with the disparity, the science of the artificial as its link to nature, and artificial intelligence for the creation of knowledge. In this chapter we show that the sciences of the artificial and computer intelligence also hold the key to an understanding of the disparity between individual behavior and market outcomes. When seen as human artifacts, a science of markets need not be built from the science of individual behavior. We outline how, in the 1990s, computer simulations enabled us to discover that allocative efficiency—an important characteristic of market outcomes—is largely independent of variations in individual behavior under classical conditions. The science of the artificial suggests such independence and points to its benefits:

This skyhook-skyscraper construction of science from the roof down to the yet unconstructed foundations was possible because the behavior of the system at each level depended on only a very approximate, simplified, abstracted characterization of the system at the level next beneath. This is lucky, else the safety of bridges and airplanes might depend on the correctness of the "Eightfold Way" of looking at elementary particles.   (Simon 1996, p. 16)

Substantive and Procedural Rationality

In 1935, Simon faced the problem of understanding the allocation of the city budget between maintenance by the parks department and programs run by the public schools in Milwaukee. He could not see how the marginal benefits of two activities could be assessed, and how these incommensurables might be compared, much less equalized, according to the prescriptions of neoclassical economics (Larkey 2002). Economics assumes that agents choose the options they prefer most from their opportunity sets, and thus requires that they know the opportunity set at the time they choose. Simple algebra leads to the equalization of the marginal benefits as a logical consequence of this process.

Simon used "substantive rationality" as the label for such behavior. It is not clear how an individual is to achieve substantive rationality without knowing his opportunity set. What could the agent do when he knows but one option, and must search further—an economic decision in itself—to generate more options? Simon postulated that an agent starts out with an initial level of aspiration about his welfare and is willing to accept an option that satisfies him by attaining this level. Acceptance of an option concludes the search; rejection leads to lowered aspirations, search for another option, and application of the same stopping rule. Simon (1978) called this process "procedural rationality."

Field and laboratory observations support the descriptive validity of procedural over substantive rationality in human agents. They are rational in the sense of choosing what is best, but only boundedly so in the sense of choosing from a limited opportunity set in relation to their aspiration level. Yet economics routinely assumes that individuals choose from their opportunity sets to maximize their welfare, not merely to satisfy their aspirations. This is true not only of the elegant neoclassical foundations in general-equilibrium theory, but also of applications in the theory of money, industrial organization, trade, labor, etc. Why build these theories from demonstrably false assumptions about agent behavior?

The positivist answer to such a question is that the descriptive validity of the model is not relevant as long as the model predicts well (Friedman 1953). Such answers are unsatisfactory because our models serve not only to predict but also to articulate our understanding of various phenomena, and to convey that understanding to others. The understanding of phenomenon is crucial to science; prediction without understanding does not build science. We show that the sciences of the artificial point to a better answer.

The Sciences of the Artificial

Artifacts comprise elements, each with its own inherent properties, governed by natural law. A boat has timber; a shirt has cotton or wool fiber; and a shoe has leather, along with other elements; which may be artifacts themselves. In natural sciences we analyze the elements of interest; in sciences of the artificial we synthesize artifacts from elements to attain goals or perform functions. In science, natural things simply are; it is not meaningful to ask how they ought to be. Of the artifacts, we can ask both how they are and how they ought to be.

Natural law governs the inner and the outer environments of artifacts, as well as the interface between the two (figure 1). The presence of the goal or intent of its creator or user distinguishes an artifact from nature. How well an artifact fulfills these goals depends on the interface between the two environments.

A twig lying under a tree becomes an artifact when a chimpanzee picks it up and inserts it into a termite hill to extract food. Titanium alloy created to meet the performance demands of supersonic aircraft

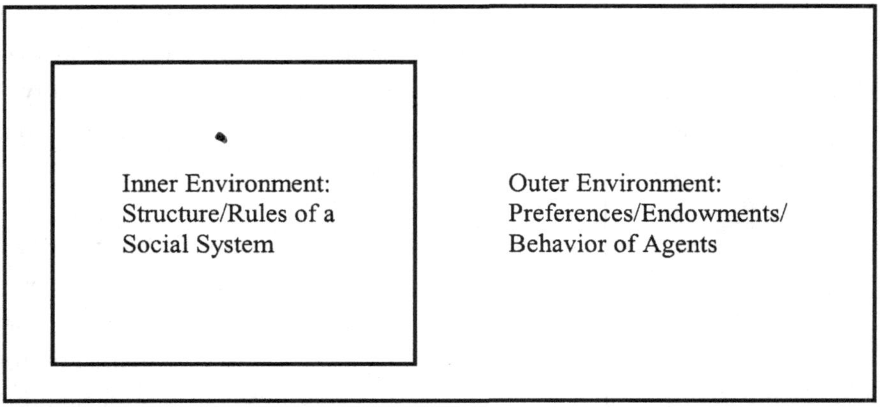

Figure 1
A social system as an artifact with inner and outer environments.

does not exist in nature. Both the twig and the alloy follow the laws of nature. The twig exists in nature; the titanium alloy is manufactured to meet the performance specifications of the aircraft. Both are artifacts to their creators and users.

It is possible to understand and predict the changes in the performance of an artifact as a function of the characteristics of its outer environment, contingent only on a few critical features of the inner environment.

The boundary between the inner and outer environments of an artifact is drawn by reference to the purpose behind its design, or its presumed function. If we were interested in all possible aspects of the relationship between the inner and the outer environments, the two would have a one-on-one correspondence. However, we are typically interested in only some limited aspects of this relationship for an artifact. This coarseness of interest creates redundancy in the correspondence: many inner environments may stand in a given functional relationship to a given outer environment, and many outer environments may also stand in a given functional relationship to an inner environment. The chimpanzee may use not only a twig but also a straw or a thin bone to extract termites from their hill. A twig may be used not only to get termites but also ants or honey from hard-to-reach spaces.

Important parts of the debate about the assumptions of economics are rooted in confusion about the roles of inner and outer environments of an artifact. For artifacts of physical substance, such as cars, cameras, or cities, the boundary between inner and outer environments is easy to see. For social artifacts without physical substance, the boundary is not so obvious. Consider markets as an example.

Markets as Artifacts

Markets are artifacts created by humans through social evolution or design. While both natural and artifactual phenomena are subject to the laws of nature, we can see all artifacts from a functional or teleological perspective.

Simon's characterization of artifacts suggests that in order to develop a science of markets and other such social systems it is useful to draw the boundary between their inner and outer environments. Market structure or rules lie inside; the agents, defined by their endowments, preferences, and decision rules, lie on the outside. The usefulness of an artifact arises from its outcomes' standing in a desired relationship with the outer environment. The outcomes are determined by interactions between the inner and the outer environments under natural law. The choice of inner environment of the artifact generates the outcome function. The inner environment remains largely unnoticed by most users, usually attracting attention only when it is stretched beyond its limits and the outcome fails to stand in the desired relationship with the outer environment.

The rules of a market define its inner environment. These include a language consisting of admissible messages its participants can send, a mechanism to define and implement the distribution of these messages, a law of motion that defines which messages are valid in each state of the market, and a rule to allocate resources as a function of messages (Smith 1982).

In a supermarket, for example, the seller sends messages about his willingness to sell through price labels. The buyer sends the messages about his willingness to buy at that price by transferring the appropriate quantities to his shopping cart and presenting it at the checkout counter. Price messages from the seller are made available to all buyers in the form of posted prices. Messages from the buyers are supposed to be available only to the checkout clerk, though it may be difficult to keep other buyers from looking at the cut of beef in the adjacent cart. The buyer cannot send a buy message when the store is out of stock. The allocation rule consists of payment of the sum of prices of groceries in the cart to the store and transfer of groceries to the customer. The inner structure of other markets, such as a stock exchange or bidding for construction of a municipal bridge, can be similarly defined by their rules.

Resource and information endowments, preferences, and decision rules of the participating agents form the outer environment of a market. The seller in a supermarket has information about estimated demand for each good at various prices. He chooses the goods, their prices, and how they are displayed, using his decision rule to seek his goals, e.g., profits. Buyers combine the information about the prices and other relevant attributes of various goods with their tastes and budgets, and use their own rules to make buy decisions.

The interaction between these inner and outer environments of the market results in the transfer of money from various customers to the store's cash register or bank account, and transfer of grocery baskets of varying composition to the customers. Prices and quantities of various items of grocery, the amount spent by each customer, the grocer's profit, and the net gain in satisfaction of the customer are some of the other outcomes of the market. We can assess a market as an artifact by examining how the outcomes of interest to us change as a function of the inner and the outer environment of the market.

We design a market by choosing its rules (inner environment) so a desired relationship between the outer environment and the selected outcomes is obtained. If the rules of the market arise from social evolution, we assess the functionality of this artifact on the basis of that relationship. Since the outcomes and the outer environment of any artifact are multi-dimensional, it is rarely possible or desirable to look at a complete mapping between them. We choose only a few critical features of the outcomes and outer environment to make the assessment. In designing a car seat for infants, for example, the safety of the child (the outcome) in car accidents of varying intensity (the outer environment) is an overriding consideration; matching the texture of the seat materials is not.

In neoclassical economics, the outer environment of a market is typically represented by the supply and demand conditions. Aspects of the outer environment not captured in supply and demand, such as the decision-making processes of the agents, are assumed to take simple and idealized forms. Allocative efficiency, price, and distribution of gains from trade are the prominent aspects of market outcome that receive attention in this tradition.

Many critical aspects of the outer environments of markets are unobservable in the field. The unique facility of computers in modeling the behavior of systems and their components and the use of the artificial intelligence paradigm helped identify which market outcomes are causally dependent on which attributes of their inner and outer environments.

New Knowledge from Simulation of Markets

Simon asked: How can a simulation ever tell us anything that we do not already know? It may help us compute the consequences of combinations and interactions among components of a system that may be too difficult to work out otherwise. In the case of markets, traders interact with other traders within the confines of the rules of the market. Even if the behavior of traders were well defined, their interactions can be quite complex, making it difficult to characterize the market outcomes in all except the simplest of market designs. Hence the theoretical prominence of the Walrasian auction, which is hardly seen in practice anywhere. Laboratory simulation of auctions with profit-motivated human subjects, often executed on a network of computers to implement the market rules, enables us to characterize the market outcomes of a variety of existing and new market designs.

Beyond the ability to compute what would otherwise be difficult or impossible, computer simulations can help us discover knowledge in a more important way:

Artificial systems and adaptive systems have properties that make them particularly susceptible to simulation via simplified models.... Resemblance in behavior of systems without identity of the inner systems is particularly feasible if the aspects in which we are interested arise out of the *organization* of parts; independently of all but a few properties of the individual components. Thus for many purposes we may be interested in only such characteristics of a material as its tensile and compressive strength. We may be profoundly unconcerned about its chemical properties, or even whether it is wood or iron. (Simon 1996, pp. 16–17)

Computer simulations have served this role in helping us to analyze market artifacts and to discover and understand how, at the interface of their inner and outer environments, the elemental forces of want and scarcity interact through the laws of statistics. Simulations also reveal that a key property of fundamental concern in economics arises from the *organization* of its inner environment, largely independent of the decision-making behavior of individuals who constitute their outer environment. Let us turn to this discovery.

An Exploration with Zero Intelligence

Many investigative reports and the press blamed the stock market crash of October 1987 on program trading. Skeptical of such claims, I designed and taught a course on program trading at Carnegie Mellon University, hoping to learn in the process about the inner workings of double-auction markets and the structure of trading strategies used in them.[1] Dhananjay Gode and I wrote double-auction software (Market 2001; see Gode and Sunder 1994) for human as well as robot traders. Each student in the class could trade from the keyboard or could let a proxy trading strategy he wrote in the form of computer code replace him. Figure 2 shows the price paths generated in three different trading sessions with identical market demand and supply conditions. The feasible range for prices was 0–200, and the market demand and supply functions intersected in the price range 82–86.

The first panel in figure 2 shows the time series of prices in a market where students traded among themselves under a promise that a part of their course grade would be proportional to the number of points earned by each trader. These data simply replicate the results of many classroom auctions with profit-motivated students conducted over the past half-century (e.g., Chamberlin 1948; Smith 1982; Plott 1982). After some initial variability, double-auction prices and allocations in classical market environments settle down in the neighborhood of the predictions of theory, even with a mere handful of traders. When subject rewards are not linked to the points earned in the auction, such markets still tend to settle down to the same predictions, albeit less reliably so (Jamal and Sunder 1991).

The second panel of figure 2 shows the price series observed in a market in which each human trader had been replaced by an artificially intelligent robotic proxy in the form of a computer program written by the trader. In this market, the prices started higher, close to 100, in the middle of the price range 0–200, and settled down to a level slightly below the equilibrium range of 82–86. A significant amount of excess volatility persisted even after several periods. These programs seem to "learn" more slowly than their human progenitors; even after several periods, they make many more bids and offers per transaction than human traders do.

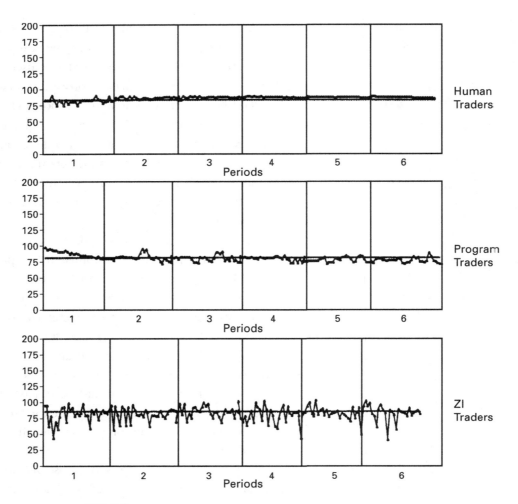

Figure 2
Price series from three market simulations. Source: Gode and Sunder 1994.

Examination of the student-written codes reveals a large variation across the artificially intelligent trading strategies. We cannot be sure what decision rules the human traders who wrote these codes used for trading with their fingers. From the individual bids and offers we can infer that the trading rules embedded in the computer codes were quite distinct. Business students found it difficult, both conceptually and technically, to express their intended trading strategies in the form of state-contingent and dynamically learning computers code. They pressed us for our own trading strategy so they could trade against it—and beat it.

Through several weeks of this program trading course, we had used the allocative efficiency of the markets (total profits earned by all traders as a fraction of the maximum total profits that could have been earned) as an index of the overall quality of students' coded trading strategies as they evolved after competing in successive class sessions. Until this point we had believed that as students learned better to formalize and translate their thinking into computer code, both the price path and allocative efficiency should converge to their equilibrium values. After all, when the uninitiated students trade with their fingers, prices and efficiency of the markets come close to the equilibrium values within 10 or 15 minutes of trading. Within five weeks of the course, the allocative efficiency of markets with artificially intelligent traders crept up slowly from around 60 percent to 90 percent. Students' coded strategies were getting smarter, making fewer errors (their program taking an action the author had not intended under the circumstances). We thought it was just a matter of time before the codes would become as smart or smarter than their authors, and markets populated by them would achieve 100 percent allocative efficiency.

Meeting the students' challenge to the instructor for a coded strategy presented two problems. Gode and I knew little about what is a good trading strategy in a double auction (Wilson 1987); such learning itself had motivated the design and offering of this course. We wondered if our inability to write a winning strategy might raise questions about our suitability for teaching the course. We were not sure if beating the instructor's strategy would energize or demoralize the class; we knew it would demoralize us.

Toward the end of the term, we finally wrote a trading strategy. The bottom panel of figure 2 shows the results of a market consisting entirely of clones of this program. The market demand and supply remain unchanged.

This market exhibits more variability in prices than the previous two. The strategy consists of one line of computer code: if you are a seller with a cost of, say, 40, pick a uniformly distributed random number between 40 and 200 and submit it as an "ask"; if you are a buyer with a value of, say 135, pick a uniformly distributed random number between 0 and 135 and submit it as a "bid." This strategy makes sure these traders—later labeled "zero-intelligence" (ZI) traders—do not trade at a loss but keep spewing new proposals. No maximization, no memory, no learning, no natural selection, and no arbitrage. Yet, prices in this market also converge to a level near the equilibrium prediction of the neoclassical model.

Our motivation for the ZI strategy was part jest: it was sure to lose to the student strategies, but we could still save face with such an obviously simple and silly strategy. But it also arose from partially formed ideas after hours of watching the bids, asks, and transaction prices of double-auction trading on dynamically moving charts of Market 2001 computer screens. Human traders learn quickly enough for their markets to achieve almost 100 percent efficiency. Markets with artificially intelligent traders seem to fail only because these traders get stuck doing nothing in a contingency their authors had not anticipated. What might happen if the traders keep trying to trade without losing money? We did not know. Human experiments could not answer the question. Computers, with their ability to model the micro-level behavior of traders in any manner we want, helped us find out. And the answer surprised us.

Introduction to the elements of economics derives competitive equilibrium as an outcome of the individual striving to maximize their personal gain. From Adam Smith to the modern mathematical derivation of the first fundamental theorem of economics, this maximization is etched into our economics consciousness. In laboratory experiments with human traders that we, following others, have conducted, rewarding subjects on the basis of their performance to encourage them to maximize their rewards is an important part of the method. Yet we found that prices in this market converged without any attempt by the traders to maximize.

Examination of the allocative efficiency of the markets held an even greater surprise for us: efficiency of the third market with zero-intelligence traders is almost the same (about 99 percent) as the efficiency of the first market with profit-motivated human traders. We may not fully understand the decision rules of the human traders, but there is no mystery about the behavior of the ZI traders. We know for sure that they do not maximize; they are programmed merely to pick prices randomly with an opportunity set defined by a no-loss constraint. This is analogous to Becker's (1962) consumers whose random choices from their opportunity set in commodity space generate a downward-sloping demand function. The ZI traders, who bear little resemblance to their human counterparts in their motivation, cognitive equipment, or decision rules, yield market outcomes that are virtually identical in allocative efficiency—the critical performance feature of the market artifact.

Simon had developed and validated the bounded rationality theory of individual decision making decades earlier. These results suggest that the achievement of high levels of efficiency under classical conditions may place minimal demands on individual rationality—no maximization and not even bounded rationality is necessary. If individuals simply refrain from throwing their money away by making "obviously stupid" trades given their local information, allocative efficiency approaches its maximum.[2] After a decade of mathematical modeling, reprogramming of robots, analyses of data, and more simulations, what are the findings of this work?

Some features of market outcomes are largely robust to variations in the decision-making behavior of the agents who participate in them. Allocative efficiency, a key measure of market outcomes, is one such feature. Adam Smith's conclusion that the allocative efficiency arises from individual pursuit of self-interest may be more general than it appears. Efficiency is achievable in double-auction markets even if agents act randomly within their budget constraints. Random choice within one's opportunity set is, at best, only a weak form of "pursuit of self-interest" (Gode and Sunder 1993a).

The use of the maximization assumption to derive market equilibria in economics and the findings from cognitive psychology that individuals cannot and often do not know how to maximize need not be seen as mutually inconsistent. Market institutions[3] may be society's way of dealing with the human cognitive limitations. In classical environments, markets can approach the aggregate maximum even if the individuals do not know how to.

Efficiency of markets is primarily a function of their rules. Most of the efficiency arises from two basic rules: traders forced to abide by their proposals and giving priority to proposals that are disadvantageous to their originators (i.e., to high bids and low asks). Contrary to the teachings of standard textbooks, the shapes of market demand and supply in extra-marginal region influence allocative efficiency (Gode and Sunder 1993b, 1997).

As the market demand and supply conditions change, the expected loss of efficiency has an upper bound. This bound is generated by a tradeoff between the magnitude and the probability of efficiency loss associated with the displacement of intra-marginal traders by extra-marginal ones. This market-level tradeoff is independent of the individual tradeoff between a proposal's profit and its probability of being accepted.

Double auctions are more efficient than one-sided auctions such as sealed-bid auctions because the former require more conditions to be fulfilled for an inefficient trade to occur. On the one hand, auctions that batch or accumulate bids and asks before picking the highest bid and the lowest ask are more efficient than auctions where a transaction occurs as soon as a bid exceeds or equals an ask. Such auctions have lower probability of allowing the extra-marginal traders to displace the intra-marginal traders; others things being the same, call markets are favored over continuous auctions. On the other hand, efficiency is higher if traders can observe market data (e.g., call auctions in which the bids and asks are made public in real time, as compared to call markets in which they are not made public). Public bids and offers allow the intra-marginal traders to promptly outbid or undercut the extra-marginal traders, again reducing the probability of efficient reducing displacement of intra-marginal traders.[4] In asset markets where the value itself is discovered through the market process, continuous markets have the advantage of faster price discovery and the disadvantage of lower allocative efficiency.

Single-market findings about double auctions generalize to a set of multiple interlinked markets. If inventories are maintained between the markets, the effect of market discipline weakens and efficiency drops (Bosch and Sunder 2000). The partial equilibrium result on the achievement of Pareto-efficient outcomes is replicated with ZI traders in a simple general-equilibrium setting of Edgeworth's Box for two commodities (Gode, Spear, and Sunder 2001).

Double-auction asset markets with state uncertainty and imperfect information converge to the equilibrium are derived by assuming that the traders are profit-maximizing Bayesians, irrespective of whether the traders are actually (1) Bayesians, (2) empirical Bayesians, or (3) biased heuristic traders who use adaptive heuristics well known to be biased (Jamal and Sunder 1996, 2001).

Walrasian tatonnement is a valuable static model that captures the asymptotic behavior of markets, but it does not organize the data from the process of arriving at equilibrium well. The ZI model is a simple model that does a reasonable job of capturing the dynamics of markets, and organizing the data from the early part of trading well. The two models, in combination, may do a better job than either can do alone in helping us understand the markets.

Conclusions

Markets are powerful social institutions. They probably evolved in human societies because their efficiency had survival value. We can usefully distinguish between the inner and outer environments of an artifact. The former are designed to obtain a degree of insulation across variations in the latter, so the artifact can serve the function for which it is created or used. The inner environment of markets is defined by their rules; their outer environment includes the behavior of agents.

A claim that the predictions of the first fundamental theorem in economics are approachable in classical environments without actual or attempted maximization by participants might have been met with skepticism until recently. Thanks to a largely serendipitous discovery using computer simulations of markets, we can claim that weak forms of individual rationality, far short of maximization, when combined with appropriate market institutions, can be sufficient for the market outcomes to approach the predictions of the first fundamental theorem. These individual rationality conditions (labeled zero-intelligence) are almost indistinguishable from the budget or settlement constraints imposed on traders by the market institutions themselves. They are even weaker than Simon's concept of bounded rationality.

ZI traders are only an important first step toward using computer simulations with artificially intelligent traders to explore the structural properties of markets. Such simulations—the "wind tunnels" of economics—have already given us interesting discoveries. For example, we now know that the market level tradeoff between the level and the probability of execution of an ask would exist even if no trader included such a tradeoff in his strategy. Much more remains to be done.

As social artifacts, markets are the arena for the interplay of demand and supply. The functionality of markets can be assessed by their robustness to certain environmental variations and responsiveness to others. We prefer markets to be robust to variations in individual cognitive capabilities and responsive to their wants and resources. If creation without a creator and designs without a designer are possible, we need not be surprised that markets can exhibit elements of rationality absent in economic agents.

Notes

1. In a double auction, a buyer can submit a price at which he is willing to buy (make a bid), and a seller can submit a price at which he is willing to sell (make an ask). If another buyer bids a higher price, it becomes the market bid; if another seller asks a lower price, it becomes the market ask. A buyer is free to accept the market ask; a seller is free to accept a market bid; and such acceptances consummate a binding transaction. The auction continues for a specified period of time.

2. Von Neumann (1956) points out that the link between the details of the components of a system to the performance of the system can be quite weak; only a few aspects of a component may be functionally relevant to the system.

3. See also North 1990.

4. See also Cason and Friedman 1998.

References

Becker, Gary S. 1962. Irrational behavior and economic theory. *Journal of Political Economy* 70: 1–13.

Bosch-Domenech, Antoni, and Shyam Sunder. 2000. Tracking the invisible hand: convergence of double auctions to competitive equilibrium. *Computational Economics* 16, no. 3: 257–284.

Cason, T., and Daniel Friedman. 1978. Price formation and exchange in thin markets: A laboratory comparison of institutions. In P. Howitt et al., eds., *Money, Markets, and Method.* Elgar.

Friedman, D., and J. Rust. 1993. *The Double Auction Market*. Addison-Wesley.

Friedman, Milton. 1953. The methodology of positive economics. In *Essays in Positive Economics*. University of Chicago Press.

Gode, D. K., and Shyam Sunder. 1993a. Allocative efficiency of markets with zero intelligence traders: Market as a partial substitute for individual rationality. *Journal of Political Economy* 101, no. 1: 119–137.

Gode, D. K., and Shyam Sunder. 1993b. Lower bounds for efficiency of surplus extraction in double auctions. In D. Friedman and J. Rust, eds., *The Double Auction Market*. Addison-Wesley.

Gode, D. K., and Shyam Sunder. 1994. Human and artificially intelligent traders in a double auction market: Experimental evidence. In K. Carley and M. Prietula, eds., *Computational Organization Theory*. Erlbaum.

Gode, D. K., and Shyam Sunder. 1997. What makes markets allocationally efficient? *Quarterly Journal of Economics* 112, no. 2: 603–630.

Gode, D. K., and Shyam Sunder. 2000. Double Auction Dynamics: Structural Effects of Non-binding Price Controls (version revised in March). Working paper, Yale University.

Gode, D. K., Stephen Spear, and Shyam Sunder. 2001. Convergence of Double Auctions to Pareto Optimal Allocations in Edgeworth Box (version revised in November). Working paper, Yale University.

Hayek, Friederich A. 1945. The uses of knowledge in society. *American Economic Review* 35, September: 519–530.

Jamal, Karim, and Shyam Sunder. 1991. Money vs. gaming: Effects of salient monetary payments in double oral auctions. *Organizational Behavior and Human Decision Processes* 49, June: 151–166.

Jamal, Karim, and Shyam Sunder. 1996. Bayesian Equilibrium in Double Auctions Populated by Biased Heuristic Traders. *Journal of Economic Behavior and Organization* 31, no. 2: 273–291.

Jamal, Karim, and Shyam Sunder. 2001. Why do biased heuristics approximate Bayes Rule in double auctions? *Journal of Economic Behavior and Organization* 46, no. 4: 431–435.

Knight, F. H. 1947. The planful act, part VI. In *Freedom and Reform*. Harper.

Larkey, Patrick D. 2002. Ask A Simple Question: A Retrospective on Herbert Alexander Simon. Working paper, Carnegie Mellon University.

Leijonhufvud, A. 1993. Towards a not-too-rational macroeconomics. *Southern Economic Journal* 60, no. 1: 1–13.

North, Douglass C. 1990. *Institutions, Institutional Change, and Economic Performance.* Cambridge University Press.

Plott, C. R. 1982. Industrial organization theory and experimental economics. *Journal of Economic Literature* 20, December: 1485–1527.

Plott, C., and V. Smith. 1978. An experimental examination of two institutions. *Review of Economic Studies* 45: 133–153.

Rothschild, E. 1994. Adam Smith and the invisible hand. *American Economic Review* 84, no. 2: 319–322.

Simon, Herbert A. 1947. *Administrative Behavior.* Free Press.

Simon, Herbert A. 1978. Rational decision making in business organizations. *American Economic Review* 69: 493–513.

Simon, Herbert A. 1996. *The Sciences of the Artificial,* third edition. MIT Press.

Smith, Vernon L. 1982. Macroeconomic systems as an experimental science. *American Economic Review* 72, December: 923–955.

Smith, Vernon L. 1991. Rational choice: The contast between economics and prsychology. *Journal of Political Economy* 99, no. 4: 877–897.

von Neumann, John. 1956. Probabilistic logics and the synthesis of reliable organisms from unreliable components. In C. E. Shannon and J. McCarthy, eds., *Automata Studies.* Princeton University Press.

Wilson, R. 1987. On Equilibria of Bid-Ask Markets. In G. Feiwell, ed., *Arrow and the Ascent of Modern Economic Theory.* Macmillan.

Personal Recollections from 15 Years of Monthly Meetings

Raul E. Valdes-Perez

I had the personal fortune to know Professor Herbert Simon since 1986, meeting with him monthly in my role as his computer science Ph.D. student, and since 1991 as a faculty member of the computer science department. After my graduation, I asked him whether he would accept continuing our meetings to discuss research and science in general, and he graciously agreed. We met around twice monthly for an hour in his Psychology department office over fifteen years. Hence, I have both good data and a good internal model of what Simon believed in science, although my recollections below should fairly be judged susceptible to my own biases and imperfect memory.

I will organize my personal observations around notes that I took during a lecture by Simon on the nature of research as part of Carnegie Mellon's computer science department Immigration Course in 1986, which introduced new doctoral students to faculty research projects as well as to broader issues, such as addressed by Simon's lectures. Simon gave this Immigration lecture nearly every year, and I attended many more of these over the following years. The 1986 version made the most impression on me, being a new student.

By no means do I imply from these notes that Simon, whom I could never bring myself to call "Herb" although most people did, believed that there is only one way of doing science. At least at the stage of his research career when I knew him, he was anything but dogmatic, since he always allowed for different research styles and methods. Consistent with this liberalness, a favorite criticism of his was the casual way in which using the English article 'the' implied a unique property, as in "the key creative discovery." Simon liked to stress that scientific discoveries always involved different creative stages often carried out by different people: formulating the problem, finding the right approach, actually solving the problem, placing it within the context of existing knowledge, explicating the relationship to other fields, and so on.

"A research problem is a question, not a topic."

Ask graduate students what they are working on, and most will reply with a topic like artificial intelligence, human memory, or Bayesian networks. Probing further will get you sub-topics, and probing still deeper will extract tasks like a faster algorithm, a less memory-intensive one, data on human performance during recall, and the like. Instead, Simon emphasized formulating a question, partly I suppose because one can evaluate a question from many angles without actually doing any work on it. If the question is rejected, for example, by means of some of the tests in the next items below, then one saves much effort that is better expended elsewhere.

Another benefit of seeking a question is that one can, according to one's taste, emphasize finding a novel question. It is easier to make rapid progress when the question is new, because one doesn't have to improve on the many previous attempts to answer a question that is already well established. Of course, thinking about questions requires the student to have a good big picture of his or her discipline, in terms of what questions are of interest to the discipline or to science in general. This checklist provides some help in evaluating scientific questions.

One of my favorite examples of a once-novel question that was plainly available for anyone to formulate is: Why are the male testes always outside the body cavity in mammals? By finding an interesting, tractable question that nobody else has thought of, even modest progress will be a solid contribution.

In Simon's view, questions didn't need to be very specific. He was fond of examples like "What happens when you configure the world in this novel way and provide such-and-such stimulus?" which, according to him, fit the discovery of Ohm's law. One of Simon's earliest questions, from his own doctoral research into the processes of decision making, was "How do playground administrators allocate their budgets?" The empirical observations that led him to his celebrated theory of bounded rationality began there, according to his autobiography.

"What would an answer to the question look like? How would you begin work on the problem?"

Simon's favorite example here was always a gravity shield. How to construct one is surely an interesting question, but if you cannot conceive of what form the shield will take, then you can scarcely figure out how to begin work on the problem.

From Simon's own research, another example is: Can one develop a cognitive model that would simulate, in humanly plausible and inspectable steps that are faithful to the historical facts, a celebrated discovery from the history of science? Answers to this question, as Simon and his students/collaborators Langley, Bradshaw, and Zytkow showed in their 1987 book *Scientific Discovery*, take the form of a computer program whose operation is consistent with knowledge in cognitive science, that explains the available historical circumstances about the discovery, and does not pre-suppose knowledge or data on the part of the discoverer that he or she did not possess.

"What test will determine whether the question was answered?"

I don't remember specific examples, but from other conversations with Simon, I believe that the many research articles whose titles begin with "A Framework for" suffer from this problem: What test would show whether you have the right framework? My search within the INSPEC literature database (computer science, physics, electrical engineering) for titles containing the word 'framework' turned up 11,785 articles, so there is no shortage of them.

Simon had a general suspicion of articles whose titles begin with "Towards," presumably because he believed that authors should publish their conclusions when they arrive somewhere interesting, not when they've identified a direction and ventured a step or two. (INSPEC turns up 12,644 "Towards ..." articles.)

"Would anybody care whether I solved the problem?"

Working on problems that nobody cares about, no matter what creativity is required to solve them, is risky. Of course, the importance of the problem and its solution could emerge later, but probably most students do not have the well-formed scientific taste to pick the eventual winners. Simon doubtless intended this point and the others as heuristics that pointed the way to fruitful discovery, but which could be violated successfully.

I am reminded of another favorite theme of his: that the advice contained in popular proverbs often come in contradictory pairs, which shows their heuristic nature. For example, "Haste makes waste" and "Don't put off for tomorrow what you can do today." Context is important.

"Does the present state of the art make the research feasible?"

I don't remember Simon supplying specific examples here, but I think he would agree that research in theoretical computer science that intended to prove that P equals NP (or its denial) was not very feasible, since there possibly was not enough theoretical knowledge available to make the problem soluble soon. An example closer to his own research would be attempts to show specific workings of the brain when the instruments to make the needed measurements have not been invented.

"If the field is crowded, what is my secret weapon that makes me think I can solve the problem where others have failed?"

I remember being surprised when hearing this, since it seemed to stress a competitive aspect to scientific research which, given my first-year student's idealism, seemed misplaced. However, failure and me-too success aren't much rewarded in science, so it's hard to dispute the heuristic wisdom of the advice. Simon pointed out then, and always, that "I'm smarter than other people" wasn't an acceptable answer, since it's rarely true. Much better answers could involve having access to unique apparatus that other people lack or, of course, possessing a new idea.

"Working on several tasks at once is good in order to avoid ruts."

This was in reply to a question (mine) from the audience, about how to avoid getting stalled in one's research. I don't know whether Simon really intended this advice to apply to graduate students, who after their initial course work are usually absorbed by one project, or to senior researchers who have the luxury of developing several simultaneous projects.

There is a relation between this advice and Simon's own research into the cognitive processes that underlie scientific discovery. As is widely known, Simon hypothesized that scientific discovery, as practiced by human beings, makes use of the same mental capacities that ordinarily problem solving does, whether it involves doing crossword puzzles, solving exam problems, or inventing new cooking recipes. In fact, Simon argued that, if nothing else, assuming a same mental faculty was the right hypothesis for reasons of parsimony or Occam's Razor, i.e., of not multiplying entities beyond what are needed to explain the facts. In his view, there were no facts that proved that the mental discovery processes of great scientists were qualitatively different than the everyday mental processes of less celebrated people doing less exalted problem-solving tasks.

Like any theory, Simon's hypothesis that scientific discovery *was* problem solving needed to be checked against the facts. In his view, the only significant hard fact about scientific discovery was that discoverers often reported that the insights that led to a major discovery happened suddenly while attending to something else, the so-called Eureka sensation or effect. So how could Simon's problem-solving hypothesis account for the Eureka effect?

Simon's explanation began by noting that discoveries came only after working on a problem for some time. His idea was that problem solving (also known as heuristic search in problem spaces) leads the researcher in different directions, all of which are unsuccessful if the problem is yet to be solved. When the researcher puts the problem aside for a while and later starts, he begins in a new direction while leveraging all the clues and understanding of the problem gained so far. Thus, the new direction of reasoning can lead quickly to a definitive insight and a Eureka sensation.

Simon would not have claimed that this explanation of the Eureka effect is "true." In fact, it is difficult to test. Rather, it simply fulfilled the need for a hypothesis, scientific discovery as problem solving in this case, to admit a plausible explanation of whatever hard facts are available about the studied phenomenon, here, scientific discovery.

So, Simon's own research was consistent with this advice: work hard on a problem, but practice putting it aside as well.

"A Ph.D. thesis is a 'progress report' that reports progress you have made on a problem."

A consequence of this dictum is that research topics that are of an all-or-nothing character, i.e., the student either wins a grand prize or has nothing to show for it (except perhaps a consolation Master's degree) are very risky. I think that science students in longer-established fields understand this better than computer science or artificial intelligence graduate students, many of whom would set up very ambitious but practically insoluble research problems. Put another way by P. B. Medawar: science is the art of the soluble.

"Outstanding discoveries happen by luck, but only to prepared minds and with sufficient effort."

This was not an original remark, but worth repeating to aspiring researchers. Among Simon's favorite examples was the discovery of Penicillin by Fleming, who famously noticed dead bacteria where living ones were to be expected. A less-prepared mind might have ignored the surprise and thrown out the Petri dish, but Fleming persevered, leading to his discovery of the anti-bacterial properties of penicillin.

This dictum hit home with great personal clarity in the context of a modest discovery I made some years later. I had been collaborating with a Bulgarian linguist Vladimir Pericliev, whom I had met at a Stanford symposium on scientific discovery that Simon and I had organized in 1995, on the problem of reconstructing, in computational terms, the logic underlying a discovery process that was popular in linguistics research of the 1950s and the 1960s (so-called componential analysis). In the componential analysis of the kinship terms used by a human language, the linguist would try to formulate concise descriptions of the kinship terms (e.g., English uncle, cousin, sister-in-law, etc.) that would demarcate each from every other term, using the attributes of sex, birth, marriage, and other relations between the kin and the speaker. This concern with conciseness, understandability, and demarcation led to the following discovery.

In preparation for a trip to South Florida, I was casually browsing the web pages of the University of Miami and came across this statement: "The University of Miami is the youngest of 24 private research universities in the country that operate both law and medical schools." At once it occurred to me that, given a database of peers—such as universities and their attributes, a computer program could be written to generate such *niche* statements, which expressed concisely and in grammatical English how a single, chosen database entry was interestingly *unique*. This task turned out to be a new data-mining question to ask about a database, which seemingly has never been approached in any systematic way, despite the plethora of niche statements that are appear everywhere, at least in American culture, not excepting scientific culture. Time will tell how important this new data-mining question is, but there are promising applications of the idea in science, such as in genomic data analysis—in what interesting way is a specific gene unique?

Following Simon's dictum, this writer could have seen the University of Miami statement two years earlier and not given it a further thought.

"To stimulate the imagination, arm yourself with knowledge from many fields in order to approach the task from different angles."

Simon made a practice of having lunch at an open table with faculty members from other university departments. I recall him saying that a favorite conversational tactic was to ask "What's new in your field?" If his lunch mate reported a new topic of interest in another field, in which Simon had expertise to bring, he could read the pertinent literature, formulate his own ideas, and submit them for publication, whether the field was something he had ever published in or not. In his last years, Simon began to take an interest in theoretical, qualitative questions in developmental biology and how to approach them from an evolutionary viewpoint that his previous work in other fields (e.g., economics) prepared him to answer. I did some programming for him in Mathematica on simulations of his ideas, but lack of time prevented my supporting him much in his efforts. Of course, Simon did not rely only on lunch mates for new ideas.

Not everyone had the breadth of knowledge and confidence to do research in fields with any previous track record. The advice above refers to the other direction, in which knowledge of techniques from other fields could be newly imported into one's own discipline.

"If I had my druthers, the department would accept no graduate students with undergraduate degrees in computer science."

Simon felt very strongly that computer science departments erred by accepting mostly students with little backgrounds in anything besides computer science. He did not change this opinion in later years, since we talked about it often. He believed that students with little outside knowledge to draw on would tend to follow the research steps already laid out by others. Also, interdisciplinary research, which Simon of course championed, would be stunted, since few such students would seek outward-looking opportunities. Needless to say, many other faculty disagreed with him. Today almost all computer science graduate students, at least at Carnegie Mellon, have almost entirely computer science backgrounds.

I will end my remarks with some anecdotes about conversations that greatly helped me understand how Herbert Simon thought about research.

Simon introduced the idea of *satisficing* in artificial intelligence: people solve everyday problems by spending some effort gathering information followed by making a decision that leads to a satisfactory outcome. In his autobiography *Models of My Life*, he tells about his field observation of how playground administrators solve the problem of deciding what to spend their budgets on. Contemporary thinking was that they found an optimal solution by considering their constraints and resources and optimizing their choices. As a student, I asked Simon whether one couldn't construe their decision-making processes in terms of optimizing, within which their time, probability of finding information, and other factors could be included in the optimization criteria. Simon replied that one could always conceive any problem as an optimization problem, but thinking in that way would lead the researcher to a very different path, such as estimating unknowable probabilities, quantifying the space of different purchasing decisions (which are boundless), and so on. The researcher who instead viewed the decision problem as one of *satisficing* would try to identify the heuristics and information-gathering steps used in practice, perhaps try to find better heuristics if his goal was to improve human decision making, and so on. Very different research would ensue. Simply put: conceiving of the problem in different ways led to different research, and Simon believed that the more fruitful research would be based on the *satisficing* interpretation. The question of whether decision makers *truly* optimized or not was problematic and not to pursued scientifically, since what test would answer it?

As a student, I read many of Simon's early papers, chosen somewhat at random, simply because I was intrigued by the man and his work. In the early 1950s he wrote an article that used the formalism of differential equations to model aspects of social interaction. Upon finishing the article, it struck me as excessively conjectural, hard to test, and generally uncharacteristic of the Simon that I knew. At my next meeting I asked why he had written such an article. He replied that his goal had always been to introduce more rigor into the social sciences, and in the early 1950s differential equations were available to him, but not computers. When he came into contact with computers, Simon quickly recognized them as the formal tool he was seeking, since computers were a highly flexible experimental instrument that he could use to model intelligence or other social science phenomena.

I wrote only a few minor, short papers with Simon, since my own research on scientific discovery did not attempt to model human processes in any way, but to improve on them using computers, which was of interest to Simon but was not something he did himself. But once when we were discussing how to conclude an editors' introduction for a special issue of a journal, Simon asked "What would Cicero write?" I never did figure out precisely what Professor Simon meant by that, since he just wrote the conclusion himself, and quite well, as always.

Epilogue

A Soft Goodbye

James G. March

We celebrate a life within a protocol
Of sorrow. A friend is dead and we alive
Must weep our speeches in his shadow. I've
No eloquence that's adequate for this, just small

Cold casseroles of memories he left behind:
A freezing night in nineteen fifty-three,
The Hotel Taft, when I was young, and he,
I met a truly extraordinary mind.

We worked together three productive years.
That's all. Just three. But many more we had
As friends, I grateful for the myriad
Of inspirations breathed within his atmospheres.

For more than fifty splendid years since he began
To write, he's been our definition. Herds
Of eager students copy all his words,
But they can never ever replicate the man.

Computer scientist. And psychologist.
But to list just two of them would be to err.

Miscellaneous philosopher.
Sociologist. And economist.

In every discipline he occupied, a gem.
The disciplines were his; he was not theirs.
They covered him with prizes, but all the chairs
He held were honored more by him than he by them.

For he was not at all an ordinary man.
A bold, precise, seditious mind, he stood
Before authorities and said he would
Rework their favorite theories, make then better than

They were. And that is what he did. He was a kind
Of unremittingly irreverent youth
Who looked for beauty as he looked for truth
And found them both within a science of the mind.

A man ferocious when engaged in argument,
Not inclined to compromise a bit;
Though once or twice, I'm told, he did admit
He might, perhaps, be wrong—to a limited extent.

I've known, throughout my life, great scholars to admire
In academe, but I will never see
Another one as bountiful as he.
Ideas burned in him like paraffin afire.

A glorious mind. A glorious man. In retrospect,
He died the way he lived, impatiently,
Not waiting for the rest of us to be
Prepared for it. Impetuous, quick intellect,

Not pausing to allow the rest of us to get
Prepared, but rushing forward to the end
As though life were a paper he could send
To a journal. Well, suppose we don't accept it yet.

Suppose we tell him to revise and resubmit,
Keep the essence as it was except
Prolong the ending more, so we'll accept.
That life was nourishment for us, please add to it.

Too late. The winter winds of time have swept away
A rock. Too suddenly to comprehend,
A gentle man, an honest man, a friend
Is gone, his recollection cherished every day

With love and tears. Like flowers robbed of their butterfly,
We miss his mind, his straight Wisconsin style,
His humanness, his graciousness, his smile.
To Herb, in thankful memory, a soft goodbye.

About the Contributors

Albert Ando (1929–2002) *Professor of Economics and Finance, University of Pennsylvania Research Associate, National Bureau of Economic Research*

Kenneth Arrow *Joan Kennedy Professor of Economics and Emeritus Professor of Operations Research, Stanford University* Professor Arrow received the Nobel Prize in Economic Science in 1972 for his work on general equilibrium and social choice. He writes: "In my intellectual journeys, I went from mathematical statistics to economic theory (at a graduate school where it was held in low repute). I found in Herb Simon another who saw the chief subject of social science to be the social and individual responses to uncertainty."

Mie Augier *Postdoctoral fellow, Stanford University* Dr. Augier is interested in the history of behavioral approaches to economics, particularly as those approaches were manifested in the 1950s and the 1960s around Carnegie Mellon University. She is working on an intellectual biography of Herbert Simon.

William Baumol *Professor of Economics, New York University; Senior Research Economist, Princeton University* Professor Baumol has worked in many areas, including theory of the firm, welfare economics, productivity and growth, economics of the arts, environmental economics, antitrust, and regulation. Although he is a dedicated theorist, he has always emphasized the tradeoff between the simplicity of workable theoretical models and the resulting gulf between them and reality. A disquieting example is the behavior of humans that is not always what theoretical analysis deems "rational" or "optimal." Working with real firms, he has often encountered apparently "irrational behavior" and actions that at best approximated "optimally imperfect decisions."

Philip Bromiley *Curtis L. Carlson Chair in Strategic Management, Carlson School of Management, University of Minnesota*

John Conlisk *Professor of Economics Emeritus, University of California, San Diego* Professor Conlisk's early interests were in economic growth, the distribution of income, and negative tax experiments. His use of adaptive dynamics as an approach to behavior led naturally to strong later interests in bounded rationality.

William Cooper *Foster Parker Professor of Finance and Management Emeritus, Red McCombs School of Business, University of Texas* Specializing in modeling managerial and social processes, Professor Cooper has authored, co-authored, or co-edited 476 professional and scientific articles and 22 books. A member of the Accounting Hall of Fame and a Fellow of the Econometric Society and the American Association for the Advancement of Science, he holds honorary D.Sc. degrees from Ohio State University and Carnegie Mellon University and a Doctor Honoris Causa degree from University of Alicante.

Richard Day *Professor of Economics, University of Southern California* Professor Day's early work developed "recursive programming" models for simulating production, investment, and technological change in agriculture and industry. That work led to explorations in dynamic theory concerning economic change when agents are boundedly rational, when economic behavior is adaptive, when markets work out of equilibrium, and when economic structure evolves. Those explorations led to explorations of models of market adjustment, business cycles, growth, and economic development in which irregular, random-like behavior is generic and can be characterized in statistical terms. He co-founded the *Journal of Economic Behavior and Organization* and served as its editor from its inception in 1980 until 2001. At present he is completing a collection of essays on economic growth and a book on macroeconomics.

William Dill *Consultant on management and higher education* In 1967, Dr. Dill left the faculty of the Graduate School of Industrial Administration (GSIA) at Carnegie Mellon University to manage the design of education programs at IBM. Subsequently he was a dean at New York University, a team leader in the founding of a school for experienced managers in China, and president of Babson College and two other colleges. Through his work, he has tried to guide faculties and shape programs to honor Simon's tenets: curiosity to know, courage to integrate across disciplines, and imagination to help students put ideas into practice.

Giovanni Dosi *Professor of Economics, Sant'Anna School of Advanced Studies, Pisa* Since 1992 Professor Dosi has been Editor for Continental Europe of *Industrial and Corporate Change*. He is an Honorary Research Professor at the University of Sussex. His interests include the modeling of evolutionary dynamics and technological change.

Peter Earl *Senior Lecturer in Business Economics, University of Queensland Co-editor, Journal of Economic Psychology* Professor Earl has authored or edited, alone or with others, fifteen books, including

The Legacy of Herbert Simon in Economics (Elgar, 2001), a two-volume collection of reprinted articles.

Massimo Egidi *Professor of Economics, University of Trento; Co-director, Laboratory of Computable and Experimental Economics* Professor Egidi's main research interests relate to the study of boundedly rational behaviors in organizations and institutions. His research includes laboratory experiments on individual and team problem solving, and correlates with computer simulations to yield better understanding of decisions in complex environments.

Edward Feigenbaum *Kumagai Professor of Computer Science Emeritus, Stanford University* Professor Feigenbaum did his Ph.D. work under Herbert A. Simon at Carnegie Institute of Technology (now CMU) in 1956–1959. In the 1960s he pioneered the development of the Expert Systems field. In the 1980s, he participated in the start up of several companies that commercialized expert systems technology. During 1994–1997, he was Chief Scientist of the U.S. Air Force. In 1986 he was elected to the National Academy of Engineering. In 1995 he was awarded the highest research honor in Computer Science, the Turing Award of the Association for Computing Machinery.

Julian Feldman *Professor, School of Information, University of California, Irvine* Professor Feldman received his Ph.D. from the Carnegie Institute of Technology (now Carnegie Mellon University), working with (among others) Herbert Simon.

Katherine Simon Frank *Former Coordinator of Advising, Sociology Department, University of Minnesota* Mrs. Frank (Herbert Simon's eldest child) is independently investigating and writing about motivating factors of participant-activists in the 1964 Berkeley Free Speech Movement.

Shane Frederick   *Assistant Professor of Marketing, MIT Sloan School of Management*   Professor Frederick received his B.S. in zoology at the University of Wisconsin and his Ph.D. in decision sciences at Carnegie Mellon University. His research interests include intertemporal choice, heuristics and biases, contingent valuation, and preference elicitation procedures.

Gerd Gigerenzer   *Director, Max Planck Institute for Human Development, Berlin*   In Professor Gigerenzer's view, most decisions are based on fast and frugal heuristics constructed from elementary building blocks in the "adaptive toolbox." The motto of his book *Bounded Rationality: The Adaptive Toolbox* (with Reinhard Selten, 2001) is "to promote bounded rationality as the key to understanding how actual people make decisions without utilities and probabilities." The program is outlined in *Simple Heuristics That Make Us Smart* (1999, with Peter Todd et al.).

Robert Goodin   *Professor of Social and Political Theory and of Philosophy, Research School of Social Sciences, Australian National University*   Previously, Professor Goodin taught at the Universities of Essex, Maryland, Strathclyde, and Oslo and at the California Institute of Technology. He is founding editor of the *Journal of Political Philosophy* and sometime co-editor of the *British Journal of Political Science* and of *Ethics*. The most recent of his many books and articles on political theory and public policy is *Reflective Democracy* (Oxford University Press, 2002).

Harold Guetzkow   was a friend of Herbert Simon from the time they were undergraduate classmates at the University of Chicago in 1933–1936. Guetzkow worked with Simon at Carnegie Mellon University in 1950–1957 (first as an associate professor, later as a full professor), and they remained friends after Guetzkow left for Northwestern University.

Charles Holt   studied with Paul Samuelson at the Massachusetts Institute of Technology and with Milton Friedman at the University of Chicago while earning four degrees in electrical engineering and economics. He then faced the challenge of heading up a research team at Carnegie Mellon University that included Franco Modigliani, Jack Muth, and Herbert Simon.

Yuji Ijiri   *Robert M. Trueblood University Professor of Accounting and Economics, Graduate School of Industrial Administration, Carnegie Mellon University*   Professor Ijiri came to Carnegie Mellon University in 1961 as a doctoral student and has been at that university ever since then except in 1963–1967, when he was on the faculty of the Stanford Graduate School of Business. As a student, he took Herbert Simon's most influential course, Mathematical Social Science. Later he had the privilege of co-teaching the course and publishing five articles and a book with Simon.

Daniel Kahneman   *Eugene Higgins Professor of Psychology and Professor of Public Affairs, Princeton University*   Professor Kahneman has studied the bounded rationality of human judgment and decision making for several decades.

David Klahr   *Professor of Psychology, Carnegie Mellon University*   Professor Klahr was head of the Psychology Department from 1983 to 1993. His current research focuses on the development and teaching of scientific reasoning skills and his most recent books include *Exploring Science: The Cognition and Development of Discovery Processes* (MIT Press, 2000) and *Cognition and Instruction: 25 Years of Progress* (with Sharon Carver; Erlbaum, 2001). He is a fellow of the American Psychological Association and of the American Psychological Society and a member of the governing board of the Cognitive Development Society.

Kenneth Kotovsky   *Professor of Psychology, Carnegie Mellon University*

David Kreps   *Holden Professor of Economics and Senior Associate Dean, Stanford Graduate School of Business; Senior Professor by Special Appointment, Berglas School of Economics, Tel Aviv University*   Professor Kreps's written work has concerned dynamic economics, with a strong secular trend away from mathematical theorizing and axiomatic choice theory to dynamic financial markets, dynamic games, and adaptive learning, to blends of social psychology, organizational sociology, and transaction cost economics, particularly concerning employment and human resource management.

Pat Langley   *Director, Institute for the Study of Learning and Expertise; Head, Computational Learning Laboratory, Center for the Study of Language and Information, Stanford University; Consulting Professor of Symbolic Systems, Stanford University*

Axel Leijonhufvud   *Professor Emeritus, University of California, Los Angeles; Professor of Monetary Economics, University of Trento*   Born in Stockholm, Professor Leijonhufvud obtained his Ph.D. from Northwestern in 1967. Partly under the influence of Robert Clower, Leijonhufvud produced a dissertation which was to profoundly affect macroeconomics for the next decade: *On Keynesian Economics and the Economics of Keynes* (1968).

Brian Loasby   *Professor Emeritus, University of Stirling*   After studying economics at Cambridge, Professor Loasby held appointments at Aberdeen, at Birmingham, at Bristol, and (for many years) at Stirling. His work has focused on the connections between knowledge and organization, in economies and the history of economics, drawing on Smith, Menger, Marshall, Schumpeter, Hayek, Shackle, and Simon (among others). His book *Knowledge, Institutions and*

Evolution in Economics was joint winner of the Schumpeter Prize in 2000.

Michael Lovell   *Chester D. Hubbard Professor of Economics and Social Science Emeritus, Wesleyan University*   Professor Lovell was trained mostly as a conventional economist—the only exception from conventionality in his graduate career was an optional assignment of a paper in Simon's book *Models of Man*. He was a colleague of Herbert Simon during the six years he taught at the Graduate School of Industrial Administration Carnegie Mellon University.

James March   *Professor Emeritus, Stanford University*   Professor March is a student of organizations, decision making, and political institutions. He was on the faculty of the Carnegie Institute of Technology from 1953 to 1964. He collaborated briefly with Herbert Simon to produce a book (*Organizations*) that is cited frequently and read occasionally.

Luigi Marengo   *Professor of Economics, Faculty of Law, University of Teramo*   Professor Marengo's main research interests concern the theory and modeling of bounded rationality in individual and collective decision making, the economic theory of organizations and institutions, and applications of adaptive learning models to market behavior.

Pamela McCorduck   is the author or co-author of eight published books. Two are novels and five are focused on the intellectual impact of computing, especially aspects of artificial intelligence. Among her books are *Machines Who Think*, *The Fifth Generation*, *The Universal Machine*, and *Aaron's Code*. Her books have been translated into all the major European and Asian languages, and her articles have appeared in journals ranging from *Cosmopolitan* and *Omni* to the *New York Times* and the *Michigan Quarterly Review*. She was a contributing editor to *Wired*.

George Miller   *Professor Emeritus of Psychology, Princeton University*

Franco Modigliani (1918–2003)   At MIT since 1962, Professor Modigliani was well known for his work on monetary theory, capital markets, corporate finance, macroeconomics, and econometrics. He received a J.D. in 1939 from the University of Rome and a D.S.S. in 1944 from the New School for Social Research. He was the author of ten books, five volumes of his collected papers, and numerous articles for scholarly journals. He was the recipient of the 1985 Nobel Prize in Economic Science.

John Muth   graduated from Washington University in 1952 with a degree in industrial engineering. He then entered the Graduate School of Industrial Administration at the Carnegie Institute of Technology. Where, as a research assistant, he was assigned to the Planning and Control of Industrial Operations project. After graduating, he joined the faculty. He moved to Michigan State University in 1964, then to Indiana University in 1969. He retired in 1994 and moved to the Florida Keys.

Joseph Pitt   *Professor of Philosophy and head of Department of Philosophy, Virginia Polytechnic Institute and State University*

Jason Potts   *Lecturer in Economics, University of Queensland*   Dr. Potts studied at Lincoln University in New Zealand. *The New Evolutionary Microeconomics*, a book based on his Ph.D. dissertation, shared the 2000 Joseph Schumpeter Prize.

Roy Radner   *Leonard N. Stern School Professor of Business, New York University*   Professor Radner did his undergraduate and graduate work at the University of Chicago, receiving an M.S. in mathematics and a Ph.D. in mathematical statistics. Before joining New York University, he was a Distinguished Member of the Technical Staff at AT&T Bell Laboratories, Professor of Economics and Statistics at the University of California at Berkeley, and a member of the Cowles Foundation for Research in Economics at the University of Chicago and Yale University. His research interests include a strategic analysis of global climate change, theories of information processing and decentralization within firms, a statistical evaluation of data-mining procedures, and models of extortion by government officials in developing countries.

Paul Samuelson   *Institute Professor Emeritus, Massachusetts Institute of Technology*   Professor Samuelson was educated at the University of Chicago (B.A., 1935) and at Harvard, where he obtained his Ph.D. in 1941. He has been at MIT since 1940. He also served as a government economic adviser on several occasions. He received the Nobel Prize in Economics in 1970.

Reinhard Selten   *Former Professor of Economics, University of Bonn*   Professor Selten still serves as the Director of the Experimental Economics Laboratory at Bonn. In 1994 he shared the Nobel Prize in Economics with John Harsanyi and John Nash. His main research interests are game theory with its applications to economics, political science and biology, experimental economics, and the theory of bounded rationality.

Vernon Smith   *Professor of Economics and Law, George Mason University*   A research scholar in the Interdisciplinary Center for Economic Science, and a Fellow of the Mercatus Center, Professor Smith received his bachelor's degree in Electrical Engineering from the California Institute of Technology and his Ph.D. in Economics from Harvard University. He has authored or co-authored over 200 articles and books on capital theory, finance, natural resource economics, and experimental economics.

Shyam Sunder *James L. Frank Professor of Accounting, Economics, and Finance, Yale School of Management*

Ferenc Szidarovsky *Professor of Systems and Industrial Engineering, University of Arizona* Professor Szidarovsky graduated from the Eotvos University of Sciences in Budapest. He holds two Ph.D. degrees, one in mathematics and the other in economics. As a Hungarian professor, he participated in several international research projects. In 1987 he immigrated to the United States. His main research interest is systems theory and its application in analyzing dynamic economic systems. He is the author of 16 books and more than 150 journal articles.

Raul Valdes-Perez *President and co-founder, Vivisimo, Inc.* Dr. Valdes-Peres has been a member of the computer science research faculty at Carnegie Mellon University since 1991, developing new methods for computational knowledge discovery and applying them to the natural and social sciences. He began working under Herbert Simon as his Ph.D. student in 1986. After graduating in 1991, he continued meeting regularly with Professor Simon until his passing.

Oliver Williamson *Edgar F. Kaiser Professor of Business, Economics, and Law, University of California, Berkeley* A 1963 graduate of the Ph.D. program at the Carnegie Institute of Technology, Professor Williamson is the author of *Markets and Hierarchies* and *The Economic Institutions of Capitalism*, as well as many other books and articles on transaction-cost economics and on general issues relating to economics, law, and organization theory. Herbert Simon was a member of his doctoral dissertation committee at the

Carnegie Institute, and they remained friends and not-always-in-agreement-about-the-details colleagues for the rest of Simon's life. He credits Simon with having "permanently altered" his research career.

Sidney Winter   *Deloitte and Touche Professor of Management, Wharton School, University of Pennsylvania*

Name Index

Printed in the United States
by Baker & Taylor Publisher Services